ELEMENTS

OF

POLITICAL ECONOMY.

BY

ARTHUR LATHAM PERRY,

ORRIN SAGE PROFESSOR OF HISTORY AND POLITICAL ECONOMY IN WILLIAMS COLLEGE.

Quid pro quo.

SEVENTH EDITION, REVISED AND ENLARGED.

NEW YORK:

CHARLES SCRIBNER AND COMPANY,

654 BROADWAY.

1872.

RIVERSIDE, CAMBRIDGE:
STEREOTYPED AND PRINTED BY
H. O. HOUGHTON AND COMPANY.

To

MY ONLY BROTHER,

BAXTER EDWARDS PERRY, Esq.,

OF BOSTON,

WHOSE FAITHFULNESS TO HIS CLIENTS IS ONLY SURPASSED BY

HIS KINDNESS OF HEART,

IS

This Edition of my Book

FRATERNALLY INSCRIBED

TABLE OF CONTENTS.

CHAPTER VIII.

CHAPTER IX.

CHAPTER X.

CHAPTER XI.

CHAPTER XII.

CHAPTER XIII.

CHAPTER XIV.

CHAPTER XV.

CHAPTER XVI.

ANALYSIS OF CHAPTERS.

CHAPTER I.

ON THE HISTORY OF THE SCIENCE.

CHAPTER II.

ON THE FIELD OF THE SCIENCE.

CHAPTER III.

ON VALUE.

CHAPTER IV.

ON EXCHANGE.

CHAPTER V.

ON PRODUCTION.

CHAPTER VI.

ON LABOR.

CHAPTER VII.

ON CAPITAL.

CHAPTER VIII.

ON LAND.

CHAPTER IX.

ON COST OF PRODUCTION.

CHAPTER X.

ON MONEY.

CHAPTER XI.

ON CURRENCY IN THE UNITED STATES.

CHAPTER XII.

ON CREDIT.

CHAPTER XIII.

ON FOREIGN TRADE.

CHAPTER XIV.

ON THE MERCANTILE SYSTEM.

CHAPTER XV.

ON AMERICAN TARIFFS.

CHAPTER XVI.

ON TAXATION.

ELEMENTS OF POLITICAL ECONOMY.

CHAPTER I.

HISTORY OF THE SCIENCE.

POLITICAL ECONOMY is the science of exchanges, or, what is exactly equivalent, the science of value. Properly to unfold this science, requires an analysis of those principles of human nature out of which exchanges spring; an examination of the providential arrangements, physical and social, by which it appears that exchanges were designed by God for the welfare of man; and an inquiry into the laws and usages devised by men to facilitate or to impede exchanges. The science, accordingly, is built up partly on facts of consciousness and partly on facts of outward observation. When its propositions are strictly deduced from acknowledged principles of human nature, and are shown to be consonant with the structure of the world and of society; when they are simply and logically set forth in a system; and when, in their light, human institutions and laws relating to exchanges are correctly explained and estimated; then the science of value is soundly based and orderly unfolded. An attempt to base and to develop the science of value thus will be made in the following pages; but before that work is fairly entered upon, it will be well to take a preliminary glance at the history of the science, and to trace the steps by which successive inquirers have brought Political Economy to its present stage of development.

While labor is as old as the race, and exchanges are as old as society, and while doubtless in all ages individual inquirers have tasked their minds with some portions of the subject, Political Economy as a science can hardly be said to have existed till within a period comparatively recent. Men exchanged among themselves services and commodities, and found their account in exchanging, long before the dawn of authentic history. The first commercial transaction on record dates back about two thousand years before Christ. It was the purchase by Abraham of the cave and field of Machpelah. "And Abraham weighed to Ephron the silver which he had named in the audience of the sons of Heth, four hundred shekels of silver, current money with the merchant." All this implies at that early day fixed conditions of trade. There were merchants as a class. Silver by weight was already a medium of exchange passing from hand to hand. It was current money with the merchant. In the absence of written documents a bargain was made in the presence of living witnesses. It was "in the audience of the sons of Heth, before all that went in at the gate of his city, that the field and the cave were made sure unto Abraham for a possession." An earlier passage in the life of Abraham shows that gold as well as silver was already reckoned an article of merchandise. It is said that Abraham departed from Egypt "very rich in cattle, in silver and gold."

Homer makes no mention of money, as he undoubtedly would have done had he been acquainted with it, but there are many passages in his poems that indicate a brisk direct exchange of products as characteristic of those times and countries. There was also then and there a sort of common measure of things exchangeable. Various things are mentioned in these poems as being worth so many *oxen*. The twenty-seventh chapter of Ezekiel gives a vivid picture of the immense commerce centering in Tyre. Nineveh, according to the prophet Nahum, "multiplied her merchants above the stars of heaven." Herodotus makes the probable statement that the Lydians of lesser Asia were the inventors of coined money; and the same writer describes with minute accuracy the caravan routes by which Carthaginian enterprise penetrated the interior of Africa for the sake of a trade in dates and salt and gold-dust and slaves. The records of the voyages of Hanno and Hamilco show the Carthaginians daring unknown seas also in the interests of traffic; coasting outside the pillars of Hercules, southward to the mouths of the Senegal and Gambia, and northward to the British Isles. Athens, Alexandria, Venice, Lisbon, Amsterdam, London, and New York, have been among the busy marts on the Mediterranean and the Atlantic, while counterparts to their activity in trade have existed in all ages in the farthest east.

The earliest writer known to us who treated economic subjects at any length is Xenophon. Before the middle of the fourth century before Christ this accomplished Athenian published a treatise "On Ways and Means." This early essay, not indeed on

Political Economy, but on some of the subjects with which that science has to do, contains, together with much that is fallacious, some sound and liberal principles. Its object is to propose methods for enhancing the prosperity of the Athenian State. Praising the soil, the climate, the mines, the coins, the commercial position of Athens, Xenophon suggests that the State offer various encouragements to the settlement of aliens, in order to swell the active population and increase the revenue from the aliens' tax; that merchants and shipmasters of all nations receive special honors in the city, in order to attract more of them thither and thus augment the income from duties on imports and exports; that prizes be offered the presidents of the courts to expedite the trial of commercial causes; that inns, warehouses, and marts for the sale of goods be erected at the public expense for the sake of the rents; that government as such undertake commercial enterprises; that especially the silver mines be worked on the most extensive scale, as well on government account as by private and joint-stock adventurers, so that the State might enjoy direct profits in addition to the prices and the twenty-fourth part of the produce of the mines purchased by individuals; and that finally a council of peace be instituted, by whose mediation war might be avoided, and the State, in the enjoyment of durable tranquillity, enter gradually upon these measures of national improvement, which, moreover, ought to be begun and continued by consulting the ancient oracles, and by supplications to the gods. Xenophon also wrote a treatise entitled "The Householder," in which there is a discussion of the various parts of domestic economy, and a pretty full treatment of the subject of agriculture.

Plato in the eleventh and twelfth chapters of the second book of his "Republic," admirably sketches one important principle of the science, namely, the necessity men are in, from their multifarious wants, of uniting in society, in which each individual may devote himself to that branch of industry for which he is best fitted, and then by exchange supply his remaining wants. "More will be done, and better, and with greater ease, when every one does but one thing, according to his genius, at the proper time, and when at leisure from all other pursuits." But this speculative view is adduced to account for the origin of a political state, and is so far from being carried out to its practical applications either economically or politically that Plato goes on to advocate community of goods in the leading class of his ideal state, and the exclusion of husbandmen and artisans from all share in the government.

Aristotle is sometimes called the father of Political Economy. He is certainly the father, if not of the science, of this name of the science, which name, however, he uses in a very different sense from that in which it is now used. At the opening of the second book of his "Economics" he distinguishes economy into four kinds, the regal, the satrapical, the *political*, and the domestic. By the first he means the central, and by the second the provincial, administration of a great empire like that of Persia; by the third, the administration prevailing in free states; and by the fourth, what we also mean by domestic economy. It is in the last sense, as indeed the name (οἶκος, *family*, and νόμος, *law*) implies, that the ancients generally conceive of economy; and hence, although Aristotle is the first to use the term political economy, it is not so much in his "Economics" as in his "Ethics" and "Politics" that we find his real contribution to our science. According to Aristotle's division of the practical sciences, Ethics treat of the nature and welfare of man apart from the social relations; Economics view him under the social relations of the family; and Politics under the social relations of the state. In all three of these treatises accordingly of this transcendent thinker are to be found acute definitions, shrewd remarks, and pretty copious information, relating to the proper science of Political Economy. This, for example, is a perfect definition of property: — "*But by property we mean everything, of which the value is measured by money.*" (Ethics, IV. i.) The proper boundary line between economy and morals is drawn as follows: — "*Whenever there is no agreement made about the service performed, those who confer a favor freely for the sake of the persons on whom they confer it, cannot complain; for the value of it is not measured by money, and no equivalent price can be paid.*" (Ethics, IX. i.) The same chapter accurately describes the ultimate phenomenon of value as between the two persons exchanging: — "*For each fixes his mind on that which he happens to want, and for the sake of that will give what he does give.*" Aristotle understood, as well as any one understands at present, the function of money as a measure: — "*Money, therefore, as a measure, by making things commensurable, equalizes them; for there could be no commerce without ex-*

change, no exchange without equality, and no equality without the possibility of being commensurate." (Ethics, V. v.) In direct opposition to Plato's proposed community of goods, he insists strongly upon the rights and benefits of private property (Pol. II. v); apprehends the true origin of money, and that it is, in common with all other forms of property, a mere means, no more than they, an end in itself (Pol. I. ix.); and estimates agriculture highly, as the ground of all other arts, and as most favorable to health, morals and good government. (Econ. I. ii.) Still Aristotle was not wholly emancipated from the prejudices of his time. Remarkable as was his sagacity in matters economical, he yet held views incompatible with a sound and complete science of economy. For example, these: — "*And indeed the best regulated states will not permit a mechanic to be a citizen; for it is impossible for one who lives the life of a mechanic or hired servant to practice a life of virtue.*" (Pol. III. v.) "*For usury is most reasonably detested, as the increase of our fortune arises from the money itself, and not by employing it for the purpose for which it was intended.*" (Pol. I. x.) "*It is clear then that some men are free by nature, and others are slaves, and that in the case of the latter the lot of slavery is both advantageous and just.*" (Pol. I. v.)

There appear to be three principal reasons why the Greeks, who were so intellectually capable of it, did not develop any true system of Political Economy. In the first place, their affairs of private life were wholly subordinate to those of public life; and, consequently, the varied forms of private and associated industry could not win that attention, which, at present, they are able to compel. To the Greeks the State was everything, and the individual only that which the State allowed him to be. In the second place, the institution of slavery threw its shadow over most of the branches of industry. It was inevitable that employments committed mainly to slaves should seem mean to the free. Only agriculture and commerce, carried on on a large scale, and scarcely these, escaped this damaging influence. Even Aristotle, who says, "*The best nation is a nation of farmers*" (Pol. VI. iv.), says also, "*Neither should they who are destined for office be husbandmen.*" (Pol. VII. ix.) It lessened no man's consideration, however, in the public opinion of the Greeks, to have any kind of industry carried on on his account, provided he did not work at it with his own hands. In the third place, the constant recurrence of wars interfered sadly with the free expansion of industry.

Nevertheless, the Greek States showed practical good sense in their economical regulations. They fell into no such egregious follies as have marked the legislation of modern states. There was no interdicting the exportation of raw materials; no favoring of manufactures at the cost of the agricultural class; no prohibitions on the export of specie; no efforts to preserve a factitious balance of trade; and no duties on imports except for purposes of revenue. The usual customs' duty in the port of Athens was two per cent. of the value of the goods. The duty laid by Athens in the ports of her subject-allies was generally five per cent.; and when in a few exceptional cases the rate was raised to ten per cent., it was regarded as extortion. In all essential respects, therefore, there existed freedom of industry and freedom of trade.[1]

We should expect beforehand that the more practical Romans, lovers of law and order, and exhibiting to the world many of the high qualities of citizen life, would make some valuable contribution to the science of exchanges. In this we are disappointed. Though in the earlier and better days of Rome, agriculture was highly esteemed, the blighting institution of slavery brought labor, the mechanical arts, and commerce more and more into disrepute. The lands were tilled by slaves. Slaves became the artisans of the country. As always happens under such circumstances, the freemen, the citizens, came to feel themselves above such degrading occupations. It is pitiful to hear Cicero declaim against the noble rights of labor. In the "De Officiis" there is a whole paragraph of condemnation for those branches of manufacturing and commercial industry which ought to be regarded not only as honorable but as the life and strength of the State. One sweep of his pen pushes out of the pale of respectability the whole class of mechanics. "All artisans are engaged in a degrading profession," says he. Again, "there can be nothing ingenuous in a workshop." Trade and commerce fare no better at his hands. When carried on on a small scale they are to be regarded as disgraceful; when on a large scale they must not be greatly condemned! When social prejudices and views of labor like these are promulgated by the foremost man of his time, the best educated and the most liberal,

[1] See Boeckh's Public Economy of Athens, and Heeren's Ancient Greece, chap. x.

there is no longer room for surprise at the lack of Roman contributions to Political Economy.

Moreover, the Roman moralists regarded the accumulation of wealth as undermining those virtues in which they placed the perfection of character. Cato, the censor, in his denunciations of luxury, which is the result of accumulation, was a representative of the whole class of moralists. Their position ought not to surprise us for two reasons. First, the stream of the Roman wealth, much of it at least, proved a curse and not a blessing, not because wealth is not a blessing, but because its waters instead of being diffused everywhere, rushed at once into a few huge reservoirs — there was no natural and general distribution of it. Second, the source of most of the wealth was as illegitimate as its absorption by the few great families. It did not come from the peaceful and gradual development of the national resources; it came from conquests, from tributes, often from official extortion from the provincials. A comprehensive theory of value will hardly be helped forward in connection with such moral notions, such views of labor, and such methods of gain, as prevailed at Rome.

In all that related, however, to the proper acquisition and exchange of property, and to the management of the ordinary sources of national income, the Romans exhibited a strong sense of justice, together with moderation and practical wisdom. They taught the world something in the matter of taxation. They opened up new sources of revenue, from which governments still think it useful to draw. They levied duties in their ports as a simple expedient of taxation. They knew nothing of what has since become famous under the name of Protection. The rate of the duties in Cicero's time was five per cent. of the value of the goods; in the time of the emperors, two and one half per cent.; and the highest duty known to the Roman custom-house was twelve and one half per cent. Augustus introduced an excise-tax of one per cent. on the value of all things which were sold. The same emperor laid a tax of five per cent. on legacies and inheritances. There was a tax on bachelors. In the provinces at least, a door-tax was sometimes exacted. The public lands, the mines, the salt-works, and especially the tributes, were the remaining sources of income.[1]

The confusion consequent upon the breaking up of the old Roman empire; the settlement of the barbarian nations in the seats of the ancient civilization; the gradual growth of feudalism, than which no system could be more hostile to a free and varied industry; the almost exclusive occupation of men's minds during the Middle Ages, with religious questions, and with the intricacies of the disputatious schoolmen; the prevalence of the monkish idea that contact with the world was contaminating; the fact that the universities were under the control of the clergy, who only allowed in them a meagre curriculum of scholastic studies together with the civil law; and the fact that war and rapine, rather than the supply of their mutual wants, gave occasion to the intercourse of nations with each other; all these contributed to divert attention for centuries from the subject-matter of the science of exchanges,

[1] See articles "Vectigalia" and "Portorium" in Dict. of Antiquities.

In our survey thus far, if we have found little positive light thrown as yet upon the science of value, we have at least discovered some of the reasons why such light could not be thrown. Absence of investigation and discussion however does not necessarily imply the lack of a theory. In truth, there was a half-developed theory of value, which exerted a prodigious influence, certainly from Cicero's time, even down into the seventeenth century. It is remarkable that this earliest general doctrine of value, which I shall venture to call the *Bullion Theory*, came into currency in direct contravention of the great authority of Aristotle. That philosopher taught clearly that money is but an instrument towards a further end, and derives all its importance from being an *instrument;* but the later less acute observers, perceiving that gold and silver were the money of all civilized nations, fell into a curious mistake in regard to the nature of money, and came to give to these metals a factitious importance by regarding them as the *real and only wealth.* They overlooked the fact that these metals are a commodity, that they owe their value to efforts and desires just as other commodities do, and that they are bought and sold like all other commodities. With useful products of any kind one can always buy gold and silver. To trade is nothing but to barter one commodity for another, — to exchange corn for silver and silver for corn. Unless the trade is fraudulent, the one is equally valuable with the other; and it would seem as if the simple consideration that men are willing to part, and do constantly part, with gold and silver to buy other things, would have been fatal to the prejudice that the precious metals are the only wealth.

There were however two things that seemed to sustain the Bullion theory. One was, that money is always the measure of value. "How much is it worth?" The answer comes, so many dollars. Dollars are the denomination in which value is reckoned, just as degrees of the thermometer are the denomination by which heat is measured. The difference between value itself and the measure of value — between a bushel of wheat and that round measure by which we determine that there *is* a bushel — seems obvious enough; but money has this peculiarity, it is not only a measure of value, but, so far as this expression is ever true of any one commodity, it has value in itself. There is no heat in a thermometer, and no wheat in a bushel-measure, but a dollar is not only a dollar measure, but a dollar value, and we can see how the fact that dollars both had value and were the measure of all other values, gave some plausibility to the notion that the dollars were all. The other thing that made the Bullion theory plausible was the use of gold and silver as the universal medium of exchange. They came to be such medium simply in consequence of their convenience and their nearly uniform value; and because they were such a medium, everybody wanted them, and whoever had them could get with them whatever else he wanted. Because the great thing was to get money, men seemed to think that money was the only thing to be got!

I cannot find that the Bullion theory had anything better to support it than these two deceptive pillars; and yet for a very long period, and by many well-informed men as well as by all the unthinking, it was considered to stand upon an immovable founda tion. The commercial policy that sprung from this theory was obvious and well-nigh universal. If gold and silver are the only wealth, then by all means keep the gold and silver in the country! Get all you can in, and let as little as possible out! Accordingly very early the nations passed laws to prohibit the exportation of gold and silver. We learn from Cicero, incidentally, that this was done repeatedly at Rome. In one of his orations he says, "The Senate solemnly decreed both many times previously, and again when I was consul, that gold and silver ought not to be exported." According to Adam Smith, there are ancient acts of the old Scotch Parliament, which prohibit under heavy penalties the carrying gold and silver *forth of the kingdom.* The same thing was done by France and England, and probably by every other nation in Europe. Spain tried this experiment of prohibition under noticeable conditions. She had domestic mines, but also became proprietor in the sixteenth century of the rich metallic treasures of Mexico and Peru. The precious metals were literally poured into her bosom. Their export she prohibited under the severest penalties. The prohibition was largely futile, since these are things that can easily be smuggled out. So far as the prohibition was effective the metals in consequence sank rapidly in value. They are only good to buy with; and as the Spaniards were not allowed to buy with them abroad, they soon found that they could buy relatively little with them at home; which, of course, increased the smuggling out. Spain persisted in this policy until her commercial decay proved to her and to all the world, not only the folly of such attempts to obstruct the natural current of commercial circulation, but also the important truth that national wealth consists not in the mere abundance of gold and silver. Had the Bullion theory been correct, to encourage the importation of the precious metals, and discourage their exportation, would have been the high road to national prosperity. But the Bullion theory was not correct; and the clearness of our views in Political Economy will largely depend upon our thorough emancipation from the prejudice that gold and silver are any more valuable or any more desirable than the products for which they exchange. They constitute a part, but only a small fractional part, of the values of any country.

The discovery by the Portuguese of an ocean path to the Indies in 1497, and the general waking up of the European mind during the next century, gave a vast impulse to commerce. On the last day of that century, Dec. 31, 1600, Queen Elizabeth chartered an exclusive company entitled "The Governor and Company of Merchants of London trading into the East Indies." They were empowered to export all sorts of goods free of duty for four years; and also to export foreign coin or bullion to the amount of £30,000 a year, £6,000 of the same being previously coined at the mint; but they were at the same time put under obligation to import, within six months after the completion of every voyage except the first, the same quantity of silver, gold, and foreign coin that they had exported. The enemies of the Company soon complained that this last condition was not complied with, and that it was, besides, highly injurious to the public interest, and *contrary to all principle*, to allow gold and silver to be sent out of the kingdom.

The advocates of the Company, on the other hand, though they did not venture to assail the doctrine that wealth consists in gold and silver alone, took narrower ground, and asserted that the export of money is advantageous, whenever the articles bought by it and imported, are chiefly reëxported to other countries and sold for as much money as was originally carried out; and also whenever the export of coin, and the consequent import of commodities, occasions, though indirectly, a greater value of exports from home of native products. Thomas Mun, a writer of that period, quoted by Adam Smith, compares the trade of the merchant exporting gold and silver, to the seed-time and harvest of agriculture. "If we only behold," says he, "the actions of the husbandman in the seed-time, when he casteth away much good corn into the ground, we shall account him rather a madman than a husbandman. But when we consider his labors in the harvest, which is the end of his endeavors, we shall find the worth and plentiful increase of his actions." In these excuses now set up for the exportation of bullion we may mark the beginnings of a second general commercial theory, which is usually termed the *Mercantile System*. This child of the bullion theory became in turn the cause of the death of its parent. The advocates of the East India Company gradually learned to take broader ground, and at last boldly contended that bullion was nothing but a commodity, and that its exportation should be made as free as that of other commodities. These views gained strength; many eminent merchants not connected with the Company adopted them; and in 1663, the House of Commons repealed the statutes prohibiting the exportation of foreign coin and bullion, and gave the Company and private traders liberty to export them in unlimited quantities.[1]

The Mercantile System, though, as compared with the previously existing bullion theory, it was a considerable step in the progress towards sounder opinions, was itself fallacious in principle and pernicious in action. It gave its care, not indeed to prevent the direct export of the precious metals, but to make the general exports of a country greater than its imports, so that a balance should come back in gold and silver. The sole aim of the system was to preserve what was called the *Balance of Trade.* A famous phrase this, the balance of trade! The legislation, the politics, the diplomacy, and the wars, of nearly two centuries were full of it.

By the balance of trade was meant the excess of the value of the commodities exported over the value of the commodities imported, which excess, it was supposed, would always come back in the form of gold and silver. Hence unlimited pains were taken to make the exports greater than the imports, and the excess was regarded as the measure of a country's commercial prosperity. Various devices were employed to make the exports great and the imports little. To increase the amount of exports, bounties were offered to domestic producers, to encourage them to sell as much as possible to foreign countries. With the same end in view, the raw materials of domestic manufactures were forbidden to

1 M'Culloch's *Commercial Dictionary,* Art. East India Company.

be exported, so that the finished products, thereby rendered greater in amount, might help swell the exports. Colonies were planted with similar intent, that the mother country might find an open market there, and swell her exports. To diminish the aggregate of imports, prohibitions were laid on the bringing in from abroad articles which could be made or grown at home; and heavy restrictions imposed on imports from those countries with which the balance was supposed to be unfavorable, while the same articles, perhaps of an inferior quality, were admitted on easier terms from countries with which the balance was supposed to be better. Thus everything was sought to be regulated in view of an imaginary balance of trade. The Mercantile System was the prolific mother of those commercial restrictions, those attempted regulations of manufactures, those doctrines of monopoly, of corn-laws, and colonies, which have fettered industry almost up to the present time.

The particular fallacies that lurk in the Mercantile System, and the tortuous and cramping policy that grew out of it, will be more fitly discussed at a later stage of our inquiries; this is a proper place to indicate in general that the whole system is based on a misapprehension. It overlooks entirely the mutual benefit to the parties of every act of exchange, without which benefit the exchange clearly would not take place at all, and makes the whole advantage of commerce consist in a certain balance of gold and silver, which comes back to that one of the parties which has managed to part with more of its own commodities. It seems strange that it did not occur to those people, that, if it were worth while to trade at all, the benefits of the trade were rather to be measured by the amount and value of what was received, than by the amount and value of what was parted with! Moreover, the system takes for granted, that traders carry forth goods to foreign countries to receive back goods *and* bullion worth as much, — less goods, indeed, and the balance in bullion. Why on that principle should the goods be carried forth at all? The labors, the risks, and the exchanges all made; the goods and the balance received; and the country just as well, but no better off than before! The whole wisdom of the Mercantile System was to sell as much as possible and buy as little as possible, — a wisdom which is evident folly, inasmuch as it is not possible to sell without buying, or to buy without selling. The sound reason, that justifies the East India Company in exporting the metals or other commodities, and at the same time condemns the Mercantile System, is, that the goods purchased by the exports are of greater worth, when imported, than what was exported to pay for them.

The leading commercial nations of Europe, nevertheless, fell into the meshes of the Mercantile System. Portugal, Spain, France, Holland, and England, all gave their attention to the balance of trade, all laid restrictions on the natural freedom of industry, and all applied the system rigidly to their colonial dependencies. These restrictions on trade, especially on the importation of manufactured goods, and on the exportation of corn and raw mateirals, to say nothing of the bounties which the people were taxed to pay, were to the last degree vexatious and onerous; while the penalties for their infringement were in many cases cruel and even barbarous. Various writers in the different countries, and particularly in England, where the laws in question were, perhaps, the most oppressive, began to attack the mercantile theory and the policy that had grown out of it. And it is to this series of writers in long succession, some overthrowing one false position, and some another, one establishing a truth here and another there, that we owe the gradual development and present state of the science of Political Economy. The science has gradually emerged from the waves of thought dashing and roaring around the Mercantile System. It is still necessary, at least on the continent of Europe and in the United States, to combat some of the remains of the old mercantile legislation. England is believed to be the only country which has erased from her statute-book the last vestiges of the system. This she has done in direct consequence of the skill and power with which the political economists have guided the public opinion of that country; and it is on account of their success, as well as on account of the superior numbers and weight of English thinkers in this field of inquiry, that it is proper now to consider first the English contributors to the modern science of Political Economy. We shall then attend to what the French have done towards building up the science; and, with a few remarks on the Italian and German writers, shall close this sketch with a brief recital of American views and writers.

It is not necessary in a book like the present to go into much detail respecting individual authors, or their claims to priority of discovery in the realm of economical truth. This has already been well done by Mr. McCulloch in the "Introductory Discourse" prefixed to his admirable edition of Adam Smith's "Wealth of Nations," to which I am indebted for some of the facts and thoughts already stated, and soon to be stated, in this chaper; and will doubtless be exhaustively done in Mr. Macleod's "Dictionary of Political Economy," of which one volume has already appeared. My object is to give a brief but just outline of the labors of the principal thinkers, with the practical aim of preparing my readers for a better apprehension of the discussions which follow.

Omitting the pamphleteers, who not seldom struck upon an important truth here and there in their zealous debates on questions of taxation, trade, poor-laws, or other point of government policy; and who are to be regarded as the pioneers in economical discovery, pushing their way into the wilderness in one direction and another, and thus, as it were, piloting the great writers who came after,—John Locke may first be mentioned, whose "Two Treatises of Government" were published in 1690, in justification of the English Revolution of 1688, in which he incidentally illustrates the distinction between utility and value, and all but establishes this one of the fundamental truths of Political Economy, namely, that value is the birth of effort, and not the gift of Providence. He says:—"*For it is labor indeed that puts the difference of value on everything;*" again:—"*Whatever bread is worth more than acorns, wine than water, and cloth or silk than leaves, skins or moss, that is wholly owing to labor and industry;*" again:—"*It is labor then that puts the greatest part of value upon land, without which it would scarcely be worth any-*

thing;" and once more: — "*Supposing the world given, as it was, to the children of men in common, we see how labor could make men distinct titles to the several parcels of it for their private uses.*"[1] These passages are an early, if not the very earliest, statement of a truth destined in our own day to transform the face of the science of economy; but Locke himself was hardly aware of its pregnant nature, and did not deduce from it the conclusions which it is well able to bear. In the controversy concerning the recoinage of silver money in the same reign, Locke did good service by his tracts on money, in preventing the lowering of the currency standard, and in diffusing sound principles (not unmixed with several errors) on the nature of money. He justly taught that it was as absurd for the State to attempt to fix the price of money, as to fix the price of cutlery or broadcloth.[2]

David Hume, more distinguished as a historian and writer on strictly philosophical subjects, must yet be mentioned with honor in any sketch of the rise of the science of economy. He was the friend and forerunner of Adam Smith. His Political Essays were published in 1752. The titles of some of these are as follows: — "Of Commerce," "Of Money," "Of Interest," "Of the Balance of Trade," "Of the Jealousy of Trade," "Of Taxes," "Of Public Credit." In these essays are to be recognized, not only the clear-flowing style which makes it always a pleasure to read Hume's "History of England," but also liberal sentiments largely emancipated from the fetters of the mercantile system. The views pro-

1 Locke, book ii. sections 39, 40, 42, 43.

2 Macaulay's England, chap. xxi.

pounded are interesting even where they are not sound. Of commerce, he says, "*Foreign trade, by its imports, furnishes materials for new manufactures; and, by its exports, it produces labor in particular commodities, which could not be consumed at home. In short, a kingdom that has a large import and export, must abound more with industry, than a kingdom that rests contented with its own commodities. It is therefore more powerful, as well as richer and happier.*" I am aware of no earlier hint of the great truth afterwards fully developed by Say, that there can never be a general over-production, than these words from the same essay:—"*If strangers will not take any particular commodity of ours, we must cease to labor in it. The same hands will turn themselves towards some refinement in other commodities which may be wanted at home; and there must always be materials for them to work upon, till every person in the State who possesses riches, enjoys as great plenty of home commodities, and those in as great perfection as he desires;* WHICH CAN NEVER POSSIBLY HAPPEN." The absurdity of the then current notions concerning the Balance of Trade is triumphantly exposed by Hume, in the essay under that title; and in the conclusion of the essay on the Jealousy of Trade, occur these noble words:—"*I shall therefore venture to acknowledge, that, not only as a man, but as a British subject, I pray for the flourishing commerce of Germany, Spain, Italy, and even France itself.*" Hume throws some new light on the subject of Money; although his discussion of it is marred by the assumption, that a less quantity of the metals would answer every purpose of commerce as well as a greater, and have as much value; which would only be true on the supposition that the less quantity cost as much effort to produce it, and its minuter subdivisions were as convenient in exchange; — a false assumption from which he deduces this very false inference: — "*Were all our money, for instance, recoined, and a penny's worth of silver taken from every shilling, the new shilling would probably purchase everything that could have been bought by the old; and domestic industry, by the circulation of a great number of pounds and shillings, would receive some increase and encouragement.*" Are men, then, usually willing to consider $\frac{11}{12}$ equal to $\frac{12}{12}$? Besides, Hume did not attempt to analyze value, or to ground comprehensively the science of Political Economy.

That attempt was first successfully made by Dr. Adam Smith, Professor in the University of Glasgow, who published in 1776 his great work on the Wealth of Nations, in which many of the more important propositions of the science are established beyond the reach of controversy. It will be noticed that the publication of this work took place in the very year in which American Independence was declared; and it was itself a sort of declaration of independence of the false principles and foolish policy of the Mercantile System. Like the document of Jefferson, it excited universal attention: like that, it marks an era; and the results in the economical world of the treatise of Smith have been scarcely less striking and beneficent than the results in the political world of the document of Jefferson. Indeed, the merits and originality of Dr. Smith are so great, that he has frequently been called, as Aristotle has been by others, the father of Political Economy It is not just that that title should be borne by either the one or the other; the science has grown up very gradually, and through the contributions of a great many thinkers; but the most prominent name among them all is now, and doubtless always will be, the name of Adam Smith. He goes over the whole ground, endeavors to bring the principles discovered by others and those first demonstrated by himself into one harmonious system, and by means of historical information makes his book as interesting as it is instructive by reason of scientific discussion. He exalts labor, shows the immense advantages of its division, and advocates its unshackled freedom in all departments; he unfolds the benefits of commerce, and mercilessly exposes the weak points of the restrictive and regulating devices of the mercantile system; he discusses money, capital, profits, wages, rent, taxation, and public expenditures. A book with such a scope, and published at such time, of course contains many errors; but the wonder is, not that there are so many, but that there are not more. A groundless distinction made between productive and unproductive labor; the including of vendible commodities only in the field of value; a preference given to agriculture over other forms of production, and to the home trade over foreign trade, a misapprehension in regard to the nature of rent; a want of clear perception of the difference between utility and value, and a consequent partial confusion in the whole doctrine of values; an occasional inconsistency with its own principles, as when allowing that a State may regulate the rate of interest; a lack of clear definitions; a confused arrangement of the topics discussed; and lastly, a prolixity that at times becomes tedious; are among the chief defects of the Wealth of Nations.

Most of the English writers on this subject, since the time of Dr. Smith, may be fairly said to belong to his school. They have corrected many of his errors, and made additional contributions to the science in several respects, but, in the main, have followed out his principles, and, like him, confined their discussions of value to tangible commodities. Mr. Malthus, author of a very famous theory of population; Mr. Ricardo, author of a scarcely less famous theory of rent, — both of which theories will be considered further on in these pages; Mr. McCulloch, who clearly discriminates between utility and value, but erroneously regards labor as the sole constituent in the latter; Mr. Senior, author of the able, but not sufficiently comprehensive, treatise in the Encyclopedia Metropolitana; and Mr. John Stuart Mill, whose work has been deservedly more read in this country than any of the rest, are the principal figures in the long array of writers. The definition of the science, to which, in general, they would all assent, is, The science which treats of the Production, Distribution, and Consumption of Wealth.

Mr. Horner, Mr. Thornton, and Mr. Huskisson, were the joint authors of the Bullion Report made to Parliament in 1810, in which the true principles of metallic and of paper money are stated with demonstrative ability.

Mr. Macleod, the latest English author of note in this field of inquiry, is a very able representative of what may perhaps be called the modern school of French economists. Their definition of the science is the one enforced in these pages also, namely, The science of Exchanges. This definition is drawing to itself the most recent investigators in France, England, and America; and the scientific development of it has already put political economy into a new and better posture. According to this view, exchangeability is the only quality requisite to bring any service or commodity within the sphere of economic regulation. To Mr. Macleod's "Theory and Practice of Banking" I am under obligation for some information in matters of fact, and some distinctions in matters of science, made use of in some of the following chapters.

If the French have done less than the English in building up the science of Political Economy, they have done well what they have done. They have the honor of publishing the very first general treatise under the title of "Political Economy." It was issued at Rouen in 1615. To them also is due the credit of having furnished the first writer who undertook a systematic analysis of the sources of value, and whose ingenious speculations gave rise to the first school of Political Economy. This was M. Quesnay, a physician attached to the court of Louis XV., whose book was published in 1758.[1] His fundamental positions expressed the reaction from the principles of the Mercantile System as embodied in the policy of Colbert, the famous finance minister of Louis XIV. That policy gave a decided preference to the industry of the towns and cities. M. Quesnay appeared as the champion of agriculture. His system assumes that the physical earth is the only source of wealth, and consequently that labor is incapable of producing any new value except when

[1] Adam Smith. Book iv., chap. ix.

employed in agriculture. Artisans and merchants are unproductive laborers, because there is no nett produce remaining, as in agriculture, over and above the expenses of production. The system mistook the nature of rent; and falsely though tacitly assumed that wealth consists in matter. The novelty of the theory however, its scientific shape, and the liberal commercial policy coupled with it, gave it for a time a great reputation; and it numbered among its disciples no less persons than Turgot, the financier, and the elder Mirabeau. The former, when he became controller-general of the French finances in 1774, proposed, in accordance with the principles of Quesnay, the freedom of labor at home and of trade abroad, and the substitution for existing taxes on a multitude of articles, of a single tax on land; and the latter was so far carried away by zeal for his master, that he puts his work, in point of benefit to mankind, on a level with the invention of writing and the invention of money. The numerous disciples of Quesnay were called Physiocrats, and constituted what is termed the early school of French economists. Their system is sometimes named the Agricultural System in contradistinction from the Mercantile System. Their views color many parts of the "Wealth of Nations," and afterwards exerted a predominating influence in the councils of the French Revolution.

To make the year 1776 doubly memorable in the history of this science, the French philosopher Condillac published in that year a work entitled "*Le Commerce et le gouvernement considérés relativement l'un à l'autre.*" This work was comparatively neglected at the time, and has never shared the popular favor accorded to the other writings of the same author, but the definition of the science given in it, namely, that it is the science of commerce, found many years afterwards an intelligent champion in Archbishop Whately, to whom the definition is commonly and perhaps properly referred; and this definition or one equivalent, is the one now generally accepted.

In 1803, appeared in Paris, Say's "*Traité d'économie politique*," which soon became, and is even yet, a standard work. Say is a skilful expositor of the science, an able advocate of the freedom of commerce, and the original contributor of the important demonstration that there cannot be a general glut of products — a general over-production. His doctrine of value, however, is infected with a fundamental error, namely, the confusion of value with utility, which one of his own countrymen was destined completely to expose, and to replace with the nucleus of satisfactory truth. That countryman of his was Frederic Bastiat, whose book, entitled "*Harmonies économiques*," published in Paris in 1850, carried Political Economy to a very advanced position, and is the most important contribution to the science since the time of Adam Smith. The gifted author died the same year in which his book appeared, leaving unfinished an intention to recast and complete it. It is not strictly a treatise of Political Economy, as it does not touch upon several of the most important subjects comprehended in that title, such as Money, Foreign Trade, Taxation, and others, but there is in it a masterly definition and exposition of value, and a vigorous demonstration of the harmonious mechanism of society, by which, through the agency of liberty and property, God has designed the progressive amelioration of mankind. "All legitimate interests are in harmony" is the key-note of the book. Bastiat encumbers his discussions by the attempt to use technically the term "wealth," and his chapter under that title is singularly perplexed and confused, affording again for the hundredth time an illustration of the impossibility of using that word to advantage for any scientific purpose whatever. While unfolding the laws of value in their manifold applications, Bastiat incidentally but most effectually demolishes the vagaries of communism, and establishes the right of property upon unassailable grounds. It is a pleasure to acknowledge in the amplest manner one's indebtedness to such a quickening writer as M. Bastiat is. Whoever will compare carefully with his book the following chapters on Value and Land, will see how much I have profited by his discussions; and he will also see that I have made an independent, not a servile, use of them. It is hoped that the relations of utility to value are even more clearly and ultimately put than he has put them. Not to have availed myself of the truths which he has actually established would be as unjust to science, as not also to have endeavored in the chapters on Exchange and Foreign Trade to execute the commission which he left to his readers in these words: —"*I hope yet to find at least one among them who will be able to demonstrate rigorously this proposition: the good of each tends to the good of all, as the good of all tends to the good of each; and who will, moreover, be able to impress this truth upon men's minds by rendering the proof of it simple, lucid, and irrefragable.*"[1] M. Bastiat defines Political Economy as the

[1] Stirling's Translation of the *Harmonies*, page 92.

Theory of Exchange, and Value as the Relation between two Services exchanged. His system turns on the technical use, definition, and analysis of the term *Services.* He derives all the economic phenomena out of the fundamental facts of human Wants, Efforts, and Satisfactions. Value cannot exist separately from human efforts. Utility resides in the materials and forces of Nature. "*But these natural forces, in themselves, and apart from all intellectual or bodily exertion, are gratuitous gifts of Providence, and in this respect they remain destitute of* VALUE *through all the complications of human transactions. This is the leading idea of the present work.*" Thus he himself expresses the matter.[1]

The Italian writers, though voluminous and respectable, have originated comparatively little within the field of this science. Several of them commenced during the seventeenth century to investigate the nature of money, and came to the sound conclusion that governments have no right to tamper with the standard of value used by their subjects. As early as 1764, a professorship of Commerce and Political Economy was instituted at Naples, and Antonio Genovesi, to whom Say and others would assign a high rank among the contributors to the science, was appointed to lecture in it. This was the first established professorship in this department of knowledge. A collection of the best Italian writers on the subject was undertaken, under the patronage of Napoleon, in 1803, and subsequently completed in fifty volumes octavo.

The Germans have done more perhaps for the

1 Stirling's Translation, page 62.

science of economy through their public action in the Zollverein, than through the private contributions of their numerous economical writers. The Zollverein, or Customs Union, was commenced by Prussia in 1818, and has received the adhesion from time to time of other German States, until now it embraces all of Germany except Austria. Within this broad territory, embracing a population of above 38,000,000, the duties on imports are uniform, and uniformly low; and there is no duty on exports except on paper-rags.[1] All interior custom-houses are swept away. No foreign articles are excluded; many are admitted free of duty; and those on which duty is charged are arranged in thirty-seven simple classes, the duties being always specific (generally by the hundred weight), except in the case of carriages and ships, on which the duty varies from five to ten per cent. of value. The commercial prosperity induced by these liberal regulations, the steadily enlarging revenue from these low duties, and the growth of domestic industry by the side of these practically unrestricted importations, have taught the world a more valuable lesson than often falls to the lot of an individual thinker to teach. It is true that the founders of the Zollverein were not wholly free from the prejudices of the mercantile system, but the results of the experiment so far confirm anything rather than the principles of that system. Friederich List, an early champion of the Zollverein, some time also a resident of the United States, who published in English his " Outlines of a New System of Political Economy," at Philadelphia, 1827, and "*Das*

[1] Zolltarif des Deutschen Zollvereins vom 1. Juni 1868 ab gültig.

Nationale System der politischen Oekonomie," in Stuttgart, 1841, and who, while advocating the principle of protection in his books, displayed a multifacious activity in behalf of many liberal schemes; Ludwig Stein, Professor in Vienna, an indefatigable writer and zealous free trader; and Professor Rau, of Heidelberg, a correct and forcible writer and a popular lecturer, may suffice, as examples merely, of the individual writers of Germany.

The circumstances of the United States, as well in colonial vassalage as in an independent position, their experience with almost every variety of paper money, the alternations of the national policy in respect to trade, the long continued public discussions on the tendencies and results of a protective tariff, and the efforts — State and National — which have been made towards realizing a healthful currency, have been favorable to the cultivation of economical studies. To these circumstances may now be added the pressure of a vast public debt, the opportunity of watching the operation of a national banking system, and the interest attaching to the production of gold and silver in the western half of the continent. Attention to this subject, however great heretofore, is likely to be greater in the time to come.

The Reports of the Secretaries of the Treasury, particularly those of Mr. Hamilton, Mr. Gallatin, Mr. Walker, and Mr. McCulloch, have treated many branches of the subject with marked ability. Much economical truth has been brought out also in congressional speeches, for example, in those of Mr. Webster, Mr. Calhoun, Mr. Benton, Mr. Silas

Wright, Mr. E. G. Spaulding, Mr. Amasa Walker, Mr. B. F. Thomas, and Mr. Garfield. The debate in the House of Representatives, on the tariff, during the spring of 1870, was more general and thorough and able than any previous congressional tariff debate; and the point then raised by Judge Winans of Ohio, that Congress has no constitutional right to lay duties except *to get money* with which "to pay the debts and provide for the common defence and general welfare of the United States," is a point of much importance. Congressional reports, like that of Mr. John Quincy Adams on Weights and Measures, and that of Mr. Kasson's late committee on the Metric System, have illustrated portions of the subject. The annual reports of the Special Commissioner of the Revenue, Mr. David A. Wells, have presented such facts and reasonings in relation to the national industry, commerce, and currency, as have deserved and have received the profound attention of the people. Treatises more or less formal and complete have been written by Daniel Raymond (1820), John Rae (1834), Henry C. Carey (1835–1860), Professor Vethake, President Wayland, Stephen Colwell, George Opdyke, Professor Bowen, E. Peshine Smith, Professor Bascom (1859), Charles Moran (1860), E. B. Bigelow (1861), Amasa Walker (1866), John A. Ferris (1867), George A. Potter (1868), E. G. Spaulding (1869), Horace Greeley (1870), and by many others.

The economical works of Mr. Carey are to be noticed the more particularly, because he claims as original with himself some of the fundamental positions of M. Bastiat. It is certain that these positions are common to the two writers; and it is to be presumed that M. Bastiat profited by some of the views of Mr. Carey; but there is enough that is distinctive in the two authors to justify the claim of each to both originality and merit. Among Mr. Carey's central principles may be enumerated the following: That land gains its value from labor; that, generally, poorer soils are first cultivated, then, those more fertile and difficult; that, what would be the cost of their reproduction rather than their actual cost of production, determines the value of commodities; that the interests of classes and individuals are really harmonious; that there is a tendency to increase in the wages of labor, and to diminution in the rate, though increase in the aggregate of the profits of capital; that the advancement of society corresponds to the degrees of association and liberty in it; and that the prices of land, labor and raw materials tend to approach the prices of finished commodities.

Mr. Amasa Walker's "Science of Wealth" has already passed through several editions, and is a very high authority on all questions of Political Economy. On the subject of Currency it is particularly original and full. Wages, Trade, and Taxation are also subjected in it to admirable analysis and discussion.

A second edition of Professor Bowen's "American Political Economy" has been recently published. As his treatment of the various questions of Money was the strong point in the original edition of 1856 so his copious discussion of the recent financial experience of the United States constitutes a chief merit in the book as it now appears.

CHAPTER II.

FIELD OF THE SCIENCE.

WHEN Adam Smith taught Political Economy in the University of Glasgow, it was as a branch of moral philosophy, and the substance of his "Wealth of Nations" was delivered first in the form of lectures, which made up a part of his moral philosophy course. That course was divided into four parts: the first comprising natural theology; the second, ethics, or what Paley terms the science of duty and the reasons of it; the third jurisprudence, or that part of morality which relates to justice; while in the fourth part he examined those political and social regulations which are founded on expediency, and which tend to increase the prosperity and power of a State.

Now, expediency is so radically distinct from duty that there is no need of proving that Political Economy is not to be reckoned a part of moral philosophy at all. The idea of obligation, on which the science of morals is founded, and the idea of value on which the science of economy is founded, are totally distinct ideas. There is one word that marks and circumscribes the field of morals. That word is Ought. There is one word that marks and circumscribes the field of economy. That word is Value. Political Economy does not aspire to place its feet upon the ponderous imperatives of moral obligation. It finds a solid and adequate footing upon the expedient and the useful. As a science, it does and must discuss and decide all questions upon economical grounds alone. As a science, it has no concern with questions of moral right. If it favors morality, it does so because morality favors production. It favors honesty because honesty favors exchange. It puts the seal of the market upon all the virtues. It condemns slavery, not because slavery is morally wrong, but because it is economically ruinous. Moral science appeals only to an enlightened conscience, and certain conduct is approved because it is right, and for no other reason. Political Economy appeals only to an enlightened self-interest, and exchanges are made because they are mutually advantageous, and for no other reason. Each of the two sciences, therefore, has a distinct basis and sphere of its own. The grounds of Economy and morals are independent and incommensurable.

Every science, however, has its points of contact with other sciences; and this is particularly the case with Political Economy in relation to moral science, and is the reason why the two have sometimes been confounded. The sound conclusions of the one are harmonious with the sound conclusions of the other. Both work together for the good of men, for the amelioration of their condition. Their spheres, though distinct, nevertheless touch each other. Duty and interest lie alongside. The ultimate analysis of property, for example, will, as we shall see, lead the inquirer into the higher region of moral science. In legislation also, the question is frequently at the same time an economical and a moral question. Dr.

Wayland has observed that "almost every question of the one science may be argued on grounds belonging to the other." But the grounds themselves, it is important to remark, must be seen to be, and must be kept, distinct.

In the next place, the very name of the science indicates that it is a political, that is, a social science. It relates to men in a state of society, and not to men in a state of isolation. The hermit, who neither buys nor sells, who neither gives nor receives anything in exchange, is not amenable to the laws of Political Economy. So far as men satisfy their own wants by their own efforts without exchange, they stand outside the pale of this science. Under those circumstances the idea of value could neither have birth nor being, and of course there would be no such thing as a science of value. Robinson Crusoe came to lead a very tolerable life upon his desolate island by means of his own industry. He worked, but then he worked to satisfy his own wants directly. He did everything for himself. He had no opportunity to buy anything, sell anything, exchange anything. The whole course of such a life could never have developed the idea of value, and the record of the whole experience of such a solitary individual would require no such word as value. If God had made men so that their varied wants would best be met by applying their own efforts to satisfy these wants directly, without the intervention of exchange, there would have been, there could have been, no such science as the one to which attention is now directed. In that case, men would live, if they lived at all, in perfect isolation. Every man would satisfy his own desires by his own efforts. There would be no society, and no exchange.

But it is evident at the very first glance, that the Creator has not made men thus. Society is God's handiwork. It is the most complicated and the most wonderful, as it was the final, work of his hands. The first man, as he stood alone in Paradise, was indeed a wonderful structure, — wonderful in his body, and in all his mental and spiritual powers. But it was not good that the man should be alone. Society must be provided for; and in providing for a society of human beings, God impressed upon that organization, as upon all others, its own proper and peculiar laws. These laws embrace its entire organization, in its lower, as well as in its higher, parts. They cover the phenomena of exchange, just as they cover the phenomena of morals; and no intelligent observer can watch their working, when left intact and free, without being stimulated and gladdened by the beneficent results to which they lead. If the footsteps of providential intelligence be found anywhere upon this earth, if proofs of God's goodness be anywhere discernible, they are discernible, and are found in the fundamental laws of society. Certainly, if every man could satisfy all his desires as well, by putting forth his efforts to that end directly, he would do it. He would grow his own food, make his own clothes, write and publish his own newspaper, be his own doctor, in one word, perform all needed services for himself. But God has so ordered it that he cannot do this. He cannot, in a state of isolation, with all his efforts, procure for himself one thousandth part of the comforts which he easily procures for himself by less efforts, througn exchange. Society and exchange are, under God's ordination, matters of necessity, if men are to rise in a scale of comforts perceptibly above the brutes. And the reason is this. There are obstacles, in all directions, to the satisfaction of men's desires If the desires are to be met, these obstacles are to be surmounted. But if one man undertakes to surmount any considerable number of these obstacles, he miserably fails. His powers are not adequate to the task; and hence we say, that in a state of isolation, men's wants exceed their powers. But, if he devote himself to surmounting one class of obstacles, as, for instance, those in the way of procuring suitable clothing, his powers are adequate to this, he soon acquires skill in it, he learns to avail himself of the gratuitous help of Nature, and the facilitating processes of art, he is able to realize large products along his line, and is now in position to offer valuable services to society. Meanwhile other men have been devoting themselves each to another class of obstacles, have concentrated effort and skill upon them, have succeeded by the help of Nature and art in surmounting them, and now offer their valuable services to society.

Now, then, these services are mutually exchanged in all directions, and men find, as it is God's clear design that they should find, that, by making given efforts along one line, and exchanging them for corresponding efforts along other lines, they obtain vastly greater satisfactions for their various desires than they could obtain by direct effort. Why? Because there is now a vast increase of useful products in existence. Here we have reached, provisionally, the true explanation of the gains of exchange. It is not so much that by exchange men get better and cheaper articles, as it is that they get more of them. By the division of employments, which is only possible under a system of exchange; by the fact that, under free exchange, men avail themselves of all the varied advantages of Nature and position; the number and variety of useful products created, the number and variety of the services which men are able to render to each other, are immeasurably augmented. More is produced, more is to be exchanged, and therefore there are more satisfactions of all men's desires. Political Economy, therefore, which unfolds the reasons and the laws of exchange, finds its only field in a state of society. It is truly a political, that is, a social science.

In determining now more definitely still the field of our science, we will look at some of the leading definitions of it which have been given by different writers. Mr. Senior defines it "the science which treats of the nature, the production, and the distribution of wealth." Mr. McCulloch regards it "the science of the laws which regulate the production of those material products which have exchangeable value, and which are either necessary, useful, or agreeable to man." Archbishop Whately gives it the name of "catalactics, or the science of exchanges." Among several equivalent definitions which he is at pains to give, Mr. Mill places first,—'the science which treats of the production and distribution of wealth, so far as they depend upon the laws of human nature." The French writers give definitions somewhat broader. M. Storch says it "is the science of the natural laws which determine the prosperity of nations, that is to say, their wealth and civilization." M. Sismondi regards "as the object of political economy the physical welfare of man, so far as it can be the work of government." And M. Say defines it as "the economy of society; a science combining the results of our observations on the nature and functions of the different parts of the social body." Mr. Carey defines it "the science of the laws which govern man in his efforts to secure for himself the highest individuality and the greatest power of association with his fellow-men." And lastly, Mr. Macleod offers the definition, — "the science which treats of the laws which govern the relations of exchangeable quantities."

It will be noticed that in several of the preceding definitions the term wealth is introduced as a part of the definition. This word wealth has been the bane of Political Economy. It is the bog whence most of the mists have arisen which have beclouded the whole subject. From its indefiniteness, and the variety of associations it carries along with it in different minds, it is totally unfit for any scientific purpose whatever. It is itself almost impossible to be defined, and consequently can serve no useful purpose in a definition of anything else. It has been much debated, for example, among political economists, whether the term wealth includes anything more than material products, such as houses, lands, metals, tools, food; or whether the skill of artisans and the services of professional men are also to be reckoned as wealth. Some include under the term only material products; others, as Mr. Mill, widen the signification so as to take in those immaterial services which result in an increase of material products; while others still, with evident violence to the current meaning of the word, include under it all things, whether material or immaterial, for which something may be obtained in exchange. Thus the meaning of the word wealth has never yet been settled; and if Political Economy must wait until that work be done as a preliminary, the science will never be satisfactorily constructed. It is simply impossible, on such an indefinite word as this at the foundation, to build up a complete science of Political Economy. Moreover the word wealth includes the two distinct ideas of value and utility, — ideas which must be kept perfectly distinct, or else there is no sound thinking and no sound conclusions within this field. Men may think, and talk, and write, and dispute to weariness, but until they come to use words with definiteness, and mean the same thing by the same word, they reach comparatively few results, and make but little progress. And it is just at this point that we find the first grand reason of the slow advance hitherto made by this science. It undertook to use a word for scientific purposes which no amount of manipulation and explanation could make suitable for that service. Happily there is no need to use this word. In emancipating itself from the word wealth as a technical term, Political Economy has dropped a clog, and its movements are now relatively free.

Of the other definitions quoted, against which the objection just considered does not lie, some embrace too little, and others embrace too much. The only one which seems to the present writer to be exactly right, is the definition given by Archbishop Whately, namely, the science of exchanges. This definition, or its precise equivalent, the science of value, gives a perfectly definite field to Political Economy. Wherever value goes this science goes, and where value stops this science stops. Political Economy is the science of value, and of nothing else. To determine with distinctness what value is, to separate it from some things which have often been confounded with it, and thus to lay a foundation for the science at once satisfactory and complete, will be the work of the next chapter. But it is in order at this point to call attention to the second grand reason of the slow advance hitherto made in this field of inquiry. Value is a relative word. It is usually defined as purchasing-power, that is to say, the value of anything is its power of purchasing other things. It is not an independent quality of one thing, as hardness is a quality of a stone, but it is a quality of one thing as estimated in a corresponding quality of something else. It is not a quality, in and of itself, of gold, but a relation which gold holds to other things which gold will buy. The notion of value is not conceivable except by a comparison of two things, and what is more, of two things mutually exchanged. Political Economy therefore is based upon a relative idea, and has to do from beginning to end with a relation. Now in this there is an inherent difficulty, and a difficulty too which can never be obviated. It lies in the very nature of the subject. Men much more readily apprehend an absolute idea than a relative one. They more easily follow a discussion touching the independent attributes of single objects, such as length, breadth, thickness, and many others, than a discussion touching value, which is not an attribute of any one thing, but a relation subsisting between two things. I am not aware that this difficulty has ever been remarked on by any writer, but I am at the same time very sure that it constitutes the principal difficulty in this class of inquiries, and has been the main reason of the tardy progress hitherto made in them.

In thus circumscribing the field of Political Economy, I am not disposed to deny the possibility of a more comprehensive science than this is as thus defined, or of even a number of sciences, as yet undeveloped and unnamed, whose inquiry might be, under what intellectual and physical conditions, men, whether as individuals or as aggregated in society, might obtain the greatest amount of physical comforts, or the highest degree of individuality, or the widest control over the powers of nature. Several of the definitions cited above imply more general inquiries than are relevant in a proper science of exchanges; and a good deal of the discussion in almost all books that professedly treat of Political Economy is drawn from territory that lies outside the strict limits of that science. Whatever others have done, or may hereafter undertake to do, I propose solely to investigate the motives and the conditions that govern men in their *exchanges*. Such investigations have a definite field of view; and if properly pursued, will lead to a statement of those laws that constitute the Science of Value. To these, then, we next proceed; and first of all, to an analysis of Value itself.

CHAPTER III.

ON VALUE.

If I take up a new lead-pencil from my table, for the purpose of examining all its qualities, I shall immediately perceive those which are visible and tangible. The pencil has length, a cylindrical form, a black color, is hard to the touch, is composed of wood and plumbago in certain relations to each other, and has the quality, when sharpened at the end, of making black marks upon white paper. These qualities, and such as these, may be learned by a study of the pencil itself. But can I learn, by a study of the pencil itself, the *value* of the pencil? Is value a quality? By any examination of its mechanical, or by any analysis of its chemical properties, can I detect how much the pencil is *worth?* No. The questioning of the senses, however minute, the test of the laboratory, however delicate, applied to the pencil alone can never determine how much it is worth. These methods will discover the *qualities* that belong to the pencil as such, but I must take another method altogether to determine its *value.*

Will the origin of the word Value help in finding a method by which I may discover the value of the pencil? The word is derived from the Latin verb VALERE, *to pass for*, *to be worth.* There is a hint of a *comparison* in the original meaning of the term itself. Will the current use of language assist me any further in finding out the way to learn the value of my pencil? In current language, when the value of anything is asked, the answer always comes in the terms of something else. We ask, How much is it worth? The answer is, so many cents or dollars. The cents or dollars are very different things from the things whose value we inquire after; and thus we see again more clearly that value implies a comparison of two distinct things; and, if so, of course it is useless to try to ascertain its value by a study of the pencil alone. But what kind of a comparison between two things is needful, in order to ascertain the value of either? There is no use in laying down a certain number of cents by the side of the pencil for the purpose of fixing its value, as we lay down a carpenter's square by the side of a stick to ascertain its length; because the cents have no common physical quality with the pencil, as the square and stick have in common the physical quality of length. A simple comparison determines the relative length of the square and the stick, and it makes no difference in the result whose the square is or whose the stick is. A borrowed square is just as good to determine length as any other, since that circumstance does not affect the terms of the comparison: also, one man is competent to make the comparison, and it is not needful that he be the owner of either of the things compared.

But is a man who does not own a thing competent to fix its value? And is a man who does own a thing competent to fix its value by himself alone?

The true answer to these questions brings out two peculiarities of that comparison by which value must always be ascertained. Besides the two things compared, there must be always two persons comparing, and each of these two persons must be virtually the owner of one of the things compared. Because I think my pencil is worth fifteen cents, is it therefore worth fifteen cents? Somebody else must think so too before that fact can be announced. Also, the comparison that two thieves make between two pieces of stolen goods would not go far in public estimation towards fixing the value of either piece of goods. Somebody, then, who owns the cents, must make a comparison with somebody else who owns the pencil, or the value of the latter is not likely to be truly ascertained.

But besides such a comparison, essential as this is as towards the end in view, another step is needful before I can announce the value of the pencil. Not simply a comparison but an *action* also is necessary. I think it is worth fifteen cents; an owner of cents, with whom the comparison is made, thinks so too; is it therefore worth fifteen cents? That is more than I can tell yet. I say to him, Will you take it and give me fifteen cents for it? He replies, I think it is worth it, but I am not ready to give that sum for it this morning. The value of the pencil is not yet determined. In order to that there must be an actual EXCHANGE of the pencil for the cents. There must be two things, two persons, a comparison, an actual exchange by which each person shall receive in fact or in ownership that previously held by the other, — each rendering something *for the sake of* the thing received, before the determinate *value* of anything is possible to be stated. There may be expected value, estimated value, but actual value there is none, until a real exchange has settled how much the value is. The value of anything is something else already exchanged for it. Value is not simply a relation subsisting between two things, but an actual fact established in connection with those two things. *Quid pro quo* is the universal formula of value. The pencil is *not* worth fifteen cents, because I have not yet succeeded in obtaining that sum in exchange for it.

Not dealing in pencils, nor liking to chaffer, and finding it a little troublesome to discover what the value of the pencil *is*, I ask myself what its value *was* when I purchased it? That is an easy question. Two days ago I paid for it the sum of ten cents, United States currency. It was the storekeeper and I. I owned the cents and he owned the pencil. We compared these two pieces of property together, and agreed to change ownership in them. I gave him the cents for the sake of the pencil, and he gave me the pencil for the sake of the cents. How much is my pencil worth? I do not know. How much was it worth two days ago? Ten cents exactly.

If this preliminary view be just, it is clear that value is not in any true sense a quality residing in any one thing, but is a relation of mutual purchase established between two things. Nevertheless, it is often convenient to regard value as a quality inhering in a commodity or service. The convenience of such expressions as, "the pencil has value," "gold has value," is so great, that science will not consent to forego the advantage of using them, even though they are not scientifically accurate. Science justly prefers to make her language intelligible and popular, even at the hazard of perpetuating a misapprehension. On such subjects as these, she is compelled in part to use language as she finds it; but she is culpable if she does not fix at the outset with absolute distinctness the meaning of her terms, however popularly current, and then use the terms, always in the same sense, never confounding a term with other terms of a similar but not identical significance. In allowing, therefore, such expressions as, "gold has value," I do not use the term in any other than its defined sense, I do not imply that value is a simple quality, but I employ shortened forms of expression long consecrated by usage, and avoid circumlocutions sure to become tedious. So also, by using language that may imply that value exists before it is realized in an actual exchange, I do not admit that value exists independently of an exchange; men employ foresight, put forth exertion, practice abstinence, in reference to a future realization of value: it is proper, at any rate it is necessary, to speak of them as already employed upon *value*, and of value itself as a purchasing-*power* residing in this or that. A concession to the exigencies of language is not a departure from the exactness of science. It is not, accordingly, true, speaking strictly, that value is a quality of gold in the sense in which weight is a quality of gold, because circumstances are easily conceivable, and have often occurred, under which gold would have no value at all. To the crew of a boat abandoned at sea, among whom the last biscuit had been rationed out, a bag of gold belonging to one of the men would not purchase a biscuit belonging to another. The inherent qualities of the gold are present. It is still hard, and yellow, and heavy But valuable it is not. It will not purchase anything. Value, therefore, is not an inherent and invariable attribute, but is the relative power which one thing has of purchasing other things. This power in any one thing will vary according to time and place and circumstances. It may cease altogether, as in the case just supposed, or it may rise under other circumstances to a very high degree; but whenever it exists, it exists with reference to some other thing, which either is, or is supposed to be, exchanged with it. Ten cents had the power of purchasing my pencil, and my pencil had the power of purchasing ten cents. In this transaction the idea of value is developed. A similar transaction first introduced that idea into the world, and the endless succession and variety of such transactions have kept the idea in the world, and will keep it here till the end of time. Value, then, speaking strictly, is not an independent quality of the pencil, any more than it is an independent quality of the cents. Both are necessary in order that the value of either may be conceived of. The value of the cents is estimated, is measured by the pencil; and the value of the pencil is estimated, is measured by the cents. In one word, value is always relative, and never absolute. To say that anything has an absolute value is a simple contradiction in terms.

But why was I desirous to part with good United States money for the sake of the pencil, and the storekeeper to part with a good pencil for the sake of the money? The answer to this question will ground the science of value on the unchanging principles of human nature. I experienced a want which the pencil was adapted to satisfy. He experienced a want which the money was adapted to satisfy. But between my want and its satisfaction, both of which were personal to me, there lay an effort, to be made either by myself or by somebody else in my behalf. So, between his want and its satisfaction, both of which were personal to him, there lay an effort, to be made either by himself or by somebody else in his behalf. If I had chosen to do so, I might have made the direct effort necessary in order to supply myself with a pencil. I might have made the pencil for myself. It would indeed have been a long and tedious process, would have required a learning of two or three trades, a journey to some plumbago-bed, the working and preparation of the mineral, and various other subordinate processes; still, in the course of half a life-time it might perhaps have been done, and I might by direct efforts have supplied myself with a pencil as good as that which I purchased. So, too, the storekeeper, unless the laws had prevented it, might have procured for himself by direct efforts the metal cents which I gave him in exchange for the pencil. He might have dug the ores for himself, refined, alloyed, and minted them. Had we chosen respectively to take this course, and each been able to satisfy his own particular desire by his own unassisted efforts, the processes in either case would have had no relation to Political Economy. There would be in each case a want, an effort, a satisfaction, but there would be no exchange. As a matter of fact, however, we exchanged the efforts which lay between our respective desires and their respective satisfactions. I desired a pencil, he relieved me of the effort necessary to make it, and I experienced the satisfaction. He desired the cents, I relieved him of the effort necessary to procure them, and he again experienced the satisfaction. We each experienced our own desires, and our own satisfactions, but we exchanged efforts. Precisely in this exchange of efforts arose the phenomenon of value. I parted with my cents, which had cost me an effort, in order to satisfy my desire for a pencil, because my effort, represented in the cents, was less than the effort it would cost me to create the pencil. The shopkeeper parted with the pencil, which had cost him an effort, in order to satisfy his desire for the cents, because his effort, represented in the pencil, was less than the effort which it would otherwise cost him to procure the cents. We exchanged efforts, therefore, for our mutual advantage.

The principles of human nature, then, on which the laws of value are grounded, are these: Men have desires, are capable of making efforts to meet these desires, and experience a satisfaction when the desires are met. These three are indisputable and universal facts. But while the desire and the satisfaction are strictly personal to one man, that is to say, belong to him and cannot be communicated to another, it is not so with efforts. Efforts are exchangeable. You have a desire, I make the effort to meet it, and you again experience the satisfaction.

On the other hand, I have a desire, you make the effort to meet it, and I again have the satisfaction. We exchange efforts, but experience our own satisfactions. Desires, efforts, satisfactions, constitute the one circle of Political Economy, and value arises in every case from a comparison of two corresponding efforts. Efforts are naturally irksome. Everybody wishes to realize as large a satisfaction as possible from a given effort. If, by making that effort for another, a larger satisfaction will be realized than by expending it directly for one's self, there is an immediate and pressing motive to make the effort for another, and to reach the satisfaction, not directly, but indirectly, that is, by exchange. A precisely similar motive actuates that other person. If his given effort will realize more for himself by being put forth for the first man, and by accepting the first man's effort in return, he too will be anxious to exchange efforts with the first. There is a mutual advantage in thus exchanging. A given effort realizes better satisfactions for each of the parties, and the reason for exchanges is thus seen to spring from the most active and invariable principles of human nature.

The exchange of the cents for the pencil, and the pencil for the cents, is a simple case of value, but it is not the simplest. In this case there is an exchange of one commodity for another commodity, the idea of value is instantly developed, and we say that the pencil is worth ten cents, or, what is exactly equivalent, ten cents are worth the pencil. There are two things in every exchange, — that which is parted with and that which is received. Attention should be constantly directed to both. Many errors in science, and numberless mistakes in legislation, have arisen from not attending to this circumstance, as if it were the glory of trade to sell rather than to buy, whereas it is not possible to sell without buying, because the pay must be taken for what is sold. In every exchange, therefore, of commodity for commodity, the value of each is expressed in the other, and the relation between the two purchasing-powers is adjusted. This is the common case. The trade of all past ages, and the present commerce of five continents, presents us, in principle, with nothing different from this. The commerce of the world is substantially barter, that is, the exchange of commodities for commodities; and, though many purchases and sales may intervene, and money may play its part in facilitating the exchange, and many forms of credit may come in, before the transaction is finally closed, these do not alter in the slightest particular either the notion of value or its laws. Each repeated purchase and sale presents us over and over again with the same phenomenon, namely, the equalization through exchange of two purchasing-powers. This is value, and is the sole subject of our science.

The simplest case of value, however, will throw light upon the more complex ones, and will be found to include them. Two farmers, who are neighbors, find, on talking over their respective crops, that one has more hoeing and less haying this year than usual, and the other less hoeing and more haying. A says to B, "Come over and help me hoe in June, and I will go over and help you hay in July."

B agrees. It is a mutual advantage. And so, to use the old expression, which is better here than any scientific terms could be, they change works. B does a service for A, and A does a service for B. The two services balance each other. They are mutually exchanged one for the other; and in the very proposal thus to exchange them the notion of value is conceived, and in the exchange itself value is both produced and measured. B's help in hoeing is worth A's help in haying.

This exchange of one service for another service presents the simplest case of value; and I now proceed to show that it essentially includes all other cases. If it can be shown that value is always and everywhere the same thing, that it is always and everywhere THE RELATION OF MUTUAL PURCHASE ESTABLISHED BETWEEN TWO SERVICES BY THEIR EXCHANGE, Political Economy will be seen to possess one grand characteristic of the great sciences, namely, simplicity. This can be shown. There are only six cases of value conceivable, because there are only three kinds of things that are ever economically exchanged. These latter are, 1st. Material Commodities, like the pencil; 2d. Immaterial Services, like those of the teacher; 3d. Forms of Incorporeal Property, like a United States bond. We may have, then, first, an exchange of commodity for commodity, as the pencil for the cents; second, of commodity for service, as five dollars for the advice of a lawyer; third, of commodity for some form of incorporeal property, as a Waltham watch for a copyright; fourth, of service for service, as in the case of the two farmers just mentioned; fifth, of service for an incorporeal, as a year's work for a five hundred dollar bond; and sixth, an incorporeal for an incorporeal, as a bond for so many railroad shares.[1] What is mutually transferred in all these cases is the ownership or property in something. Material products may or may not be passed over to the purchaser at the time of the sale, but the *ownership* goes over to him in all cases. Personal services, unlike material products, are not commonly resalable by the purchaser; sometimes they are, as when one hires out for a time his own hired man. Most species of incorporeal property are transferable at will, as bank checks, patent-rights, and promissory notes. But this transfer of ownership, a feature in all cases of value, though less obviously so when simple services are rendered, does not present the best aspect for the complete understanding of value. That aspect is presented through the term *services.*

It is mutual services, as well as mutual ownership, that are exchanged in these six cases; and the word services carries us deeper into the central phenomena of value. Thus the client, with five dollars in his pocket, is just as much in position to do the lawyer a service, as the lawyer is in position to do him a service. The counsel is serviceable to the client, and the dollars are serviceable to the lawyer, and so they exchange. And just so when commodities are exchanged with each other. The hatter serves you with a hat, and the shoemaker with a pair of boots, and you serve them with six dollars each; or if the hatter be in want of boots, and the shoemaker of a hat, they serve each other with their respective prod-

[1] Compare Macleod's Banking, page 9.

ucts. In every case of value, therefore, without exception, what is really exchanged, whether a commodity intervene or not, are mutual services; and value is then produced, and only then, when two persons are in position to render each other a service; and the respective services being rendered, that is exchanged, and the balance being struck, we have the value of one expressed in the other.

Do I, then, obliterate the old distinction between services and commodities? Yes, I do, as far as the laws of value are concerned. I use the term "service" in a broad sense, which includes the specific sense and something more. I mean by it, *the rendering of anything for which something is demanded in return.* People sometimes do for others what are called services, out of sympathy, from benevolence, from duty; but the characteristic of these is that they are free; nothing is demanded in return. These, therefore, fall in the sphere of morals, and are outside the pale of Political Economy. There is no such thing as exchange proper within the field of morals, and there is nothing else but exchange proper within the field of economy. This principle alone marks the boundary-line between the sciences referred to. A service, then, in the language of this science, and as the word will henceforward be used in these pages, is anything rendered to another in view of a return, and for the sake of a return. The man who furnishes you a barrel of apples, does you, in this sense, a service equally with the physician who attends upon your fever; and you pay them both on precisely the same principles. You render to each an equivalent service in return. To pay them money is to render them a service, just as to furnish you apples and medical advice were a service to you. Whether a commodity, as apples, intervene or not, is, as far as value is concerned, a matter of indifference. The more specific use of the term "service," as opposed to a commodity, is indeed convenient, and will, doubtless, continue to be used: the broader sense is exceedingly useful, and, by its aid, we clear up the whole subject of value.

This ultimate definition of value, namely, that it is the relation of mutual purchase established between two services, is substantially, but not in form, the definition of M. Bastiat. Mr. Macleod's definition is also excellent, though I cannot give it the preference:—"*The value of any economic quantity is any other economic quantity for which it can be exchanged.*" If the question relate to the value of any *specific* thing whatever, Mr. Macleod's answer is perfect; if the question be, What is *Value?* the other answer seems to me to be equally satisfactory. The reasons why we may feel complete confidence in it will appear in a more and more striking light as we proceed, and until we conclude.

In the first place, this definition covers naturally and easily all those anomalous cases of value which have been so hard to reduce under any other general view. Take for instance the case of the value of the diamond. The English school, and especially Mr. McCulloch, claim that labor is the source of value, and that the purchasing-power of everything is proportioned to the labor which it has cost. But, take care. There must be error in this statement. Value is not always proportioned to the mere labor the thing has cost. Often it is. Frequently it is not.

For example, as I am strolling along the sea-shore I accidently perceive a splendid diamond among the pebbles. It is but a moment's labor to appropriate the prize, but do I on that account sell my diamond for one dollar less to the jeweller or the prince? No. I am now in position to do a great service to anybody wanting a diamond. I demand a large service in return, and get it. I say to the man who wants it, give me ten thousand dollars for my prize, and you shall have it. It would be poor mercantile logic for him to reply: Your labor is not worth more than one cent a minute, and it did not cost you but one minute's labor to get that gem, and certainly one cent, therefore, is a fair price for the diamond. He rather reasons in this way: Can I by going myself to the diamond-bearing regions, or in any diamond market elsewhere, procure for myself so good a gem as this by a less sacrifice than ten thousand dollars. He resolves this question mentally; and, if negatively, I am sure of getting my price. In that case I am offering him a service worth at least ten thousand dollars. No one else is in position to render him the same service at so favorable a rate. If, on the other hand, there be other diamond dealers offering gems as good as mine for less than ten thousand dollars, then I have pitched my demand too high; my service is not worth that sum, because there is some other person ready to render the same service for a less sum. The value of my diamond, therefore, is proportioned, not to the labor which it has cost me, but to the service which I am able to render to the purchaser with it, compared with the service which he is able to render to me. I take advan tage of his desire for the diamond, and crowd up the price as near as I can to the point at which he will either forego the possession of a diamond altogether, or can obtain a similar one from some other party. He takes advantage of my desire for the money, and crowds down the price as near as he can to the point at which I can either find another purchaser, or should prefer to retain the diamond myself. The comparison and adjustment of these two, my service to him and his service to me, fixes, for that sale, the value of the diamond.

And here we must stop to notice what an exceedingly good word the English language provides us with, in this term *service*. It explains perfectly all anomalous, as well as all common cases of value. It combines in its own proper meaning all the elements which make up and which vary value. First, it implies always two persons, the person rendering and the person receiving the service. Next, it always implies some effort on the part of the person rendering, and some satisfaction on the part of the person receiving the service. Thus when one service is spoken of there are always implied two persons and two things, and the two things are the effort of one person and the satisfaction of another. But when two services are spoken of as exchanged, as is always the case in Political Economy, there are implied, as before, two persons, each of whom makes an effort for the other, each of whom is recipient of a satisfaction which comes from the effort of the other, and each of whom estimates in the light of his own satisfaction that which is received as compared with that which is rendered. It is this reciprocal estimation alone that constitutes value; and it is the excellence, I may almost say the glory of the term service, that it gathers up in its own signification all the elements which go to determine value, and which ever vary its amount. As here is the very kernel and core of our science, illustration will be well bestowed at this point. Let the parties be A and B, in position to render each other a mutual service. A has a desire which B's effort can meet, and B has a desire which A's effort can meet. Up to the point when the exchange takes place there are only four elements that play any part in the transaction as preparatory to it, namely, two desires and two efforts. In the act of exchange itself two other elements come into being, namely, two relative estimates, A's estimate of B's effort for him as compared with his own effort for B, and B's estimate of A's effort for him as compared with his own effort for A. As a result of the exchange, and as that for the sake of which the whole series took place, there appear two other elements, namely, two satisfactions. Here is the whole of it. Now, then, any change in any one of the first four elements will vary value; and there is nothing else in the world that can vary it. If A's desire for that which B is ready to render be lessened, the other elements remaining the same, A's estimate of B's effort as compared with his own is lessened, and value is at once affected. If A's desire be increased, other things being equal, his estimate of B's service as compared with his own is increased, and value is affected. Just so any diminution or enhancement of B's desire for that which A is ready to render, acts at once upon B's estimate of A's effort as compared with his own, and consequently acts at once upon value. Again, any change in either effort as compared with the other, such as its becoming more or less onerous than the other, will of course affect the estimate of the one as measured by the other, and of course also will vary value. These first four elements then are not only the elements out of which value subsequently springs, but also are the elements any change in any one of which, the others remaining the same, will tend to vary value, and without a change in some one of which, relatively to the others, value never will be varied. The term services expresses just these elements which play and vary as preparatory to the realization of value. Value itself is realized from the adjustment of the fifth and sixth elements, that is to say, from the equalization of A's estimate of B's service with B's estimate of A's service. This adjustment also, together with the remaining elements, the two satisfactions, are all implied in the expression mutual services, or, if you please, two services exchanged. If any of my readers object to this paragraph as abstract, I have only to reply that it is no more abstract than the subject-matter; and if any of them find difficulty in the relative nature of the transaction unfolded, in the fact that the views and comparative estimates of two persons must be kept in mind throughout, I can only say, that this science starts with a relation and has to do with a relation every step of the way to the end. This is the one intrinsic, unavoidable difficulty that lies at the threshold of the science; and whoever, by taking pains at the outset, familiarizes this difficulty to his thoughts, and thus overmasters it, will walk thenceforward with positive pleasure through the whole economic domain. And if there ever was a science grateful for a word, as lessening its inherent difficulties and helping explain its phenomena, Political Economy, which has wandered these twice forty years in the wilderness of wealth, thankfully accepts in the term service its latest and most important gift.

In the second place, the definition of value which is here given expands the field of Political Economy to its natural limits. Even Adam Smith, and the English economists generally, while defining wealth as consisting of material commodities only, have experienced a difficulty in excluding from the domain of the science certain mere services, and in denying that value resides in these services. Some have endeavored to avoid the difficulty in one way and some in another. Some have stigmatized those who render a mere service to society as unproductive laborers, and have gifted with the title of productive laborers all those who bring forward some vendible commodity. John Stuart Mill, as we have seen, enlarged his definition of wealth so as to take in all those sorts of mere services whose action goes directly to swell the volume of material commodities. It is conceded then that value resides in some services; why not then in all services which are put forth for the sake of a return? Why allow value to a service which comes to be embodied in a commodity, and deny the term to another service just as necessary to our comfort that is not thus embodied? Why class the brick-maker as a productive laborer, and refuse the epithet to the hod-carrier, without whose help the bricks would never reach their ultimate destination? The truth is there is no ground for this distinction; and the very difficulty which the various writers have found in trying to make it, is a pretty sure proof that it ought not to be made at all. By making its definitions such that value can only be supposed to reside in tangible commodities, Political Economy excludes itself, without any good reason, from a large portion of its own field. Let us see if there be any good reason. For example, a man buys a spelling-book for his boy, for the sake of his learning to read. He then hires a teacher to teach him to read. According to the usual definitions the spelling-book has value, while the service of the teacher has none. But why has it none? It has to be paid for, certainly, as much as the spelling-book has to be paid for. There are two separate exchanges; first, of money for the spelling-book, and second, of money for the service. Both are made with the same object in view, namely, that the boy may learn to read. The want of a spelling-book and the want of a teacher are the two external obstacles in the way of reaching that object; and the father overcomes them both by similar means, that is to say, by an exchange; and there is no such difference in the two transactions as will justify or even tolerate the distinction sought to be made between them. The teacher sells his service. The shopkeeper sells his book. The father renders a service to each equivalent to that received from each. Political Economy now claims jurisdiction over both transactions alike, and affirms value as truly of the service as of the commodity, and more truly of the service than of the commodity, inasmuch as it stands ready to prove that so far as value resides in any commodity it resides there simply in virtue of the human services which have been concerned in its production and which will be subserved by its exchange. What is ultimate, therefore, in all exchange, is services and not commodities; and the services which are bought and sold in every department of life, the services, for example, of the lawyer, the physician, the clergyman, the teacher, the editor, the musician, fall as much within the province of Political Economy as the traffic of commodities in the market-place. Our science asserts its claim of jurisdiction wherever services are mutually exchanged.

A third advantage of the definition of value now given, and one closely connected with the last, will be seen in the fact that it frees the discussion from a perplexing error which has long infected this class of inquiries, namely, that value is somehow or other connected with matter. This notion has controlled the definitions of wealth; has led, as we have just seen, to groundless distinctions among services; and has taken possession of language so thoroughly that no judicious writer will attempt at this late day to dislodge it from that strongest of the citadels of error. Rather than disturb the current nomenclature of business he will allow such expressions as these to stand: Gold *has* value, strawberries *have* value. But it is very easy to show that value does not reside in matter, or in any form of matter, but only in human services exchanged; and that, therefore, value is never of God's creation, but always of men's exertion. We shall see abundantly, before we finish the chapter, that utility is one thing and value quite another. No effort of men can add one particle to the existing matter of the globe, but it has been supposed that the efforts of men, by changing the form of existing matter, impart the quality of value to it, and that thenceforth the value remains fixed in the matter itself. The efforts of a woodman, for example, with the coöperation of nature, can transform the stock of a tree into wooden bowls, and value is now supposed to reside in the vendible bowls, and the current language is, that each bowl *has* a value of fifty cents. Why has it a value of fifty cents? Clearly enough, to reward his *service* who felled the tree, and sawed the block, and then hollowed out the bowl. But the service having been employed upon the matter, and being embodied in it, is not what is really sold now the matter, and not the service? I answer, No. What is really sold is the service, and not the matter. And this, which at first sight might not be thought important, but which is really very important, becomes apparent as soon as we reflect that any changes in the conditions of the service instantly affect the value. Our woodman has on hand a stock of one hundred bowls, which he offers for sale at fifty cents apiece, as fairly rewarding his personal services in their production. But, unknown to him, an enterprising neighbor has invented a machine which enables him to make bowls in every respect equal to the others, and to offer them at twenty-five cents apiece. Whoever now wants a wooden bowl can have that service rendered him for twenty-five cents return. The first man finds that he cannot sell a bowl for over twenty-five cents, and that his stock of one hundred has sunk at once in value from fifty dollars to twenty-five dollars. What is the matter with his bowls? The matter is not in the matter. The matter is all there, and the form of the matter is all there, but the value is just one half escaped, because the service which he can render to a buyer by a bowl has been, by the enterprise of his neighbor, just one half lessened. Value then follows the fortunes of services, and varies as they vary, just as much when they have been employed upon commodities, as when they are independent of them, and we see that the value resides in services compared, and not in matter at all.

I now proceed to indicate the manner in which language came to be used in such a way as gives color to the notion that value resides in the commodities rather than in the services. An instance will bring the whole subject before us clearly. In many parts of the United States delicious wild strawberries may be had in their season for the simple picking. The pastures and meadows are open to every comer, and the strawberries are considered to belong, not to the owners of the fields, but to any one who takes the labor of picking the fruit. Let us suppose that my family are fond of the berries, and that no member of it likes to undergo the labor of picking them, and that I hire some girl, who offers her services for the purpose, to go to the fields and gather some of the fruit for us. When she returns I pay her for her service. She does not conceive of any value residing in the strawberries themselves. Neither do I. She makes a series of efforts for the gratification of my family, and is paid for her efforts. Language recognizes the true state of the case, and she does not say now that she *sells* us the berries, and we do not speak of *buying* the berries of her. She thinks only of her service, we think only of her service, she is paid only for her service: language is exact in the premises. The next day, as the girl is about to go for us again, my neighbor says to her, "You bring me as many, and I will pay you as much." The third day, a second neighbor makes a similar bargain with her, and she brings strawberries for the three families, and is paid in each case for her service. The girl, on the fourth day, taking it for granted that we shall be likely to want strawberries that day also, does not wait to be sent, makes no bargain for her services beforehand, but goes and gathers the fruit. This time there is a change of language when she comes to my door. She now offers to *sell* me *strawberries*. "How much are they worth?" I ask. She names probably the same sum which she had before received for the service of picking the same quantity. She could not materially increase it, because there are doubtless other girls who are ready to render the service which she before rendered, at the same rate. But attention is now drawn away from the service to the berries, and the idea of value is attached to the berries, and language adopts the illusion, and says, "the *berries* are worth so much." Who does not see, however, that the transaction is substantially the same as before? Who does not see that it is only by a figure of speech, convenient indeed, but still only a figure, that the berries are now said to *have* value? If there be no difference in the last case as compared with the former cases in the two desires and in the two efforts, it is plain to reason that there can be no difference in the value, and consequently no difference in that which is really sold. But my desire for the berries, my effort as represented in the price paid, her desire for the money, and her effort as represented in the picking, are all just as before. She expected me to take them, and I took them as before. The value, therefore, the purchasing-power, resides not in the berries, but in the service; that is to say, in that which she renders as compared with that she receives; and it is only a freak of language which leads us to suppose otherwise. This is but a simple instance, but the principles of the instance are applicable to all commodities whatsoever. It is only mediately and figuratively that commodities can be said to have value at all; and if we use the common language, and say that they have value, we must always remember that they have it simply and solely in consequence of the human services which have been employed upon them, and which may be subserved by them, as related to those other human services for which they may be exchanged. If this be true, and it seems to me certain that it *is* true, it throws a flood of light upon the whole field of value. More attention must be given hereafter, in Political Economy, to persons, and less to things. Man and his wants, man and his efforts, become at once the chief topics, while the material products on which efforts are employed, and which minister to wants, sink in relative position. It follows also from this distinction, that there is not so much difference as is commonly supposed, when a man works for others, and when he sets up for himself, — between a journeyman and a master. The journeyman sells his services, and the master sells nothing more or other than his own services. The services of the master may not be manual, they may be merely supervisory, or they may be connected with the use of his capital; but the finished product, when it is ready for the consumer, represents the aggregate of the human services which have been employed upon it, and whoever sells it, sells those services, and its ultimate value is determined, as all other value is, by a double comparison, the purchaser's comparison of the service of the product to him with that which he renders, and the seller's comparison of the service he receives with that of the product. Service for service, in the last analysis, rather than commodity for commodity, is the rule of value and the law of exchange.

It may be observed, in the fourth place, that a principal merit of the definition of value insisted on in this chapter, is the discrimination which it allows between utility and value. It is absolutely essential that these two ideas be not confounded. But they are confounded in all the earlier writers on wealth. The word wealth itself inextricably confounds them. Whole discussions in Adam Smith are marred by his not consistently attending to the distinction, which he himself draws in one place, between "value in use and value in exchange:" meaning by the former expression simple utility. Say mixes up the two ideas even more completely than Adam Smith does; and the errors of the two writers in this respect gave rise to the twentieth chapter of Mr. Ricardo's book,[1] in which the difference between utility and value is pretty clearly unfolded. Mr. McCulloch, too, always insists upon this difference, and correctly maintains that the distinguishing characteristic of utility is, that it is gratuitous; although the theory of value of each of these writers is too narrow, unduly restricting the field of Political Economy by assuming that value rigidly inheres in commodities only. The example of these writers shows that the distinction referred to can be made even under their definition of value, but it is not so easily and practically made as under the true definition, because in the true definition attention is inevitably drawn to two persons, instead of to one thing, and utility, which is simple capacity to gratify any desire, is neatly discriminated, even in the nomenclature itself, from the mutual efforts by which the mutual desires are met. The word service enables us to draw the distinction, and to hold it fast.

Utility, then, is the capacity which any thing or any service has to gratify any human desire whatsoever. Political Economy has nothing to do with the estimation in which different desires are held by a philosopher or a moralist. It is enough to constitute for it utility, if anything will meet anybody's desire or serve anybody's purpose. In this sense, which is the etymological and only just sense of the word, ardent spirits have utility just as wheat has utility. The same thing may have no utility for one man, a low utility for another, and a very high utility for a third; since the first has no desire for it,

[1] Principles of Political Economy and Taxation.

the second a feeble, and the third a strong desire for it. Desires are personal to individuals. There is no common standard with which they may be compared. They are not exchangeable. Utility is the capacity which anything has of meeting any one of these desires at any time or in any place. But some things have this capacity in a high degree which are never exchanged, which are never bought or sold, and which consequently can have no value. The air we breathe, the light in which we recreate ourselves, the water we drink from the spring or brook, all have the highest utility, but no value. They connect themselves with no service. We give nothing for them. They, and such as they, are the direct gifts of God. They are gratuitous.

But utility is always present in all value also, since it is an element in all service; and the utility that appears in connection with value is always derived partly from Nature and partly from man. It is impossible to say, in any given case, how much is attributable to Nature and how much is attributable to man. It might seem at first sight, as if, in the case of the diamond, or in the case of the strawberries, the utility were wholly the gift of Nature, but the diamond undiscovered among the pebbles, and the strawberries unpicked upon the meadows, can hardly be said to have utility, much less value. The human service that fits each of these to meet a present desire is an essential contributor to their utility. On the other hand it might seem as if the utility of a painting were wholly referable to the art of the painter; but the tenacity of the canvas, the flexibility of the brush, and the brilliancy of the colors, are the contribution of Nature. Although, therefore, all utility that ever appears in connection with value is partly due to the efforts of men, it is none the less essential to clear thinking in this department to separate distinctly in the mind the utility from the value. The utility of a service may be great and its value little; the utility of a service may be great and its value also great. They are distinct things. They become, as it were, commingled in the service rendered, but the utility is one thing, and the value a distinct thing. Utility is ultimate: value is mediate. Utility is absolute with reference to the individual: value is always relative. The utility involved in every valuable service is derived from two sources, — the free contribution of Nature, and the onerous contribution of man; but the value of such services in general tends perpetually to become proportionate to the onerous human contribution, and not to the aggregate utility. If the service be unique, if only one person or a few be in a position to render it, no useful principle can be laid down, which shall discriminate the two components of the utility; but in respect to the vast mass of services, of which a market rate can be predicated, it is very clear that the competition with each other of those who are ready to render them, will fix the current value at a point which shall just about compensate for the onerous elements involved. That portion of the utility which is the free gift of Nature will be very nearly a common factor in that whole set of services. The action of competition will eliminate this common factor, and tend constantly to determine value on the basis merely of what man has done to impart utility to those services. Thus, if ten men bring ten horses to the market to exchange against money, though the utility of the horses be derived in large degree from the free gifts of Nature, yet there are some of the owners who will be willing to part with their property at a price that will compensate them for what they themselves have contributed towards that utility. The action of these will tend to fix the price of the whole ten. There is no tendency in value, then, to proportion itself to the aggregate utility of a service, but there *is* a tendency in value to proportion itself to the aggregate of the onerous human efforts represented in a service.

This principle, which I deem important, perfectly accounts for the low value of many services, which may be said nevertheless to have a high utility. The girl brings delicious strawberries to my door in summer. Their utility is great, their capacity to gratify my palate and that of my family is exquisite, but her effort in picking and bringing them is relatively little, and therefore it is little that I pay her. She cannot charge me one farthing for all that has been done for the fruit in the wonderful laboratory of Nature. Should she attempt to do so, there are doubtless other girls willing to bring me the fruit for a fair equivalent for their personal efforts only. Utility and value, then, are different things; we must certainly believe this, when we see some things, as air, possessed of the very highest utility and no value at all; and other things, as strawberries, possessed of a high utility and a low value.

The history of economy is full to a surfeit of the theoretical errors and of the practical blunders which have come from confounding value with utility; and from not attending to the fact that all utility, until some human service has been mingled with it, is absolutely free. God is a Giver. He gives sunlight, and air, and water, in abundance. He gives the earth, with all its materials, and with all its powers, and with all its spontaneous fruits, gratuitously to man. At the very first, He gave to man, "dominion over the fish of the seas, and over the fowl of the air, and over every living thing that moveth on the earth." So far forth as these gifts minister directly to men's wants, there is utility indeed, but no value. But since, for the most part, human services are required to mould these gratuitous materials, to harness these gratuitous powers, to make these gratuitous fruits and animals available for use, and since services for this purpose are exchanged among men, value springs up in connection with these utilities, but must not be confounded with them. The utilities, disengaged from the service, are free. God never takes pay for anything, and has not authorized anybody to take pay in his behalf; what is paid for is the service of man, and not the bounty of Nature. Even the powers of Nature which men avail themselves of by machinery, such as water, wind, and steam, all work for nothing: water gravitates, and wind blows, and steam puffs, for nothing. These all, and such as these, help to create utilities, but ultimately no value. Value is in the service which makes the machine, and in the service which tends it, but in the power which moves it, unless that power be human muscle, there is no value.

Value must be carefully distinguished from Price.

The price of anything is its purchasing-power expressed in money; the value of anything is its purchasing-power expressed in any other purchasing-power whatever. Price is a relative word, but specific; value is a relative word, but general. When we speak of the price of a service, we mean the sum of money which that service will buy; but when we speak of the value of a service, we mean the command in exchange of that service over other services generally. Thus, we say, "This coat is worth twenty-five dollars;" that is its price. The value of the same coat never could be completely expressed, because it would require a comparison not only with hats and gloves and boots and vests, but with all other things which are ever exposed for sale. Therefore, for convenience' sake, value is commonly reduced to price. By knowing the price of various things, we readily compare their value relatively to each other. Thus, when we know the price of the coat at 25 dollars, and of gloves at 2, of hats at 5, and vests at 10 dollars, we easily determine the value of the coat as estimated in gloves, hats, and vests, namely, that its value as compared with theirs, is respectively 12½, 5, and 2½ times theirs. The value of anything may remain nearly uniform while its price may greatly vary. At the present writing (1871), the prices of almost all commodities are much above the normal rate, because the currency of the country is much depreciated as compared with gold; but the value of these commodities, that is to say, their power of purchasing each other, is just about as it was before the depreciation began. All other commodities have risen in relation to the one commodity, money; or, which is the same thing, money has fallen in purchasing-power in relation to all other commodities; and there is in consequence a universal rise of prices; but it would be a total mistake to suppose that values have risen. A bushel of corn, now selling at one dollar, will buy no more labor, or hay, or cloth, than it used to buy when it sold for less than one dollar a bushel; because the labor, hay, and cloth have risen in relation to money in the same proportion as the corn has; while in relation to each other no changes have supervened. Services and commodities, with few exceptions, exchange with one another at the old rates, — value is unaltered; but exchange for money at much above the old rates, — prices have risen. Moreover it is not possible that there should be any general rise or fall of values, as there may be a general rise or fall of prices. A rise in the value of anything implies a fall in the value of those things with which you compare it; that is to say, if it will buy more of them, they will buy less of it. Its rise in value implies their fall in value, and conversely. Every rise in value of any service involves a corresponding fall in other services; and every fall in value of any service involves a rise in value of other services; and therefore, a general rise or fall of values is impossible. Nothing is more common than a rise or fall of value in particular services. Suppose, for instance, an improvement in machinery by which broadcloth can be made with one half the former effort, and that no change has been made in the efforts requisite to make the gloves, hats, and vests of our former example, and no change in the views of those who wish to exchange them. The coat will sink at once to about half its former value, not only in relation to gloves, hats, and vests, but in relation to everything which does not happen to be affected by a similar depressing cause. It is correct to say that the value of the coat has fallen. As estimated in gloves, hats, and vests, its value now is only 6¼, 2½, and 1¼ times theirs, respectively. But while coats have fallen in relation to the other commodities, the other commodities have risen in relation to coats; and if similar improvements should be made in the machinery by which gloves, hats, and vests are made, so that one half less effort will bring these also to market, views of parties as before remaining unchanged, they will exchange now for coats exactly in the same ratios as at first, namely, 12½, 5, and 2½, respectively, for 1. As soon as the improvements affect all the commodities equally, value stands just as it did before the first improvement was made. Views of the parties remaining the same, it is only an advantage or disadvantage affecting some services and not others, that will vary their value in exchange: whatever affects them all equally will have no effect upon value. Thus, a universal rise of wages in any country, provided they rise in all departments of effort equally, will have not the least effect upon value; and we have just seen that a universal rise of prices at present experienced in this country, has no effect whatever upon the general purchasing-power of services in exchange, but is only a token that the one commodity, money, has fallen relatively to them.

It only remains in this elementary discussion of

value to inquire whether there is, or can be, any measure of value — any standard, by a comparison with which we may determine the general purchasing-power of different services. It has commonly been supposed that there is such a measure, and political economists have expended a great deal of strength in endeavoring to discover what it is. The results have hardly been commensurate with the zeal and patience of the search. Adam Smith seems at one time to regard labor as the best measure of value, that is, the quantity of labor which any commodity will buy as the best gauge of its power to buy commodities in general. At another time he seems to think that corn is a better measure of general exchange value than labor. Others have thought that price furnished the best attainable standard of comparison; in other words, that the quantity of gold or silver which anything will purchase, will best enable us to determine the quantity of all other things which it will purchase. Others still have supposed that the cost of production of any commodity would give the most accurate rule by which to decide the value of the commodity, that is, the degree of its command over purchasable articles generally. But the truth is, a measure of value in the sense in which it has been sought after by these writers, is something impossible to be realized. It never would have been sought after, unless value had been supposed to be a rigid quality inhering in commodities, and, when once placed in them by whatever process, to be invariable. We have seen, however, that value is not a quality inhering in any one thing, but is a relation subsisting between two services which two persons are in a position to render to each other; and that this is not an inflexible relation, but is variable by any change in the views of the two persons, by which either of them puts a different estimate upon the service about to be rendered as compared with the service about to be received. We have seen sufficiently already, that there are four things, and only four, any change in any one of which will vary value; and that these four things are two desires and two efforts, the two desires belonging to two persons, and the efforts made by two persons each for the other. Now these four elements are in their very nature so liable to vary, and as a matter of fact do so constantly vary, that no man who clearly perceives what value is, will waste time and ingenuity in searching for an invariable standard of that which in its nature is variable and relative.

But while no reliable measure of value is possible to be found, there are certain limitations and principles of much importance which ought to be given in this connection. Since the foundation of value lies partly in the effort made by the person serving, and partly in the effort saved to the person served, and since in every exchange each of the parties is reciprocally serving and served, the outermost limitations of value are easily seen. A and B will not exchange services, unless the effort which each renders to the other is less onerous than the effort which each would have to make if each served himself directly. It costs a certain effort for me to bring water from the spring; I am willing to pay a neighbor for bringing it for me, but I should not be willing to make a greater effort for him in return than the effort is to bring it myself; neither should I be willing to make an effort for him which I regarded just as onerous as the bringing the water: unless there is some service which he will accept less onerous to me than that, I shall continue to bring the water for myself. On the other hand, he will not render the service to me of bringing the water, unless it be less onerous to him than the doing that for himself which I am ready to do for him. This principle, applicable to all exchanges whatsoever, draws on the one side the outermost line, beyond which value never can pass. It may be asserted with confidence that no man will ever knowingly make a greater effort to satisfy a desire through exchange, than the effort needful to satisfy it without an exchange. Moreover, within this outermost limitation which is made by the comparative onerousness of the respective efforts, there is a second limitation of a similar kind. To pursue the same illustration, while I should never make an effort for another in return for his bringing the water, greater than that required to bring it myself, the return effort may be very much less than that effort, and may sink down to a point, below which I can get no one to bring the water for me. Suppose I estimate the effort required to bring the water myself as 10; and that there are several persons who would be glad to do that service for me for a return service which I estimate as 8; and that there are two persons who are willing to do it for something which I estimate as 6; and that there is only one person who will do it for a return service which I regard as 5. It is evident that the extreme limits of the value of that service to me are

10 and 5. Higher than 10 it cannot go, lower than 5 it cannot sink. I should render the service estimated as 8, rather than forego having the water brought for me; but I shall render the service estimated as 5, just as long as there is any one person who will make the exchange with me on those terms. If he declines the exchange, I fall back on one of the two persons in the class above him, and value rises now from 5 to 6. It will be steadier at 6 than it was at 5, because there are two persons ready to render the service at that rate. If each, however, in turn should give out, I should then be obliged to fall back upon the larger class ready to serve me for a return service of 8. At this point the value would be very steady from the presence of numerous competitors anxious to serve me at that rate, and it could by no possibility rise above 10. Between 10 and 5 the value may fluctuate, but it cannot overpass these limits in either direction. Therefore we may say that the maximum value of any service in exchange is struck at the point where the recipient will prefer to serve himself, rather than make the exchange; and the minimum value of any service in exchange is struck at the point below which the recipient cannot get himself served. These two limits, it will be observed, are found in the two elements which we have called efforts.

But there are also limitations of value in the two elements which we have called desires. In the foregoing illustration, it is supposed that my desire for the water is all the while of uniform strength, and the desire of each of the three classes willing to serve me for the return service is uniform also, though each class makes a different estimate of the comparative efforts. Let us now suppose that the efforts on either side remain invariable, but there is a change in the element of desire. Any capacity in anything to gratify any desire of anybody is utility. For simplicity's sake, let us look only to the one man who was ready to bring the water for a return service which I estimated as 5, and suppose that he is the only man who will do me the service on any terms. Let now the utility of the water to me be increased, and let him know that fact, all other elements remaining as before, and he can crowd up the value of his service towards 10, according to the intensity of my desire. Of course he cannot crowd it over 10, but the limit below that will now be determined by the relative strength of my desire. On the other hand, if my desire be as before, and the two efforts as before, and his desire for my return service be increased, and I know it, and I the only man who can render him such a service, I can crowd down the value of his service below 5, according to the intensity of his desire. Of course I cannot crowd it down below a point, which we will call 3, at which, rather than continue his service at that rate, he will forego the exchange altogether. But value may vary between these limits, 10 and 3, according to the varying intensity of our mutual desires. If it should so happen that both these desires, my desire for his service and his desire for mine, should increase simultaneously and proportionably, value would not be affected; the exchange would go on at the same rate as before. Or if both desires should diminish simultaneously and proportionably, value would not be affected. The same is true of efforts. If both efforts suddenly become twice as onerous, or one half as onerous as before, the desires remaining the same, the value of the two services estimated in each other would stand just as before. Thus we see that the natural limits of value, and all the variations in value, are to be sought for and will be found in the play and interaction of the four elements out of which value itself springs.

We shall now be able to understand clearly what is meant by Market-Value and its variations, and also the action of Supply and Demand. Market-Value is the rate at which services of all sorts are exchanging at the present time in the various departments of society. What determines that rate? What determines that corn is now selling in the market for 1 dollar a bushel? Two desires come in to determine it, — the desire of people for corn, and the desire of farmers for money. Two efforts come in to determine it, — the effort of farmers to raise and bring a bushel of corn to market, and the effort of people to secure 1 dollar in money. The presence of corn in the market, or its being ready to be immediately brought there and offered in exchange for money, constitutes what is called a Supply of corn; money offered, or ready to be offered, in exchange for corn, constitutes what is called a Demand. This is commercial language, and is sufficiently accurate, although it must be remembered that each commodity in reality constitutes a Demand for the other, and is a Supply in reference to the other. But, speaking commercially, the money ready to be offered for commodities is the Demand,

and the commodities ready to be exchanged for money are the Supply. What, then, is the law of market-value? The law of market-value is the equation of supply and demand: that is to say, the rate of the exchange is adjusted when money enough is offered to take off within the usual times the commodities on hand. Demand and supply are thus equalized, and the current market-rate is determined. If demand for any reason becomes quickened, and the supply not increased, there is competition among buyers for the stock in market, and market-value tends to rise. If demand becomes sluggish, the supply remaining the same, there is competition among sellers to dispose of their stock, and market-value tends to sink. So far it is the action on value of the element of desire, which expresses itself through demand. How far can this action go? Demand being increased, supply remaining the same, value rises: how far does it rise? In the *ratio* of the increased demand, say some; if the demand be one third increased, the value will be one third higher. By no means is this true. The value may rise far higher than that proportion, or it may not rise in anything like that proportion. It depends upon circumstances, and upon the nature of the commodity. We must remember that demand not only acts upon value, but value acts upon demand. As value rises, the number of those whose means or inclinations enable them to purchase at the new rate is constantly diminished. There are ten persons who may wish an article at one dollar, of whom not over four will wish it at two dollars, and perhaps only one at three dollars.

Every rise in value then, under the influence of increased demand, tends to cut off a part of that demand, that is, to lessen the number of those who will purchase at the increased price; and the value will rise only to that point, whatever it be, where an equalization takes place between the supply and demand, between the quantity of corn, for example, offered at the enhanced rates, and the quantity of money in the hands of those willing to exchange it for corn at the enhanced rates. Thus we see that every rise or fall of demand, and the consequent rise or fall of value, tends to check itself. An increased demand for any article or service, other things being equal, enhances its value; but the enhanced value in turn lessens the demand by lessening the number of those who will purchase, and the new market-rate is struck at the point of equalization between the old supply and the new demand. Just so, if demand is slackened, value declines; but declining value in turn increases the demand by bringing the article within the range of a larger number of purchasers, and the decline is arrested at the point of equalization between the new demand and the old supply, and a new market-rate is determined. Everything oscillates under the variations of demand, but the point of stable equilibrium, if I may use the expression of anything so unstable as market-value, the point of stable equilibrium is always the equation of supply and demand.

In the preceding paragraph we have supposed supply to remain unchanged, and have followed the law of value through the variations of demand, which, money being invariable, as is here supposed, expresses the element of desire. Supply expresses the element of efforts, and market-value varies with the variations of supply. We have seen that every rise or fall of demand tends to check itself, and will check itself even without variations in the supply; but it is commonly checked at an earlier point by variations in the supply. A brisk demand enhances value, and enhanced value commonly stimulates supply, and increased supply checks the rise. A slack demand lowers value, and lowered value commonly lessens the supply by the action of holders and speculators, — holders withdrawing their stock for a better market, and speculators buying now when the article is cheap, to store away till it shall be dearer. Thus rise of value from increased demand is doubly checked; first, by restricting the number of purchasers, and second, by increasing the supply: the fall of value from slack demand is doubly checked; first, by enlarging the number of consumers of a now cheaper article, and second, by diminution of supply by the action of holders and speculators. This law of the equalization of demand and supply, thus doubly and harmoniously working, is perhaps the most comprehensive and beautiful law in political economy. But we must note the action on value of changes in supply only, demand continuing steady. If the supply be short, and cannot be increased at all, as is the case with choice antiques and certain gems and paintings by the old masters, value may rise to any point, and will be struck, as before, at the precise point of equality of the demand then existing with the supply there offered. The French government paid, in 1852, 615,300 francs for a painting by Murillo, which had belonged to Marshal Soult. The genuine Murillos are comparatively few, and their number cannot be increased, and their merit causes a strong desire to possess them, and their value rises in consequence of the limitation of supply to a point beyond which no one purchaser can be found. When this painting was offered in Paris for sale, many parties were anxious to purchase it, but the equation of demand and supply was reached, and its value was determined only when one party distanced all other competitors and offered a sum greater than any one else would give. There was one painting; there could be but one purchaser; value rose under the influence of demand, and could not be checked by increase of supply; and the equation was complete when the demand was practically restricted to one party, and that the highest bidder. The same principle controls all sales of this sort.

If the supply, instead of being absolutely limited, can only be increased with difficulty, or after the lapse of time, similar but less extreme results will be observed. Suppose pianos are selling in any community at $300 each, and there are twenty persons in that community who wish a piano immediately, and that there are but fifteen pianos on hand, and the number cannot be increased for six months. The value will rise above $300. How much above? To that point, whatever, it be, at which only fifteen of the twenty will be willing to purchase at the new rate. The equation of supply and demand will be reached by a rising value which cuts off five competitors This is the principle, working only roughly indeed in practice, — working only by the estimates and good judgment of dealers, — but the principle is this. A better illustration of this class of cases is, perhaps, the grains and other products of the earth. When these have been gathered there is no more home supply for a year. Any deficiency in the crops will raise their value, not at all in the ratio of the deficiency, but according to the relations of the diminished supply to a new demand. It will depend on the facility of importation, and other causes, but it has frequently happened that an estimated deficiency of crops amounting to one third has doubled and even quadrupled the usual prices.[1]

In the only remaining, and far more numerous class of cases, in which the supply of commodities and services can be readily and indefinitely increased, every rise and fall of value is speedily checked by the action of supply; and the comprehensive and harmonious law already referred to keeps value in this class of cases comparatively steady.

The general theory of value has now been given. While we shall find no case of value, or its variations, which this theory does not cover and explain, we shall find particular principles which act in certain cases upon demand and supply, and thereby act upon value. We have now seen what value is; how it arises; the elements which alone can vary it; and the universal law which limits it.

1 Tooke's History of Prices. Quoted by J. S. Mill.

CHAPTER IV.

ON EXCHANGE.

The strength and safety of our conclusions in Political Economy are derived from the simplicity and certainty of the forces at work. No man has ever denied the great facts that lie at the basis of exchange. That men are possessed of desires, that efforts are necessary in order to meet these, and that satisfactions are the result, are propositions universally admitted. From these simple truths spring all the laws of our science. Efforts are exchangeable. One man may and does put forth the effort necessary for the satisfaction of another man's desire. But since the effort is not for himself but for another, and since to put forth efforts is not naturally agreeable to man, and never becomes so, except in connection with the satisfaction to which they minister, he will demand for his effort some corresponding effort made for him. This is a simple fact. No man will work for you for nothing. If you think he ought to do so, there is no law against your trying to induce him to do so.

How now does it happen that society is one vast hive of buyers and sellers, every man bringing something to the market and carrying something off? We speak of the commercial classes, but all classes are commercial. Everybody exchanges. You do something for me, and I will do something for you, is the fundamental law of society. From this results the division of employments, and all the various professions. Every man brings his own product and exchanges with society as best he may. The farmer brings his produce — and exchanges. The mechanic brings the product of his skilled labor — and exchanges. The laborer brings his strength, and the teacher his knowledge, and they are ready to do service — for a consideration. The merchant, the physician, the lawyer, the clergyman, the editor, the lecturer, the singer, the actor, and so on to the end of the list, are all in position to render services to society, and justly expect to receive an equivalent service in return. Indeed, when we look out upon society, the most striking thing we observe about it is, that these exchanges are going on, in a thousand directions at once, determining all employment and professions, reaching everywhere and permeating everything, and all this the more rapidly and perfectly as knowledge and civilization advance. Since, therefore, as a matter of fact, men do constantly put forth onerous efforts to satisfy other men's desires, in order to receive back from them the results of corresponding efforts in return; since this mutual exchange of services is everywhere present in society, not in the market-places only, but in every department of life, there must be in this exchange some great GAIN. We now inquire particularly what this gain is. What is the motive that leads men universally to exchange?

The answer to these questions will bring us to the gratifying conclusion that the laws of exchange are based on nothing less solid than the will of God. The desires of men are not only various in kind and indefinite in degree, but also tend to increase in variety and extent by the progress of knowledge and freedom. To the gratification of almost all these desires, however, there are obstacles interposed, some of which are physical and some moral; and these obstacles are so great in all directions, that the powers of the individual man are utterly incompetent to surmount them. They mock at his weakness, and throw him back upon his destitution. Without association with his fellow-men, there is no creature so helpless, so unable to reach his true end, as is man; and therefore it is, that the impulse to association is one of the strongest of our natural impulses. Men come together, as it were by instinct, into society; and, associating themselves together in a society, it is very soon discovered, not only that there are various desires in the different members of the community which are now readily met by coöperation and mutual exchange, but also that there are very different powers in the different individuals in relation to those obstacles which are to be surmounted. There is a vast diversity in natural gifts. One man has physical strength, with no mechanical ingenuity; another combines with a feeble body a wonderful knack for contrivance; a third has a philosophical turn, liking to examine into the laws of nature; and a fourth has a bent and genius for traffic. Now, then, Nature speaks in this diversity of gifts in as loud a voice as she can utter, in favor of such a degree of association and exchange as shall allow a free development of these varying capacities, while they work upon the obstacles to the gratification of men's wants which are appropriately opposite to them. Mr. Carey is right in his principle that the degree of individuality depends on the degree of association, each advancing hand in hand with the other; but he seems to me to be wrong while he lacks confidence in the natural forces at work tending to the highest degree of association and consequently to the highest degree of individuality. There is no social force stronger than interest, and interest is driving society continually to exchange, and to a wider and wider application of the principles of exchange, that is to say, to a higher and higher degree of association, which allows of course a continually freer development of individuality. When interest fails as a motive power, at least in this department, it is vain to appeal to or to trust an inferior and factitious motive power.

It is interest that leads men to exchange. It is because a given effort put forth for another, in view of a return, realizes more of satisfaction than when put forth directly for one's self, that exchange ever takes place. Why does it realize more? BECAUSE THERE IS DIVERSITY OF ADVANTAGE BETWEEN DIFFERENT MEN AND BETWEEN DIFFERENT NATIONS, IN DIFFERENT RESPECTS. All exchange depends on diversity of relative advantage; and diversity of relative advantage exists by God's appointment among individual men, and among the nations. Reserving this national diversity for a later discussion, it is very clear that a diversity of advantage in different things displays itself as between the individuals of every community large and small. There is no village in which one man has not an advantage over his neighbors in the making of coats, another in the shoeing of horses, another in the curing diseases, another in the keeping a school; while each of those neighbors may have an advantage over each of these in some other art or avocation. This diversity of advantage in various directions depends, in every advanced state of society, partly upon diversity of original gifts, partly upon concentration of personal effort upon the one set of obstacles that lie in the path of a single branch of business, and partly upon the use, and familiarity in the use, of the gratuitous forces of nature which lend their aid towards overcoming these obstacles. As the result of one or two or all of these, one man comes to have a legitimate advantage over others in his own branch of business, whatever it is; and the others come to have a legitimate advantage over him in their own branches of business, whatever they are; and if he has desires which their efforts can satisfy, and they desires which his efforts can satisfy, nothing more is necessary to a profitable exchange between them than this relative advantage at different points. The tailor and blacksmith can profitably exchange their respective efforts just as soon as each has a relative superiority to the other in his own trade, provided of course each has a desire for the product of the other; and the greater the relative superiority of each to the other, the more profitable is the exchange to both. This is a point of considerable consequence, and will repay some pains in illustration. If the blacksmith can shoe horses only a little better than the tailor could shoe them, and the tailor make coats only a little better than the blacksmith could make them, there will be only a slight advantage in their mutually exchanging efforts. For the sake of definiteness, let us say, that the tailor's capacity in making coats is 6, and his capacity in shoeing horses is 5; and the blacksmith's capacity in shoeing horses is 6, and his capacity in making coats is 5. Each has a relative superiority to the other of 1, and if they exchange, there is an advantage of 2 to be divided between them. Now let us suppose that each, by exclusive devotion to his own trade, by developing his latent skill and ingenuity, and by availing himself of all the forces of nature at his command, comes to have a capacity in his own business of 15, his capacity in the other business remaining as before at 5. Each now has a relative superiority to the other of 10, and when they exchange there is an advantage of 20 to be divided between them. The motive to an exchange, and the gain of an exchange, are ten times greater than they were before. Therefore we lay down the principle, as universally applicable to all exchanges, that the greater the relative superiority at different points, the more profitable do exchanges become. If this principle is just, and I flatter myself that it will be found to be just, it follows, that every man who has anything to exchange, is directly interested in the success of his fellow-citizens, that every trade finds its advantage in the increasing development of other trades, and that all discoveries and inventions by which Nature is made to pay tribute to any art is, restrictions apart, so much clear gain to the world at large. In the light of sound principles, what has been sometimes called the jealousy of trade is simply silly.

All exchange, then, depends on difference of relative advantage, because without some difference of relative advantage, each party could serve himself directly just as well as he could be served by the other party, and there would be no motive at all for an exchange. As soon as there is any difference of relative advantage, there begins to be a motive for an exchange, and a gain as the result; and the motive and the gain become stronger and greater as the difference increases; so that the gains of exchange are the greatest in that state of society in which the freest opportunity is allowed to every individual to employ his peculiar powers in work for which he is best fitted, in which desires are so various and employments so diversified as to give a chance for all kinds of efforts, and in which men avail themselves to the utmost of those natural advantages and gratuitous powers which lie open to their disposal. Freedom, association, and invention, are the three things which make exchanges as profitable as they can become, and which will carry society, so far as exchanges can do it, to the highest pitch of prosperity. Of these by far the most important is freedom, because, where freedom is conceded, association and invention follow in time by laws of natural sequence. By freedom is meant the right of every man to employ his own efforts for the gratification of his own wants, either directly or through exchange. Each man's right of freedom is limited of course by every other man's right of freedom which he is not at liberty to infringe; and also, in certain respects, by what is called the general good, of which the judge must be the government under which he lives. Under these limitations, which limit in common all other rights, the right of exchange is just as much of a right as the right of breathing. It stands on the same unassailable ground. Every man has a natural, self evident, and inalienable right to put forth efforts for his own well-being; and whenever two men find that by exchanging efforts with each other, they can better promote their own happiness, they have an indisputable right, subject only to the above limitations, to exchange; and it is a high-handed infringement of natural rights, a blow aimed at the life and source of property, when any authority whatever interferes to restrict or prohibit the freedom of exchange, except that act be justified by a solid proof that other private or public rights which are as well based as the right of exchange are infringed thereby.

Happily, since governments have become more enlightened than formerly, they perceive for the most part that they have no right to interfere with this natural right of their people, and also, that, by interfering with it, they would do them an incalculable injury. The only motive to a mutual exchange of services, is always and everywhere the mutual benefit of the parties. After every fair exchange, each party is richer than before, has more satisfactions, otherwise there would be no exchange. I esteem the service

I receive more highly than the service I render, otherwise I should not render it. The man to whom I render it esteems that service more highly than the service he renders to me. We are both gainers. And since almost everybody in every community has something to exchange,—either service or commodity, and nobody exchanges except in view of a gain, it is clear that free exchange benefits everybody, and harms nobody. Moreover, under a system of free exchange, every man is allowed, under the stimulus of self interest, to follow the bent of his own mind, to work away at those obstacles to the gratification of human desires which he feels himself best able to overcome, and to avail himself of all those helps in his work, of which Nature offers to him a full store. Under these circumstances, obstacles give way in all directions: the amount of material products produced and offered for exchange is vastly augmented; the number and variety and excellence of the services proffered is indefinitely increased; the diversified and rapidly increasing desires in such a community are readily met by exchange; all peculiar facilities are taken advantage of, and the difference of relative advantage becomes great in all directions, and a new day of industrial and commercial prosperity is ushered in. Under freedom all men have the greatest possible motive to produce, because they can dispose of their efforts to the best advantage. They can purchase with these efforts what they will, and when they will, and where they will. Thus freedom leads to extended association, and, speedily also, to the invention of machinery and all labor-saving appliances. Therefore, since free exchange indefinitely multiplies, in number and variety, the services which men may render to each other; since, by means of it, men's satisfactions bear a larger and larger proportion to their efforts; and since the only possible motive to an exchange is a mutual benefit of the parties, no reason can be given, no good reason ever has been given, why exchanges should not be the freest possible.

After long centuries of meddlesome and vexatious interference with the freedom of industry and the rights of exchange, by limiting the number of apprentices to each artisan, by dictating what should and what should not be manufactured or grown, by attempting to determine what should and what should not be imported and exported, and by arbitrary burdens on certain classes, and arbitrary privileges granted to others, the more enlightened nations of the world have come at length to perceive that wealth and power and progress are dependent on free exchange, at least within their own boundaries. Common sense reigns now, for the most part, in this thing, within the limits of the individual nations. When Bonaparte brought half of Western Europe under French dominion, the previously existing custom-houses and toll barriers of the interior fell as by a stroke, and free trade became the rule between French, Dutch, Germans, Italians, and Spaniards, — all who were subject to his sway. But when his vast empire was dissolved into its original independent kingdoms, up shot the custom-houses again, around all the petty frontiers, and each State was busy to reimpose on itself the fetters which his powerful hand had broken.[1] Just as if the benefits of exchange depended on the accident that the parties to it are subjects or citizens of the same government!

Opposed to free exchange are monopolies. A monopoly is a legal restriction imposed by the government upon the sale of certain services or commodities. This restriction is ostensibly laid for the benefit of certain persons or classes, and limits of course the competition to which they would otherwise be subject in their business, and tends therefore artificially to raise the value of that which the privileged few offer for sale. If the view be limited to these persons alone, monopolies would certainly seem to be advantageous, but what of the purchasers and consumers of their wares? They all are obliged to pay a higher price for what, were it not for the monopoly, they could obtain at a cheaper rate, since the only object in laying the restriction, is to enhance the price for the benefit of those possessing the privilege. Monopolies, therefore, infringe the right of exchange, are unjust and odious in their nature, and are in practice abominable. Nearly all governments have been chargeable, at times, with successful attempts to make things thus artificially dear to the mass of the people. Queen Elizabeth called the power of granting patents of monopoly to her favorites "the fairest flower of her garden." Towards the close of her reign, her abuse of this power had reached an intolerable height, and some of the most necessary articles of life, such as salt, iron,

[1] Senior. Page 177.

calf-skins, vinegar, lead, paper, and many others, were in the hands of patentees, and could only be procured at exorbitant prices. In 1601, the House of Commons met in so angry and menacing a mood, in consequence of this abuse, that Elizabeth was obliged to promise at least, that the monopolies complained of should be abolished. The famous Act of Parliament of 1624 declares that all monopolies, grants, letters patent for the sole buying, selling, and making of goods and manufactures, shall be null and void. This Act effectually secured the freedom of industry in England; and in the opinion of excellent authorities, has done more to excite the spirit of invention and industry, and to accelerate the progress of wealth in that country, than any other in the statute book. The Act excepts, however, patents for fourteen years to the true and first inventors of new manufactures within the realm, and also the grants by Act of Parliament to any company, for the enlargement of foreign trade. Under this exception, the East India Company possessed, up to 1834, the exclusive right to vend tea in England. During the last years of this monopoly, and notwithstanding the quantities of tea smuggled into the country, the people of England paid more than $7,500,000 a year for their tea beyond the price at which tea of equal quality was sold, under a system of free competition, in Hamburg and New York. Opium is still, for purposes of revenue, a government monopoly in British India. In France, tobacco is a close monopoly in the hands of government for revenue purposes. It is noticeable that monopolies never realize to their possessors the full pecuniary advantage of which the public are robbed by their action. Thus, while Englishmen paid $7,500,000 *extra* annually for their tea, the Company, by their own showing, did not realize much more than half that sum from their privilege; owing to the inertness of their servants removed from the stimulus of competition. "The spirit of monopolists," says Gibbon, "is narrow, lazy, and oppressive. Their work is more costly and less productive than that of independent artists; and the new improvements, so eagerly grasped by the competition of freedom, are admitted by them with slow and sullen reluctance."

A second form of monopoly is that in which governments by restrictive duties try to exclude foreign competition in certain articles, leaving the domestic dealers open only to home competition. This is done in connection with, sometimes under color of, levying duties for revenue. Duties laid for this purpose, however, as we shall see more fully hereafter, are very different in principle, amount, and action, from those properly laid for revenue. They violate a natural right of exchange, as the others do not, and are always followed by injurious consequences. Sometimes the hope of unusual gains from producing an article whose foreign supply is thus restricted, seduces capital and labor from other profitable channels and concentrates them upon this business; and the home competition, thus artificially stimulated, becomes intense and feverish, the business is overdone, an element of distrust and unsteadiness is introduced, the weaker houses are ruined, and only the stancher firms tide over the depression consequent upon overdoing, and control the market for a while at a monopoly price. But the losses of home competitors; the losses of those who would otherwise have been foreign competitors; and especially the losses of those home producers who would have exchanged products with those foreign competitors, overbalance many fold these gains. Sometimes, again, home competition is even less active after the imposition of such duties; and then the manufacturers and dealers, relieved, in great measure, from the stimulus of competition, are less on the alert for improvements, less attentive to the quality of their goods, less compliant to their customers; and the consumers are obliged, not only to pay a tax levied for the benefit of the monopolists, but also an additional tax on account of their want of enterprise and spirit.

Very different is the third form of monopoly, that involved in the granting of patent-rights and copyrights. Society does well in protecting, by law, inventors and thinkers in the sole use of their respective productions for a limited time. Otherwise, men would have less motive to think and to invent; since in that case only the public-spirited and the rich would or could devote themselves to an important branch of the public progress. A patent or copyright is merely a return service which society renders for a service received. It violates no man's right of property, as an ordinary monopoly does, but is a provision to protect a right of property. In the United States a patent lasts for seventeen years, and is not reissued. A copyright lasts for twenty-eight years, and may be renewed by the author, his widow, or children, for fourteen years longer.

CHAPTER V.

ON PRODUCTION.

While it is impossible to make discussions in Political Economy amusing, it is also impossible intelligently to conduct them without constantly coming to conclusions which are most cheering. We shall find a gratifying law underlying the operations of production, which demonstrates that God designed man to be a producer, and to produce under conditions of constantly increasing advantage. The world with its forces, and man with his motives, are so admirably constructed, that these conditions of increasing advantage cannot fail, under freedom, to redound to the benefit of the masses of men. We will first determine what production is, and then the cheering law that underlies it.

Every man who puts forth an effort to satisfy the desire of another, with the expectation of a return, is, in the language of Political Economy, a Producer. The Latin word *producere* means *to expose anything to sale*. Our derived word *to produce* means the same. A Product is anything thus exposed, that is, a service ready to be rendered. Adam Smith, who is sometimes called the father of this science, used these terms in a restricted sense, and thereby almost unfitted them to do their proper work. He confined production to the occasioning of changes in material objects. He gifted with the title of producer the farmer, the mechanic, the miner, the hunter, and fisherman, because they bring to the market a material commodity; and refused the honor of the term to those who render simple services, however essential. This is wrong. It proceeds from an inadequate analysis of value. That which is produced, that with which we have to do, is not matter but value. They who originate value are producers. But we have seen that value is not an attribute of matter, but a relation of services. The service may be employed upon matter, may be embodied in it, but what is really sold is not the matter, but the service; and services are all the time being sold, as those of the singer, the teacher, the clergyman, which have no connection whatever with matter. These services have purchasing-power, these persons originate value, and therefore, they are producers. Certainly, in an inventory of all values, a certain part would be found connected with material objects, but not the largest part. Our language must be broad enough to cover all the cases. Therefore, Production is the rendering of any service for which something is demanded in return.

Now let us examine the underlying law of Production. Production is effort. But efforts are irksome. Is there, then, no way to lessen efforts, to make them less onerous, and, at the same time, more productive? Yes, thank God, there is! We may bring to our aid the gratuitous help of Nature! The world is full of powers which we may employ to facilitate our work. For example, at first people ground their grain by hand; and it was a weary, weary task to sit cramped at the mill all day, and turn, and turn, and turn.[1] The effort was great, and the result was small. At length it occurred to somebody that the weight of water would turn a wheel, and that the wheel might turn the mill-stones. Once thought of, the water-wheel was soon an actual fact. Instead of human strength, Nature works now, and what is better, works for nothing! Man's service is still needed, he feeds the hopper, tends the bags, but he does not ache so badly! Nor is this all. One day's labor is now vastly more productive. More grain is ground, bread comes easier to the poor, and the wheel which free water turns blesses its millions with a cheapened product!

Let us take another illustration. The old hand-loom was the only means antiquity knew of for procuring clothing. The shuttle was thrown by human muscle. Every thread cost a throw. This work was mostly done by women. The word wife is supposed by some to have been first derived from the word *to weave.* While the slave woman sat on the ground, and turned the handle of the mill to grind the grain, the wife was exalted to the dignity of the loom, and worked away at the monotonous task, thread by thread, thread by thread. Doubtless the hand-loom was a great improvement on the earlier processes, and was itself gradually improved as the centuries went by, each improvement being the substitution either of a gratuitous force of Nature for an irksome human effort, or an easier process of art for a more laborious one. Every step of improvement was a lessening of obstacles with reference to a given satisfaction. All the way up to

[1] Exod. xi. 5; Isa. xlvii. 2.

our present admirable machinery — the power-loom, which weaves, as if by magic, while a child can tend it — every step has marked a lessening of efforts relatively to utilities. The utility, the satisfaction, the yard of cloth, has cost less and less of human effort, not only to the producer, but, through exchange, to everybody. Accidental causes in different countries may interrupt this progress for a little time in any single direction, but the law will soon assert itself again in spite of these causes. And this progress, thus briefly illustrated in the two cases of flour and cloth, has been going on, and is constantly going on, in all directions; more strikingly, perhaps, in the production of material commodities, in which the powers of Nature may be indefinitely applied by machinery, but at the same time there are no services of any kind which are not facilitated in some degree by the progress of knowledge and experience; and the benefits of this increasing advantage come home, through exchanges, to everybody; and, consequently, the satisfactions of all bear a larger and larger proportion to their efforts.

This, then, is the underlying and benevolent law of production, that God has placed freely at men's disposal such materials and forces in Nature, that, availing themselves skilfully of these, onerous efforts bear a less and less proportion to realized utilities. Men have a strong motive to substitute, whenever they can, force for muscle, machinery for labor. The farmer who used to cut all his meadow-grass with a hand-swung scythe, then rake it up with a hand-drawn rake, and then pitch it into the loft with a handfork, now mows and rakes and pitches with a machine. And it is a beautiful consequence of this law, that all improvements in machinery, all inventions, all substitution of Nature's forces for human labor soon become the common property of mankind. Patent rights speedily expire by their own limitation, secret processes are sure to become known, and the competition of the different men who, under a system of freedom, will be sure to use these gratuitous helps, will compel each of them to sell their product at a rate graduated only by the actual human service rendered; so that, the liberal gifts of Nature, though seemingly monopolized at first by ingenious men, are not long intercepted in their descent towards the masses of mankind. An invention of great merit even at first does not benefit the patentee alone; as a patentee, his interest leads him to lower the price of his product, to bring it within the reach of a wider circle of consumers; and so soon as the patent has expired, the benefit has at once a wider reach. The steam-engine, for example, has long been common property. There are, indeed, certain features of the more perfect engines still restricted in their manufacture by the rights of individuals, and this will always be so while invention continues busy, but the perpetual tendency in all inventions is from individual property towards a common right. And it is here in place to remark, that the application of machinery to all departments of production, and the introduction of improved processes of every name, can hardly in the first instance be prejudicial to any, and are sure ultimately to be beneficial to all.

What is the effect on values of these processes now made easier in all directions? Clearly, since value is nothing but the relation between two services exchanged, no effect at all is produced on values, if the improvements have gone on equally in all directions. Everything exchanges just as before. If the improvements have not gone on equally, then the value, that is, the purchasing power, of those products is diminished in whose production the improvements have been relatively greater. As the service has now diminished, the value, other things being equal, has diminished along with it. For such a service less can be demanded in return. The utility of the product, on the other hand, that is, its capacity to gratify desire, remains as before. A less effort produces the same utility. The portion of effort thus set free, however, is not probably idle. It will be still put forth to create a larger number of products of the same kind, each one of which indeed has less purchasing power than before, but the aggregate value of which is much greater than before. For example, when machinery is employed in the making of gloves, which before were cut and stitched by hand, the value of a pair of gloves, estimated in anything whose production has not been altered by a similar improvement, will infallibly decline; but the aggregate value of all the gloves made in the establishment will be greater than before, because otherwise there would have been no motive to introduce the machinery. Does, then, the machine originate value, contrary to the doctrine in the chapter on value? Not strictly. The machine originates utility, since each pair of the now increased number of gloves has the same utility as a pair of the former fewer number; and the maker is able to render a service to a greater number of persons than before; and it is true, that, for a time, especially if the process be not yet generally applied in glove-making, before value has a chance to adjust itself to the new state of things, he will realize extra gains; he will obtain, in part, the old price for his product, and it would seem, in this case, as if the machine created value. Nevertheless, it is only a transitory state of things. Just as soon as machines come to be generally employed in the business, value adjusts itself, through competition, to the real human service rendered, and the extra gains of the first operators are cut off. The gain of the reduction has now become permanent to all consumers of gloves. It is this interval between the old price and the new which gives to producers the margin for their enterprise, and a sharp spur to invent and adopt improvements. The improvements once become general, the gain redounds to the whole community. The value then of all services which have been facilitated by improved processes, is constantly being lessened relatively to services not equally facilitated; and here we gain the first glimpse of a truth, which will afterwards appear in the clearest light, namely, that the value of commodities tends to decline as compared with human labor, and therefore, that there is inwrought into the nature of things a tendency towards the elevation of the masses of men in a scale of comforts.

A leading proposition of production is the following: — *Production may go on indefinitely in all directions without ever a fear of reaching a general glut of products.* This proposition was first fully developed by Say, in the fifteenth chapter of his well-known treatise on "Political Economy," and the proof of it, and some of the consequences of it, are well worthy of our attention. I shall put the proof of it in this form: the desires of men which the efforts of other men can satisfy, are unlimited in number and indefinite in degree; and therefore, mutual efforts can continue to be put forth in exchange, until these unlimited and indefinite desires of all men are all met — a goal which never can be reached. This proposition demolishes at a stroke the fallacy which pervades Dr. Chalmers' book on "Political Economy," namely, that the universal market is limited, and therefore, were it not for the unproductive consumption of the rich and luxurious, and the equally unproductive consumption of wars, there would soon be a general glut, and production must cease for the lack of a vent for its products. What constitutes a market for anything? This, that somebody desires the service thus offered, and is willing to render a return service acceptable to the offerer. Only two things can limit the universal market, first, a lack of desires, and secondly, a lack of return services. But there can be no lack of desires at any time, and there will be the greatest plenty of return services where production is most busy and most universal. Therefore, again, no general glut of products is possible to occur. A truth which we have already seen in another connection, reappears here as a consequence of this proposition, and will reappear again and again, namely, that all persons are interested commercially, as well as morally, in the prosperity of other persons, and each nation which has anything to exchange, is directly interested in the prosperity of all other nations; because the more production everywhere, the better market everywhere. A market for products is made by products in market.

But while no such thing as a general glut of products ever did, or ever can occur, a glut in respect to certain services is very common. Through want of foresight, or miscalculation, particular services are offered in too great abundance, or of a kind not adapted to the demand, and in respect to these the market is truly said to be glutted. This frequently happens with editions of books; more copies are printed than can be sold at remunerative prices. Also when fashion changes, the goods which were fashionable, but are so no longer, are apt to be in excess of the demand. The only precaution that can be taken to avoid losses of this character, is the cultivation of foresight, by studying as accurately as possible the nature of human desires, and the changes that have been observed to take place in them. This constitutes mercantile sagacity; and the most successful producers in all departments are those who best develop this sagacity, who adapt their services to the existing and coming demand, who, to excellence in the substance of their services, add taste and attractiveness to their form, who tend rather to lead the fashions for the many than follow in their wake. The field of production is like the billowy and heaving sea: to navigate most successfully requires foresight, a wise courage, a power of adaptation to varying circumstances, skill to veer and tack when the wind changes, and a will to run before a favoring breeze with all sails set. Produc-

8

tion, as a general rule, is no dead level of monotonous exertion; since its sphere is life with its wants, man with his desires; and there is scope for the development of ingenious mind in almost all of its departments. Since all exchange is due to the diversity of relative advantage, whoever develops his powers of observation, of application, of adaptation, to a higher point, and avails himself more skilfully of all peculiar facilities, will reap a larger share of the harvest of exchange.

The immense increase of production, and the superior perfection of products consequent upon what he calls the Division of Labor, was fully pointed out by Adam Smith. The chapter in which this author treats of the division of labor, has always been the most famous, and is still one of the most interesting in the "Wealth of Nations." We have already seen how exchange is stimulated and made profitable by the diversity of employments, and by the application of all peculiar gifts to the corresponding obstacles which lie in the path of production: this is the more general truth of which Adam Smith's principle of the division of labor is a specific part. He means by this term the dividing up of a process or employment into particular parts, so that each person employed can devote himself wholly to one section of the process. The proposition is, that by means of the division of labor, the processes of production are vastly facilitated. He cites, as an illustration, the manufacture of pins. One man draws out the wire, another straightens it, a third cuts it, a fourth sharpens the points, a fifth grinds it at the top for receiving the head. The making the heads consists of two or three distinct operations, each confided to a single person. The remaining processes are similarly divided up, and the result is, according to Dr. Smith, that in a single establishment, employing only ten persons, 48,000 pins are made in a day, while if each man went through all the processes himself, he could hardly make twenty pins a day, or two hundred for the whole establishment. Perhaps a more striking illustration of the division of labor may be found in the art of watch-making. According to evidence brought before a committee of the British House of Commons, there are one hundred and two distinct branches of this art, to each of which a boy may be put apprentice; and when his apprenticeship is expired, he is unable, without subsequent instruction, to work at any other branch. The watch-finisher is the only person, out of the one hundred and two, who is able to work in any other department than his own. The causes of increased efficiency imparted to production by the division of labor are reduced by Dr. Smith to three: —

1. The improved dexterity, corporeal and intellectual, acquired by the repetition of one simple operation.

2. The saving of the time which is commonly lost in passing from one species of work to another, and in the change of place, position, and tools.

3. The invention of a great number of machines which facilitate and abridge labor in all its departments. Because the simple task which complete division of labor gives to each operator is precisely what machinery may most easily be made to per-

form, and what the operator, if intelligent, will be most likely to devise machinery for. Add to these advantages of the division of labor these other: —

4. The saving of the waste of material, partly as the result of this improved dexterity; and frequently, also, as the result of the shorter time required to finish up the product.

5. The more economical distribution of labor by classing the operatives according to their strength, skill, and experience. The easier parts may be performed by women and by children, whose labor is less expensive; the ruder parts by ruder hands; and only the more difficult processes by the most skilful workmen, who must be highly paid. Next to the first, this advantage is the most important.

6. There is a saving in tools. The various implements, being now in constant use, yield a better return for their original cost; and therefore their owners can afford to have them of a better quality, and this, too, facilitates production.

7. It brings the producers and consumers into more intimate and safe relations. The division of labor between the wholesale and the retail trade is of great advantage. The retailers know their local markets, and supply them without loss or waste from the wholesale reservoirs. The wholesale reservoirs neatly control the various streams of production, according as demand is slackened or intensified. Thus, for example, a large city is daily supplied with fresh meat, without the loss, perhaps, of a hundred weight.

There are some disadvantages resulting from this division of labor: —

1. The work becomes in some departments monotonous and irksome, while some variety of occupation would afford relief by employing different muscles, or different faculties of the mind.

2. There is some tendency to dwarf the mental and corporeal powers, through exclusive attention to one part only of a complicated process.

3. When this part has been learned, and long made the means of a livelihood, a person has less power to adapt himself to change of circumstances, and becomes too much dependent on the continuance of the business in that form.

The degree to which the division of labor can be carried, depends in part upon the extent of the market, and in part upon the nature of the employment. To recur to Dr. Smith's illustration of the pins: if the market would only have received 24,000 pins a day from that establishment, instead of 48,000, the division of labor could not have been carried to the same extent, because if it had been, the men would be idle one half the time. In that case, some of the men would be dismissed, and some of the separate processes be combined, and production would be less efficient from the limitation of the market. Production, therefore, is most profitable when the market is broad enough to allow a full division of labor, and complete employment to all the operatives; and, the market being presupposed, is more likely to be profitable in large establishments than in small; because, (1) the division of labor can be carried to a fuller extent; (2) more perfect machinery can be afforded; (3) relatively less superintendence is required; and (4) the scraps and ends of a large business are frequently of sufficient importance to justify one or more subordinate branches of business in connection with the main business. For example, a large saw-mill may profitably furnish lath as well as lumber, since the refuse boards and slabs may go to lath. A wholesale butchering establishment of neat cattle might profitably have, in connection with the sale of meat, a tannery to dispose of the hides, a comb manufactory to dispose of the horns, a glue manufactory to dispose of the feet, a stall for the hair, which is useful in plastering, while the offal might be chemically disposed of in fertilizers.

The nature of the employment also limits the degree to which the division of labor may be carried. Agriculture, for instance, allows less of this division than most other departments of production, because its various operations cannot, from the nature of the case, become simultaneous. When the sowing is once done, the producer must wait some months upon Nature, till his agency is again required in the reaping. This fact, that agriculture can be less facilitated by the division of labor, and by the use of machinery, than most other departments of material production, constitutes one ground of an important truth, which we shall hereafter perceive stands also on another and firmer ground, the truth, namely, that agricultural products tend constantly to rise in value as compared with other commodities.

CHAPTER VI.

ON LABOR.

It is a curious thing, and one that draws after it very important consequences, that physical labor consists simply in moving things. When a man works with his hands, all that he does, or can do, is to produce a series of motions. Human muscles are only capable of two things, namely, producing motion, and resisting motion. All the marvellous results of human labor in all the world, have flowed from so simple a matter as the contraction and expansion of muscle. Work is motion, and weariness is weariness of muscle. The world of materials is so cunningly constructed, that, when they are moved into right position the powers of Nature do the rest, and objects of utility are the result.

When the pioneer fells a tree, he moves his axe through the trunk, and then the power of gravitation seizes the tree, and brings it to the ground. He produces a series of motions upon the tree, but the final motion, by which the century-girdled oak comes crashing to the earth, is not of his producing. Nature does that. Wool, cotton, and flax, have by nature a certain tenacity of fibre. Man moves these fibres in certain relations to each other by an instrument called a spindle, and the result is thread. Then the threads are moved in certain relations with each other by an instrument called a shuttle, and the result is a web of cloth. The tailor moves his shears through the cloth, and then his needles, and the result is a coat, — the object of utility for which all these processes were gone through with. The farmer first moves the ground, then moves his seeds into it, moves his sickle through the standing corn, moves his corn to the granary and mill, moves his meal from the mill to the larder, at which last point the housewife begins to operate upon it in a new series of motions. She moves the meal to the kneading-trough, and, having well moved it there, moves it to the oven, and, from the oven, after due interval, moves it to the table, at which point production ceases, and consumption begins.

Physical labor, then, is, and can be, nothing but this, *an effort, by which materials or implements are moved with reference to a given result.* Nature furnishes all the materials, and all the primary qualities of which we avail ourselves in production. She coöperates at every step. We pay her absolutely nothing for all she does. All we can shirk off our own shoulders, and throw upon hers, is so much clear gain. And it is a most happy circumstance that this is being done more and more completely in the production of nearly all commodities. Nature is good, to use a commercial term, for all she can be made to carry.

Now, since motion is the only thing which man is required to furnish in the production of commodities, he naturally looks around for helps in this matter. The first thing he lighted on, as a help to produce motion, was the domestic animals. The ox, the ass, the horse, were doubtless domesticated in the very beginnings of society. Men want these animals to produce motion for them — simply that. And as they can be used in so many different places, and for such a variety of purposes, and are so cheaply reared, they are exceedingly convenient as a motive power, and will probably never be superseded. The discovery and application of the great motive powers of water and steam have scarcely occasioned a lessened demand for the earlier and humbler motors, oxen and horses. Some of my readers will probably remember the time, when the introduction of railroads was opposed by some people, on the ground that the value of horses, and the business of teamsters would thereby be destroyed. Experience has demonstrated in this case, as it does in all similar cases, that improved machinery, and improved facilities of all kinds, so far from harming any class of persons permanently, are likely to be a gain to all classes of persons. At least, they only are harmed, who stupidly hold on to the old methods.

Labor, having employed from a very early time as a motive power the domestic animals, secured after a while, as inanimate auxiliaries, the water-wheel and the windmill; and, much later, the steam-engine. It is a point that has scarcely been noticed, even if it has ever been noticed at all, that all these auxiliaries, whether animate or inanimate, produce simple motions of the same kind as, and only supplemental to, the motion produced by a human arm. The most ponderous engine merely reduplicates that which the arm of a child is capable of; while in point of delicacy and firmness of touch, perhaps no machinery has yet been devised which can subdivide and apply this motion as skilfully as the human fingers can. It is said, that some of the lace made wholly by hand, is finer and more delicate than any yet woven by machinery, although the introduction of machinery into lace-making has cheapened th product, according to Dr. Ure, to about $\frac{1}{50}$ of its former cost. What we call power, then, however produced, is simple motion. But in order to subdivide these motions and apply them to the various purposes of production, implements of all sorts are needed, and implements, as we shall see in the next chapter, are always the gift of capital. But no power however mighty or however delicate, and no implements however perfect, can ever dispense with some portion of human labor. Not until machinery can be taught to think, to adapt means to ends, will human labor cease to play a chief part in production. These therefore, are, and always will be, the three requisites of material production: LABOR, POWER-AGENTS, CAPITAL.

Besides physical labor, there are the various forms of mental efforts put forth by men to satisfy the desires of other men, and with reference to a return. So far as exertion, physical or mental, is put forth for amusement, or for a pure benevolent motive, it has nothing to do with Political Economy. *It is only exertion which demands for itself something in exchange, that is technically labor.* Labor, which is primarily mental, such as most professional labor, the labor of the editor, the teacher, the architect, has of course little connection with motion or with commodities. But it is not on that account less useful or less valuable. The exchange of simple services depends on the same principles, gives rise to the same phenomena, and is amenable to the same science as all other exchanges. One man, as the violin-maker, offers services in which a commodity intervenes; another, as the violinist, offers services in which no commodity intervenes; each has gained in his own art a point of relative advantage as compared with other men, and these doubtless have gained some point of relative advantage as compared with them; each, by the sale of his respective service, meets some desire of the buyer, and is paid on the same principle as the other. The violin-maker of Cremona, who sold his instruments for five hundred francs apiece, was no more and no less a laborer, in the language of our science, than Paganini, who sold an hour's playing in the theatres for five thousand francs.

Having now seen what labor is, let us pass to the principles that determine its remuneration. I can see no reason why the purchasing-power of labor is not determined in the same way as the purchasing-power of all other things; and, if so, there is no difficulty in pointing out the general law of wages. I go back constantly to first principles, because I believe that first principles really control everything. Chance effects there most certainly are; but, as they happen now on one side and now on the other, they balance each other, and leave all the great working forces unaffected. For the sake of convenience, a distinction may be made at this point between professional and common labor, — a distinction which is not indeed very definite, but which is sufficiently so for the purpose in hand. The wages of professional labor of all sorts run up and down upon a scale whose extremes are much wider apart than the extremes of the scale which marks the variations in the wages of common labor, while at the same time the principle that determines the value of both forms of labor alike is the principle that determines all other value, namely, the law of Supply and Demand. The wages of professional labor, however, are so far different from the wages of common labor as to demand a somewhat distinct treatment. Why could Daniel Webster demand a fee of a thousand dollars for attending to a single case in court, Paganini a like sum for an hour's playing on a violin, and Jenny Lind at least as much for an evening's singing in a concert? Because there was in each case a strong demand for a peculiar service, and only one person in the whole world who could render that service, at least in the same perfection. The demand was large, the supply was small, and the value consequently great. The highest efforts of professional skill will always receive a high reward, whenever there is one person even, who, together with a strong desire for the product, has also the power to give a service in return; and especially whenever there are many persons who have a similar desire and power, to whom, as in the case of Paganini and Jenny Lind, the service can be rendered in common without lessening the satisfaction of each individual. That the supply is small in these higher regions of skilled effort, is due partly to the fact, that Nature is not lavish in her gifts of peculiar talents, and partly to the fact, that those who have received have assiduously cultivated them, and have reached in consequence a high point of relative advantage. These persons have what may be called a natural monopoly in their respective fields of high effort, because there are few others who have the natural gifts and the acquired skill which enable them to come in competition with them. But the objections which lie with such force against artificial monopolies, cannot be urged at all against a natural monopoly; for, if the road to excellence be open to all, and no artificial obstructions thrown in the paths of any, there is no blame but rather praise for him who distances all competitors, and demands for services of peculiar excellence a large remuneration. John Sartain is a superior engraver: he enjoys a natural monopoly in the highest walks of that art; the wages of his labor are very high; yet nobody can complain of this, since he has had no factitious privileges, but has fairly attained his excellence under freedom. Exchange rejoices in all diversity of advantage that is the birth of freedom, but reprobates with all her force advantage that is gained by artificial restrictions, because artificial restrictions always infringe on somebody's right to render services for a return; and the right to render services for a return is the fundamental conception in the right of Property. The wages of professional labor, then, are determined by the relations between the demand for such labor and the supply at hand; and are usually higher than the wages of common labor, because the supply of such laborers is restricted by the lack either (1) of appropriate original gifts, or (2) of the requisite industry, or (3) of the means of suitable education and training.

Within the great law of supply and demand, there are several important subordinate principles, which go to vary the wages of both professional and common labor, principally through their action upon supply; and it is now in order to consider these, before we pass to consider the wages of common labor. In common with all the writers who have succeeded him, I shall avail myself freely at this point of the labors of Adam Smith. That writer considers that there are certain circumstances in the employments themselves, which either really, or at least in men's imaginations, make up for a small pecuniary gain in some, and counterbalance a great one in others.

1. The agreeableness or disagreeableness of the employments will have an influence in determining the rate of wages paid to those who engage in them. The more agreeable employment will attract the larger number, and will experience in consequence the press of competition, and the rate of wages will be lessened by the increased supply of laborers. The more disagreeable employment will feel less the pressure of numbers, and will secure, other things being equal, a higher rate of remuneration in consequence. Among the elements which, in spite of the diversity of natural tastes, make any employment agreeable or disagreeable to the laborers, are (1) the less or greater exertion of physical strength required, (2) the healthfulness or unhealthfulness of the labor, (3) its cleanliness or dirtiness, (4) the degree of liberty or confinement in it, (5) the safety or hazard of the employment, (6) the esteem or disrepute of it in public opinion. To illustrate

each of these in order, the stone-mason, the glass-blower, the scavenger, the factory operative, the worker in a powder-mill, the smuggler, will each receive a larger compensation owing to the peculiar element of disagreeableness involved in his employment; and he will be able to demand and secure it through the action of the disagreeableness upon the supply of such laborers. Of all these elements, public opinion is perhaps the most operative; and if this be favorable to an employment, and some social consideration be attached to it, and only common qualifications be required for it, the wages in it will infallibly be low. This is probably the main reason why so many young women prefer to teach, rather than be employed in mills, shops, or offices, and why the wages of female teachers are so pitifully low; although each of the elements of agreeableness specified above may also contribute something towards the same result. If a business be decidedly opposed to public opinion, it must hold out the inducement of a large reward, or nobody will engage in it. This explains the abnormal gains of the slave-trade, the liquor-business, of gambling-houses, and of lotteries.

2. The easiness and cheapness, or the difficulty and expense, of learning different employments, will have an influence on the rate of wages paid in them. The more quickly and cheaply one can learn to perform the duties of a place satisfactorily, the less, so far forth, will be his wages; because there will be many who will compete with him in rendering such services; the more time, difficulty, and expense involved in learning a business, the larger, so far forth, will be the wages secured by it;

because fewer persons have the means, the foresight, the patience, to prepare themselves for such an avocation. This is the principal ground of the difference in the wages of skilled and unskilled labor. The artisan has, at least, given time, and the professional man has given both time and money, to fit themselves to render the services which they now offer to society; and it is right, therefore, for them to demand a higher rate of compensation than is accorded to operatives and common laborers. But a right to demand does not always carry along with it an ability to secure: in this case it does, through the reduction of numbers which these obstacles at the entrance occasion, and the consequent weakness of competition. To put a boy apprentice to a trade, requires on the part of the parents a foresight, an ability to get on without his immediate help, and sometimes an amount of money for his board and clothes, which all parents do not possess; and consequently, the number of skilled artisans, who must learn when they are young if at all, are relatively few compared with common laborers, and are able to realize a much higher rate of wages than they. In the professions, if we confine our attention to those persons who are thoroughly trained for them, we shall find a higher rate of compensation still, and one made higher on the same principles; although we must here bear in mind the counter-working influences which tend to increase the competition in the professions, namely, the respectability which attends them, the desire of knowledge for its own sake which is gained in connection with them, the instruction wholly or in part gratuitously offered to those in course of preparation for them, and the desire to do good, without regard to pecuniary reward, which actuates many who enter upon them.

3. The constancy or inconstancy of employment is a consideration that affects wages. If the employment be such that it can only be carried on during nine months of the year, the wages of the day or month will be greater than they would be if it could be carried on during the twelve months. The laborer looks to the aggregate earnings of the year, and will hardly take up a trade which affords employment but a part of the time, unless some compensation can be found in the higher wages for that time. This is the chief reason why the day's wages of the mason and the house-painter, in this climate at least, are higher than those of the carpenter or smith. The coachman, also, may stand by his horses half the day or night, with no call for his services, and must have, therefore, a proportionably higher fare from those whom he does transport. In general, it is found that men prefer a constant employment with a lower rate of wages, than an inconstant one, with a prospect of higher pay for the particular jobs actually done, and because they prefer that, those who take up with the other are able to secure a higher rate of pay in their less eligible avocation. Counter working this, however, are the desires which many men have, for intervals of leisure in their business; and the opportunity to make these intervals subservient to another branch of business or means of livelihood.

4. The amount of trust involved affects wages. Men in responsible positions secure a higher rate of

pay for their services than can be accounted for, except by a reference to the unwillingness of people to intrust great interests to others, unless they are men of established character for probity. Such men, men who combine all the other requisites for an important post, with a well-known honesty, are comparatively rare; and, when they are found, will receive a very high compensation for their services. Treasurers of corporations, cashiers of banks, and holders of trust-funds generally, are examples in point. Shall we say, then, that men offer their honesty in the market, as they offer their skill, and are paid for the one as for the other? No! Their skill has been acquired to sell, and for no other reason; but their honesty, if it be genuine, has another basis altogether; and he who is honest, simply because honesty is the best policy, is not honest at all! The very characteristic of honesty is that it cannot be bought! It has a moral, and not a mercantile foundation. In point of fact, a man who has the full confidence of his fellow-citizens, as an honest man, and at the same time all the other qualifications requisite for a post of high pecuniary trust, is in position, partly on the ground of his honesty, to render a high service, and will receive for that service a high reward; but I protest, in the name of morals, against the notion that honesty is a marketable article: it is rather an underlying element of moral character, which fits men indeed to render certain services, but the honesty is maintained, not for the sake of the service, but has an independent basis of its own. So, also, most people would prefer a deeply religious man for a preacher and spiritual guide, but it is a perversion of language to maintain that in rendering these services a clergyman sells his religion. It is true that he sells services to the appropriate rendering of which his personal piety contributes one element; but the piety is not nourished for the sake of the services, but for its own sake, and it must not be confounded with that which is sold. Accordingly, while the clergyman's vocation is sacred, and belongs to the sphere of religion, his salary belongs to the sphere of exchange, and its determination is wholly a business transaction. This distinction ought to be better understood than it is; and both clergymen and people need to be reminded that the spiritual things belong to one sphere, and the carnal things to another. The amount of a clergyman's salary, and the time and mode of its payment, are matters of pure business; and the clergyman himself is to blame if he does not attend to them, and insist on them, on business principles.

5. The probability of success in any employment is a circumstance that has some influence on the rate of wages paid in it, through the action of this probability on the numbers of those who enter upon it. If success is problematical, fewer will engage in such a business, and those who do engage in it and succeed, will reap a very high reward. Ten boys, for example, put to the blacksmith's trade, ordinary capacity being presupposed, will probably every one succeed in becoming a tolerable workman; but of ten boys of the same capacity put apprentice to an engraver, probably not over three would ever reach any high degree of skill and success; and therefore,

the pressure of numbers will be felt much more in the former than the latter art. So also, those who take jobs by contract, and who consequently assume some risks, are usually paid at a higher rate than those who do work by the day. It is true that this is owing partly to the fact that the contractor commonly uses his own capital, and must therefore be paid profits as well as wages, and also that the wages of superintendence are due to him as well as ordinary wages; still there is a residuum of difference which can only be accounted for by the risk he runs of a successful issue. The difference in wages from this fifth cause of variation, would be greater than it is, were it not for the overweening confidence which most men have in their own good luck. This confidence is seen in the rush which is always made for newly discovered mining regions, and in the facility with which even yet lottery tickets are sold. It is demonstrable beforehand, on the doctrine of chances, that no lottery ticket is worth so much as it is sold for, and yet men buy on in spite of the demonstration; and experience in California and at Pike's Peak, has sadly taught how excessive was the confidence in their own success of the men who flocked to those new El Dorados.

6. Custom and prejudice and fashion, have something to do with the determination of wages in some departments. Custom, especially in former times, has been very operative. The current fees of lawyers and physicians have been largely dependent on custom, competition merely coming in to decide how many such fees a man should get, rather than lessening the amount of each particular fee. Cus-

tom determines the wages when men take farms on shares. But competition is now breaking down custom in all directions, and will soon, I think, reign supreme over the economic field. Prejudice is closely allied to custom, and has some voice still in adjusting wages, as may be seen, perhaps, in women's wages, crowded down to a point unreasonably low, as compared with the wages of men. Custom and prejudice may yield the field, but fashion, which is one form of competition, will always have an influence over wages. They who lead the styles in any department whatsoever, will always offer their services to society at an advantage to themselves, and their rate of compensation will be legitimately higher than the average rate.

7. Legal restrictions and voluntary associations are another cause acting on wages, by acting on the supply of laborers. Laws inhibiting or promoting immigration, laws appointing the fees and salaries of officials, tariff laws, whether prohibitory or only restrictive, unequal taxation, and so on, all have an agency in adjusting wages. Governments are coming, however, much more freely than formerly, to leave everything except the wages of their own servants, and those things which they choose to tax, to the simple and safe action of supply and demand. The guilds of the Middle Ages, and the trades' unions of our own day, are examples of voluntary associations for the sake of regulating the wages of the members by combined action. The restrictions in the old guilds, limiting the number of apprentices to each artisan, determining the time a man should serve before he could become a master, and

so on, were very onerous, and have mostly passed away. The trades' unions in this country cannot be commended, because they tend to destroy the freedom of personal action, and bring all workmen to one level of wages. The spirit of Political Economy, which is the spirit of freedom, is against such associations for such purposes. If any man has a service to render, let him offer it freely, and make the best terms he can with whoever wants it.

Having looked at the principles that determine the compensation of skilled labor, and also at some causes tending to vary the wages both of skilled and common labor, we pass now to a consideration of those principles more particularly applicable to the wages of common labor. All value, as we know, is a resultant of two desires and two efforts, and is variable by any variation of either desire or either effort. When the laborer offers a series of efforts to another person, he does so in virtue of a desire for something which that other person has to give, for food, clothing, money; and the other person has a desire for the efforts of the laborer, and is willing to give in return the food, clothing, money, or whatever it may be. The more laborers there are who offer their service to this person, the more likely he is to obtain the service at a cheap rate, since there is a competition among the laborers to secure that food, clothing, money, and so on, which he offers in return for the service: the more persons, on the other hand, who offer food, clothing, money, and so on, to the laborers there present, the more likely are the latter to receive a high rate for their efforts, since there is a competition among employers to secure such efforts. The number of employers and the amount of that which they offer as return for such efforts, constitutes the demand for laborers; the number of laborers willing to render service for what is thus offered in return, constitutes the supply of labor: the current rate of wages of common labor is determined by the adjustment, that is, the equalization of the demand and supply. In what we have said thus far in relation to wages, we have referred chiefly to causes acting on the supply of laborers, rather than on the demand for labor: we must now look in the other direction, and anticipate the discussions of the next chapter, so far as to say, that all capital constitutes an immediate and pressing demand for labor. Whoever desires a service which a laborer can render, and lays by something to pay for that service, creates that instant a demand for labor; and especially, whoever accumulates raw materials which laborers are to work up, builds, buys, or keeps machinery which laborers are to tend, or puts himself in position to suffer loss by the ownership of lands, ships, or other property whatsoever, unless laborers be employed to make them productive, creates thereby an instant demand for labor. All such accumulations whatsoever, destined in the owner's mind to be employed in further production, all implements, buildings, and improvements, designed to assist labor, and raw materials which labor must work up, are capital; and capital must be constantly united with labor, or the owners will suffer an inevitable loss. The presence of capital anywhere constitutes a demand for labor. The more capital there is anywhere, the stronger the demand for labor; and capital, therefore, is the poor man's best friend. Mr. Carey regards the laborer as at a disadvantage compared with capital, because the laborer must at once dispose of his product, or starve; which seems to me a superficial view of the relation, because capital submits to an instant loss when it declines to employ labor. Capital does not like to lose its profit any more than the laborer likes to lose his bread. In a true and general view, the one is under just as much pressure to employ laborers, as the other to get employment. They come together of necessity into a relation of mutual dependence, which God has ordained, and which, though man may temporarily disturb it, he can never overthrow.

Labor, then, takes itself to the market to effect an exchange with capital. It is only capital that employs labor. Now, the terms of the exchange, that is to say, the average rate of the wages of common labor, will depend on the number of laborers compared with the amount of capital there present. The aggregate of all the forms of capital there present, helps to make up in the mind of the capitalist his motive for employing labor, because the more he has invested in buildings, machinery, and materials, the more urgent is the necessity to employ laborers, in order to make the investment productive; although only a part of the capital is free to be offered in payment of wages. Demand for labor is constituted, strictly speaking, by that part of the capital which is available to be offered in the form of wages, but it is clear, that, as a rule, demand, that is, the portion of capital designed for the payment of wages, may increase under the influence of increased desire for laborers, and an increased desire for laborers is a necessary consequence of the increase in the aggregate of capital. Whether the portion designed for wages *will* increase or not, on an increase of capital, will depend on the number of laborers. It is certainly possible that capital may go on increasing, while the wages-fund (the portion designed for wages) may remain stationary, or even diminish, owing to the competition of an increased number of laborers, and the diminished compensation going to each. The number of laborers remaining the same, and intelligently comprehending their position, the size of the wages-fund will necessarily keep pace with all increase of aggregate capital. This point of connection between the two, this influence of the whole capital on the desire for laborers, and consequently on the wages-fund, is a point which I do not remember to have seen noticed by anybody, yet which is obviously of much importance in unfolding the relations of labor to capital. Now, wherever there is capital there is a wages-fund, and we have just seen what the connection is between the whole capital and that portion of it which is ready to be devoted to the payment of wages. If we call this portion of capital, or wages-fund, a dividend, and the number of laborers a divisor, the quotient will be the general average rate of wages at that time and place. This principle invariably determines the current rate of wages in any country. If the laborers are few relatively to the amount of capital, there will be a large dividend, and a small divisor, and infallibly a large quotient. In the reverse case, when laborers are many as compared with the capital that seeks to employ them, the large divisor and small dividend will surely give a small quotient. In the first case, capitalists will compete for laborers, and wages will go up. In the second case, laborers will compete for employment, and wages will go down.

We see now what we are to think of many remedies popularly recommended for low wages. When wages are very low in any country, or in any department of labor, there are some who think that the government ought to interfere to better them, at least to designate a minimum below which wages shall not go ; others propose that strong public opinion be brought to bear upon employers, to induce them to give sufficient wages: others still maintain that combinations among the workmen themselves, for the purpose of dictating the rate of wages to the employers, would be an appropriate and effective remedy. Every one of these is a delusion, and so is every other proposal that ignores the law of wages just established. That which pays for labor in every country, is a certain portion of actually accumulated capital, which cannot be increased by the proposed action of government, nor by the influence of public opinion, nor by combinations among the workmen themselves. There is also in every country a certain number of laborers, and this number cannot be diminished by the proposed action of government, nor by public opinion, nor by combinations among themselves. There is to be a division now among all these laborers of the portion of capital actually there present. Suppose there has been free competition on both sides, and that the average rate of wages as thus determined, is one dollar per day for each laborer. Suppose that everybody thinks that this is insufficient, and that government accordingly issues a decree that wages thereafter must be one dollar and a half per day to each laborer. This decree has no tendency to increase the size of the wages-fund; *that* is determined by the general productiveness of labor, and by the division, under free competition, between wages and profits; if the decree, therefore, were carried out, as it never could be, the result would be that only two thirds of the laborers there present could be employed at all, and the remaining third must be supported by charity, or starve. The wages-fund is only sufficient to give to all the laborers a dollar a day, and if the government enforces a new distribution at a rate one third higher, then one third of the laborers cannot be employed at all. There is no use in arguing against any one of the four fundamental rules of arithmetic. The question of wages is a question of Division. It is complained that the quotient is too small. Well, then, how many ways are there to make a quotient larger? Two ways. Enlarge your dividend, the divisor remaining the same, and the quotient will be larger: lessen your divisor, the dividend remaining the same, and the quotient will be larger. All accessions to capital, all investment of profits in an enlarged business, all saving from expenditure for the sake of further production, will increase the dividend, and, the number of laborers continuing as before, the rate of wages will rise. Or, if there be no accessions to capital, the wages-fund consequently standing as before, and the number of laborers be diminished, as by emigration to new fields of effort, or by enlistment in armies, the divisor will be lessened, and the rate of wages will rise. The reversed suppositions will give, of course, reversed results, and wages will go down.

Though not in the way proposed, there is a way in which government may act most beneficially upon this matter of wages. By faithfulness to its peculiar trust, that is to say, by making the rights of person and property as secure as possible, it gives an impulse to enterprise, a spur to industry, makes the desire of accumulation effective, and thus indirectly but most powerfully contributes to the increase of capital, to the fund out of which wages are paid. Also, by fostering the means of education, and by the diffusion of knowledge among all classes, government acts beneficially upon the laborers, to make them intelligent, to impart to them that character and self-respect which fits them, in exchanging services with capital, to demand and secure their full rights in the exchange. It is not denied that capital takes advantage of the ignorance and immobility of laborers, and sometimes secures their services at a less rate than the just relations of capital to labor then and there would indicate, but the remedy for this is not in arbitrary interference of government in the bargain, but in the intelligence and self-respect of the laborers which shall fit them to insist on a just bargain. In this whole sphere of exchange, the just and comprehensive rule always will be, that when men exchange services with each other, each party is bound to look out for his own interest, to know the market-value of his own service, and to make the best terms for himself which he can make. Capital does this for itself, and laborers ought to do this for themselves, and if they are persistently cheated in the exchange, they have nobody to blame but themselves. Government should give them all facilities for intelligence: they should give themselves a character, and cherish a hearty self-respect, which there is nothing in their position to diminish: towards such laborers, capital occupies no vantage ground in an exchange of mutual services.

Public opinion can do something towards bettering the wages of labor, in countries where they are low, by organizing means to assist the laborers in distributing themselves at points where their services are most in demand. Societies in our seaboard cities, whose object it is to aid immigrants to pass on from those cities where labor is very abundant, to the country towns and to the West, where it is relatively much less so, are commendable in their purpose and spirit. So also are emigration societies, in countries situated as Ireland has been, where centuries of misgovernment combined with centuries of ignorance, produced a temporary pressure of population on the means of support. Where such pressure exists, as it does also in China, it is a good thing for public opinion to be favorable to emigration to newer and more fortunate countries, and liberally to assist in the distribution of labor to those points, wherever they may be, where capital is ready and anxious to employ it.

It may surprise some who are familiar with books on Political Economy, that I do not here adduce the influence of public opinion in restraining population as favorable to wages, and inveigh against the force of that spring of population which the Creator has coiled up in the nature of man, as compared with the weakness of that power by which the earth produces sustenance for man. Mr. Malthus, and other economists, have discussed at length the tendency in the law of human fecundity to outstrip in its results the law of diminished returns from land; and have expressed an apprehension that the time may come when the earth shall be unable to support her children. They have enlarged upon the well-known fact that in the United States population doubles every twenty-five years; and have calculated that, at this rate, the inhabitants of every country would, in the course of five centuries increase to above a million times their previous number; that the population of England, for example, would, at this rate, in that time, exceed twenty million millions, — a population which could not get standing-room there. Such a rate of increase certainly needs to be checked; and Mr. Malthus divides the checks to population into the positive and the preventive. The first increase the number of deaths, the second diminish the number of births. The principal positive checks are war, famine, and disease; the principal preventive check is prudence. Of course it is better that the check which limits fecundity should come into play, rather than those which decrease longevity; and these writers are at pains to inculcate upon the laboring classes prudence in marrying, and temperance after marriage. These discussions are interesting in themselves, and have attracted much attention; but I cannot regard them as particularly pertinent to discussions on wages. God has endowed mankind with a strong impulse towards procreation. But experience has shown that it is not too strong for the purposes for which it was given. Experience has also shown that, as society advances, and men come more and more under the influence of reason, and affection, the preventive check comes silently and effectually into operation. Experience has shown also that food and comforts have more than kept pace with the stride of population; since the inhabitants of the world, as a whole, were never so well fed and clothed and housed as now. The abstract antagonism of the law of the increase of population with the law of the increase of food is admitted; but HE who is author of the laws is author also of natural counter-workings of them; so that a practical *tendency* towards their coming into conflict is denied. Each human being is as much constituted by Nature to receive services as to render them, and each is as likely as any of the others to become a capitalist; and therefore the law of population, the maladministrations of men aside, has no scientific relevancy to the question of wages. Whenever population has pressed on food, reasons for it are apparent outside of natural laws.

But will not strikes accomplish that for the raising of wages which neither government nor public opinion can effect? A strike is a combination among workmen for an increase of wages. They agree to stop work altogether until their employers shall comply with their terms, and raise their wages to a certain definite sum. It is not to be denied that workmen thus possess, under many circumstances, a very considerable reserved power which they can bring to bear upon their employers. When the processes of production are going briskly forward, when the manufactory is thoroughly furnished with competent hands, and profitable orders are in waiting, it is no laughable thing for the owner to be told, of a cloudy morning, that his hands have all stopped work, and refuse to lift a finger, until he shall agree to pay them wages at a rate which they themselves dictate. Of course, his first impulse is to discharge every man of them, and endeavor to fill his factory with new hands But this he cannot always do. At best it will take time. Meanwhile his wheel or engine must be idle, customers be lost, orders unfilled, and profits nowhere. And so, many an employer has surrendered to a strike, when he felt that it was all unjust, rather than undergo a still greater loss. It is admitted that workmen may sometimes strike and gain their point, but it is none the less true for all that, that strikes are false in theory and pernicious in practice; that they spring from utter misapprehension of the true principles of wages; that they embitter relations between employers and employed which ought to be cordial and free; and that they rarely or never are permanently advantageous to the workmen themselves.

In the first place, then, strikes are false in theory. It is a very old adage, that it takes two to make a bargain. Express this in the language of Political Economy, and it will take this form: When two men have mutual services to exchange, let them come to a fair agreement as to the terms on which they will exchange. Certainly, let each make the best terms he can, but let the bargain always be free. If one party, who happens to have the power to do it, uses compulsion upon the other, it ceases to be a bargain at all, and becomes a sort of robbery. If, driving with my good horse along a lonely road, I meet another man driving an inferior one, and he, being the stronger man, compels me to exchange horses, it may be all very well for him, but I protest that it is no bargain. It is robbery. Now, workmen bring a certain valuable service to the market, just such a service as the capitalist wants, and he has to offer just such a service as they want, namely, wages. Now let them come to a free and fair agreement on the terms of their exchange. Let the workmen by all means make the very best terms they can; let them insist to the last penny on all which they can get elsewhere, for the value of their service is determined, as the value of every other service is determined, by what it will bring. Let the employer do the same. Let a fair bargain be struck. There is no objection to this kind of striking; and the more intelligence and skill and self-respect a workman has, the better prepared he is to strike the bargain and secure his just due. If the employer will not yield him this, let him have done with it at once, and go elsewhere. Or, if a just bargain has been struck, and afterwards circumstances shall so alter that he thinks he can rightfully demand more, let him frankly demand it, remembering always that it is an exchange he has to do with, and that it takes two to make a bargain. If he does not get for his service what he thinks he ought to get, let him quit. He has a perfect right to quit. All this is legitimate and fair and above board.

But a strike is wholly different. This brings compulsion into play. A combination among workmen to leave an employer in the lurch, and especially a combination which forces into its ranks by cajoling or menaces, those who are unwilling to join it, is of itself a confession of the injustice of the claim. If the claim be just, there is no occasion to extort it. If the value of the service rendered be equal to the sum demanded, if this can be obtained elsewhere, there is no need of consultation and conference, combination and conspiracy. Let each man go quickly where he can get the most for his service. The fact that this is not done, that means are brought to bear upon the employer which are not ordinarily used in bargains, — means of the nature of a threat — that the justice of the claim is not relied on in a case where, more than anywhere else, justice can enforce itself, that full and free explanations are not had, that no notice is given, that great damage is expected by their action to accrue to the employer, all this seems to forget that the transaction between employers and employed is a case of pure exchange, a simple bargain of one service against another service. Therefore, I say, that strikes are false in theory.

But this is not the worst of it. Strikes are pernicious in practice. And the grand reason for this is they tend to lessen the wages-fund. The production of all material commodities is a joint process. Capital and labor both conspire in it. The gross returns belong wholly to the capitalists and the laborers. The profits of capital and the wages of labor are paid out of these returns and from no other source. It is for the interest of both capitalists and laborers that these returns be as large as possible, because they are wholly divided between the two, and if the whole be large the parts will also be large. Profits being taken out, the rest is wages-fund; or, more strictly speaking, wages-fund being taken out, the rest is profits. It makes no difference practically that the wages have been advanced to the laborers while the production was still going forward, since the wages really come out of the proceeds of the joint process. The capitalist never means to pay wages out of his previous accumulations, and ought not to be expected to do so, and were he obliged to do so, it would soon be worse for the laborers, since these accumulations are the only stock which supports labor. It is not only just but needful for the laborers, that wages shall be paid out of the proceeds of that on which labor is now expended. Whatever, then, tends to lessen these proceeds, necessarily lessens the wages-fund. Any interruption of the process of production by strikes, any want of full and hearty coöperation between the two parties to the joint process, will, if continued, infallibly make the wages-fund smaller.

Suppose it takes three months to realize the returns in some branch of manufacture. If, when the workmen are paid off at the end of one three months, they all strike at the beginning of the next, and both parties hold out for three months, what is now the chance for higher wages? It shall go hard even if they get as much as before. And why? Because the mill has stood idle, and the owner has lost three months' profits on the whole investment connected with the mill. They have lost wages for three months, and now when they come to begin again, they may not be able to wait, as before, till the end of the cycle, and their wages must be advanced out of a fund smaller than it would have been but for the strike. The employer usually advances wages out of his own, or borrowed capital, expecting to be repaid from the results of current work. Sometimes his mere expectation of large returns acts favorably on the wages-fund. But this employer has lost profits and customers by the strike, and his business is disarranged. His workmen by inflicting a loss upon themselves have found an opportunity of inflicting a loss upon him. Their loss is undoubtedly the greater of the two. Therefore, I say, strikes are commonly, and almost necessarily, a disadvantage to the workmen themselves. The case just put is a strong case to show the principle involved, but all interruption whatever to the processes of production by strikes, all consequent embittered relations between employers and employed, all want of hearty working together of the labor with the capital, tend to diminish the gross returns, and consequently, both the wages-fund and profits. As far as this point is concerned, there is no sense or reason in the common jealousy of workmen towards employers. There is no real antagonism between them. Their interests lie along the same line. They are partners in the same concern. Workmen who are intelligent, prudent, skilful, will infallibly get their due. Employers who are humane, urbane, fair, will find their account in it.

In discussing labor and wages, it will be noticed that I have made no reference to a subject a good deal agitated at present in Europe and somewhat also in the United States, namely, to coöperation. This is a scheme originating with laborers themselves, under which they combine, either to purchase their necessaries in common and hence at cheaper rates because avoiding all profits of middle-men; or, more especially, to engage in joint production, the workmen furnishing the capital; all being copartners, and of course all sharing *pro rata* the profits of the concern. All this is well; and in countries where laborers are under traditional disabilities, it may be very promotive of their welfare; but any one can see that no new economic principle is involved in it. The workmen unite the character of capitalist and laborer in their own persons, and both receive wages and share profits; but the principles which determine the amounts of each are the same as if the two went in opposite directions. The practical success of the scheme will depend in each case upon the question whether there be any of the workmen of sufficient organizing and executive ability to carry it through. Workmen should have a chance to do this everywhere: it is done essentially whenever two or more workingmen organize a firm to carry on any business. In the United States the greatest freedom prevails; there is nothing to hinder any laborer from becoming a capitalist; nearly all our capitalists were formerly laborers; the savings-banks are open for the smallest gains; and the shares of most joint-stock companies are open to everybody who has means to buy them. There is only one consideration that seems to justify in this country any special jealousy of laborers as such, towards capitalists as such; and that is the fact, that the legislature does sometimes confer, by means of corporate charters, and otherwise, certain extraordinary rights upon capital. So long as capital and labor rest solely upon their natural rights, neither can have the advantage of the other; but so far forth as advantage is given to capital by law, it is unjust to labor, and ought to be vigilantly watched and counteracted by laborers. The legislature, whether state or national, cannot be too scrupulous in this whole matter. The proper limits of legislative action upon economical subjects are pretty narrow. Capital and labor should both have the utmost liberty of action compatible with social security; and the *equal rights* of each will, in general, best be reached by leaving both to take care of themselves, subject only to general laws relating to person and property. If the legislature yields to special claims of capital, it must expect to hear labor also knocking at its doors. If capitalists "strike" for artificial profits by means of a protective tariff, why may not laborers "strike" for artificial wages? The former have set the latter a bad example. Much of the recent discontent of labor has come from this greed of capital demanding and securing for itself special privileges. Let alone. Legislatures are not wise enough to say how many hours per day adult laborers shall work, or how many dollars per day capitalists shall pay them. To attempt to do either is an economic abomination.

CHAPTER VII.

ON CAPITAL.

THE three requisites of production are labor, power-agents, and capital. Of the first we have now learned what can be learned, without attending in turn to its counterpart — capital; of the second we have learned already that all the powers of Nature work gratuitously in the service of man; and of the third, we are now to learn what it is, how it arises, how it works, and what its influence is upon the progress and amelioration of society. Political economy is able to show that there is no natural opposition of interest between capitalists and laborers; that capital is just as dependent on labor as labor is dependent on capital; that each is equally interested in the prosperity of the other, and that thus a deep and admirable harmony subsists in this part, as in every other part, of the social organism.

Capital is any product reserved to be employed in further production. This definition will be found to cover all the cases, to obviate many difficulties, and to take the life out of many disputes. Mr. Carey defines capital as the instrument by means of which man obtains mastery over Nature, including in it the physical and mental powers of man himself, and thus needlessly confuses the boundaries between capital and labor. It is much simpler and better to define labor, as has already been done, as physical or mental exertion for the sake of a return, and to define capital, as is now done, as any product outside of himself reserved by man for further production. There are many products devoted to immediate consumption; that is to say, to the gratification of present desires, without any reference to the rendering of future services by means of their help. Such products are not capital. They are a portion of the wealth of the community, they are valuable, but capital they are not. All capital is wealth, but all wealth is not capital. Only that portion is capital which employs, assists, and pays for labor. All raw materials are capital, all machinery is capital, all funds destined to purchase these, and all funds destined for wages, are capital. As all values reside in services exchanged, so all capital resides in services accumulated with reference to an ultimate exchange. It is only in the intention of the owner that capital can be discriminated from other products destined by him for the gratification of himself and his family, or for benevolent purposes. Take a hardware manufacturer, for example, and he has a stock on hand of finished hardware, a part of the proceeds of which he will put back into his business in the form of materials, tools, and wages, and another part will go in the form of personal and family expenditure, and it is only his intention that discriminates the first part, which is purely capital, from the second part, which, as far as he is concerned, is not capital at all. It may indeed become capital in the hands of those to whom he pays it out; and will become so, in case they destine it as an aid to further production in their several lines of business. The whole mass of capital, then, in any country, is the whole mass of those products, of whatever kind, which are destined in the mind of their owners to be retained as an aid towards rendering future services to society.

How does capital arise? We have seen that there are obstacles which lie in the way of the gratification of men's desires in all directions, and that these obstacles can only be removed by human effort. When a man devotes himself to one set of these obstacles, with a view to surmount them, he is not long in discovering, that if he had certain tools, his work would be greatly facilitated; and having discovered that, it will not be long before he will attempt himself, or induce others to attempt, to invent such tools. The beaver gnaws down the tree with his teeth, from generation to generation; but man is a being more nobly endowed than the beaver, and no sooner had he occasion to fell trees, than something of the nature of an axe suggested itself to his ingenuity. It is true, that his earliest attempts at axe-making were probably of the rudest sort, but just as soon as anything was devised, whether of flint or shell or metal, that rendered easier the labor of felling a tree, capital made a beginning along that line of obstacles. Among the more gifted races, progress in this direction was perhaps more rapid than we are wont to think it was, since Tubal-cain, even in the times before the flood, is said to have been "an instructor of every artificer in brass and iron." At any rate, we are at no loss to explain the origin of capital: it is found in the motive that exists everywhere, and that always existed, to lessen, if possible, a given irksome effort that is the condition of a given satisfaction. And this origin of capital gives the key-note to its universal use and indefinite expansion. Tools are invented and employed for no other reason than this, that, by means of their help, the human effort is lessened relatively to a given satisfaction. The powers of Nature, such as those which make the grain grow, bring the tree down, turn the water-wheel, impel the locomotive, and send the message round the world, all stand ready to slave in the service of man; but in order to make their aid available for human purposes, there must be a plough, an axe, a wheel, an engine, an electric machine. These, and all other implements whatsoever, from the tiniest needle to the most ponderous engine, are products created and retained for the sake of further production. They are capital. They are not capable of yielding in themselves an ultimate satisfaction to human wants, but they mediate between the powers of Nature, which they enable us to make available for our purposes, and those ultimate satisfactions. Nature furnishes all the powers, and all the natural qualities of objects, but labor can go but a very little way towards making these available for the satisfaction of human wants, without the aid of implements and contrivances which are produced by labor; and which, being retained as an aid to future labor, are capital. Since it requires tools to make tools, the progress of capital at first was very slow; but, since every advance in mechanical contrivance makes still further advances easier, there is a natural tendency, which facts abundantly exemplify, to a more and more rapid progression in the number and perfection of all implements of production. The same motive that impelled to the first invention, has impelled to the whole series of inventions since, and will constantly impel to further inventions till the end of time. This motive, — and there is no motive that actuates man more universal, — is, to lessen the onerous effort of human muscle, and to throw upon the ever-willing shoulders of Nature more and more of the burden of production. Every step of this progress gives birth to a larger and larger proportion of satisfactions relatively to efforts; marks an increasing control on the part of man over the powers of Nature; and gives promise for the time to come of greater advantages still in both these two directions. And it is because capital brings gratuitous natural forces into service, and the more so as capital progresses, that the value of those things created by the aid of capital tends constantly to decline as compared with the value of those things, in whose production capital less conspires; and in the chapter following the next will be developed from this point one or two important laws of value.

Now, then, having seen what capital is, and the human motive that brings it forward in production, we next inquire after its remuneration. *The remuneration of capital is technically called profits:* just as wages are technically the remuneration of labor. The present proposition is, that profits are the legitimate reward of a service, just as much, and in the same sense, as wages are the legitimate reward of a service. The distinctive service of the capitalist as such, as distinguished from the service of the laborer, consists in his voluntary *abstinence* from the use and enjoyment of that which he contributes in aid of further production. If a man puts a thousand dollars, which he might spend upon his immediate gratifications, into a machine to be used in his business, the money immediately becomes capital; the owner practices abstinence, and for this abstinence justly expects a reward. This reward we call profit. The expected profit is the only motive for the abstinence. He will not be content simply to get his thousand dollars back, for that he has now: he must have his thousand dollars with a profit. Suppose A to be a manufacturer of flax fabrics, B to be a farmer in his neighborhood, and C an expert mechanic acquainted with the current modes of spinning and weaving flax. A has a capital of $10,000 invested in his business, in buildings, machinery, materials, and wages-fund, which nets him $1000 a-year clear profit. At the end of the year, the question with him is, whether he shall spend this $1000 unproductively in immediate gratifications, or, adding it to his capital stock, increase his business with it. If he concludes to do the latter, he must forego the use and enjoyment of his $1000 for the present, he must practise abstinence; and this he will not do, and ought not to do, except in view of increased profits to accrue from his business at the end of the next year. If more flax is to be spun and woven in his factory, more money must be invested to buy more materials, to pay more laborers, or to pay for more or better machinery. His contribution to the prospectively increased production is $1000, transformed by his intention from simple property to capital, devoted to production by a voluntary abstinence from its present use and enjoyment, in view of a future reward or profit. It is a service rendered by one man to a joint process to be performed by many, and gives him a just claim to a portion of the product. Is exertion irksome? So is abstinence. Are wages legitimate? So are profits. B as a farmer might devote all his fields to growing food and fruits for the gratification of himself and family, but since A now wants more flax fibre for his factory, he gives up a part of his acres to growing flax, and this becomes a part of A's capital in the form of raw material; and the money received for it may become capital in B's hands by being spent either in agricultural improvements, or in buying additional land. The mechanic C, by giving time, exertion, and money to the work, may invent an improved machine for spinning flax, to be introduced into A's factory. The machine becomes a part of A's capital, and the money paid to C for his machine is partly wages, a reward for the labor bestowed on its construction, and partly profits, to replace to C the money used in making the machine, together with a reward for his abstinence from the use of this money until the machine was sold. Thus we see that capital, whether in the form of wages-fund, materials, or implements, is always the result of abstinence; and that whoever abstains from the present enjoyment of anything, in order that that something may contribute to a future production, renders an essential service; and, consequently, that the reward of such abstinence, or profit, is just as legitimate as are wages. This is very clearly seen in the common case in which one man loans capital to a second, to be used by that second in his own business. Brooks has a thousand dollars in hand which he is at liberty either to enjoy unproductively, or to employ himself productively, with the assurance of a profit; but is willing to forego the use of it for a year in favor of Smith, who is anxious to enlarge his business. Brooks' abstinence is a clear service to Smith; and at the end of the year, therefore, Smith not only refunds the thousand dollars borrowed, but also sundry other dollars besides as a specific reward for this specific service. If Smith keeps the money ten years or twenty, it is no more than just that he should pay this sum every year till the principal is refunded, because the service is every year repeated, the abstinence is still practised in his favor. Therefore, capital once acquired by abstinence, becomes, if the abstinence be continued, a legitimate source of perpetual revenue to the owner, as well as a perpetual source for the maintenance of laborers. Whoever transforms his property into capital, establishes thereby a permanent fund whence he may draw an income, and laborers support, in perpetuity; because the capital, though constantly disappearing in production, as constantly reappears in products, with profits added: a fact which shows the folly of the popular opinion which regards more favorably the man who spends his money freely and unproductively, than the man who, turning his money into capital, building a mill, or making other permanent investments, creates by that means a fund in the community, out of which permanent wages and permanent profits can be paid. The strength of the motives to abstinence in any country will depend largely upon the character of the government, and the organization of society there; these motives being generally strongest where liberty of action, equality of privileges, and security of property are the greatest.

We turn now to the relations of capital to labor, and to that law of the distribution of the products between capitalists and laborers, which was first promulgated by Mr. Carey, and which of itself fully justifies his claim to be regarded as an important contributor to the science of Political Economy. As I regard some of the positions of Mr. Carey as fundamentally erroneous, and shall freely animadvert on them in that view, I wish at this point to bear testimony to his great merit as the original discoverer of the beautiful law of distribution, in the light of which the future condition of the laboring classes in all countries, if they are only true to themselves, seems hopeful and bright. Capitalists are interested in profits, and laborers are interested in wages; is there, then, as is commonly supposed, a deep-seated antagonism between them? None whatever. No profits can be realized unless labor be united with the capital, because it is labor alone that works up the raw materials, tends the machinery, and disposes of the products. Capital not united to labor remains barren, giving birth to no profit, nay, itself commonly becoming less. At any rate, the idle mill and hoarded gold yield no profit. Without the profit there will be no capital; since no man will practise abstinence without the hope of a reward: but without the labor there will be no profit; and therefore the very presence of capital in any community, constitutes of itself a demand for labor. The more of capital in any community, the greater the demand for laborers, since it is through laborers alone that the profits are realized. But the greater the demand for laborers, the greater the reward of labor; and, therefore, laborers as such, are interested in nothing so much as in the increase of capital, and in the strength of those motives to abstinence, out of which capital springs.

Capital must have laborers. Laborers desire remunerative employment. It is the old case of values over again. Labor offers a service to capital, and capital offers a service to labor. They exchange to the mutual advantage of both, and one is as independent as the other. The workmen may hold up their heads. They offer an honorable service on which capital is absolutely dependent for its existence. They offer a service as legitimate and as respectable, as that of the clergyman who preaches their sermons and baptizes their children, and are paid on precisely the same principles. Let no employer feel too much exalted towards his workmen. The money he renders them is no whit better than the work they render him. The exchange is honorable, and the parties to it on the same level of advantage. They are as necessary to him as he is necessary to them. As a capitalist he cannot exist without them; as laborers they cannot exist without him. He is one blade of the shears, they are the other blade, and it takes both blades to cut. It is absurd to ask which blade cuts most, because there is no cutting at all, unless both blades work together

More than this. Capital and labor are not only essential to each other, but also each is bettered by the prosperity of the other. If capital realizes a good round rate per cent., every capitalist is anxious to enlarge his business, whether as lender or active operator, and employ as much of his wealth as possible, as capital. This process increases capital. If men constantly put their profits only back into their business, which, under a high rate per cent., they will be pretty sure to do, capital rapidly increases. But increase of capital is, in its very nature, an increased demand for laborers. An increased demand for laborers, other things being equal, infallibly raises wages; just as an increased demand for anything else raises its value. Therefore, laborers are directly interested in the prosperity of capital, because the prosperity of capital leads to its increase, and its increase leads to higher wages. As a matter of fact, high profits and high wages, so far from being incompatible, usually accompany each other.

But is the capitalist equally interested in the prosperity of laborers? I think so. That he has to pay high wages is not necessarily a dead loss to him. This is no game of grab, in which what one gains another loses; it is a case of joint production, in which two parties conspire, and in which whatever helps to enlarge the gross amount produced, helps to increase the share falling to each party. If then, as they undoubtedly do, high wages tend to make the workmen more intelligent, industrious, frugal, and inventive, they are not a loss to the capitalist, but a gain. Larger gross returns are thereby secured.

Improved intelligence and skill of workmen affect production, just as improved machinery, secured by the aid of capital, affects it. Both alike enlarge the aggregate of products to be divided between capitalist and laborer. Now, in the division of products thus rendered larger in amount, what hinders capital from getting a fair share? When a firm is prosperous, are not all the partners benefited? All that is produced is to be divided; if more is produced, more is to be divided. Intelligent, industrious, skilful workmen, are best for production, are best for the capitalist, and therefore, high wages, which tend to make them so, and which are a consequence of their being so, are to be paid without grudging. When the matter is sifted to the bottom, it is seen that capital is as much interested in the prosperity of labor, as labor is interested in the prosperity of capital. All legitimate interests are in harmony.

I am now prepared to prove that all increase of capital, while it redounds to the benefit of capitalists, redounds in a still higher degree to the benefit of laborers. The demonstration is Mr. Carey's, and is the law of distribution above referred to. The proof is this. The rate per cent. of profits invariably goes down as a country grows older and richer. This is a simple fact of history, which no one will dispute. It has been exemplified alike in ancient and in modern times, so that one is at a loss whence to take the best examples, when all the examples are so good. In England, three centuries ago, the legal rate of interest was ten per cent., while now the average rate is barely four in that country, and lower still in Holland. During the first years of mining operations in California, from eight to fifteen per cent. a month, with security of real estate, was paid for the use of money, which enormous rates have now declined to rates not much higher than those paid in the States along the Mississippi River, and in these also the rates are constantly approximating those current in the older Eastern States. It may be assumed, therefore, as an indisputable fact, that, as capital increases, the rate per cent. for its use tends steadily to decline; but, while less profit is received on every hundred, there are also more hundreds, and consequently, there is an absolute gain to capitalists as a class, and both an absolute and relative gain to the laborers. Let us take to figures. Let $100,000,000, while the rate of profit is six, and $500,000,000, when it has fällen to four, be expended in payment of simple wages. So far forth, the value of the products to be divided yearly, will be represented respectively by $106,000,000 and $520,000,000. In the first case, $6,000,000 is profits, and $100,000,000 is wages. In the second case, $20,000,000 is profits, and $500,000,000 is wages. Here is an absolute gain to capitalists. Profits have gone up from six to twenty millions, are more than three times as great as before. But wages have gone up both absolutely and relatively. They have risen from one hundred to five hundred millions, and are *five* times as great as before. Profits have risen in the ratio of one to three, but wages in the ratio of one to five. This arithmetical example is put for the sake of illustration, but the principle holds good in every case where the rate per cent. goes down in consequence of the increase of capital, and therefore the advantages of ever enlarging capital are even greater to the laborers as a class than to the capitalists themselves. Most assuredly, if capital now takes less out of every hundred, more is left to labor. Profits and wages are reciprocally the *leavings* of each other, since the aggregate products created by the joint agency of capital and labor are wholly to be divided between them. This demonstration is extremely important; for it proves beyond a cavil, that the value of labor tends constantly to rise, not only as compared with the value of the material commodities which, by the aid of capital, it helps to create, a truth we have seen before, but also as compared with the value of the use of its co-partner capital itself; and therefore, that there is inwrought in the very nature of things a tendency towards equality of condition among men. God has ordered it so. Self-interest is indeed the mainspring of movement in the economic world; but no man can labor intelligently and productively under its influence, without at the same time benefitting the masses of men. His very savings, productively employed, are the poor man's wealth.

It only remains to speak of the forms which capital assumes, and to divide these, in general, into circulating and fixed capital. Circulating capital comprises all those products, the returns for the sale or consumption of which are derived at once and once for all. Such are generally (1) all raw materials; (2) funds destined for wages; (3) completed products on hand for sale; and (4) all commodities bought and held for the sake of resale. Fixed capital comprises all those forms of capital which are purchased or held with a view of deriving an income from their *use*. Such are generally (1) all tools and machinery; (2) all buildings used for productive purposes; (3) permanent improvements in land; (4) all investments in aid of locomotion, such as railroads, canals, ships, and everything subsidiary to these; (5) all products loaned or rented, or retained for that purpose; and (6) the national money. "The test of fixed and circulating capital is the inquiry, Are returns secured by the retention, or by the transfer, of the particular product? Tools in the hands of him who uses them are fixed, in the hands of him who manufactures them, circulating capital."[1]

As civilization advances, and the aggregate of all forms of capital enlarges, there is a tendency towards a relative increase of fixed capital, as compared with circulating. This disproportion would become greater than it actually does become, were it not for the fact that almost all forms of fixed capital are subject to a rapid deterioration of value, due partly to usual wear and tear, and partly to the progress of improvements, in consequence of which, what is old soon becomes antiquated. In nothing, perhaps, is actual cost of production so useless a guide to present value, as in machinery, and other forms of fixed capital. New and easier methods are being constantly invented, and the result of their introduction is to lessen the value of the old apparatus, and consequently to lessen the value of the aggregate accumulations of fixed, as compared with the current value of circulating, capital. Production looks perpetually to ends; and estimates means just in proportion to

[1] Bascom's Political Economy, p. 71.

their present efficiency to reach the end proposed. If the end can be reached by a cheaper process, in any department, the value of the former means will fall; and the value of the former results secured by these means, other things being equal, will fall also. It has been estimated, that at the present time, the proportion of circulating capital to fixed in France, is one to eight; in England, one to three; in the United States, three to five; proportions which are believed to be much higher in favor of fixed capital than formerly obtained in those countries.[1] It is also worthy of notice that a too rapid and general conversion of circulating into fixed capital may prove temporarily injurious to large classes of persons. If all carriage-makers, for example, instead of selling their carriages outright, and making new carriages with the proceeds, should let them out on hire, receiving their value only in instalments, it is evident that they could not make so many carriages as before, and that their workmen would suffer by the change of method. So too, if, while a national debt is being contracted for war expenditure, general business become dull, and capitalists, preferring the steady income from the national bonds to the uncertain gains of business, largely invest their circulating capital in bonds, it is very clear that many laborers would suffer a disadvantage. In the same view, a mania for building railroads, or any other impulse, by which large masses of floating capital are suddenly transformed into fixed capital, will surely be followed by some temporary distress.

[1] Carey's Social Science, iii. 56.

CHAPTER VIII.

ON LAND.

The crucial test of a definition, a generalization, a theory, is found in those seemingly anomalous cases with which all science has to do, and which come with such apparent reluctance under her pains-taking classifications. If a definition given, or a generalization propounded, reduce into order these outlying cases without violence, as well as cover easily the more central phenomena, there is at once created a strong presumption of their truth. Does it cover all the cases? Does it account for all the observed facts? These are tests of definitions and of theories. The questions relating to the value of land and of its products have been among the most vexed questions of Political Economy, have exercised a vast amount of ingenuity, have led to careful and commendable observations and investigations in the whole field of agriculture, while the diverging views that have been taken, the arguments adduced, the conclusions drawn, and the spirit manifested, in these discussions, form the most unrefreshing portion of the history of the science. These questions, however bitterly debated in the past, are approaching, even if they have not already reached, a satisfactory solution. The value of land and of the products of land have been almost uniformly regarded in the theories of wealth as anomalous matters, to which peculiar principles are applicable, and from which certain conclusions are deducible, which color and modify results and prospects in the whole field of value. Adam Smith, Ricardo, McCulloch, Senior, and Mill hold substantially one set of views on land and its rent. Carey and Bastiat hold views on that subject almost totally at variance with the English writers; it seems to me that the means are at hand for combining what is true in these opposing views in a clear and consistent manner, and for settling the dispute. I feel sure that both parties are right in many respects, and are wrong in some respects, and am not without some hopes of being able in this chapter to reconcile the difference, and to show that the value of land and the rent of land are not anomalous cases of value, but arise from human services rendered and exchanged, just as all other value arises, and vary under the same laws as vary all other values.

A series of propositions, and discussions under them, will bring out what seems to be the truth in this whole matter.

1*st. The whole earth with all its productive powers was given to men gratuitously of God under the simple direction that they replenish and subdue it.*

No provision was made for particular ownership. The whole earth, thus bestowed without partiality upon a whole race, had in all its spontaneous products a great utility, but, for a time, no value whatever. The spontaneous fruits, when gathered by any person, might become thereby possessed of value from his effort expended, but to the land itself, on which no human efforts had been expended, the idea of value could not have attached. No man would have *thought* to say to another under such circumstances, This field is mine: give me something for it, and you shall have it; and if he had, that other would not give it, because such fields were open on every hand to his occupation gratis. It is not in human nature to render anything for something which may be gratuitously obtained; value has no place in a sphere where everything is free. But it is well worth while to notice, that under God's command, the earth was not only to be replenished but *subdued.* Under this word subdue, and under the work implied in that, came in the first idea of ownership in land. When a family commenced this work of subjugation upon a piece of land, when they enclosed it, settled on it, tilled it, in any way whatever improved it by an expenditure of their own toil, then first dawned upon their minds the idea of possession, then first began the land to be possessed of *value*, since now the family would justly say to another, If you want this field, you must give us an equivalent for what we have expended on it. If the transfer took place, is it not very plain that what was sold, was not the inherent qualities of the soil, but the services which had now been expended in its amelioration? The first family received the soil and its powers gratuitously, and then expended a series of efforts on its improvement; but a similar series of efforts bestowed on other gratuitous land in the neighborhood would make it as eligible as this now is; if, therefore, the family insisted on more than an equivalent for their exertions actually bestowed on the land, the other would reply, For as much labor as you have given to your land, we can make other free land as good as yours, consequently we can give you no more than a fair equivalent for your efforts. The *value* therefore of the parcel sold, would be determined, not by the gratuitous elements involved, but by the onerous elements involved, that is to say, by the efforts already made by the first family in connection with the land, as compared with the efforts of the second involved in the remuneration offered. It is not possible in the nature of things that God's bounty to the whole race should be thwarted by any number of individuals through exclusive appropriation on their part of this bounty. What they received gratuitously, they must gratuitously transmit; what they have wrought of permanent improvements on the land, they may justly demand a recompense for, and can secure it. By their expenditure of efforts they have saved to the purchaser a like expenditure of efforts, and for these they can demand, and he will be willing to concede, a recompense; but if they go further, and demand pay for the natural qualities of the soil which God gave and they have not improved, for the sun that shines, and the rain that falls on it, the demand is blocked at once by the common sense of the purchaser. He replies: There is land enough in its natural state, with inherent qualities as good as yours, the same sun shining on it, and just as much blessed rain falling on it, which I can have for nothing. I cannot give you something for that which costs you nothing, and which I can get for nothing.

As long as there is abundance of land still open

to occupation, everybody will concede that this line of argument is just, and that the general value of land cannot rise above the estimated measure of the human efforts actually bestowed on its improvement. Though less obvious at first, the principle is just as true after all the land has been taken up. Improved farms are always for sale in every country, lands once appropriated and ameliorated are perpetually changing hands, and men enough are always found willing to part with land, as with everything else, for what it has cost them. If some proprietors are unreasonable enough to try to intercept God's gifts bestowed alike on all the generations, and endeavor to exact a price for their land made up of compensation for what they and their predecessors have done upon it, together with something added for what God has done for it, their cupidity is instantly thwarted by the readiness of others to dispose of their land for a fair equivalent of their onerous exertions. Human motives are such, and everything is so providentially arranged in this department, that men cannot sell God's gifts; it would be derogatory to the Giver, if they could.

What might be thus inferred from the nature of the case, is abundantly confirmed by facts. As a matter of fact and experience, lands are absolutely *valueless* until some portion of human effort has been expended on them, or in reference to them. They may have utility, but they have no value. Nobody will give anything for them. The United States government has been selling for years some of the best lands in the world for one dollar and a quarter an acre, and this after the lands have been surveyed at government expense, local governments provided for the settlers, and mail facilities and other privileges guaranteed to them. The same government is now giving away similar lands in homesteads to actual settlers, merely taking for the title-deeds nominal fees, whose aggregate amount does not begin to meet the expenses incurred in connection with these lands. If lands had value, independent of human exertions, then would the English companies and individuals who received grants in the seventeenth century of vast tracts of as fertile land on this continent as the sun ever visited in his diurnal revolutions, have become rich as Crœsus; but these companies and individuals did not become rich at all, but rather poor. The amount realized from the sale of their lands fell far short of reimbursing the expenses of colonization; and, after incurring debts and endless vexations, most of the companies and proprietors were glad to be rid of their lands at any price. It is a current proverb now in regard to wild lands at the West, that the more a man has of them the worse off he is; and it is a maxim also in the newer settlements everywhere, that improved lands are worth the present value of the improvements and no more. And Mr. Carey is at pains to prove at great length that the value of lands in all old countries is now vastly less than they have cost of actual human efforts in their subjugation and improvement; less, because the progress of capital and inventions enables similar work to be done now at much less outlay. We conclude, then, that the value of land follows the law of all other values; that it arises only in connection with human efforts; that the utility in land sold is due in part to nature and in part to man; that the utility from nature does not commonly affect price; that landed property rests back, like all other property, its ultimate defence upon the right of making efforts for one's own welfare and of not parting with these efforts except for an equivalent; that land and the use of it have value because the proprietor can by them render a service to somebody else; and finally that the value and the rent of land vary, like all other values, under the law of supply and demand.

2*d*. *The powers of all land, under more laborious culture, agricultural skill remaining the same, are subject to the law of diminishing return; in other words, increased labor upon it, though increasing the aggregate return of produce, does not secure an increase proportioned to the increase of labor.*

This is the fundamental proposition on which Ricardo, and the English writers generally, lay such stress, and on which they found the law of Rent, and the necessity of restraints on population; while Carey and Bastiat, impliedly if not expressly, deny the proposition, and of course, the inferences deduced from it. In my judgment, the proposition cannot be logically denied. The law of diminishing return from land is a law of Nature, and has played a very important part in the occupation and culture of successive portions of the earth's surface. The proof of the proposition is all the better for being short. If by doubling the labor on a piece of land, double the produce could be secured, and by quadrupling it, quadruple, and so on, there would be no reason why any man should ever cultivate more than a square acre, or even a square rod. He has a strong motive to confine his culture to a small space, just so long as the amount of produce is in the ratio of the labor expended, because there is less locomotion of tools and fertilizers and crops. The fact that he extends his culture from one acre to another, and then to distant acres, notwithstanding the inconveniences and expense of transportation, is an irrefragable proof of the proposition in question. Increase of agricultural labor and expenditure on a given space of land will secure a larger amount of produce; but as a general law, the increased amount will not be proportioned to the increased expenditure. If it were thus proportioned, if the law of diminishing return did not exist, then, for purposes of agricultural production, a square acre is as good as a continent.

It is through this law of diminishing return, that the Creator has secured the gradual occupation by men of almost the whole earth. There is a strong tendency to leave the old acres to advance upon new, the old countries to emigrate to new, whenever the returns begin to bear a more unfavorable ratio to the labor bestowed. The farmer will advance from the first to the second acre as soon as he thinks that more produce can be obtained from it by a given amount of labor than can be got by a like expenditure of additional labor upon the first acre, allowance being made for the increased inconvenience; and so, cultivation has gradually extended itself, and men have become dispersed over the whole earth. Other principles leading to dispersion have undoubtedly coöperated, but this is the fundamental one, operative at all times, changing the course of population, and consequently of empire.

Mr. Carey seems to think that this proposition is dependent on another, and endeavors to break down this by an attempt to break down that other. That other proposition is, that in the course of occupation the best lands are entered upon first, and that afterwards recourse is had to the poorer soils. He attempts to prove that the exact reverse of this is the historical fact, that cultivation has always been begun upon the poorer soils, and that afterwards the river bottoms and strong lands have been drained and cleared and tilled. This discussion, however interesting in itself, is irrelevant as far as the law of diminishing returns is concerned, because that law is nowise dependent on the order in which soils of different productive power are entered upon in cultivation; it is true of all soils, whether rich or poor, whether entered upon in the order of their fertility, or in the inverse order; and I cannot help thinking that Mr. Carey puts upon this matter of the order of occupation, which he asserts has always been from the poorer to the richer soils, an estimation altogether disproportioned to its importance. Whenever men have entered upon new countries, they have undoubtedly selected those lands first which seemed to them most eligible, reference being had of course to their present means of subduing them; and whether these lands proved ultimately to be better or worse than other parcels which they might have chosen, is a point, which, however determined, has no effect to disturb the fundamental proposition in hand.

3*d*. *The operation of the law of diminishing returns is retarded by all improvements in agriculture.*

The discovery of new and more available fertilizers, the invention of better agricultural implements, the light thrown by chemistry upon agriculture, the consequent adoption of better methods of culture and rotation of crops, the more perfect adaptation to the various soils of the kinds of produce sought to be raised from them, all these and similar improvements tend to increase the ratio of the produce to the labor, and disguise the law just established. The lands that are now under cultivation may be made, under more skilful modes of culture, to yield indefinitely more than at present, and the vast still uncultivated lands of the world may come to render an incalculable quantity of food to the world's population; but yet, as improvements are naturally less continuous in this than in some other departments of production, as invention has less play, as there is less opportunity for the division and coöperation of labor, as nothing can materially shorten the time during which the fruits of the earth must ripen, the value of agricultural products tends to rise relatively to manufactured products generally. Labor, for a reason already given, and produce, for the reasons now given, have risen and tend steadily to rise, as estimated in general commodities.

4*th*. *The rent of land is the measure of the service which the owner renders to the actual cultivator, and does not differ essentially in its nature from the rent of buildings in cities, or from the interest of money.*

Mr. Ricardo's famous doctrine of rent, is for substance, this: there are some lands in every country whose produce just repays the expenses of cultivation, and consequently yields no margin for rent; and the cost of production on these rentless and poorest lands under cultivation, will determine the price of the produce; and as there can be but one price in the same market, the produce raised on more fertile lands will be sold for the same price, and this price, besides paying the cost of production, will yield a rent rising higher according as the land is more fertile; so that the rent paid on any land is always a measure of the excess of productiveness of that land over the least productive land under paying cultivation; and therefore, an increased demand for food in consequence of increased population, and the higher price resulting, will force cultivation down upon still poorer soils, or else compel a higher culture for less remunerative returns on the old soils, according to the law of diminishing returns, which in either case will raise the rents on all the soils above that grade that just repays the expenses of cultivation; so that it is the sole interest of landlords, as such, that population should be dense and food high, their interest being directly antagonistic to that of the other classes of the community.

This very ingenious and complicated theory, which is supported by many other authoritative names besides that of its author, is too mechanical and rigid to be a good scientific statement of universal facts. It is true that, if 150 bushels of wheat are raised each with x hours' labor, and 50 each with $x + y$ hours' labor, and 200 are wanted, the price of the whole, offered at once, will not be below the rate

$x + y$ for the whole 200; but this fact is not sufficient to make the price of food and the rent of lands anomalous cases of value, and it never would have been supposed so, had not England been under infamous corn-laws which forbade importations, and made everybody tributary to landlords. If a war breaks out, and the founders have only 150 cannon on hand, which cost x, and the order comes for 200 to be delivered at once, of which fifty will cost $x + y$; the founders will as certainly be paid for the whole 200 at the rate $x + y$. When the trade in corn is free, the Ricardo law of rent loses its formidableness, and the simple law remains, applicable to all products that have a market-rate, that that rate must be sufficient to compensate the cost of that portion produced with greatest difficulty, otherwise that portion would not be produced. Of course, those who produce at the greatest advantage will realize extra gains from this market-rate, so far forth as their advantage does not depress the market-rate. So far as lands are taken on shares, or on permanent leases, or so far as their products are exchanged directly against other commodities and services, the law of Ricardo has little application. As a matter of fact, too, there is often more than one price in the same market-town; and prices, and especially prices of agricultural products, are varying all the while from other causes than those affecting the cost of production. The following seems to me to be the whole truth in regard to rent. That portion of utility in lands that is the free gift of Nature is mostly a common factor eliminated from value by the action of competition, as in the horses and strawberries, by which illustration was made in the chapter on Value. A parcel of land of extraordinary fertility, or extraordinary beauty, or holding an extraordinary mine or water-privilege, is assimilated in the law of its value to other unique products. Its price, whether at sale or rent, is only gauged by the service which the owner can render the purchaser by it. Still, the efforts, care, and abstinence of its owners, or of others, have made up an essential part of the present utility of the parcel. Of such things no market rate can be predicated, because competition has no play. With these unimportant exceptions, the rent of lands is a simple recompense for the use of a productive instrument, made such by human efforts. The owner has become proprietor of all the results of the onerous exertions put forth upon that land, or in any connection with that land, and allows the lessee the use of these results. Because the owner practises *abstinence* in the lessee's behalf, *rent* is substantially the same as *profits;* and as gross profits include the wages of superintendence, so rent also partakes of the nature of wages, so far forth as the owner still takes an active supervision of his property. Proximity to markets, degree of fertility, state of improvements, and the variations of supply and demand, will influence rent.

5th. That division of land is best for purposes of production, which gives farms approximately equal in size to the cultivators; and the best tenure is the fee-simple.

Taking the last part of the proposition first, the fee-simple is better for production than any other tenure, because when one owns the land he tills, he takes a greater interest in it, it is his own, he has a constant motive to improve it, to make the production from it as great as possible, since all it produces is his own. If men work from motives, and if the energy and persistence of the work be proportioned to the constancy and press of the motives, then will the fee-simple most certainly make the aggregate of produce greater than any other tenure of land. Moreover the fee-simple immeasurably improves the character of the cultivators. The masses of men are educated and developed by nothing so much as by the ownership of land. It tends to make them industrious, thrifty, independent, hopeful of the future, anxious to give their children better privileges, as well as better lands, than they themselves had. The testimony on this point is abundant from many countries, and it all goes to show that the peasant proprietor is a happier and more virtuous, as well as a more industrious and productive man, than the mere tenant and farm-laborer; while similar testimony, as well as common observation, proves, that lands under the copyhold tenure, or leased at will, are far inferior in point of improvements and production, to contiguous lands held in fee-simple. The zeal of absolute ownership, especially if it be a limited ownership, has been observed to produce almost magical effects, as well upon character as upon lands, transforming after a while the poorest into excellent lands, and thriftless and desponding laborers into frugal and enterprising proprietors.

The practical play of the fee-simple draws after it such a division of lands into farms moderately large and approximately equal, as can be shown to be most favorable to the largest aggregate production. Wherever there is no primogeniture and no entails, and owners can consequently sell a part or all their lands, whenever it is their interest to do so, lands naturally fall into those hands which are most capable of using them productively, because such persons can afford to pay more for them than anybody else; and the division that follows this impulse of self-interest and this freedom of exchange is likely to be into farms tolerably equal in extent and moderately large. Such a division has naturally taken place in New England, in the Middle States, and at the West; while in the South, the institution of slavery led to the system of large plantations and few land-owners, which system, I believe, will now, under the auspices of freedom, give way to the better system of small farms and numerous proprietors. That the latter system is more profitable in reference to production, as well as advantageous in point of national character and a broadly based and sound development of the national resources, is evident from a few considerations, and has been exemplified distinctly in the diverse experience in this respect of France and England. 1. When the mass of the agricultural population are owners of the soil they till, the motives to productive cultivation are brought to bear most universally. These motives are interest and hope. There is a high pleasure in possession, and in self-guided exertion, a strong stimulus to get as much as possible from the land, and at the same time to keep good and ever improve its condition. When the great body of the land of any country comes under the action of such motives as these, then will the amount of production be the greatest. 2. Aristotle quotes from "the African" the saying that the best manure for the land is the foot of the owner; a saying which is often attributed to Dr. Franklin, and which is as true as if its origin did *not* date back some centuries before Christ. Franklin had read Aristotle. Personal supervision, to be most effective, must be limited in its sphere; and the best agricultural knowledge and skill becomes comparatively weak when it attempts to exhibit itself on too broad a surface. Because a man can cultivate one hundred acres better than any of his neighbors, it does not prove that he will cultivate fifty acres additional to them better than a neighbor of inferior skill, who is the owner of those fifty and no more. 3. The possession of small freeholds educates and gives energy to the masses. That educates a man which calls forth varied efforts of intelligence and will. To protect and advance his own interests, to attend upon the seasons, to watch and wait, to foresee and plan and labor, all this will secure that a nation of freeholders will never be a nation of ignorant, indolent barbarians. 4. National strength is best secured and maintained wherever there is a broad basis of independent yeomanry to lean back upon when heavy taxes are to be raised and strong blows of battle are to be struck in behalf of the nation.

France and England are instructive examples in this whole matter. In France, since the abolition of all entails and primogenital rights by the revolution of 1789, and under the action of the law requiring the equal partition of a man's landed estate among his children, the lands have become subdivided into small parcels, averaging about fourteen acres to each owner. Out of a population of 37,500,000, 8,897,000, or nearly one fourth, are proprietors of land either in town or country. Of improved and unimproved lands there are in France about 122,500,000 acres owned by individuals. The number of different lots of land, however, is about 140.000,000, or considerably less than an acre, on the average, to each lot. About ten of these lots, on the average, are included in one assessment of the land-tax; the whole number of such assessments being 14,123,117. Of these fourteen million assessed properties, more than seven million are worth less than $1,000; more than two million are worth between $1,000 and $2,000; nearly two million more are worth less than $3,000; while only 53,000 properties are worth more than $100,000. The estimated value of all these lands is $31,000,000,000; and the annual net income $937,500,000. These figures, which are all taken from the official returns of the French government for the year 1866, are very significant of the beneficial results of the land system of France. In point of a regular increase of agricultural products; in point of an industrious, frugal, cheerful peasantry; in point of a very general desire and ability to purchase land; in point of showing that subdivision ceases so soon as the lands, if divided further, would be less profitable in production; in point of pauperism; in point of national strength and weight, in spite of a centralized and repressive government; in point of an ability in the peasantry to loan to government, in an exigency, large sums of money in the aggregate; a long experience has shown that the practical workings of this division have been most happy.

In England, on the other hand, the monster-farm system prevails, the small proprietors have mostly disappeared, the law of entails and leases ties up the landed estates from sale and division, less than 150 persons own one half of all the lands in England; and not more than ten or twelve persons are in possession of one half of all the land in Scotland. The national results of this system are what we should expect they would be. There are upper and middle, and lower and lowest classes, but a homogeneous English *people* are not to be found. Particular results are seen, in part, in what has been justly called the irretrievable helotism of the laboring classes; in almost eleven hundred thousand paupers in England and Scotland alone in 1867; in an annual poor-rate for 1866 in the two countries of $35,000,000, raised by taxation; in unmeasured inequality in fortunes and comforts; in the lack, felt alike in war and peace, of a large class of sturdy yeomanry, the strength of a State; and in a consequent sinking of relative position, power, and influence, former times being held up with the present, as compared with France and the other first-class powers. No degree of merit in the other parts of the English system, can ever compensate the want of just and broadly liberal laws of land. Still, the merits of other parts of the system are alleviating results even here. Pauperism is declining. Wages are rising. The annual poor-rate is growing less. The proportion of paupers to the whole population in England in 1867, was, in round numbers, one to 20; in Scotland, one to 25; proportions much less frightful to contemplate than those which prevailed previous to 1842.

The "encumbered estates law," applicable only to Ireland, passed by Parliament in 1848, has had the beneficial effect of multiplying the number of landed proprietors in that island. Under this law there can be brought into market, in whole or in parts, estates encumbered with debt, and thus shut out from improvement. "The proceeds of the sale are paid into the Court of Chancery, to be distributed by that court as equity may require, between the owner, his creditors, the various encumbrancers, the heirs at law, and all other interested parties."[1] Thus millions of acres of heavily mortgaged lands have passed from the hands of their nominal owners into the hands of absolute proprietors, whose title is perfect because parliamentary, and whose interest and zeal are said to have changed already the face of their lands. In the first five years of this system, more than one tenth of all the landed property in the island was sold in the Irish Encumbered Estates' Court; and the land thus sold was divided into about five times as many distinct estates as before. Up to 1870, the value of the lands sold in this way amounted to $170,182,015. The proportion of paupers to the population was only one to 80 in 1867. Recent parliamentary legislation has relieved the Irish of their forced tribute to the English Church; and the hope may be indulged that Ireland has already entered upon a period of substantial improvement and prosperity.

[1] Bowen's Political Economy. 1st ed., page 521.

CHAPTER IX.

ON COST OF PRODUCTION.

WE are now in position to be able to analyze the cost of production, and to bring forward some supplementary matters relating to value, which could not be properly discussed, until the subjects of labor, capital, and land, were, at least in their ground principles, understood. While we were inquiring, in the chapter on value, whether such a thing as a measure of value were possible, it was remarked that some political economists have thought that the cost of production of any commodity is the most accurate measure of its general purchasing-power; and it might have been added, that these writers consider that there is such a thing as *natural* value distinct from market value, that natural value is the cost of production, and that market value oscillates perpetually around that, and tends constantly to return to it. How far these views are just, how far cost of production constitutes a law of value within the all-comprehending law of demand and supply, is the point to which attention is now directed.

It is noticeable, that while almost all people put forth onerous efforts to satisfy the present and immediately prospective wants of other people, in view of receiving back from them corresponding efforts to satisfy their own present and immediately prospective wants, there are some people, who have both foresight and capital, who set to work to make preparations in reference to services which they expect to render some time in the future; and it is evident that this matter of the cost of production has an especial bearing upon those classes of production in which permanent investments are made, looking to future rather than to present exchanges. It becomes necessary to attend to cost of production simply because cost of production is sometimes an exact measure of one of the elements out of which value springs, namely, the element of effort. When a surgeon, for example, charges fifty dollars for cutting off a man's leg, cost of production is an impertinent phrase in relation to such a service, and is no measure of the effort; but when a capitalist invests $20,000 in a cutlery establishment, hires all his labor, and at the end of the year has produced 5000 knives, cost of production has a definite meaning as applied to each one of the knives, and is an accurate measure of the one element of effort, which goes, together with other elements, to determine its value. It is not true at all that cost of production alone determines the value of the knife, or is a measure of the value of the knife, but it *is* true that, in this case, and in all cases in which a commodity is produced by a definite capital invested for a fixed time, and by labor wholly hired, or estimated as hired, the cost of production is an exact measure of one of the four elements which go to determine value, namely, of one effort. Now let us suppose that when these knives are exposed for sale, no such return efforts are offered for them as are estimated by the maker as compensatory and remunerative. He may, in order to avoid a still greater loss, sell his knives below the cost of their production, but it is evident that he will not go forward at present in his enterprise of making knives. He will suspend operations, or withdraw from the business; and his action in this respect will affect the supply of knives to lessen it; and the next equalization of demand and supply will be likely to adjust a market value more favorable to knife-makers. Or if, when the knives are exposed for sale, they meet with an exchange at very remunerative rates, our capitalist is now stimulated to increase his production, to put back his profits into his business, and perhaps to invest in it additional principal. His action in this respect will affect the supply of knives to increase it; and the next equalization of demand and supply, or if not the next, some subsequent one, will be likely to adjust a new market value less favorable to knife-makers. Thus it is seen, that absolute cost of production influences value not directly, but remotely, through its influence on supply. To suppose and to say that the cost of production of one commodity determines its value in an exchange with another, is to perpetuate the old mistake of ignoring the second commodity, is to reiterate the fallacy that value is an independent quality of one thing, is to confuse the whole subject of value. When the writers referred to speak of the "natural value" of any commodity, they mean its absolute cost of production; but, at this stage of our inquiry, it surely cannot be necessary to repeat the thought already so often expressed in substance, that an analysis of one component part falls far short of determining the resultant of four component parts. I do not think the expression "natural value" is calculated to be useful. From the very meaning of the word "value," if it is to have any consistent meaning at all, there can be no other kind of value than market value, that is, value in exchange.

But while all this will doubtless be conceded to be just, there are other points of view in which the cost of production of any commodity comes to be a very important matter. From its obvious relations to supply, already exemplified, it is constantly, though indirectly, influencing the value of the commodity itself; and in respect to permanent investments, looking solely to future production, it becomes the main inquiry; because, while the cost of production can never determine the purchasing-power of the product, it is always one element in determining it; and also, especially, because the improvements which are all the time being introduced into the mechanical and other processes of such production, which improvements always tend to lessen the cost of the product, have the effect to lessen the value of all permanent investments, unless similar improvements be inaugurated in connection with them. The march of improvement is so constant, that old machinery and old processes are rapidly depreciated; and a calculated cost of future production in one establishment is almost sure to be disturbed by new labor-saving inventions in other similar establishments, which will be able in consequence to offer the commodity at a lower rate than the rate estimated; in which case the value of the product will not conform to the estimated or even actual cost of production in that establishment, but will pitilessly fall to the point at which similar commodities are offered by the more fortunate producers. For these reasons we must inquire carefully after the elements of cost of production.

These elements are two: cost of labor, and cost of capital. These are the only onerous elements that enter into production. Assisting the processes are, indeed, the natural powers of land, water, wind, steam, electricity, and so on, but as these are always gratuitous, they form no element of cost. Labor must have its wages, and capital must have its profits, and also a sinking-fund from which to replace the original capital when worn out or expended. It will be in vain to search for any other ingredient of cost than these two.[1]

1. By cost of labor is meant, of course, its cost to the employer, and not to the laborer himself, in reference to whom the phrase would have no definite meaning. Now, if we make an exhaustive analysis of the cost of labor to the employer, we shall find that there are three things, and only three things, that go to determine its cost. 1. Efficiency of the labor. 2. The rate of nominal wages paid. 3. The cost of that in which the wages are paid. To illustrate each of these in order:— If a capitalist hires two men to work for him at the same rate of wages, and if the one is twice as efficient a laborer as the other, the cost of his labor to the capitalist is one half less than the cost of the other's labor. The first element of the cost of labor is its efficiency. If a capitalist, accustomed to pay one dollar a day, is

[1] Compare J. S. Mill's Political Economy, book iii. chap. 4.

now obliged to pay one dollar and a half a day to his laborers, their efficiency remaining the same, the cost of labor is increased in the ratio of 2 to 3. The second element is nominal wages. If that commodity, whether money or other, in which wages are paid, varies in cost to the capitalist, the cost of the labor compensated by that commodity, nominal wages and efficiency remaining the same, is varied thereby of course. We shall discover in the next chapter that the value of money is by no means invariable, as we have already learned the variable nature of all other values, and accordingly the third element of cost of labor is the cost of that in which the labor is paid. It is easy to see that there is nothing else, aside from these three things, that can ever affect the cost of labor. This analysis is not given here for its own sake merely, but for some ulterior purposes, of which the first is to show, how various are the ingredients that enter into the computation which men ought rationally to make before engaging in extended enterprises of production. They must make calculations on the prospective cost of production, since that is one element that will determine the value of their future product. In doing this they must calculate the cost of labor, and the cost of capital; and the cost of labor alone involves, as we have just seen, three variables, no one of which can be safely neglected in the supposed estimation.

The second purpose is to explain from the analysis, that a great diversity of nominal wages may exist in different countries without necessarily affecting the cost of labor. If English wages, for example, are, nominally, one half wages in the United States, it is very poor logic to jump to the conclusion, that the cost of labor in England is one half less than in the United States. That will depend partly on the efficiency of the labor, and partly on the cost of that in which the respective labor is paid. If English laborers are only one half as efficient as American laborers, then a difference of one half in nominal wages, cost of money in the two countries being the same, will occasion no difference at all in cost of labor. Because nominal wages in England are lower than with us, many people think and maintain, that the English have an advantage over us, whereas it is notorious, and admitted even by themselves, that American labor is more efficient than English labor, and therefore there is no such difference in cost of labor as the difference in nominal wages would indicate, even if there be any difference in cost of labor at all. Just at this point great confusion has existed in the popular mind, and some by no means harmless fallacies are still current, arising from the want of a due analysis of the cost of labor. It is probable, all the elements being allowed for, that the cost of labor in one country is not very widely different from its cost in other countries; because, if there were much difference, there would be a greater difference than is actually observed in the rate per cent. of capital; and this conclusion is strengthened, when it is remembered, that in those countries in which the cost of labor is supposed to be low, as in England, the rate per cent. of capital is also low; and in those countries, as the United States, in which the cost of labor is supposed to be high, the rate per cent. is also high. Before leaving this point, I wish to remove one or two causes of misapprehension, which have frequently infected discussions of wages. The terms "high and low wages," are often used ambiguously; some meaning by the words, a high or low nominal rate; others, a high or low degree of comforts enjoyed by the laborers, as the fruit of their wages; others, still, as Ricardo, using the words high and low in relation only to profits, in which last sense, if wages are high, profits are low, and conversely. In the first two senses, wages and profits may both be high, or both be low, at the same time and place, but not in the last sense. When the first sense is meant, the expression should be *money wages;* when the second, *real wages;* when the third, *relative wages.* Had this nomenclature been adopted and consistently employed, many an angry dispute and many a false conclusion would have been avoided. Also, it has been thought by some, that high money wages create high prices of commodities, that is to say, that things are dear because laborers have been paid a high price for their agency in producing them. This does not follow. Their labor may be very efficient, and may be assisted by first-rate machinery, and the price of the commodities may be low, although the money wages may be high. Money wages must not be confounded with cost of labor, because it is only one element of cost of labor. A higher cost of labor in any department of production, other things being equal, will tend to raise the price of the product, but not higher money wages alone. Price is value expressed in money, and general rise or fall of prices is usually due to changes in the currency. An inflated currency produces universally high prices, as well of labor as of commodities, and for the same reason of labor as of commodities, and it is a superficial view which supposes, that, of these two effects of a common cause, one is a cause of the other. On the other hand it is sometimes supposed, that the exact reverse of this takes place, and that money wages become high simply because the commodities which the laborers consume have become high. This is an error similar to the other. If an inflation of the volume of the current money of the country has supervened, then the price of labor rises by the same impulse that carries up the price of commodities. Both are effects; neither is the cause of the other. But if the currency has remained sound and stable, a high price of any of the commodities consumed by the laborers, has no tendency, that I can perceive, to raise the rate of money wages. The higher price of those commodities may have arisen from deficient harvests, or from a higher cost of labor in those departments, from inequality of taxation, or other similar causes; but no one of these enables capital to share the gross proceeds of production on better terms with labor. Neither money, nor real, nor relative wages can rise, as I see, merely from high prices of the commodities which the laborers consume. It seems to me, accordingly, that much clear light is thrown from this analysis of the cost of labor upon the whole vexed question of wages.

The third ulterior purpose of presenting this analysis is briefly to unfold the principles according to which the division between wages and profits is practically made. It was Mr. DeQuincy who first called profits the *leavings* of wages; but this is only true when by wages is meant the *cost of labor*. The gross products created by the combined action of capital and labor belong in common to the capitalists and laborers, and are to be divided between them in some way, and the analysis in question enables us to perceive just how they are divided. Cost of labor being deducted, the rest goes to capital as a matter of course, and the proportion of this part to the whole capital marks the per cent. for the given time. If this part falling to capital is large for every hundred invested, the rate per cent. is high; if small, low. The efficiency of labor and the state of the currency being as before, a rise of money wages will lessen profits, but no rise of money wages accompanying increased efficiency of labor, or resulting from inflated currency, has a tendency to lessen profits at all. The capitalist as such is interested in having cost of labor low, but not in low money wages necessarily, because a low cost of labor is consistent with high money wages, and with high real wages too. Very efficient labor may be very highly paid, and yet leave to capital a high rate per cent. We here see again from another stand-point, and from a deeper view, a truth we have seen before, that there is no real antagonism but a real harmony of interests between capitalists and laborers. Both are alike interested in the combined efficiency of capital and labor, that is to say, in the amount of gross products created; and, in respect to the divis ion of this gross amount, there is no more collision of interest than in making the dividends of the year among the partners of a commercial house. The cost of labor must first be defrayed; and this depends on its efficiency, its nominal rate of remuneration, and the present purchasing-power of money. What is left is gross profits, and the relation that this bears to the whole capital invested decides the rate per cent. So far of cost of labor.

2. The second element in the cost of production is the *cost of capital;* and this also must be analyzed into three variables, no one of which can be safely neglected in a computation which has for its object to decide a prospective cost of production: — 1st, The rate per cent.; 2d, The time for which the capital is advanced; 3d, The form of the capital as liable to slow or rapid deterioration. We must look at the influence of each of these elements on cost of production.

(1.) Let us suppose that the rate per cent. at Amsterdam is 3, and the rate at New York is 7, that the cost of labor is equal in the two cities, that the time of advance is one year, and that there is no liability of the capital to wear out; a commodity made at Amsterdam with an outlay of $100 can be sold for $103, while the same commodity made at New York with the same outlay cannot be sold for less than $107. The current rate per cent. is one element of the cost of capital, and through this, of the cost of production.

(2.) The effect of the time of advance on cost of capital is more striking. Let the same supposition be continued, except that the time of advance in New York be extended to four years. The commodity will sell in Amsterdam, as before, at $103, but in New York for not less than $131. This principle is well illustrated also in the case of wine, which to reach its perfection requires to be kept a number of years. Even under the same rate per cent. which we will suppose 6, a commodity made in six months with an outlay of $100 may sell for $103; while wine grown in the same six months at the same outlay, kept five years, cannot be sold without loss for less than $133. If the period of advance be long, and the rate per cent. be high, the cost of capital from the two causes enhances enormously the cost of the product; so that, it is only countries like England and Holland, in which the rate per cent. is very low, which can successfully engage in enterprises requiring a large capital to be invested for long periods before returns are realized. This accounts for the fact that mining operations in Mexico and South America have been largely carried on by foreign rather than American capital. One million of Dutch capital at three per cent., expecting to realize returns only after twenty years, will be remunerated by a product selling for $1,806,111; but under like circumstances, American capital at seven per cent., must have a return of $3,869,685, or lose.

(3.) Most forms of capital, especially that invested in buildings, machinery, and the like, more or less rapidly wear out, and a sinking-fund must be reserved from gross profits in order to replace the principal. This is the third element in cost of capital, and through this cost, influences the cost of production, and through cost of production, affects, in the manner already pointed out, the value of the product. Suppose there are two commodities A and B produced in two establishments, in each of which is invested a capital of $11,000, in one of which is a machine costing $1000, which is wholly worn out by one year's use, and in the other a machine costing the same sum, which will last however for ten years. Let the rate per cent. be ten, and the time consumed in completing the products be one year. There is a difference in the cost of capital in the two establishments, and this difference indirectly but immediately appears in the value of the respective products. To A must be charged not only $1100, the interest on the capital at the current rate, but also another $1000, wherewith to replace the machine already worn out by the year's production. A cannot be sold without loss for less than $2100. B however will cost less. To it must be charged, as before, $1100, current rate of profit on the capital invested, and only $100 to replace after ten years' use the machine. B therefore can permanently sell without loss for $1200.

Now, then, if my readers are willing to follow me a little further along this dry and dusty road, we shall be able to draw some important conclusions in respect to value as depending on wages and profits. While we have been seeming to attend to only one of the four elements out of which value springs, namely, one effort, of which cost of production is always an exact measure whenever the effort is embodied in a commodity made jointly by paid labor and capital, we have really been attending to the other effort also whenever that effort is similarly embodied; and since gold and silver money is a commodity, like any other, we have incidentally, in this analysis of cost of production, taken some steps towards determining the value of money. Now, cost of production is made up of cost of labor and cost of capital, and the first general conclusion is, that if the cost of labor for any reason be enhanced, nothing can prevent this higher cost from taking effect and exhibiting itself in lower profits. The second conclusion is, that money-wages, or any rise or fall of them, provided they are uniform, or uniformly rise and fall, in those departments of production whose commodities exchange with each other, have no effect at all upon value, since they are common factors in two costs of production, and like all common factors, cancel each other; but any inequality of money-wages in these departments that affects the cost of labor, will have an indirect but controlling influence on the value of the commodities. The same is true of profits. So far as the rate per cent. is common to all branches of production, the capital advanced for the same period, with a similar risk of deterioration or loss, and so far as any one or all of these advance or recede uniformly and together, they do not affect the value of any of the commodities produced. But inequality in any one of these points, varies the relative cost of capital, and consequently, the cost of production, and consequently the value of the product. It is at this point precisely that there is opened up to us a clear view of the influence of machinery upon values. So far as machinery brings into play, as it always does, a gratuitous natural force, it is outside the pale of value; but since the machinery itself is one important form of capital on which rate per cent. must be paid, the more machinery employed relatively to labor in the production of commodities, the more do profits enter into the cost of production, and the more powerfully do changes in the rate per cent., in the time of advance, and in the risk of deterioration, tell upon the value of commodities so produced, as estimated in other commodities.

In other words, the more, or the more durable the machinery in the production of a commodity, the larger the element of profit in the price now absolutely reduced; on a rise of the rate per cent. therefore, the value of the commodity made by more or more durable machinery will relatively rise.

Having traced completely the influence of machinery on profits, a few things must now be said on its influence upon wages. Formerly the prejudice was almost universal, and is still wide-spread in many parts of the world, that the general introduction of labor-saving appliances does an injury to the laborers by taking away their work. So strongly has this been felt by the laborers, that in England, and especially in Ireland, mobs and riots have usually accompanied the introduction of machinery into those departments of production in which hand-work had previously prevailed. If *work* were what laborers really wanted, the prejudice in question would cease to be such, and become a sound opinion; since the only object and result of introducing machinery is to lessen work, at least with reference to a given product; and the laborers, to be consistent, should not stop with opposing new inventions, but should destroy all forms of existing capital, that there might be work a plenty for simple human hands. What the laborers really want, however, is not work, but wages, or rather, those commodities for which their wages are expended; and the question is, whether labor-saving processes tend to lessen, not work, but work's remuneration. There is no form of proof that I know of, which amounts to a moral demonstration that the substitution of machinery for labor cannot lessen the laborer's wages; the opposite has perhaps sometimes happened, and is possibly liable to happen, especially in agriculture, in certain transitory states of society. But the general appeal can be made to experience with all safety. As a matter of fact and experience, it has not been found true that the introduction of improved processes, the substitution of Nature's forces for human muscle, has deteriorated the condition of laborers in those departments into which the inventions have been brought, or the condition of laborers generally. Exactly the reverse has usually taken place; and wages are apt to be highest rather than lowest in connection with the most and the most durable machinery, and higher rather than lower, after the introduction of more and better machinery. Operatives in manufactories, for instance, are, as a rule, better paid than farm laborers; and better paid in the first class than in the inferior establishments. Teamsters, in this country at least, and I suspect in all countries, are as well to do as before the construction of railroads. So of spinners, weavers, and artisans of every name. In explanation of these general facts, it may be noticed, (1) that labor is always required in the construction and repairs of all kinds of labor-saving appliances, and so far forth, a new market for labor is opened up in place of any loss of market possibly resulting from their introduction; (2) these forms of capital always tend to cheapen the products which they help to create, and such products because they are cheap find a wider circle of consumers, and more must be produced to supply a now broader market, and so far forth the demand for labor may be stronger than it was before; (3) These improvements cheapen also the commodities consumed by the laborers themselves, and therefore a given rate of wages now secures for them a higher grade of comforts. Combining these observations with the law of distribution already pointed out, and the conclusion is fairly established that the effect of machinery is, and will be, rather favorable than otherwise to the laboring classes.

Now, as a result of this entire discussion, attention must be called to a generalization, which has been more or less fully noticed by several writers, and with the presentation of which, this branch of the subject will be concluded. Since, by the aid of the different forms of capital, and such a division of labor as that every part of it is made most efficient, the cost of production of most kinds of manufactured articles tends to decline as compared with the cost of production of food and raw materials, in whose production these advantages are less perfectly attainable, there is a constant tendency towards approximation in the value, and, if money remain unchanged, in the price, of raw materials and of finished products; and in the degree of this approximation will be found a gauge of the success with which gratuitous natural forces and improved facilities of art have been made available in production. This single statement, clearly perceived in its grounds, grasps and holds the principal results of our discussions thus far. Examples of the principle offer themselves on every hand. Let us look at cotton cloth; an example somewhat marred at the present moment by the consequences of the late civil war, and disguised by a depreciated currency; but which, allowance being made for these, is an excellent illustration. At the opening of this century, the average price of raw cotton was just about twenty cents a pound; at the middle of the century, and onwards, the average price was just about ten cents a pound. At the first period, although accurate tables are wanting, the average price of cotton cloth could not have been less than sixty cents a yard; at the second period, it could hardly have been more than ten cents a yard. The absolute price of raw cotton diminished in the interval in the ratio of 2 to 1; while the absolute price of cotton cloth diminished in the interval in the ratio of 6 to 1. Relatively to a yard of finished cloth, the raw material greatly rose in value, since at the first it took three pounds to buy a yard, and at the last but one pound. There was a marked approximation all the while of the price of the finished product towards the price of the raw material; in other words, less and less difference of price was due to the cost of manufacture, which lessening cost marks the ever-increasing efficiency in the production of commodities of the gratuitous powers of Nature applied through machinery. According to Dr. Ure, the introduction of machinery into the manufacture of lace, lessened the cost of that product in the ratio of 50 to 1; and thereby, and to that degree, approximated the price of a pound of such lace towards the price of a pound of the cotton from which it was made. Food, raw materials, and labor, and the last more than the other two, tend steadily to advance in their power to command, that is, to buy, most kinds of finished products; and therefore, the millions who labor with their hands, and the other millions who own the soil and till it, have already advanced, and will still more advance, in a scale of comforts, with the advancing centuries.

In the opening paragraph of this treatise it was stated, that to unfold the Science of Political Economy in a proper order and completeness would require three things: namely, first, an analysis of the principles of human nature out of which exchanges spring; second, an examination of the relations of men to the physical earth and to each other, by which God's design is manifest that exchanges should be practiced; and third, an inquiry into the laws and usages devised by men to facilitate or impede exchanges. According to this plan, the first and second general branches of the subject have now been treated, and we pass to the third, beginning with Money.

CHAPTER X.

ON MONEY.

There is no use in saying that money is such a mysterious and complicated agent that nobody can understand it. That is the language of indolence. Money is wholly a matter of man's device; it was invented, just as any other instrument is invented, to accomplish a certain purpose; and it would be strange if men cannot comprehend what men themselves have devised. In all departments of God's works, indeed, we constantly meet with what cannot be fully comprehended nor perfectly fathomed, because an infinite mind has been there at work upon an infinite plan. But there is no such profundity in the works of men; unfathomableness is not an attribute of human skill; and since money is an instrument devised by men to aid them in accomplishing a certain purpose, it is as unreasonable to pretend that it is incomprehensible, as it would be to pretend that the steam-engine is incomprehensible. I hold it for certain that whatever men have devised, men can comprehend.

The general purposes which money was designed to answer, and which it is found admirably to fulfil, are best perceived under the supposition that there were no money. Exchanges began, and were profitable, long before money came into existence. Men first exchanged services directly for each other, without the intervention of any medium. This form of trade is called Barter. Hiram, king of Tyre, furnished to Solomon a certain quantity of cedars from Lebanon, and Solomon, in return, furnished the Tyrians a certain quantity of wheat and oil. This may serve as an instance of barter, although money had been in current use long previously to that transaction, as is seen in the purchase by Abraham of the cave and field of Machpelah, for which he weighed out four hundred shekels of silver, current money with the merchant. It is obvious, however, that while barter is a great deal better than no exchanges at all, there are inherent difficulties in that form of exchange. Under pure barter, exchanges are pretty much limited to those parties each of whom is in position to render to the other such services, and in such quantities, as the other stands in direct and immediate need of; it is not enough, under these conditions, that a man should have a service to sell, but also he must find a man who wants that specific service, and more than this, a man who not only wants that specific service, but also has a service to render in return, such as the first man wants. If A has wheat which he wishes to exchange for a coat, he must find a party who wants wheat, and who also is in position to render a coat in exchange for it, and moreover who wants just as much wheat as will pay for a coat, no more and no less; if he wants more, he may have nothing to render in exchange for the excess which A is willing to accept; if less, A may have nothing which the other wants, besides wheat with which to help pay for the coat. Even in the simpler states of society, the inconvenience, loss of time, and deterioration of commodities involved in direct barter, are very great, and in more advanced states of civilization would be intolerable, if it were possible, as it is not, for society to become advanced under those conditions. Exchanges are so limited in time, place, and variety, association is so hampered, and the development of all peculiar talents so impeded, under a system of simple barter, that one of the initial steps in the progress of all societies has been to hit upon some expedient to lessen these intrinsic difficulties; and so to facilitate exchanges. This expedient has been the invention of money, that is to say, the selection of some product, which, by general consent, instead of the particular purchasing-power of common commodities, should have a universal purchasing-power; so that, whenever anybody has anything to exchange, he may first exchange it for this product, whatever it be, and then with this product purchase at any time and place, whatever he may want. Money makes no alteration in any law of value, but merely substitutes for convenience' sake in every transaction in which it plays a part, a universal for a specific purchasing-power; a book, for example, has a specific purchasing-power; there is somebody who wants it, and is willing to give a sum of money for it; and the owner by the sale of it parts with a product which has only the power to purchase something from a few persons, and receives a product which has the power to purchase something from all persons; it is not true to say that the book is worth more than the money, or the money is worth more than the book, because they are just worth each other, as is demonstrated by the sale; but it is true to say that the seller of the book has substituted in the place of a limited purchasing-power, of which he was proprietor, a general purchasing-power, of which he has now become proprietor; and that the command of the money, which has no more value than the book had, does carry along with it a superior command over purchasable articles generally In one word, value in the form of money is in a more available shape for general purchasing, than value in any other form. This is the exact expression for what truth there is in the common vague remark, that money is different from all other commodities; in point of value, it is different from other commodities in just one respect, namely, while they have the power of buying some sorts of things from some persons, it has the power, derived from the usages of society, to buy all sorts of things from all persons.

It might seem, at first sight, as if the introduction of money, instead of simplifying the operations of exchange, would only complicate them, since it necessitates two exchanges, where otherwise there would be but one; but reflection, as well as experience, is able to convince us that there is no machine which economizes labor like money; no instrument which plays so important a part in production; no invention, unless it be the invention of letters, which has contributed more to the civilization of mankind. While men still exchanged in kind, and knew no other mode, the purchasing-power of a service was very much confined in place, and would not be parted with except in view of the return service actually there present, the ultimate parties to an exchange must for the most part come together locally, in order to effect an exchange; under a money system, this is no longer necessary, for it is sufficient to constitute a market for any commodity that it is wanted anywhere on the globe, the middle man, paying the seller for it in money, transports it thither, and receives back his money with a profit from the ultimate consumer. Thus money brings conveniently buyers and sellers together commercially, no matter how far separated locally. So, also, money generalizes any purchasing-power in point of time. The fruit-dealer, for example, must dispose of his product quickly, or it perishes on his hands, but by transmuting his perishable product into money, he may keep its power of purchase locked in this form as long as he lists; the money, indeed, is only good to purchase with, but it puts an interval at the pleasure of the holder between selling and buying, and with this generalized power in his pocket he may buy when he will, and what he will, and where he will. Money, too, makes any purchasing-power portable, divisible, and loanable. A man may carry the value of his farm in his purse, and may divide it up for a thousand different purchases, and especially is able to loan it in this form, to receive it back again with interest at a future day. Value in any other form than money is not generally suitable for loaning, because there are comparatively few who are willing to borrow a merely specific purchasing-power, and guarantee its return in that form with the due increase; but money, as a generalized agent, will command all services at all times, will serve at any man's bidding, and work in all sorts of harness, and therefore it is rarely difficult for men to loan any sums of money they have not immediate use for, and to make every moment of their own abstinence pay tribute in interest, and the advantages to both lenders and borrowers secured through this form of value — money — are incalculable. Thus we see the reason why governments, corporations, and individuals, when they borrow, borrow money. This general view of the uses and advantages of money will show it to be one of the most potent of the social agents, and will serve also to introduce our first specific proposition.

1. *Money is a medium of exchange.*

The word medium in this proposition, is to be taken in its etymological and strict sense, as something that comes between two extremes, and serves also to relate them to each other. Money is exchanged for other things, as a means, and not as an end; it is a very great help in exchanging all other things, but is never exchanged for itself in an ultimate transaction. Small boys, indeed, swap cents, but men, the miser excepted, who is under a deplorable fallacy of the senses, use and estimate money first as the medium which facilitates the real exchanges of society. What is really exchanged is the wheat, the cloth, the lumber, the furniture, the service of every kind, and money is but the instrument making those exchanges easy, which might perhaps go on without it, though with difficulty and loss It is somewhat like a railroad ticket. Transportation to a given place is what is really bought when one buys a railroad ticket. The evidence of the purchase is the bit of paper. It comes in as a medium between the traveller and the railroad company, and while it facilitates the real exchange, it also partly disguises it. The resemblance holds in the main feature, but in two respects the likeness fails; money is not a specific ticket for one purpose, but is a general ticket for all purposes of purchase; and secondly, metallic money stands as a value in its own right, at the same time it is serving as a medium, while the ticket does not. Still, we are all desirous to get money, not for the sake of the money, but for the sake of those things which the money will buy. We part with it freely and constantly for those things which we care more about. What we really care for is what the money will buy, is the command over all services and commodities which the possession of money insures. If we could give our own service or commodity, whatever it is, and receive directly in return the service or commodity which we want, whatever it is, there would be no need of money. This is generally inconvenient, and sometimes impossible. Therefore we introduce a middle term between the two extreme terms. Money is a good mean which helps exchange the two extremes. And the value of the money of any country is a very small fraction, probably not over one fortieth, of the value of that which it helps to exchange. By the last census the estimated value of real and personal property in the United States was, in round numbers, $16,000,000,000. The whole currency of the country in 1860 was certainly less than $400,000,000; so that the money of the country stood to its aggregate material wealth in the ratio at least of one to forty. Besides all that portion of this real and personal property which changed hands in that year, the currency helped to exchange all the simple services, as those of professional men, teachers, servants, and so on, which were rendered in that year, and which are not included in the census estimate, except partially and indirectly, so far as the returns to such services had been transformed into real and personal property. If we suppose that transactions to the value of $16,000,000,000, were concluded in this country in the year 1860, and that $400,000,000 constituted the money in circulation, then it follows that each dollar of money circulated on the average forty dollars of value, or, what is the same thing, each dollar of the circulation made on the average forty payments, in the course of the year. It is, of course, impossible to determine with exactness the aggregate value of the money exchanges of any country for any given period, but if this could be determined, and should then be regarded as a dividend, for which the aggregate money of the country were a divisor, the quotient would express what has been called the rapidity of circulation, that is, the number of times which each dollar changes hands on the average in order to effect the given amount of exchanges; and it would also express how many more times the value of that is which the money of a country helps to exchange, than its own value is. That it should express this last, however, accurately, we must suppose that the same product is exchanged by the help of money only once between the producer and the consumer. Probably the ratio of one to forty is above rather than below the true ratio of the aggregate money of the commercial nations to the money value of those products, reckoned only once, which this money helps to exchange. Therefore we see that the hub and spokes, and rim of the wheel of exchange consist of services and commodities of every description; while, to borrow the famous comparison of Hume, money is but the grease which makes the wheel turn easier. It is a vast mistake to suppose that the grease is the wheel itself.

Hume's comparison, though exact as far as it goes, and for the purposes for which he used it, is nevertheless capable of misleading the mind. It is true that money is the grease which facilitates the revolution of the wheel of exchange, but it is also true that the dimensions of the wheel itself are vastly greater than they would have been had it not been for money. Money indeed helped exchange the products that already existed at its first invention, but by far the largest part of products since have come into existence largely through the agency of money. We get quite too low a view of the function of this potent agent, if we think of it merely as an aid in circulating products that would have existed whether or no; some products would have existed whether or no, and money certainly is of great use and convenience in helping bring these to the ultimate consumers; but this is a partial and wholly inadequate view of the true function of money as a medium of exchange. The fact that such a medium is in universal circulation, and that the holders of it are ready to exchange it against any sort of services adapted to gratify their desires, exercises a kind of creative power, and brings a thousand products to the market which would otherwise never have come into existence. Since money will buy anything, men are on the alert to bring forward something which will buy money; and since money is divisible into small pieces, an incredible number and variety of small services are brought forward to be exchanged against these pieces, which services we have no reason to suppose would ever be brought forward at all, were it not for the strong attraction of the money. In this point of view, the true nature of money is best perceived, when it is considered, as it really is, as a very important portion of the capital of the world. Capital, as we have already learned, is any product reserved to be employed in further production. The circulating medium of any country is the most active, the most profitable, and the most essential of all those instruments reserved in aid of further production. The axe, the plough, the spindle, the loom, the wheel, the engine, are all instruments, are all capital, and they each aid respectively some part or parts of the processes of production; but money is a form of capital which stimulates and facilitates all the processes of production without exception. Just as we have seen that money is a form of value generalized, so is it also a generalized form of capital, that is to say, it is an instrument capable of aiding all production in every department, while every other instrument is capable of aiding but few processes in one department. Without money, there could be no thorough division of labor, because there would be no adequate means of estimating or rewarding each one's share in a complicated process. By means of money, all services, small or great, contributing toward a common product, are neatly measured and paid for by some one, who thereby becomes proprietor of the whole product; or, if the contributors choose, they may wait till the product itself is sold, and then the money received is divisible without loss to each contributor, according to the service rendered. Thus the influence of money, as capital, pervades the whole field of exchange, from centre to circumference, facilitating every transfer, and stimulating to new transfers.

Money, then, is a medium of exchange; and the question arises in this connection, how much of it is wanted? Clearly, only so much as will serve the purposes which such a medium is fitted to subserve; there should be enough fairly to mediate between the services actually ready to be exchanged then and there, and also enough fairly to call out other services, proper and profitable in the then circumstances of society, and whose only obstacle to a profitable exchange then and there, is the lack of a facilitating medium. All increase of money beyond this point, which the very nature of money itself marks out as the boundary, leads to a diminution in value of every part of it, to a consequent disturbance of all existing money contracts, to a universal rise of prices which are illusory and gainless, to unsteadiness and derangement in all legitimate business, and to a spirit of restless enterprise and speculation, which seeks to draw off the excess of money in untried and reckless experiments. These consequences from this cause have been again and again witnessed in every commercial country, and in the United States on a gigantic scale during the nine years past. I cannot help thinking that Mr. Carey, who has thrown so much light on certain portions of the field of Political Economy, is decidedly in the wrong in the view he maintains that there cannot be too much money in any country. No writer has brought out more clearly than he has, the intimate relations of money with all industrial development; but he seems at times to forget that money, essential and potent as it is, is essential and potent only as a *medium*. The real subjects of exchange are mutual efforts, mutual services, and money is the instrument merely that comes in between the real services exchanged to facilitate the exchange; and therefore it seems to me to be perfectly conclusive on the point to remark, that the quantity of money needed in any country, or in the whole world, is limited by the number of the services ready to be exchanged, to facilitate the exchange of which is the good purpose and end of money. The physical and mental powers of men, which alone give birth to services, when considered, as they must be in this connection, as belonging to a given number of men at a given time and place, are strictly limited; and although the presence of money then and there is both a stimulus and an aid to their bringing forward services of all sorts to the market, there are obvious limitations both in their powers and in their circumstances; and the quantity of money needed among them is just that quantity which will fairly act as a medium in exchanging the services which they are able and willing to render to each other. All increase in the quantity of money beyond that point would have, and could have, the only effect of increasing the nominal prices of services, without making the services themselves any greater in number or better in quality. It is with money exactly as it is with any other form of capital, allowance being made for the fact that money is a kind of generalized capital. How many ships does a commercial nation need to employ? As many as will fairly take off its exports and bring in its imports. Ships are wanted for one definite purpose; and when enough are secured to answer that purpose, all additions to the number will lessen the value, that is, the purchasing-power of ships generally. So of all instruments whatever. Enough is as good as a feast. Enough is better than more. In regard to every form of capital, the point of sufficiency is determined by the quantity of work to be done. Now, money is a form of capital, an instrument, having this peculiarity only, that it is capable of aiding to a certain extent all branches of production; and the point of sufficiency in the quantity of money for a country, or for the world, is determined by the amount of products of all kinds, otherwise ready to be exchanged, and only waiting the facilitating agency of an exchange medium. The quantity of money being given, an increased aggregate of exchanges can be facilitated by it, by means of a greater rapidity of circulation of that given quantity. $400,000,000, changing hands forty times, will effect exchanges to an aggregate of $16,000,000,000 in a year; the same sum, by a circulation doubly rapid, will effect twice that aggregate of exchanges; so that, it follows, that an increased amount of business to be done, does not necessarily require an increased volume of money but sometimes only a brisker use of that already in circulation. As in mechanics, so in money, the whole power is the product of the two factors, mass and velocity. Money is like any other tool, the more constant its use the more profitable its agency. If $16,000,000,000 of value are to be exchanged, it is very much cheaper that $400,000,000 of money should do the work, changing hands forty times, than that $800,000,000 should be employed, changing hands only twenty times. The quick movement of a small mass is better than the torpid movement of a big mass, both in what it saves of expense, and in what it presupposes of the general conditions of exchange. It only remains under this proposition to add, what will be more clearly perceived when we come to treat of foreign trade, that no enterprising commercial nation, so long as the natural right of exchange is left unimpeded, and so long as the money of the nations consists of gold and silver, or paper, the genuine representative of these, can ever lack, for any great length of time, a sufficient quantity of money to serve as its medium of exchange.

2. *Money is a measure of value.*

I hope it was made very plain, under the preceding proposition, what is meant when it is said that money is a medium of exchange. Closely commingled with its function as a medium, money has another very delicate function, as a measure of value. How important this second function is may be seen by supposing for a moment that there were no instrument in existence capable of performing it. Without a common measure of values of different sorts, it would be inconvenient, not to say impossible, to carry on traffic at all. For instance: A baker has only loaves of bread, and wishes to buy a hat, a horse, a house. How many loaves shall he give for each? Without some common denomination in which these differing values can be expressed, and by means of which they can be brought into numerical relations with each other, it would be an awkward piece of business to effect even the three exchanges; and every time he wished to purchase another article, there must be an independent calculation from different data, to decide the terms of the exchange. Introduce now some common denominations in which each of these values can express itself, and the difficulty disappears in an instant. "My loaves are worth ten cents each," says the baker. "My hat is worth ten dollars," says the hatter. The terms of exchange, then, are 100 for 1, and no parleying. So of the rest; so of everything that is ever bought or sold. Dollars and cents are the denominations in which values are reckoned, and by which they can be compared with each other numerically, just as feet and inches are the denominations by which different lengths are compared, and pints and quarts the denominations by which capacity is measured; and the builder and the surveyor would not be more at a loss in their work without the units of length, or the vintner without the units of capacity, than everybody would be at a loss without the units of value. Dollars and cents are, as it were, the language in which values express themselves; and, without some such language, the busiest marts of exchange would soon become not only a silent but a deserted scene.

The difference between money as a medium and money as a measure is one that should be clearly delineated and perfectly apprehended, because there is no such thing as adequately understanding the subject of money unless the two functions be kept distinct in the mind, as well in their single as in their commingled action. The original measure of value in France, England, and Scotland, was the pound weight of silver. No coin of that weight was ever struck; but a pound of silver was cut into 240 coins called pence. Twelve of these pence were called a solidus, or shilling. Thus as applied to silver, the symbols lb. and £ denoted equivalent weights, the former of uncoined metal, the latter of metal coined. But in course of time, *more* than 240 pence so called, and at last in Elizabeth's reign, 744 pence, came to be coined out of a lb. of silver. Yet all the while, 240 of these pence were called a £. £ and lb., both a contraction of the Latin *libra*, were no longer equivalent. The lb. of weight continued stable: the £ of money had dwindled to less than one third. Yet the *name* pound continued to attach to 240 pence, although the pence embodied a less and less quantity of silver. As the *medium* contained a less quantity of silver, so the *measure*, that is to say, the *denomination*, represented a less quantity of silver. This example will help us understand the difference between money as a medium and money as a measure. Dollars and cents perform their duties as a medium by virtue of their being commodities; they perform their duties as a measure by virtue of their being denominations. Yet the denominations, though spelled and sounded as before, vary with every change that takes place in the medium.

There are two kinds of changes to which a metallic money is liable, considered as a medium of exchange. First, a less quantity than before of a precious metal may go to a certain coin. In 1834, the gold eagle of the United States was reduced in weight from 270 to 258 grains, and the alloy increased to one part in ten from one part in twelve. This was taking out more than six parts of gold out of every 100 parts, in all the gold coins of the country. Yet the coins bore the same names as before. As a medium, other things remaining equal, their purchasing-power was diminished more than six per centum; and consequently, as a measure of other values, the denominations of these coins varied simultaneously and equally with the coins themselves. Secondly, coins are liable to change in their function as a medium from changes in the general purchasing-power of the metals themselves. If for any reason an ounce of gold will buy less of other things than formerly, the coins cut from that gold will buy less than formerly, and this change in the medium will be followed by a corresponding change in the measure. Other tables of denominations have a basis independent of the things which they measure, and are not variable by the quality or quantity of those measurable things. A French metre, for example, is an invariable unit of length the world over; so is one of Troughton's inches; but this is not true of the denominations of money at all

Pounds, dollars, guilders, francs, and their subdivisions, are denominations of *value*, which is a variable relation, and as denominations they follow the fortunes of the coins whose names they are. When the current dollar, for instance, sinks to one half, or rises to twice its previous purchasing-power, we call it a dollar all the while, the denomination perpetually shifting with every variation of the thing. The same name attaches to a shifting denomination. The denominations of value, then, are not an independent standard to which values themselves can be referred, as lengths are referred to the metre, but vary with the varying purchasing-power of the coins, so that money as a measure is only uniform when money as a medium is uniform. So indispensable, however, in all exchanges is some common measure of value, that the denominations of money, notwithstanding their variable character, are universally employed in estimating and exchanging commodities, even when no money as a medium is used.

Without reflection, it might be supposed, that, since the measure rises and falls with the medium, no practical error is liable to follow the confounding of the two functions; but it is the very sympathetic connection between the two that gives rise to the possibility of error. If the units of money were, like the linear units, inflexible, so that all variations of the medium could be instantly detected by a reference to the standard of measure, there would be no difficulty at all: I could loan a thousand dollars for one year, or ten years, and, however much the medium might vary in the interval, be sure that I should receive back just as much purchasing-power as I loaned, with the interest on the same; it might be more or fewer *pieces* than the number I loaned, which is a matter of indifference. As it is, no lender can have any such assurance. The borrower is bound to pay back with interest the same number of dollars as he received, although the dollar-medium, and hence the dollar-measure, may meanwhile have fallen or risen greatly. In the United States, for the past nine years, the current money has exchanged against gold from 110 to 285 of the one for 100 of the other; and it is very obvious that all debts of old standing, paid in this period, have been only legally, and not actually, liquidated; and that debts contracted when the depreciation was more and paid when it was less were more than actually liquidated. This, of course, presupposes, what we are not yet in a position to assume, that gold remained a proper and uniform standard. The subtle error to be avoided alike in discussion and in practice is, to suppose that money, either as a medium or as a measure, remains unchanged, simply because the name remains unchanged by which we designate its denominations.

It may be asked, why cannot this source of error be obviated? I reply, that the error may be obviated, but the source of it cannot be obviated from the nature of the case. It was shown in our chapter on Value that to find an invariable measure of value is a natural impossibility. Money, as it is the medium of exchange, is also the best attainable measure of value, and is used throughout the civilized world to compare with each other all values except its own; but since value in general, and the value of money as well, is a thing of relation, and varies with every change affecting either of the things exchanged, as much by changes affecting the things it exchanges for as by changes affecting itself, — the value of a hat, for instance, as estimated in gloves, increasing by any cheapened process in glove-making, though no change at all take place in the cost of hat-making, — a perfect measure of value is impossible. Therefore the denominations of money, which is the best attainable measure, can never have a meaning absolutely fixed, but slide up and down the scale along which the purchasing-power of money as a medium is moving, and they are consequently useless as a standard to detect any changes in the medium itself, while, the medium remaining uniform, they instantly detect the changes in all other purchasing-powers. This will always be so. The same difficulty does not occur in having a perfect measure of length or of capacity, — a perfect inch or a perfect pint. The French have a perfect system of measures and weights. Their mathematicians measured an arc of the earth's circumference, and thus determined the absolute length of a degree of latitude. Three hundred and sixty times this length makes up the length of the earth's circumference, — an invariable measure recoverable again even if it should be once lost. This measure divided by 40,000,000 gave the French nation their *metre*, which is a perfect unit for the measure of length. A tenth part of the metre cubed gave them their *litre*, which is a perfect unit for the measure of capacity. The weight of a hundredth part of a metre cubed of distilled water at the temperature of maximum density is the *gramme*, an invariable unit of weight. A linear length of ten metres squared gives the *are*, the unit of surface. A perfect measure of anything demands for its starting-point something absolute and invariable: in value there is nothing absolute; we begin with a relation, and therefore an unchangeable measure is not to be looked for. Still, it is vastly important for the interest of exchange that the accepted measure of value be as little liable to fluctuations as possible, especially in all cases in which lapse of time is involved before the exchange is fully consummated. For precisely the same reason that the bushel-measure should be of the same capacity in sowing-time and in harvest, to sell by and buy by, always a bushel, no more and no less; and the yard-stick an inflexible measure of length, the same for buyer and seller, always thirty-six of Troughton's inches, no more and no less; so, as far as it is possible in the nature of things, ought the medium and hence the measure of values to represent year in and year out a uniform degree of purchasing-power. If money had but one function, namely, to serve as a present means of exchange; if there were no credit, contracts, annuities, involving the element of *time;* if the character of the medium did not also determine the signification of the measure; then the subject of money would be easily understood, and the substance that should serve as money would be a matter of comparative indifference. As it is, the second and more delicate function of money both complicates the theme, and excludes from the category of good money all but one or two of the substances that have ever been used as money. We have just now seen the radical reasons why no money can even tolerably perform its function as a measure that is not tolerably uniform in its value as a medium. This consideration brings us naturally to our third specific proposition.

3. *Gold and silver constitute the best money.*

The purposes of money have been served in different countries and in different ages by a variety of products, according to the taste and circumstances of the people. Cattle have been employed as money among pastoral people in almost all periods of the world, and are still employed for this purpose in Africa. Slaves among the Anglo-Saxons; wampum among the American Indians; salt in Abyssinia; codfish in Newfoundland; tobacco in Virginia; wheat in Massachusetts; nails in Scotland; stamped leather among the Carthaginians, and others; bark stamped with the image of the sovereign in China; platina in Russia; copper, simple or compounded with other metals, among the ancient Romans, and most other nations; iron among the Spartans; gold and silver among all civilized nations sooner or later; have been or still are used as money. Of all these products, the two last have shown themselves to be best adapted for the purposes of money, and have come consequently into universal use in the commercial world. Experience has not only demonstrated the superiority of these metals over all other forms of money, as is shown by the fact of their universal adoption, but reason also is able to tell us why gold and silver are the best money.

(1.) *On account of their comparatively steady value.* This is the main reason, and it must be firmly grasped. There is no end to the confusion which has crept over discussions on money from the circumstance that the writers have not first of all determined for themselves with fixed clearness what value is. This must be done at the outset, if there is to be the least hope of sound results. Some writers speak of money as destitute of intrinsic value, because we cannot eat it, drink it, wear it, or make any other direct use of it. Mr. Macleod, the eminent English economist, to whom I shall acknowledge my obligations in the chapter on Credit, regards money as required only to measure, record, and transfer debts. Money is, according to him, a representative of debt. Now, I cannot agree with either of these representations. Value is value, and there is only one kind of it, and the epithet intrinsic is only used to help out a lame theory, and no such epithet is pertinent to the word value, and no one can show anything different in the value of money, either in respect to the way in which it arises, or in the laws which control it, from the value of any other commodity, excepting only the difference already pointed out, that money by the usages of society has a generalized instead of a specific purchasing-power. It is all false to speak of gold and silver money as the representative of value. It represents nothing but itself. It will buy other things certainly, and so will a bushel of wheat. Value is simple purchasing-power, and money has value because we can purchase with it, exactly as everything else has value for that very reason. Society is so constituted that a want is felt in it of some medium of purchase; this want cannot be supplied without an effort; whoever makes the effort will demand a corresponding effort made for him; when it comes to the exchange of the medium for the wheat, for example, there stand face to face, as in every other instance of exchange, two desires and two efforts; there is then, as always, a reciprocal estimation of the two services about to be exchanged, and the estimation agreed on is the *value* of the medium expressed in wheat. If the want of any medium of exchange is less felt in any community, or if the effort required to secure it be for any reason less, other things remaining the same, the value of the money will be less, that is to say, it will purchase less of other things. If the demand for money as an instrument of purchase be greater, or the obstacles in the way of its supply be increased, other things as before, the value of the money will be more. It is the old circuit over again of wants, efforts, estimations, satisfactions. The value of money arises under the same conditions as every other value, and is variable by any change in any one of the four elements which alone can vary the value of anything. Two desires and two efforts invariably precede every exchange. A change in any one of these, the rest unchanged, can vary value, and nothing else can vary it; and, as it seems to me, no person has ever shown or can show that the value of money is in any respect, save the superficial one already noticed, exceptional and peculiar. And it also seems to me that nothing more is needed in order to remove the last vestiges of the dark cloud which has so long overhung this subject, than to familiarize one's self first of all with the true doctrine of value in general, and then hold fast the truth, exemplified on every side, that the value of money is just like any other value.

Gold and silver, then, as money, have value in the same sense and for the same reason as any other productive instrument, and we must now attend to the reasons why their value is so steady.

(*a.*) On account of the comparatively steady demand for these metals. Gold and silver are wanted for two general purposes: first, to be used as money, and second, to be used in the arts; and it has been estimated that about two fifths of the aggregate quantity in the world is in the form of money, and the other three fifths in the form of plate, utensils, and ornaments. Now, so far as the element of desire controls value, the purpose for which any article is desired is a matter of indifference. The aggregate desire for it for all purposes, accompanied with the offer of something with which to buy it, constitutes the demand; and the more universal the desire, no matter for what purpose, the steadier the demand, and, so far forth, the steadier the value. It is worth noticing, as a point still too little noticed, that it is not the demand for the precious metals as coin alone that determines their general value, nor the demand for them in the arts, but the combined demand for all purposes; just as the value of barley is regulated, partly by the demand for it for food, and partly by the demand for it for malting purposes. Hence an ounce of bullion of the standard fineness, destined for the smelting-pot of the artisan, is worth within a very trifle as much as an ounce of coined money. By the law of the Bank of England an ounce of standard gold is coined into £3 17*s.* 10½*d.*, and the Bank is obliged to buy all bullion and foreign coins of the standard fineness offered to it at £3 17*s.* 9*d.* per ounce — a difference of three halfpennies. Now, gold and silver are so indispensable in the form of money, so beautiful in the form of ornaments, so well adapted to serve the purposes of luxury and love of distinction, so really useful in the arts, that the demand for them is constant and well-nigh universal; and if, in the progress of civilization, a less quantity should be desired for personal ornamentation and purposes of luxury, a greater will doubtless be required for the other uses; and so, as the demand in the past has been steady, and perhaps steadily increasing, there is every reason to expect the same for the time to come. And it contributes to the steadiness in value of the gold and silver coin, that there is at hand in the form of plate a reservoir from which a chance chasm in the coin may be replenished, or an extra demand for it answered.

(*b.*) On account of their tolerably uniform cost of production. Not desires alone, but efforts as well, regulate value. Supply is the correlative of demand; and when to a steady demand there answers a steady supply, realized under conditions of pretty uniform difficulty, there will be of course a pretty steady value. Nature herself has indicated, in a manner not to be mistaken, her intention that these metals should be the money of the nations. She has scattered them all over the earth, and so scattered them that the cost of their production has been wonderfully uniform ever since civilization and commerce began. There have been but two marked changes in the value of gold and silver throughout the commercial world in the last thousand years; the first, in the sixteenth century, in consequence of the occupation of Mexico and South America by Europeans, when the value of the precious metals diminished, silver a good deal, it is difficult to say how much, and gold considerably less; the second, in consequence of the discovery of the gold-fields of California and Australia in the present century, which, it is thought by most, has still further diminished the value of gold. With these exceptions, and similar ones are not likely to recur, these metals have always maintained and are likely to maintain a remarkable uniformity of value, on account of a remarkably uniform cost of production. Even these changes became only gradually perceptible, and did but little injury to individuals, scarcely disturbing the justice of exchange or the measure of value, except in cases of long annuities and similar obligations. A universal rise of prices soon adjusted exchanges to the new state of things.

(*c*.) On account of their quantity. The amount of gold and silver in circulation in the commercial world, to say nothing of the quantity so easily brought into circulation from the reservoir of plate, is so vast, that it receives the annual contributions from the mines much as the ocean receives the waters of the rivers, without sensible increase of its volume, and parts with the annual loss by detrition and shipwreck, as the sea yields its waters to evaporation, without sensible diminution of volume. The yearly supply and the yearly waste are small in comparison with the accumulations of ages; and therefore the relation of the whole mass to the uses of the world, and the purchasing-power of any given portion, remain comparatively steady. It is probable that production at the mines might cease altogether for a considerable interval without very sensibly enhancing throughout the commercial world the value of gold; as it is certain, from experience, that a production very largely augmented only gradually, and after a considerable interval, diminishes its value. The mass of the precious metals has been aptly compared to the heavy balance-wheel in mechanics, which preserves an equable and working condition of the machinery under any sudden increase of the power, and even when the power is for a moment withdrawn. At this point a caution is needful. Because it is affirmed that the great amount of the precious metals is a ground of their firm value, it must not be supposed that we are going beyond our general doctrine, and introducing another element, namely, quantity, besides the four elements which, as we have so often alleged, can alone vary the value of any service; quantity, in itself, is not an element capable of varying the value of anything, but taken in connection with durability, it is an element of what might, perhaps, with propriety be called the *inertia* of value, and tends to keep the purchasing-power of gold and silver where it is. Value and steadiness of value are two distinct ideas. The present value of an ounce of gold expressed in any other commodity is decided by four things alone; but other elements besides these may help determine that that ounce of gold shall have ten years from now a purchasing-power approxi mately the same as now. It will depend, of course, in the last analysis, upon the relation of the then demand to the then supply; yet the vast quantity of the precious metals in existence, combined with their durability, prevent those fluctuations in the supply which are so destructive to a steady value. It is not as with the fruits and the grains, whose value varies perpetually with the seasons, and which are so perishable that they must be sold soon or never: gold and silver are almost indestructible, and except by wear and accident, the existing mass is not liable to be lessened, and in so far as the annual production from the mines exceeds the yearly waste there is a natural provision made for the natural increase of demand, to supply the wants of the world for currency and for the arts, without much disturbing the relation of the demand and supply. The quantity, in connection with the durability of the precious metals, helps preserve to them a tolerably steady value from generation to generation.

(*d.*) On account of their fluency. Gold and silver are in demand the world over. Having great value in comparatively small bulk, they are easily transported from continent to continent; and whenever, from any cause, they become relatively in excess in any country, and thus lose there a portion of their previous purchasing-power, there is an immediate motive to export them to other countries where their power in exchange is greater, and thus the equilibrium is restored. The value of gold and silver throughout the commercial world is thus kept pretty steady by the facility with which they are carried from points where they are relatively in excess to points where they are relatively in deficiency. There is a gain in carrying them to those countries where their power of purchase is the greatest, because more commodities can be obtained for them than at home; and private motives here coincide with public welfare, since what the traders do in transporting gold and silver, with an eye to their own interest, helps maintain at home and abroad the steady value of these commodities. This law of the distribution of the precious metals by commerce, and the equilibrium of value resulting therefrom, is as natural and beautiful as the law which preserves the level of the ocean, or that which balances the bodies of the planetary system. This has come at length to be recognized by the nations, and the laws which used to forbid by heavy penalties the exportation of gold and silver are all swept away, and these metals are now free to go, and do actually go, where they can obtain the most in exchange. It is absurd to suppose that their owners would carry them out of a country, unless they were worth more abroad than at home, and therefore the prejudice which exists still in this country against the exportation of gold is a senseless prejudice. The gold is not given away; it is sold, and sold for more than it will buy at home; otherwise it would not be carried abroad. There is the same kind of gain as in all other exchanges, and this great incidental advantage in addition, that, by means of free commerce in the precious metals, their general value is kept pretty uniform throughout the world, and a chance redundancy in one currency is drawn off to supply a corresponding deficiency in another. It may be laid down as an axiom, that no country will export, for the sake of getting other things, those things which are more needful for its own welfare; and there need not be the slightest fear that any nation which cultivates its own advantages under freedom will ever lack a sufficient quantum of the precious metals. Under freedom, and so long as human nature continues what it is, these metals will go, and go in just the right proportions, to and from those countries which produce and offer in exchange those desirable services which other countries want. The greater the enterprise and skill, the keener the development of all peculiar and presently available resources, the more honorable and free the commercial system, the surer is any nation, whether it be a gold-bearing country or not, of securing the gold and silver which it needs. This is so, because *there* will be a good market to buy in, and they who have gold will resort thither to buy. But such a nation will also want to buy other things besides gold and silver, and when enough of the latter are secured for the currency and for the arts, the residue will be exported, perhaps to the very countries from which it originally came, in payment for some products which those countries have an advantage in producing. The United States is a gold-producing country, and exported in the years 1850 – 1860, both inclusive, $502,789,759, coin and bullion; and during the same period we imported from other countries $81,270,571, coin and bullion.[1] Now, there was a double advantage in that exportation. In the first place, more and better commodities were secured to the country than the gold could have bought in the

[1] Report on the Finances, 1863.

country, for otherwise it would not have been carried abroad; and, in the second place, this large sum carried abroad to various countries in exchange, not only prevented the disturbing effect on our own currency of more than doubling in ten years' time our stock of gold, thus inevitably depreciating the whole mass, but also, by causing the new gold to impinge on the whole world's stock instead of on the currency of a single nation, the shock of the new production on the measure of value, though perceptible, was reduced and deadened. The world's mass of the precious metals is comparatively torpid beneath the action of an accretion which would break down by its weight the currency of a single nation. Therefore, the fluency of gold and silver, by which they pass easily in commerce to those places where their present value in exchange is greatest, and return as easily when the conditions are reversed, tends powerfully to make their general value uniform throughout the world, and consequently to make them the best medium of exchange and the best measure of value.

(*e.*) On account of this circumstance, that every general rise or fall in the value of gold and silver tends to check itself. This principle, indeed, is applicable to the value of all commodities, but owing to their quantity and durability preëminently applicable to the value of the precious metals. The check is double in either direction. First, let us suppose that the purchasing-power of an ounce of gold or silver be rising: then, production will be stimulated at all the mines, and the more stimulated as the rise is more, and the new and enlarged supply will tend to check a farther rise, and, unless the permanent demand has been intensified, to bring back the value to the old point; moreover, when there is a rise in the value of the coin, there is a less quantity required to do the same amount of business, and the demand for gold which causes the rise tends to be checked by the rise itself, because a less quantity is needed in the currency in consequence of the rise. This supposes, of course, that the exchanges mediated by money are no greater than before. Thus a rise of value in gold and silver checks itself by natural laws in two ways. Just so of a fall in their value. Production is thereby slackened at the mines, and the lessened supply tends to enhance value; and, if the same business is to be done as before, there is a stronger demand for currency while the fall continues, and this demand tends also to restore the value. All this is in the interest of a steady value.

(*f.*) On account, lastly, of this circumstance, that a stronger demand for currency is met either by increasing the stock of coin, or by an increased rapidity of circulation of that on hand. A brisker demand for money, especially if it be temporary, does not necessarily enlarge the supply, or alter the value, but only hurry round the existing circulation. Oscillations in the demand are responded to by a slower or more rapid circulation. This tends most admirably to keep the value steady within certain limits. When enterprises are multiplying and exchanges are being permanently increased in number and variety, then there must be a larger amount of money, and this larger amount is secured in the ways already indicated, with perhaps slight disturbances of value; but the temporary ebbs and flows of business have no effect at all on the mass of money, but only on its movement, and its value consequently is not disturbed at all.

These six grounds appear to be satisfactory and sufficient to account for the superior steadiness of the value of gold and silver, so far as their value is determined by considerations relating to the metals themselves. We now proceed to the reasons additional to this why gold and silver constitute the best money.

(2.) *Because they are self-regulating.* These metals came to be, and continue to be, money, independent of the enactments of any government. Government indeed coins them for the use of the people; but coinage is nothing in the world but a public attest to the quantity and quality of the metal contained in the coin. For the trouble and expense of assaying, stamping, and thus attesting the quantity and quality of the metal in the coin, governments usually charge the depositors of bullion a small seigniorage; England indeed does not; and the United States did not till 1853; but at present, France and the United States charge respectively on gold coins, .216 per centum and .5 per centum; so that a very insignificant part of the value of coins is due to the process of coining. The value of coined money regulates itself on just the same principles as the value of wheat regulates itself, and governments are as powerless to alter the one as the other. Indeed, the coining of either metal by itself is a matter of quantity and quality alone, and not a matter of value at all: the United States say by law that a gold dollar shall consist of 25⅘ grains troy, of which nine parts shall be pure and one part alloy, but of the value of this dollar thus coined the law says nothing. It can say nothing. The coin is publicly attested so heavy, so fine, and thereafter it takes its chance as to value. All governments have now learned, after oft-repeated and always vain trials to regulate the value of their coins, that all they can do is to regulate the amount and fineness of the metals contained in them. When, however, it is designed that both metals shall circulate in the same currency, then it becomes necessary that government shall determine, as well as it can, not the absolute value of either, but the relative value of each in each. And here too the value of each, estimated in the other, regulates itself independently of edicts or enactments. If the legislators can ascertain in what proportions they are exchanging for each other in a free market, they may mark that as the legal relative value of the two, but they must not suppose that their work will not require revision from time to time.

The value of gold in silver has differed considerably in different periods and countries. Livy mentions that the relative value was 1 to 10 about 189 B. C.; Julius Cæsar is said by Suetonius to have exchanged the two on one occasion at 1 for 9; under the early Roman emperors, it was 1 for 12; from Constantine to Justinian, about 1 for 14. Herodotus mentions it as 1 to 13 in Greece, in his day, which was the fifth century before Christ; Plato, a little later, calls it 1 to 12. In England, before the discovery of America, it was about 1 to 10; in 1717, the last legal rating of the two put them at 1 for

$15\frac{1}{5}$, although Sir Isaac Newton, in his report to Parliament that year as master of the mint, shows the market rate was nearly 1 for $15\frac{1}{2}$. At that time, the rate in France and Holland was 1 to $14\frac{1}{2}$, which of course made it profitable to export silver from England to the Continent. In China, Japan, and the East Indies generally, gold has always been cheap relatively to silver (in Japan, till 1860, as 1 to 4, since then as 1 to $13\frac{1}{2}$), which accounts for the stream of silver perpetually flowing from Occident to Orient. In 1792, when the mint of the United States was established, the legal rate of exchange for the two metals was fixed at 1 for 15, which proved to be an undervaluation of gold, and tended to drive the gold coins abroad. Mr. Elliott, of the U. S. Bureau of Statistics, has shown that the average for the thirty years just prior to the discovery of the new gold fields was 1 to $15\frac{7}{8}$; that after the opening of these fields in 1848–50, gold gradually fell, reaching its minimum of 1 to $15\frac{1}{5}$ in 1859; and that since it has slowly advanced to 1 for $15\frac{3}{5}$, the point it now holds. This law of self-regulation, maintaining itself in spite of all legal enactments, led England in 1816, and the United States in 1853, to abandon a double standard of value, and practically demonetize silver by degrading the coins in weight, so that they pass current at more than six per cent. above their real value. English silver coins are degraded $6\frac{2}{33}$ per cent.; United States smaller silver coins are $6\frac{10}{11}$ per cent. less than silver dollars; and consequently, they are only legal tender in the two countries respectively for 40 shillings and \$5.00. The Bank of England is only allowed to hold silver as the basis of circulation to the extent of one fourth of the gold coin and bullion held at any one time; yet silver maintains its own value in spite of these disadvantages, and is thought to comprise about one fifth of the whole metallic circulation of the realm. Between 1853 and July 1, 1867, $53,189,216.32 in silver coins have come from the United States mint and its branches.[1]

It is convenient to have at least two metals in the currency, notwithstanding the impossibility of maintaining a steady legal relative valuation between them. Gold ought to be exclusively the standard; it ought to be the only legal tender for large sums; but silver coins are useful for the lesser exchanges, and there is no present objection to their being debased in weight so as to allow a considerable change in the market value of gold in silver without tending to export the silver coins. Another reason for the use of both silver and gold in the coinage is the increased stability in value thereby secured to the whole currency. The immense quantity in the world of both metals combined, and the opportunity of replenishing a chance deficiency of the one from the stores of the other, give, in accordance with principles already explained, a superior stability to value. Most currencies, our own included, have also a third metal or mixture of metals, to serve the purposes of the smallest exchanges, and the coins made of this are usually largely overvalued — our nickel cents of 1857 cost the government about half a cent each — and are not legal tender for debts except for very small sums.

It is, then, a principal merit of metallic currencies,

[1] Report, Director of the Mint, 1867.

that the gold and silver comprised in them determine their own value by natural laws, both relatively to each other and to all other purchasable things; and hence the quantity required in each currency of the world to do the business of that country is a matter which natural laws are perfectly competent to regulate, without any direct action of government; and governments may be relieved from the difficult or rather impossible task of determining how much money their country shall have. The distribution of the precious metals over the earth by commerce, according to the wants and circumstances of each country, is not perfectly accomplished at present by the natural laws which are competent thus to distribute them, because some of the nations use still some form of credit-money as a part of their currency, and also because all the nations have not yet come to an agreement as to the degree of fineness of the metals used in their respective coinage. These obstacles impede somewhat at present the action of the comprehensive laws which will one day be allowed to control this matter perfectly. Nature herself has made the first grand provision for the self-regulation of the money of the world, by making pure gold and silver of exactly the same quality all over the wide earth. No matter where it is mined, or when, gold is gold and silver is silver. The gold mined to-day in California differs in no essential respect from the gold used by Solomon in the construction of the Temple. So that, if the commercial nations would come to a common agreement as to the amount of alloy they will put into their coins, and then bring these coins, as might easily be done, into decimal or other easy numerical relations with each other, it would be a matter of indifference to every nation whether the coins circulating therein were exclusively national coins or not. Foreign coins, to the extent to which commerce would naturally bring them there, would have just the same circulation and credit as their own: there would not be, as now, the trouble and expense of melting up and recoinage; the balances of trade could be paid indifferently in any coinage, and, as we shall soon see, every nation would secure without friction or legal enactment its due proportion of the money of the world. We are not now so far removed from this state of things as might at first sight be supposed.

Two plans of a universal coinage for commerce are now awaiting the sanction of the world. The first, or French plan, was developed at an international monetary conference held in Paris during the great Exposition of 1867. This plan proposes, (1) a single standard exclusively of gold; (2) coins of equal weight and diameter; (3) of equal quality nine tenths fine; (4) the weight of the five-franc gold piece, 1612.9 milligrams, to be the universal unit; (5) the multiples of this unit to be decimal, or at least divisible by 5; (6) the coins of each nation to bear the names and emblems preferred by each, but to be legal tender in all. France, Belgium, Switzerland, Italy, and Greece, numbering in all 72,000,000 souls, have now a common money based on the French franc. Austria, too, numbering 40,000,000 of people, has agreed to mint a ten-florin piece equivalent in weight and fineness to the new 25 franc piece, which, in accordance with the recommendation of the conference, France has promised to issue, in order to facilitate the unification of the money of Great Britain and the United States with that of the European continent. This piece will only differ four cents in value from the English sovereign, and 17½ cents from our half eagle. It is claimed that no other plan will require so few changes and so little expense to unify the money of the world. While England would have to recoin its gold and change its standard from the present $\frac{11}{12}$ to $\frac{9}{10}$ fine, and the United States recoin and reduce the weight of its coins, it is claimed that the nations already using the French unit have $1,400,000,000 of coined gold, while England has less than $500,000,000, and the United States not over $300,000,000.[1]

The second, or American plan, has been developed by Mr. E. B. Elliott of the U. S. Treasury Department. To avoid the ugly fraction in the metrical weight of the French unit and its multiples, Mr. Elliott proposes that all the coins of his international system shall bear *simple* relations to the gramme. The new union-crown (Vereins-Krone) of Germany contains just *ten* grammes of fine gold, and the union half-crown *five* grammes. These, like the gold coins of France and the United States, are $\frac{9}{10}$ fine. Now, these crowns and half-crowns, our gold dollar, the gold franc of France and the other countries using that unit, and the gold pound of Great Britain, can

[1] Report of S. B. Ruggles to the Department of State. Mr. Ruggles was a delegate to, and evidently a leading mind in, the conference.

be very easily brought into metrical harmony with each other. By reducing the weight of fine gold in our dollar from 1.5046+ grammes to 1.5 grammes, by increasing the fine gold in the pound sterling from 7.3223+ to 7.5 grammes, and by increasing the weight of the Napoleon (20 francs) from 5.8064+ to 6 grammes fine gold, their weights, both fine and standard, would all be strictly metrical, and bear simple relations to each other, as well as to the crown and half-crown. The following equivalents would obtain, namely, 3 crowns = 20 dollars = 100 francs = 4 pounds. Each of these would weigh 30 grammes fine gold, or 33⅓ grammes standard gold. Also, 1 metrical dollar = 50 metrical pence = 5 metrical francs. These pieces would weigh 1½ grammes fine, or 1⅔ grammes standard, each. Also, 5 dollars = 1 pound, both containing 7½ grammes fine, 8⅓ grammes standard gold.

A bill to bring the coinage of the United States into harmony with this metrical and international system of Mr. Elliott, was reported to the House of Representatives in July, 1868, and is still pending in that body. It is understood that the parliament of Great Britain is more favorable to this system than to that of the Paris conference. If either system prevail, it will be a triumph of the metrical system, and so far, a triumph of France.

Now, although the Bank of England circulates a paper money partly based on government credit, and though the United States has under the national banking law a similar paper money; yet every pound or dollar of this paper money is or is to be redeemable in gold and silver; and, as more than half the aggregate circulation of Great Britain is in metallic money, and as a similar proportion is perhaps likely to prevail in the United States, the maintenance of a paper money based on credit for the home circulation alone may or may not be sound financial policy; but it is evident that it cannot, under these circumstances, substantially interfere with the self-regulation of the metallic money of the world. Nevertheless, that we may see with distinctness the scope and efficiency of the magnificent natural law which distributes the precious metals over the earth in accordance with the business-wants of each nation, let us suppose that there were no paper money; that all the nations minted their metals with a common proportion of alloy; and that the real relative value of the two were ascertained by law in the countries where both are legal tender, and were well understood also in the other countries. In this case there would be no motive to debase any part of the coinage to prevent its exportation, and all the money of all the nations would be value-money purely. Now then, money is the medium of exchange, and is wanted where the exchanges are, and not elsewhere, and goes of necessity under freedom whither it is relatively most wanted, that is to say, whither the most can be obtained for it in exchange. If the country be gold-bearing, and its people at the same time be enterprising in the production of all sorts of services for exchange among themselves, they will retain enough of their own gold to mediate their own exchanges, for the simple reason that they want it, and have services to offer in exchange for it; and if they have been allowed in freedom to develop their own peculiar advantages, no foreign nation can outbid them in the offers they are able to make for a sufficient quantity of this gold. If foreigners draw away the gold from them, it shows that the home people have less industry and less skill to produce those things which the gold-producers want. The home people have the advantage in one respect. They are on the spot. There is less expense to them than to foreigners in transporting the services offered in exchange for the gold, and also the gold received in return. If, with this advantage, foreigners can still outbid them in offers for the gold, it shows that they need it most and deserve it most, since they have had the industry and the skill to produce that which is preferred by the miners to the home services offered, and have also overcome an additional obstacle. The gold producer, like every other producer, has the right to get the most he can for his service. Whoever can offer him that most has the best right to the gold. Therefore the gold goes in the first instance into their hands, whether natives or foreigners, who offer the most for it in exchange. If the people of the gold-bearing country have equal natural advantages with others to produce those things which are wanted in exchange for their gold by those who practically work the mines, and then fail to get the gold they need, the blame lies nowhere except on their lack of industry and skill. Let not such people think to find any shelter behind natural laws. Natural laws are justly and eternally against them. If, however, they are naturally placed at a disadvantage in respect to those specific products in demand by the first owners of the gold, they are then brought into the same category with non-gold-bearing countries. They will then get their gold at second hand, and if they deserve it, will be just as sure to get it as if they retained it in the first instance. Every nation has natural advantages in some sorts of products. Just so soon as these are properly developed, it has some things to offer to the world at a better rate than anybody else can offer them. Thither, and to buy those things, will gold flow, if not directly from the gold-producing lands, then indirectly but inevitably, from those lands where the gold at present is. Under our supposition, it makes no difference where the gold came from, or what nation minted it, it is drawn by a natural force not to be resisted to that people, which, by offering services in general demand, requires gold to mediate the exchange of those services. Thus, by a law as unerring as gravitation, the precious metals make the circuit of the earth, abiding certainly in large masses within all the commercial nations, because there is where they are constantly wanted and cannot be spared, but passing off also perpetually in smaller masses from all the great centres of business towards those points where their purchasing-power for the time being is greater than at home. The one only impulse that can stir the precious metals from their usual haunts, is the belief that elsewhere they are worth more in exchanges; and hence, just as soon as the demand for a currency is fairly met in any country by the presence of gold and silver, coin ceases to flow thither as a permanent thing, but rather ebbs and flows in obedience to the ever-shifting exigencies of trade. The nation that does a large business will require a large stock of coin, will be able to pay for it, and will inevitably secure it; a nation with fewer exchanges to make will less need the instrument with which exchanges are made, will buy and keep a less quantity; and if, in the chances of trade, more comes than is needed, it flows off at once to the places where the demand for it is stronger; and thus the proportionate amount due to the commercial interests of every nation goes thither under a natural law, and abides there under a natural law. Hence the general purchasing-power of gold and silver tends steadily to an equality the world over. If it be appreciably higher in one nation than in the others, the metals are drawn toward that nation by an irresistible attraction till the equilibrium is restored. Add to this, that there is at all times a vast reservoir of plate from which any sudden or steady demand for currency can easily be supplied, and into which any fortuitous or steady superfluity can as readily be drained, and the reasons are apparent why gold and silver currencies are self-regulating in value and amount. If, on the other hand, a currency is to be of paper, independent of gold and silver, there is no self-regulation about it: we pass at once from the region of natural laws into the region of statute and enactment; somebody must take upon themselves to decide how much of this paper there shall be, — a power which could not be lodged in more dangerous hands than in those which thought themselves competent to exercise it.

(3.) *Because they are conveniently portable, divis-*

ible, and impressible. Our proposition is, that gold and silver constitute the best money; and in proof of this we have already demonstrated the steadiness of their value, and their self-regulating power; incidental to these great advantages are the material qualities of these metals, by which they are admirably fitted to be the money of the nations. Their weight is little relatively to their value. A thousand dollars in gold are not indeed carried so easily as a bill of exchange or a bank-note; and expedients are easily adopted, and always have been used, by which the transfer in place of large masses of coin is for the most part obviated; and our proposition does not deprecate at all the use of the economizing expedients of commerce; but for the money of the people, for the currency that passes from hand to hand in ordinary exchanges, we maintain that gold and silver are sufficiently portable. One troy pound of English sovereigns, which one can put in a glove-finger and carry in his vest-pocket, almost without knowing it, is worth about $230; and the experience of those countries, like France and Germany at present, where the money is mostly metallic, has not pronounced it onerous on account of its weight. At any rate, it is better to accept all the other immense advantages of gold and silver money, together with a little inconvenience as to weight, if one chooses to insist on that, than to adopt substitutes every way inferior as money, except that they are lighter in our purses.

Moreover, gold and silver differ from jewels, and most other precious things, in that masses of them are divisible, without any loss of value, into pieces of any required size. The aggregate of pieces is worth as much as the mass, and the mass as much as the pieces. For currency purposes this is a great advantage. For its utmost convenience, business requires a considerable variety of coins, and if any of these kinds be minted in quantity in excess of the demand, nothing more is required than to remint them in other denominations, and their whole value is saved to the currency in the most convenient form. It is this quality which enables coins to flow into plate whenever the metal in them becomes more valuable in the form of plate, and plate again to flow back into coins whenever the metal in it is more in demand as coin.

Lastly, these metals are capable of receiving and retaining any stamp which government chooses to impress upon them. A certain proportion of alloy, say $\frac{1}{10}$, hardens them to such a degree that they exhibit with sharp distinctness the cut of the die, and permanently retain its impress. This quality of the metals, when they are skilfully coined by the improved machinery of modern times, makes the pieces of money objects of beauty, and practically indestructible also, since the perfect circular form, the device covering the whole piece, the milled and fluted edges, make clipping without detection impossible, while the hardness of the pieces makes the annual loss of weight by abrasion scarcely appreciable. The Director of the United States Mint, in his Report for 1862, gives the results of some careful and comprehensive experiments made at the mint to ascertain the yearly loss of coins by the ordinary wear and tear of circulation. These results are exceedingly interesting and important, and throw to the winds the haphazard conjectures of a host of writers on either side of the Atlantic. On our silver coins, taken promiscuously, the average annual loss from abrasion was ascertained to be one part in 630; while the gold coins were tested separately, with this satisfactory conclusion, that the half-eagle averages a loss per annum of one part in 3550, the double-eagle one in 9000; and a cautious estimate as to the proportions of the various sizes of coin actually in circulation in the United States, made of the two metals, leads consequently to the conviction that the average yearly waste by wear on all the coins does not exceed one part in 2400. The cost, therefore, of maintaining a metallic circulation is by no means so great as it has been usually represented. An instrument in constant use that requires only $\frac{1}{2400}$ of its value for its yearly repair, and performs exceeding well the most delicate and important functions, is a cheap and durable instrument.

From these three main reasons, we conclude that gold and silver are the best money.

4. *An inferior money, so long as it circulates at all, invariably drives a superior money out of the circulation.*

This is a fundamental law of finance, and has been illustrated over and over again in every age and nation. It is as solid as the substance of truth can make it, though it looks at first sight like a paradox. We naturally think that what is excellent tends rather to displace what is inferior, but with money the exact reverse is the law, and the perfect coin of full weight, instead of driving out the light and the debased pieces, is always itself driven out of the circulation by them. The reason is obvious from the nature of money. Money is merely an instrument of exchange, and nobody wants it except to buy with, and so long as the government and the community treat light coin and full coin as of equal value, receiving them indifferently in payment of debts and of taxes, it is clear that nobody will give in payment of debts and of taxes that which is really worth more so long as that which is really worth less will go just as far. The inferior pieces will abide in a market where they will fetch just as much as the superior pieces, while the superior pieces will take on a form or migrate to a place in which some advantage can be gained from their superiority. Thrown into the crucible, or exported in commerce, this superiority immediately manifests itself; and therefore into the crucible or into the channels of foreign trade it might be confidently predicted beforehand that such money would be thrown, and all experience testifies with one voice that exactly those are the destinations of such money. Mr. Macaulay, in the twenty-first chapter of his history, mentions that Aristophanes, the Greek comic poet, in the fifth century before Christ, was the first writer who has noticed the fact that where good money and bad money are thrown in together the bad money drives out the good. The verses of the poet allude to the tendency as well known, and refer it to the naturally depraved taste of his fellow-citizens, like that which led them to entrust state affairs to such men as Cleon, whom he was satirizing; but, in truth, as we have seen, the tendency results from the common sense of men, which revolts at the idea of using a dearer instrument when a cheaper one will answer just the same purpose.

Out of a crowd of good illustrations of this law, I shall first select two which occurred in purely metallic currencies. The Dutch city of Amsterdam became in the seventeenth century a centre of trade for all Europe. The mercantile honor and solid financial ability of its merchants was proverbial all over the world; and yet it was noticed, about the year 1609, that bills of exchange on Amsterdam were always below par in other countries. The merchants had never failed to meet all the paper drawn on them with the utmost promptness, and the discount on this paper in other markets was a wonder to everybody. On search, however, it was found that the cause of all this was in the currency of the city. The extensive trade of Amsterdam brought into it large quantities of clipt and worn foreign coin, which circulated in the currency of the city, and reduced its value about nine per cent. below that of good money fresh from the mint. It was noticed, that the good money of full weight which the mint of Amsterdam poured into the circulation by wagon-loads, did not stay in the circulation; that very few of such pieces were told out in the daily exchanges; it was ascertained that they were melted up, or carried away to other countries, in either of which cases their value corresponded to the value due to their weight and fineness, while at home in the currency their value only corresponded to the average value of the depreciated coins which constituted the bulk of the circulation. Bills of exchange, consequently, drawn on Amsterdam were liable to be paid in this depreciated coin, and the exchange was against the city even more than the coin was depreciated; because, the currency in such an uncertain state was naturally valued abroad even below what it was really worth. To meet this state of things, and bring up its exchanges to par, the city of Amsterdam, in 1609, established its celebrated bank. The bank received the clipt and worn coin which was circulating in the city, at its true value according to present weight and fineness, and after deducting a small charge for expense of recoining, and another small charge for management, gave a credit on its books for the remainder. This credit was called bank-money; it represented, guilder for guilder, money actually in deposit, and money too exactly according to the standard of the mint. The city ordered that all bills drawn on Amsterdam of more than six hundred guilders' value, should be paid in bank-money; thus every considerable merchant was obliged to open an account with the bank, and make his deposit. This instantly took away all uncertainty from bills of exchange drawn on Amsterdam. They went up to par at once in every market in Europe. This was the basis of the simple and beneficent operations of the Bank of Amsterdam, an institution which enjoyed unlimited credit in the commercial world for nearly two hundred years. The convenience of this bank-money; its unvarying character; its security from fire, robbery, and other accidents; the fact that the city was bound for it; and the demand for it occasioned by the fact that every merchant must have some of it, that is, must keep an account with the bank, in order to pay his foreign bills of exchange, gave the certificate of deposit, or the bank-money, a constant premium of about five per cent. over the good coin of full weight which came into circulation without difficulty as soon as the poorer coins were drawn into the bank for recoinage.

At the close of the same century, a similar series of events occurred on a much larger scale in England.[1] The old silver coinage of England was by a rude process introduced into that country by artists from Florence as early as the thirteenth century. The pieces were shaped and stamped by the hammer. They contained some a little less and some a little more than the due amount of silver; few of them were perfectly circular; the edges were neither milled nor fluted; the image of the sovereign occupied the centre of the pieces, and the superscription ran around the edge, but not so near it as that the letters were necessarily impaired by a little clipping. Consequently it was easy to pare off a pennyworth or two of silver from the crowns, half-crowns, and shillings, and then pass them along. It became a profitable branch of industry. It was in vain that Elizabeth enacted that the clipper should be henceforth liable to the penalties of high treason. About the time of the Restoration, that is, about 1660, it was noticed that a large proportion of the silver coin of the realm had undergone some degree of mutilation. At that time a new process of coinage was brought in. A mill worked by horses fabricated the new coins on better principles. They were exactly round, and the edges were inscribed with a legend, and they

[1] Macaulay's History, Chap. 21.

were all of just and equal weight. They were thrown out into the circulation to pass current with the hammered money, and it seems to have been expected that they would soon come to displace it. But they did not. Both were received at first without distinction by the individual traders and by the public tax-gatherers. But it was not long before the milled money was noticed to be scarce. One hardly saw a piece of it in a fortnight. The horses at the mint were all the time tugging away, and the bags of fresh money were carried continually from London Tower to London town, but the new money nevertheless became scarcer every day. In the payments made at the Treasury not one piece in two hundred was milled silver, and a merchant complained that, being paid a debt of thirty-five pounds, he only got one half-crown of good money. Indeed, the money was getting perpetually worse. False coiners multiplied, and clippers abounded more and more. The penalties of an extreme law were utterly powerless to restrain the mutilation of the coins; until, at length, public opinion decidedly turned against the promiscuous hanging of clippers; officers were reluctant to arrest, and juries reluctant to convict, and the people sympathized with the sufferers as only guilty of a moderate fault. Thus things went on till 1695. The lighter the old coins became, the scarcer became the new ones; for who would pay two ounces of silver when one ounce was legal tender? The new money was melted, was exported, was hoarded, but circulate it would not. At length the lightest pieces began to be refused by some people, and other people demanded that their silver should be paid to them by weight and not by tale, and there was wrangling over every counter, and a dispute at every settlement, and the coin was really so diverse in its value that there was no longer any measure of value in the kingdom; business was in utmost confusion, society was by the ears, poor people were unmercifully fleeced, and shrewd ones grew enormously rich; and the Jacobites secretly exulted in the hope of being able to avail themselves of the prevailing discontent to overthrow the scarcely established revolutionary government of William and Mary; when, by the joint counsels of two such philosophers as Locke and Newton, and two such statesmen as Somers and Montague, the government took the bold resolution of recoining all the silver of the kingdom. An early day was fixed by Parliament, after which no clipped money could pass except in payments to government, and a later day after which it could not pass at all. It was wisely determined that the loss on the clipped money should be borne by the whole public, and not by the present holders of it; and it was estimated that £1,200,000 would be required to make up the currency to the old standard of weight and fineness; and this sum the Bank of England, just established, was willing to advance on the security of some new and good tax; and the window-tax was passed to raise the money; the old coins were rapidly drawn in, melted up, and recoined, and thereafter there was no difficulty in keeping the circulation full of milled pieces of full weight.

In mixed currencies, the financial law we are now treating has a similar, but if possible a more disastrous operation. If the paper in circulation be not nominally redeemable in gold and silver, then as soon as it depreciates below the value of gold and silver, as such paper has never yet failed to depreciate in a short time, it drives the metals completely out of the circulation, and keeps them out just so long as itself circulates, or until the quantity of such paper is so reduced and its character so improved that it rises again to a par value with the metals, in which case, though it has never to my knowledge actually occurred, the metals would come back into the currency alongside of the paper. The suddenness and the thoroughness with which the gold and silver will abandon a currency of which a depreciated, irredeemable paper forms a part, was illustrated on a large scale in this country in 1862. A gigantic civil war had been in progress in the nation for a year; difficulties and disasters had thickened around the path of the government; its financial embarrassments were of the most formidable kind; and yet, until April of that year, 1862, the paper money of the loyal States, which consisted of about $140,000,000 of bills of the various State banks, had not much depreciated as compared with coin. In January, indeed, when the national government had added to this mass of paper about $30,000,000 of demand-notes gold was at a premium of five per cent.; but as soon as the law authorizing the issue of national legal-tender notes was passed, the government drew in the demand-notes, and for a little interval the paper currency was reduced to about $140,000,000, and on the first day of April, when the legal-tenders were ready for circulation but not yet issued, the coin bore a premium of about one per cent. It had not yet in any sense abandoned the circulation. The State banks had all suspended specie payments on the last day of the preceding year, but had not yet much expanded their usual circulation. And now it is to be noticed that the steady depreciation of the paper currency of the country, both state and national, commenced at the very time when the national legal-tender notes were thrown into the circulation. All the paper was now irredeemable, and its volume was now expanded, and the depreciation began; it was liable to still further expansion, both from the absence of restraint on the circulation of the State banks and from the urgent necessities of government leading to the issue of more legal-tenders, and the depreciation continued. In May gold bore three per cent., June nine per cent., July fifteen per cent., September twenty-one per cent., October twenty-nine per cent., and December thirty-two per cent. Step by step, as the volume of the currency increased, did its value decrease as compared with gold; and what is more to the present purpose, no sooner did the depreciation become sensible, than the scarcity of coin became sensible also, and in a very few weeks' time the currency was swept utterly bare of metallic money. The gold went first, and then the silver; and a little later even the copper cents followed the example; and the government was obliged to authorize the use of its postage and revenue stamps for small change; and, until it was prohibited by law, cities, corporations, and individuals issued shinplasters and metal tokens of various kinds to take the place of the small coins. This present writing is at the autumnal equinox of 1871, but with the exception of a few of the cents, the coins have not yet returned to the circulation, for the sufficient reason that the paper-money is still depreciated as compared with them. The war is over, peace has returned, business is reviving, and a career of unprecedented prosperity is opening up before the country, but the coins have not come back, and, under the commonest principles of human nature, cannot come back, until the paper dollar of the country is equal in purchasing-power to the gold dollar, and is redeemable in that. Since April 1st, 1862, the paper money has varied from less than one to sixty-five per cent. below par, and is to-day thirteen per cent. below par.

So long as the paper money of a country is nominally redeemable in gold and silver, the operation of the law we have in hand is somewhat peculiar. In times of ordinary confidence and prosperity the paper and the coin circulate indifferently together, and an undue increase of the paper beyond the just demands of business does not indicate itself in a premium on the coin, but each part of the whole currency suffers a diminution in value, which is of course indicated in a general rise of prices. There is nothing anomalous in this, for increase of supply, other things as before, always lowers the value of anything; and the direct interest of the parties who furnish the paper leads them to increase their circulation as much as they fairly, and sometimes as much as they unfairly, can. But a market in which prices are high and gold is still circulating is a good market to sell in, and increased importations never fail to accompany a rise of prices caused by the depreciation of a mixed currency. In the home market the paper is still as good as gold, but to pay the balances in a foreign trade it is good for nothing. The natural superiority of the gold to paper appears as soon as a payment is to be made abroad. In obedience to this impulse gold naturally and inevitably goes abroad; and it has repeatedly gone abroad under these circumstances from the United States to such an extent that the parties who furnished the paper, that is to say, the banks, could no longer redeem their paper in coin, but were obliged to suspend specie payments, which is a euphonious circumlocution to express going into temporary or permanent bankruptcy. In this case also, though less directly, the inferior money pushes the superior out of circulation. I have no hesitation in calling the paper the inferior money, both for other potent reasons soon to be specified, and because at any rate it is powerless in international exchanges. There is believed to be nothing in the monetary history of the United States, as there is certainly nothing in the known principles of human nature, which does not abundantly confirm as a universal truth the proposition in hand, namely, that worse and better money being in the currency together, the worse will expel the better sooner or later; sometimes into hoards, sometimes into the melting-pot, and sometimes out of the country.

5. *A paper money is only tolerable when it is actually and instantly convertible on demand into gold and silver.*

I feel no hesitation in using the term paper-money

although many high authorities will not concede that any form of paper can be money at all. They make a distinction between currency and money. The discussions in this chapter thus far have been purposely made so general as that the principles will apply to a money of paper as well as to a money of coin. *Any form of value that circulates generally among all classes of people as a medium in their exchanges* may be allowed to be called money. The essential characteristic of money is its possession of a *generalized* purchasing power. For a reason soon to be given, gold and silver in any form have a more general purchasing power throughout the world than any form of paper can have; and yet the paper that the masses of the people accept as a medium in any country, may be regarded as money in that country. Checks, drafts, bills of exchange, and so on, are not money under the definition. This is a distinction recognized in common language, and science has no motive to disturb it. The signification of the term money merely marks the fact of a general circulation, and determines nothing in respect to the nature or usefulness of a particular medium. The word money is derived from the Latin *moneta*, the mint or place where money was coined. The mint of Rome was a building on the Capitoline, and attached to the temple of Juno Moneta, as the ærarium was to the temple of Saturn. The epithet of the goddess passed over first to the mint, and then to that which was coined there.

But while nothing seems to me to be gained by refusing the courtesy of the term money to any form of value which a people choose to employ as a medium, there is a distinction of the utmost importance between coin money and paper money. Coin money is the definite thing, which paper money promises to pay to bearer. What is a dollar? A dollar is $25\frac{4}{5}$ grains of a metal compound, of which nine parts are pure gold and one part is a hardening alloy. It is a definite *quantity* of a definite thing. Government is competent, if it pleases, to alter the quantity of gold that shall constitute a dollar; but it is not practically competent to make a dollar out of anything else than gold. Our government gave up long ago the attempt to make a dollar even out of silver. After every change in the mint laws, a dollar is, and will remain, a definite quantity of gold alloyed. What is a dollar bill? It is a promise of the issuer to pay to bearer this definite quantity of alloyed gold. There is no mystery here. A dollar is a tangible commodity. A dollar bill is a promise to give this commodity to bearer. The subject of Credit will be treated at length in the chapter following the next; but it will be plain to every reader, without a technical definition, that a promise received involves the element of credit. In an exchange proper, two services are reciprocally rendered by two persons, and the transaction is then and there terminated; but in simple credit, one service is rendered, and the return service is delayed, and usually some paper evidence that such service is due springs up in connection with the transaction. It is an exchange begun, but not yet consummated, and no matter through how many hands the paper evidence may pass, it is nothing but an obligation resting on somebody to pay to somebody the return for a service which has been actually rendered. Now the grand distinction, and one of the utmost importance, between gold and silver money and paper money is, that paper money always has in it the element of credit, while the other has in it no element of credit at all. A gold eagle is not a sign of anything, it is not the representative of anything; it stands in its own right, just as a bushel of wheat does; it is true that its only use as money is to purchase other things, but its purchasing-power is within a trifle as great whether it be in the form of money or bullion; and therefore a service that is paid for in specie closes up the transaction completely, the exchange is consummated, there is no element of delay, of promise, of credit in such an exchange. It is just as when the miller renders a bushel of corn to his neighbor, and that neighbor renders him a day's labor in return. In both cases, there is an end. But paper money is credit-money. It may be more convenient than coin money; its value, that is to say, its purchasing-power, may be equal to that of coin money; it may even in some circumstances bear a premium over coin money; but all this does not alter the fact that there is in it an unlucky element, an unstable element, an element which, as men are, is liable to some suspicion, the element, namely, of a present promise to be fulfilled in future. Paper money walks by faith, and not by sight. It is the sign, and not the thing signified. It is the representative of something, and not that something itself. It is a promise to pay, and not the pay itself. It is a credit, and not a quittance. And what makes this very certain is, that all paper money knows it to be true about itself. It bears this truth stamped on its very face. It does not even profess to stand on its own bottom, but leans consciously and conspicuously on some solid support. The French assignats promised to redeem themselves in land; the continental bills of the old American Congress were all to be paid in Spanish milled dollars; the bills of the Bank of England profess to be and are, redeemable in gold and silver; the present irredeemable legal-tender notes of the United States and the new national bank bills, are all in terms promises to pay to bearer so many legal dollars of the United States, that is, so many times $25\frac{4}{5}$ grains of gold standard fine. These promises have been long dishonored.

Since, then, the various forms of paper money even the best of them, are mere promises to pay on demand, it must be conceded that they are credit-money; and the question is narrowed down to this, whether the functions of money can be well performed by the evidences of an obligation to pay for services already received. It is not denied that such evidences frequently have value, that their value is sometimes equal and sometimes superior to an equivalent sum in gold; the question is whether in their nature they can constitute a good money. In resolving this question, it must be noticed, that the fact of indebtedness is not of itself an evidence of an ability to pay: individuals, corporations, and governments have often become bankrupt through the disproportion of indebtedness to ability. It must be noticed, also, that, in the light of human nature and experience, men in all capacities are more or less willing to accept the services of others without rendering the equivalent return, even when their obligation to render it be certified on paper; also that the willingness of people to accept, in return for actual services rendered, mere promises to pay in future, by whomsoever issued, is quite different at different times — in times of confidence and prosperity they may be readily accepted, in times of disaster and peril all men prefer payment to promise. The functions of money are two: to serve as a medium of exchange, and to serve as a measure of value. To fulfil the first office well, money should be a commodity at all times acceptable to all men in return for services rendered; to perform the second function well, money should be as uniform as possible in quality, and vary in quantity according to the shifting demands of exchange, and not otherwise; in short, vary in quantity just as a good metallic currency does vary under natural laws alone. But credit-money is unfitted by its very nature to do well these two things; first, because it never has been, and in the nature of things never can be, acceptable to all men at all times in exchange for services even within the country itself, and in international exchanges it is not acceptable at all; and second, because, as has been already shown, a steady measure of value necessitates a steady value of the money, and the value of credit must certainly be as variable as the character of the issuers for integrity and solvency. Add to this, that the value of credit-money, like the value of everything else, depends in part on the supply, and the supply will vary with the varying disposition of the people to accept it, and thus the measure of value will be varied. It is in vain to talk, as too many do in this connection, of the self-interest of the issuers, and of their honor, and so on; self-interest should keep men from becoming bankrupts, yet men do become bankrupt; honor forbids indeed the escaping from a debt, yet debts are escaped from. On principles merely, it would be as certain beforehand as any such truth can be, that credit-money, from the nature of credit, could not properly perform the two delicate and important functions of money.

We see, then, precisely, the nature of paper money. It is made up of promises made by somebody to pay to somebody else a definite weight of coined metal. All civilized countries now make a certain weight of gold or silver bullion their acknowledged standard of value; and, accordingly, paper money can only be based upon specie, since specie is the only thing that can be meant, when the promise is to pay pounds, dollars, gulden, francs. Specie is indeed a commodity, like other commodities, but then it is the only commodity that is the accepted medium of exchange in civilized countries; and therefore, all attempts to base a paper money upon land, wheat, cotton, mercantile bills, or any other valuable thing, involve a direct contradiction in terms. Our proposition is, that paper money is only tolerable when it is instantly convertible into coin; which is the same as to say, that a promise is only good when it is *kept*. An inconvertible paper money is only another name for a promise unfulfilled; and no intelligent person will ever wonder that unfulfilled promises to pay invariably become less valuable than that which they promise to pay. This is the simple secret of the inevitable depreciation of all inconvertible money, as soon as the amount of it passes a certain limit. Even a convertible money, if, by any expedients, the amount of it, together with the coin in circulation, become greater than the volume of coin alone would be then and there, will diminish in value, not indeed as compared with specie, but as compared with commodities, that is, general prices will rise. All the principles of this whole discussion hinge on the fundamental truth, that money is a *medium* of exchange. Because it is a *medium*, only a certain amount of it is ever needed at any time to do the healthy business of any country. This limit of quantity not being overpassed, paper promises to pay, provided they are only kept, will constitute a tolerable money. That this limit of quantity is apt to be overpassed, whenever paper money is used, whether it be inconvertible or nominally convertible; and also, that a paper money can never be successfully based on anything but gold and silver, the subjoined historical examples will abundantly confirm.

John Law was born in Edinburgh, in 1671, and died in Venice, in 1729. Son of a goldsmith, he received an excellent education, and early manifested an acute intellect and a talent for finance, but was also notorious as a gambler and debauchee. He was the first to give scientific form and color to the theory (a theory that is still working in many minds) that money represents commodities, and may be based upon their value. He published this theory in a tract, in 1705; but endeavored in vain to persuade the government of Scotland to found a bank upon his principles. He then carried his scheme to Paris, and was again repulsed; and after a residence in many cities, in which he gambled successfully, and talked finance to princes and statesmen fascinatingly, he returned to Paris in 1715, with his ill-gotten fortune, gained the ear of the Regent Duke of Orleans, presented to him a memorial containing many sound principles of monetary science combined with the fundamental vice of his system, and was allowed by him the next year to found a bank embodying to a certain extent the new idea. The idea may be well expressed in Law's own words:—"*Any goods that have the qualities necessary in money, may be made money equal to their value. Five ounces of gold is equal in value to £20, and may be made money to that value; an acre of land is equal to £20, and may be made money equal to that value, for it has all the qualities necessary in money.*" For a couple of years, or so, Law's bank surpassed all hopes. Based on specie *and on state debts*, it paid its notes promptly in coin, and these for a time even bore a premium over coin. Law had touched a spring till then but little known in France, the potent spring of Credit. But his whole thought, meditated on for years, could not be expressed through a private bank. The State should be a banker; it should collect all its revenues into a central bank, and attract the money of individuals to it as deposits; besides, the State has public property of vast value, on the strength of which paper money can be emitted and made legal tender; and thus the State, instead of borrowing, should lend to all on easy terms, and the profits thus accruing would lessen or abolish taxes. Nor was this all. The State should also be a merchant; the whole nation should form a commercial company, a body of traders, whose common treasury should be the State bank. Commerce by individuals creates great wealth; why should not the organized commerce of a State make everybody rich? The discounts of the bank, and the profits of the trade, would surely provide for the public service without taxation. These vast ideas were actually carried out. Law's bank became the Royal Bank, issuing a paper money guaranteed by the State and resting back upon the value of all national property. The money was receivable in taxes, nominally redeemable in coin, and made a legal tender. It actually bore at one time five and ten per cent. premium over gold and silver. People were anxious to exchange their coin for notes. Meanwhile a commercial company was formed in connection with the bank, to which the State ceded at first the monopoly of the commerce of Louisiana and of the Canada beaver trade for twenty-five years, and the soil of Louisiana forever; under the auspices of which NEW ORLEANS was founded, and named from the Regent, the patron of the grand system; and in succession, the monopoly of tobaccos, the rights of the Senegal Company, of the East India Company, of the China Company, and of the Barbary Company; until, having almost all the commerce of France outside of Europe in its hands, it entitled itself the COMPANY OF THE INDIES. Its shares rose from a par value of 500 francs, to 10,000 francs, more than forty times their value in specie at their first emission. To support such speculations, which completely turned the heads of all classes of the people, the amount of paper money reached at last the sum of 3,071,000,000 francs, 833,000,000 more than had been legally authorized to be emitted. The collapse of this most gigantic financial bubble of history was terrific. Before the close of 1720, the shares of the Company could be bought for a louis d'or, and the paper money became worthless.[1] Nevertheless, Law was a great man. His accounts in all these immense transactions were as clear as daylight. He believed in his system till the day of his death, and referred its failure to the caprices of a despotic government. His mind too much loved unity, and his plan gave too little scope to individual liberty. But the central vice of all was a mistake as to the nature of money. Money is a *medium*, and its amount cannot be increased beyond a certain limit without disaster. Moreover money does not represent the commodities which it helps to exchange, any more than ships represent the cargoes which they carry.

Thus Law's paper money ran its course in about four years. Again at the close of the century France tested the merits of paper money, and the principle that money may represent commodities, on a grand scale. As the great revolution went forward, and a scarcity of money was experienced, the National Assembly, in the spring of 1790, issued, under the name of "assignats," a paper money *based on the value of the lands* of the Church which had been confiscated to the State. The assignats were receivable in payment for these landed estates at any public sale of the same. The first emission, but not

[1] Martin's Decline of the Monarchy, chap. i. Macleod's Theory and Practice of Banking, chap. xi. Bancroft's United States, chap. xxiii. New Am. Cyclo. Art John Law.

the rest, bore interest. That issue was 400,000,000 francs — about one fifth the value of the confiscated lands. In September, 800,000,000 more were authorized, Talleyrand opposing and Mirabeau strongly urging these additional issues. "It is in vain," said Mirabeau, "to compare assignats, secured on the solid basis of these domains, to an ordinary paper currency possessing a forced circulation. They represent real property, the most secure of all possessions, the land on which we tread." Nevertheless, and though all assignats were legal-tender, they drooped. The government in alarm, while issuing on the one hand enormous quantities of the paper to meet the vast expenses of the Revolution, which quantities were swelled by skillful counterfeiters in the prisons and elsewhere, took strong measures on the other to prop up their market value; the use of coin was prohibited; a maximum price in assignats for everything was established by law; heavy penalties and at last death were decreed against those who refused to receive them at par; but it was all in vain. "They sink now," says Carlyle, "with an alacrity beyond parallel." In June, 1793, the assignats had fallen to 33, and in August to 16 per cent. Renewed confiscations kept the estimated value of the public domains far in advance of the par value of the assignats based upon them; but this had no tendency to prevent the depreciation of the assignats, because money is a *medium of exchange*, and its proper amount has no relation to the estimated value of any commodities at all. In February, 1796, the assignats legally issued had amounted to 45,500,000,000 francs, and had fallen to one two hundred and sixty fifth part of their nominal value, that is, to two fifths of one per centum. The government then offered to redeem them at 30 for 1 in "mandats," which entitled the bearer to take immediate possession at their estimated value, of any of the lands pledged by the assignats. According to M. Thiers, who is my authority in this paragraph, the mandats sold first at 15, then rose to 40, and in some places to 80, and soon sank again to 5 per centum. A decree of July 16, 1796 ended the matter by permitting any one to do business in any money he chose; and business, which had practically ceased under the paper money, revived again at the sight of the coin, which, of course, had been out of circulation. Thus the assignats had a course of about six years. The distress and consternation into which a country falls when its measure of value is disturbed and destroyed, as it was by the issue of the assignats, is past all powers of description. There can be no doubt that these assignats caused more suffering in the French Revolution, a hundred fold, than the prisons and the guillotine. It may be said that the government ought not to have issued them in such quantities. Perhaps it ought not. But there never has been a government yet, of the many which have issued irredeemable paper, which had the wisdom and the firmness to resist for any great length of time the temptation to emit large quantities. There is no stopping when once the issue is begun. The first batch of such paper usually banishes the coin from the currency. There is no way to entice it back except to call in and burn up the paper. Revolutionary governments are not generally in position to be able to do this. Ordinary national expedients are denied them. They cannot borrow. Therefore they have recourse to credit-money, which is really borrowing without interest, and when once the press is set at work it must work on with livelier speed, because just in the ratio of the depreciation is a greater amount required to meet the ordinary payments. This example is significant, because it shows the powerlessness of even the strongest and most unscrupulous governments to regulate the value of anything. The assignats were depreciating during the very months in which Robespierre and the Committe of Public Safety were wielding the power of life and death in France with terrific energy. They did their utmost to stop the sinking of the revolutionary paper. But value knows its own laws, and follows them, in spite of decrees and penalties.

The bills of credit issued by the Continental Congress during the American Revolution had a course and issue very similar to those of the French assignats. Unlike them, these were based simply upon the good faith of the people whom the Congress represented. Their vice was not, as in the previous instances, the supposition that money may be founded on the value of specific commodities; but their emission ignored this fundamental law of finance, namely, that the value of money arises as all other value arises, and is amenable to the same principle of supply and demand as other values; and their vice, consequently, was, that there was no natural limitation of their supply. Money is either an intermediate and equivalent merchandise, or promises to pay it; that is to say, gold or silver, or promises to pay them; and mere promises to pay them, such as the continental bills were, unaccompanied by any provision to pay them, have no natural limitation of supply. In June, 1775, $2,000,000 were emitted; in November, $3,000,000 more; the next February, $4,000,000 more; and in August, $5,000,000 more. The depreciation began before the next issue of $5,000,000, May, 1777. But the bills kept up to par for more than a year. As the emissions multiplied, the depreciation became rapid. In August, 1777, they exchanged with silver at 3 for 1; in February, 1779, at 10 for 1; and in November, 1779, the date of the last emission, at about 40 for 1. Early the next year they dropped out of circulation altogether. Thus their course was run in less than five years. The Congress pledged itself not to emit over $200,000,000 in all; but I suspect that that limit, as is usual in such cases, was considerably overpassed, either by design or fraud. Jefferson estimates that the nation realized from the $200,000,000, $36,367,720 in specie value.[1] Most of these bills were never redeemed.

The United States legal-tender notes which began to be issued in April, 1862, and of which $450,000,000 were put into circulation, are in their nature like the continental bills, and have been more or less depreciated from the first, and at times very much depreciated. It may be questioned whether the making these notes a legal tender has appreciated their value at all; so far as the demand for them to pay debts with has been thereby increased it has had such a tendency, but so far as it indicated a lack of confi-

[1] Jefferson's Works, vol. ix., page 259.

dence on the part of the government in the validity of its own promises the tendency has been the reverse. The faith of the people in their money is very properly more sensitive and more easily shaken than their faith in anything else; and this is one of several weighty reasons why the element of credit should not enter into the money at all. Credit is good in its place, but in the people's current money it is out of place. Hence these notes, notwithstanding their legal-tender character, have been much more depreciated than any form of the national bonds. I cannot think that good financiering would have found it necessary to issue such paper; and I am quite sure that making it legal-tender has not on the whole enhanced its value. In the Eastern and Middle States, the legal-tenders had no more acceptance at first than the bills of their State banks, which were equally irredeemable.

Between the years 1782 and 1865, there circulated in the United States a paper money consisting of bills issued by banks established under the authority of the individual States. These bills were nominally convertible into coin at the will of the holders. Some of the States required their banks to keep a percentage of specie on hand for the redemption of their bills; but most of them required only a deposit of some kind of securities with an officer of the State, on the strength of which securities the banks were allowed to issue an equivalent value in bills; and some of the States did not even require so much as this. The fallacy of founding a paper money upon public securities, will be fully exposed in the following paragraphs; it is here only necessary to observe that our proposition, if correct, condemns the money of these State banks. Some of it was better than the rest, but none of it deserved the praise of being a satisfactory money. (1.) It was liable to great and sudden contractions and expansions in volume. For instance, the volume in 1858 was $59,570,474 less than in 1857; and in 1863 $54,885,139 more than in 1862. (2.) The ratio of paper to the specie reserved to redeem it was a high ratio. The average for the whole country in January, 1863, was 4 to 1; in Rhode Island more than 12 to 1; and in Vermont more than 28 to 1.[1] Such a paper can only be called redeemable by stretch of courtesy. (3.) As a matter of fact, so soon as there began to be a financial pressure, especially whenever the exigencies of commerce withdrew gold for foreign trade from reserves already so small, the banks were compelled to confess, what everybody knew before, that they were unable to redeem their promises. Four or five times, during the continuance of the system, panics attacked the paper money, and the banks suspended specie payments. In these times of stress some of the banks did better than others; the Bank of the State of Indiana, for example, under the management of the Hon. Hugh McCulloch and others, maintained specie payments in the trying periods of 1857 and 1861.[2] (4.) The instability of the general system tended towards a reckless way of doing business, and led on to frequent bankruptcies, which became a just reproach to us in foreign countries. The banks contributed powerfully

1 Finance Report, 1863.
2 Letter of Mr. McCulloch, August 17, 1867.

in times of quiet by a system of generous loaning, on which their profits depended, to induce a spirit of speculation and a willingness to contract debts, and experienced when the reaction came, how much easier it is to loan paper promises than to fulfill them. Their inability to continue in troublous times the free loans which helped to bring them on, and their repeated failures to make good the obligation to redeem their own notes, caused incalculable losses of property. There can be no hesitation in affirming that the expense of maintaining a gold and silver money for all the wants of the whole country, might have been met many times over from the losses resulting from this bank-paper system. It is fortunate that the people concluded to abandon it.

We come now to the money of the present national banks organized under the law of February, 1863. This money is likely to be better than that last considered, because the banks issuing it are amenable to a central authority and to common regulations. They deposit with the national Comptroller of the Currency gold-bearing government bonds to an amount somewhat greater than that of the circulating notes which they receive back from him, so that the redemption of the notes may be provided for by the sale of the bonds, in case the banks do not redeem the notes. The banks are also required to hold in reserve a certain percentage of lawful money of the United States. The notes are so expensively engraved by the national government that the counterfeiting of them has proved to be very difficult. The total amount of notes authorized at present to be issued by all the banks is $354,000,000.

It might seem as if this form of money would meet our test; nevertheless, there is a vicious principle that underlies the foundation of the present system. It is just as bad in principle to base a paper money upon government debt, as upon lands, or other commodities. The evidences of government debt are usually salable in the market at some price, and so are lands, mercantile bills, and all the articles of a prices current. Perhaps the government debt is more uniformly salable than any of them; but there is no relation of a proper amount of money for any country to the amount of its national debt, any more than to the value of its lands. The absurdity of the principle is only disguised by an arbitrary limitation of it. If it is proper to base $300,000,000 of paper money on $333,333,333 of government bonds, why is it not proper to base $300,000,000 more of paper money on $333,333,333 more of the government bonds, and so on, till the amount of money shall approximate the amount of the debt? Any limit placed is purely artificial. One Congress may think that $300,000,000 of paper money is enough, another that $600,000,000 will not be too much, and the third enact a free banking law, by which all the debt may become a basis for paper money to rest on. The primary function of money, it must be repeated, is to serve as a *medium* of exchange; and the quantity of such a medium required to facilitate the exchanges in any country is impossible to be determined by law. The only safety, under our present system, is to make the amount of paper decidedly less than what is known to be the necessary amount of the whole circulating medium, and then allow coin money to fill up the deficiency in accordance with its own laws. If we could have been assured that the first $300,000,000 of this money would not be increased, and that no other paper money would be allowed, then a fair degree of confidence in it would have been reasonable; then a part of the currency would soon have become specie; and the paper might have been kept at par all the while, and we should gain something by the superior convenience of the paper, and not lose much by its inferior steadiness. But the mischief of it is, this money cannot regulate its own quantity; it is not guarded, as gold and silver are, by a natural limitation of supply; a simple vote of Congress is sufficient to increase it, as the original limit has been already overpassed by the authorization of 18 per cent. additional. After all that can be said in favor of it, it is credit-money still, and exposed to the dangers inseparable from credit-money, namely, the distrust of the people, the undue enlargement and sudden diminution of its volume, a consequent unsteadiness of value, and inconvertibility. If we are to have a national paper currency expanding and contracting under the successive tinkerings of Congress, we shall yet experience more of those evils of credit-money, from which we have suffered in the past so extensively in property and reputation, and which nothing but our exuberant and exulting strength has enabled us to outlive and to forget.

Our last example of credit-money shall be the bills of the Bank of England. This is an association of individuals incorporated under the style of the "Governor and Company of the Bank of England." The bank was a child of the English Revolution, and was incorporated by Parliament in 1694, on condition that its stockholders should loan to government, then pressed for funds, the sum of £1,200,000, on which they were promised eight per cent. as interest, and £4,000 for management, per annum. On the strength of this capital stock, which was simply so much of government debt, the bank was authorized to issue bills to an equivalent amount, but which at first could only pass from hand to hand by successive indorsements. The first charter was terminable at the pleasure of the government any time after August 1st, 1705, by giving a year's notice to the bank, and by paying the debt due to it. The bills at first were paid promptly in coin on demand; the bank became the means of increasing the credit at home and the strength abroad of the revolutionary government of William and Mary; and consequently the Whigs were the friends, and the Jacobites the foes, of the bank. The government was strengthened in a sense by its own indebtedness; for it was felt that if James II. should regain the throne, no pound of the loan would ever be paid back. "So closely," says Macaulay, "was the interest of the bank bound up with the interest of the government, that the greater the public danger the more ready was the bank to come to the rescue." As already related under the last general proposition, the silver coins of the realm were at this time much worn and clipped; the bank had received them at their nominal value; but after the recoinage began in 1696, it was obliged to redeem its bills in new coin of full weight, that is, for perhaps 7 ounces of silver received, it was now bound to pay 12.[1] Consequently its enemies made a run upon the bank by collecting its notes to a large amount and presenting them for redemption. The bank was obliged to suspend specie payments, at first partially, and then generally. In February, 1697, its notes were 24 per cent. below par. A new charter, granted just at this time, extended the term, and doubled the capital stock of the bank, one fifth of the subscriptions to which increase was receivable in bank notes. This brought up the notes to par, and made the indebtedness of government to bank £2,201,171. This second charter practically gave the monopoly of banking in England to the Bank of England, and provided that if the bank did not redeem its notes, they might be presented at the Exchequer and redeemed out of the annuity due to the bank. In 1709 the term was again extended, the capital stock again doubled, and the interest on the whole debt reduced from eight to six per cent. Each increase of the debt due from the government to the bank carried along with it the privilege to the bank of increasing by so much the issue of its notes. Here is the vicious principle in the Bank of England. *It assumes that a paper money may be properly based on a government debt.* But upon how much of that debt? A limit must be placed somewhere; and the goodness of the money will depend after all not on the debt, but upon the coin on hand to convert the money. The bills of the Bank of England have been and are a tolerable money, not so much because there is a part of the national debt behind them, as because there is gen-

[1] Macleod's Banking, vol. i., page 357.

erally a plenty of solid cash behind them. In 1716 the bank was exempted from the operation of all usury laws: why the bank only, and not other people as well, the act of Parliament does not state. In 1720, and again in 1745 when the Young Pretender made the last rally of the Jacobites, there were severe runs upon the bank; on both occasions, in order to gain time, notes were paid in shillings and sixpences. Best friends were also accommodated first, who are said to have returned the bags of money as fast as they received them. The practice of indorsing the notes became gradually disused, though the law at first did not follow the innovation. In 1759 £15 and £10 notes began to be issued. Till then there were none less than £20. The bank kept advancing various sums to government on various conditions, mostly however at three per cent., till 1782, when the debt stood £11,642,400. When England plunged into the war of the French Revolution, the bank came under the imperious will of William Pitt. His constant demands for money could not be met, and the bank at the same time give its usual accommodation to merchants. Thus the merchants were refused. The monopoly now bore its bitter fruit. Private credit wavered, and there was a run upon the bank for cash. The bank suspended specie payments in February, 1797, and did not resume them till 1821. Government and the business men of London did their best to hold up the credit of the notes during the suspension, *but they were not made a legal tender for debts.* Government received them at par for taxes, and provided that business payments in notes would be held as payments in cash if offered and accepted as such. Debtors, having tendered bank notes, which the creditor refused, had certain privileges before the law, which other debtors had not. The notes therefore had a *quasi* legalization, but not a forced circulation. The bank was also authorized at this time to issue £5, £2, and £1 notes. Cautiously issued at first, bank paper continued at par for several years after the suspension, which proves that when government possesses the monopoly of issuing paper money, and carefully limits its quantity, and both receives and pays it out at par, it may keep an inconvertible paper at par, or even by sufficiently limiting its quantity carry it above par. But this truth does not make an inconvertible paper a good money, because it does not make it a self-regulating money, and because government is not wise and firm enough to fix and maintain a proper limit. Though Parliament intended in successive acts to confirm to the Bank of England the monopoly of banking by enacting that no partnership of more than six persons should take up money on its own bills, yet the common law assured to private persons and smaller partnerships the right to do this; and private bankers multiplied after the suspension, since they were allowed to pay their notes in Bank of England notes. Thus the quantity of paper money gradually increased till in August, 1813, the Bank of England notes were at thirty per cent. discount in gold. In the following years, large numbers of country bankers failed, and their notes were reduced to one half what they had been, and Bank of England paper rose almost to par, and a partial resumption of specie payments took place in 1816. In accordance with the principles of the celebrated Bullion Report of 1810, which demon strated that the market price of gold (in paper) and the state of the foreign exchanges were the infallible indices of the value of a paper money, Parliament, in 1819, passed an act requiring full resumption of specie payments at the bank in 1823. The resumption actually took place in May, 1821. In 1829, all notes whatsoever for less than £5 were forbidden to be circulated in England. When the bank charter was renewed for the ninth time in 1833, the bills of the Bank of England were declared to be a legal tender for debts, *so long as the bank paid them on demand in legal coin;* and the same act legalized the issue of paper money by other banks (no matter how many partners) outside of a radius of sixty-five miles from London, and also legalized banks within the radius, but they could not issue paper money. From 1694 to 1711, the issues of the bank were limited by law to the amount of the debt owed to it by the nation; from 1711 to 1844 there was no limitation on the issues, only the bank was required (the suspension excepted) to pay its notes in coin on demand; but in 1844, Sir Robert Peel gave the bank through Parliament a new constitution, under which it is still managed, and which restricts its issues to £15,000,000 on the basis of securities, of which something over £11,000,000 consists of the government debt, and for all issues beyond this amount it must have pound for pound of gold and silver in its coffers. The average amount of notes in circulation is about £30,000,000, one half based on specie in reserve and one half on securities. The bank is also obliged to buy, and pay for in notes, all gold bullion and foreign coins offered to it, at the rate of £3 17*s.* 9*d.* per ounce standard fine; so that, if notes depreciate as compared with coin, they can be at once changed into coin, or bullion and coin can be changed into notes if the latter are preferred. The issue department of the bank is made quite distinct from the loaning department, which latter, receiving its notes only from the issue department, raises and lowers its rate of discount according to the state of the market, but usually keeps its rate a trifle higher than the market rate, so as to be able to act as a support to private bankers and others in case of pressure. For many years the bank has conducted its business upon the sound principle of raising its rate of discount whenever the foreign exchanges become adverse and there is a consequent call for gold for exportation, and also whenever the rate of discount in the neighboring commercial countries is a good deal higher than its own. The due proportion of the paper money to the specie in reserve is maintained through a proper regulation of the rate oi discount. The regulating act of 1844 restricted the issue department, but it did not restrict the loaning department. Gold can be drawn from the bank not simply by the presentation of notes, but also by the checks of depositors, that is, by those who have sold bills of exchange to the bank. Hence the convertibility of the notes can be kept up only by careful regulation of the rate of discount. Thrice since 1844 the government has authorized the bank to violate its charter, and to issue more notes than that allows on securities temporarily; in 1847, in 1857, and again in 1866. The propriety of this restriction has been, and is still, vehêmently debated in England; and it is an open question also whether England is any richer for the use of Bank of England bills. It shows that there is something factitious and unnatural about paper money, when so rigid a system of restraint is considered needful to prevent disastrous fluctuations in volume and value.

In my judgment, the most economical, and, taking all things into consideration, every way the best money, is the gold and silver which God has evidently designed for that purpose. This position does not exclude the freest use of those convenient economizing commercial expedients, such as bills of exchange, drafts, checks, money-orders through the post-office, and so on, which are sufficient to prevent for the most part all burdensome transfers of coin. The public has not yet reflected sufficiently on the peculiar functions of money, nor discriminated as it should the proper sphere of credit from the proper sphere of currency. Let the currency stand securely in its own right as value-money, and then the various forms of paper credit will safely come in to remove all the inconveniences and secure all the advantages of a perfectly sound, and everywhere acceptable, and a naturally self-regulating money.

6. *Government ought to leave freely to the parties concerned the rate of interest to be paid on money loaned.*

The law of Moses forbade to the Israelites the taking from one another any interest on money loaned, but at the same time it allowed them to take such interest freely of strangers; the permission in the one case going to show that there is nothing in the taking of interest in itself unjust or sinful, and the prohibition in the other being readily explainable from the general purpose of the municipal regulations of Moses, which was to found an agricultural and not a trading commonwealth, in which every family was to possess land that could not be permanently alienated or sold, in which it was a great object to maintain the personal independence and equality of these families, in which the law for the recovery of debts was very summary and effective, lessening the risk of losing the principal, and which was to be and was sedulously separated in its usages from the surrounding nations. It has been well understood for a long time that the municipal code of Moses was local and peculiar, not necessarily applicable at all to the circumstances of other States, and in no sense binding on the conscience of legislators; and yet there doubtless sprung from the prohibition referred to a prejudice against interest, and this prejudice was perhaps deepened in the Middle Ages and onwards by the conduct of the Jews themselves, who, in addition to their sin of persistently growing rich in spite of the endless disabilities laid on them by the people of Europe, always demanded, in accordance with the permission of their great lawgiver, a per cent. of interest from those strangers to whom they became money-lenders. The Jews were everywhere hated, and consequently the usury which they practised was hated also. The fundamental absurdity of forbidding in trading communities the taking of interest on sums loaned to a borrower which he was at liberty to use for his own profit, deterred the nations from going to the length of prohibition, unless it might be in the case of the hated Jews. There is a clause of Magna Charta, interesting as showing how early the children of Abraham became the money-lenders of Europe, to the effect that, during the minority of any baron, while his lands are in wardship, no debt which he owes to the Jews shall bear any interest. The prejudice against interest embodied itself in what are called usury laws. These, without prohibiting the taking of interest, prescribe a maximum rate per cent., which lenders may receive, and announce a penalty in case they take more. The penalty is sometimes the forfeiture of the entire interest, and sometimes of the entire debt.

Usury laws, however, have not sprung wholly from the old prejudice that to take interest was a great moral wrong, and the greater the more was taken; they sprung also from a false notion which used to be pretty general, but which is now at length thoroughly exploded, that governments were competent to determine the value of their own money; and there has been, and is still, a curious and harmful confusion in respect to this term, the value of money In the only proper sense of the term, the value of money means its power of purchasing services in general, and the value of money is high when a given sum of it will purchase much of general services, and low in the contrary case; but, unfortunately, the terms "high and low value of money" have also been used to denote a high or low rate of interest on money loaned, which is a very different signification, and a high or low rate of interest depend on a very distinct set of causes from those which determine a high or low value of money; nevertheless, so long as governments supposed that they could regulate the latter, it is perfectly natural that they should also suppose that they could regulate the former; and although all intelligent governments have given over the idea of being able to regulate the value of money, many of them still adhere to the idea, equally false as the other, that they are able to regulate the loanable value, or the rate of interest, at least to prevent any more than their prescribed maximum rate from being taken. Are such laws needful? Are they beneficial? Are they in accordance with sound principles, or do they violate them? Has a government any right, after it has stamped or engraved its money, and parted with it to the people in return for value received, to say that they into whose hands it has rightfully come shall only have so much under any circumstances as a reward for foregoing the use of it themselves that somebody else may have the use of it?

Let us see precisely the nature of the transaction when one man loans money to another. It is a clear case of value. The lender does a service to the borrower, and for this service justly demands a compensation. The service is this: The lender might himself use the money to gratify his own desires. It is his money; he may use it, as he pleases, for his own gratification. Or, he may himself employ it productively, and, at the end of the period, receive back his principal with the customary rate of profit. If he surrenders this advantage to the borrower, if he passes over to him the right to use this money, say, for a year, he practices what we call in Political Economy *abstinence*. For this abstinence he has a right to claim a reward, precisely as the man has a right to claim a reward who foregoes working for himself in order to work for me. This reward of abstinence is *interest*. The money-lender foregoes an advantage. He performs a service for the borrower; and, therefore, the right to interest stands on just as unassailable ground as the right to wages.

The loanable value of money varies under exactly the same conditions as every other value varies. It is determined, as every other value is, by the actual exchanges between lenders and borrowers; or, rather, by what would be the actual exchanges, if they were left free. Now for any government to compel a borrower to pay six per cent. when he might otherwise borrow for five, or a lender to take only seven per cent. when his money is worth eight, is a direct violation of the rights of property. It is a forcible and pernicious interference with the freedom of contracts. It is based on the false premise that the loanable value of money is uniform, and that government is competent to determine what it is. No value is uniform. And no government is competent to determine even the maximum price of money loaned, any more than the maximum price of commodities.

On principle, then, these are the two considerations which condemn usury laws. First, it is invidious to allow other men, in every department of business, to exchange their services on the best terms they can make, without any interference or control, and then, without rendering any solid reason for it, to deny this privilege to money-lenders, who offer just as honorable and useful services to society as any other class of men. Second, it is a false notion altogether, that the loanable value of money is, or can be made, uniform; and, therefore, a rate per cent. fixed by the government constantly infringes on the rights of property, — on the rights of the borrowers, if the rate is too high, on the rights of the lender, if the rate is too low. But there are two other considerations, each, if possible, better than these, which condemn all legal rates of interest. The first is, that such laws are rarely obeyed, and can scarcely be enforced. Common sense is outraged by a law which requires a man to part with his property at less than the actual value; and when common sense is against a law, it stands a slim chance of observance. If the legal rate be six, and the actual worth be eight, who lends at six? Not the banks. They require deposits of their customers, the use of whose money shall make up to them the difference between the legal and the actual rate. The modes of evasion are various, but they are adequate.

But usury laws, if they were not disregarded, would be even worse in their tendency than they are now. They aim, I suppose, to aid borrowers, and make it easier for them to contract loans. But are borrowers, as a class, any more deserving of the fostering care of government than are lenders? Even if it could make its interference effective, as it can not, is there any reason why government, leaving these borrowers to make all other bargains, sales, and transfers according to their best skill and judgment, should rush to their rescue only when they propose to borrow money? If they are competent to do their other business for themselves, government pays their capacity a poor compliment in undertaking to help them in the single matter of making loans; and the borrowers in turn have reason to pray to be delivered from their friends, since they, of all others, would be the men especially injured, if all the lenders obeyed the usury laws. Suppose that a borrower is in great need of a loan, and that for some reason his credit is now a little weak. Many men would be willing to loan him at nine per cent., which affords a margin for the extra risk, but at seven, which we will suppose the maximum allowed by the law, he cannot borrow a dollar, because his credit is not quite equal to the best. If, therefore, the lenders obey the law, he, and such as he, must fail. And because it is unlawful to take over seven per cent., he will be obliged to pay those who are willing to violate the law ten or twelve, to compensate them for the risk and odium of such violation, while, under freedom, he could borrow at nine. Moreover, if the loanable value of money at the time be actually nine, while the law only allows seven, many men will attempt to use their own capital productively, who would otherwise loan it, in order to realize the high rate; and this action of theirs still further restricts the loan-market and makes it more difficult to borrow. If, then, the purpose of government be to aid borrowers, no means could be more unskilfully chosen for that end than to pass usury laws, since such laws, so far as they are obeyed, have necessarily the opposite tendency; and even when violated redound to the disadvantage of borrowers, so long as the laws themselves are popularly regarded as of any legal or moral force.

Governments have shown a noteworthy inconsistency in this matter, which incidentally proves the unsoundness of their whole action. While announcing pains and penalties to those who take or pay more than a given rate, they are careful never to bind themselves down to any given rate. Governments are always more or less borrowers, and if usury laws are necessary in order to help borrowers in a pinch, there ought to be a clause in the organic law of every country, forbidding the government to pay and its lenders to take any more than a certain rate per cent. There is no such clause in any organic law. Governments wisely follow the natural market, and borrow low when they can, and pay high when they must. In the last months of Mr. Buchanan's administration, the United States paid twelve per cent. on a public loan, and could get but little at that. Sauce for the goose is sauce for the gander, and if usury laws are good for the citizens, some solid reason ought to be rendered why they are not good for the government. The truth is, they are not good for either, since natural laws are perfectly competent to regulate the rate of interest, and do regulate it substantially in spite of a factitious, impertinent, and mischief-making interference. The rate of interest has little to do with the value of money, properly so called. It depends on the proportion between the sums of money ready to be loaned in any market, and the amount wanted at that time by good borrowers in that market. Every rise in the rate tends to lessen the demand of borrowers, and every fall to enhance that demand, and thus every rise and fall of interest tends to check itself, and while the daily and monthly variations of the rate for first-class borrowers are very considerable, the general average of the rate by years, especially in England, where usury laws are mostly or wholly swept away, is remarkably uniform.

In 1867, the State of Massachusetts repealed all its usury laws, though six per cent. is to be understood in the absence of special agreement, and the result has been entirely satisfactory to all classes of the people. Rhode Island had done this previously, and has experienced equal satisfaction in the result. Other States will soon follow in their lead; and this relic of ignorance and prejudice will pass away. Adam Smith left the "Wealth of Nations" disfigured by the concession that governments might properly enough pass usury laws; but it is gratifying to be able to add, that he was convinced of his error in that by Bentham's book on usury, and fully acknowledged his conviction in the spirit of a genuine lover of truth. We conclude, then, that usury laws are needless, since interest, like all other prices, will perfectly adjust itself. They are disregarded, since lenders will loan or withhold their money according to their own keen sense of interest. They are pernicious, since they infringe the rights of property, and tend to prevent weak borrowers from having a fair chance in the market.

CHAPTER XI.

ON CURRENCY IN THE UNITED STATES.

I venture to offer to guide my readers in an attempt to trace the steps, State and national, as well the earlier as the more recent, which have been made in this country to find the way to a healthy, safe, and uniform currency. Paper money of almost every conceivable variety has been tried at one time and another; and the national government for itself, between 1836 and 1862, made the experiment of discarding every kind of paper, both paying out and demanding to receive gold and silver money only. This money it has always minted, as it has a monopoly of the coinage; but otherwise, and except as now taxing heavily State bank-bills, it has left the States and the people to fabricate and circulate whatever kinds of money they might choose.

From the first establishment of the English colonies in America, the matter of a suitable exchange-medium attracted public attention, and was found to be attended with difficulties. The colonists drew all their supplies from the mother country, and for a long time had but few native products to export in return, and consequently there was a constant tendency in the coin which reached them to flow off again to England in payment of these debts. But something must be used for the purposes of domestic exchange. Tobacco in the southern colonies, and corn and wheat in the northern, were employed for a long time as a local and legalized currency.

In 1690 Massachusetts set the first example, which was soon imitated all over the country, of issuing bills of credit, a government paper made receivable in taxes, and afterwards made legal tender in payment of ordinary debts. At first these bills, or treasury-notes, were issued, not to furnish a currency, but merely as a convenient way of anticipating the taxes, that is, to realize them at the beginning of the year, while they would be gradually paid in in the course of the year. They were like the English exchequer-bills except that they bore no interest. Afterwards, a scheme originating in South Carolina came into general favor, namely, to open loan-offices for the issue of colony-bills, which should furnish at once capital for borrowers, and a currency for the people, and the interest was to be a source of revenue to the colony.

But in whatever way issued, whether in the way of loan to borrowers, or in anticipation of the taxes, the essential and inherent vice of such irredeemable paper was soon everywhere apparent. There was a constant tendency to over-issue, and consequently a necessary depreciation. There never was a government yet, of all those which have attempted the issue of inconvertible paper, which had prudence and firmness enough to resist for any great length of time the temptation to issue such paper in excess. It always has depreciated from that cause, and it probably always will. So it was, at any rate, in these colonies thus early in our history. The bills of credit were issued profusely, and depreciated indefinitely. In 1749 Massachusetts had found paper money so utterly wanting as a measure of value, that she determined to abandon it altogether. She redeemed all her outstanding bills in cash at the current rate at which they were then exchanging.

The demands of the old French war, and the various attempts to conquer Canada, led, on the part of all the colonies except Massachusetts, to new and large issues of bills of credit, which depreciated of course. Soon after the conquest of Canada the British Parliament passed an act prohibiting to all the colonies the issue of bills of credit; but from this restraint the Revolution set them free; and, to provide means for the desperate struggle with the mother-country, there was no resource but in paper money.

In April, 1775, Massachusetts, which had disused paper money for more than a quarter of a century revived its use by authorizing the issue of colonial bills to the amount of £100,000, in sums small enough to circulate as a currency; and on the 23d of June following the Continental Congress began its fiscal operations by voting to emit two millions of dollars in continental bills of credit. Fourteen months had elapsed, and fourteen millions of continental paper had been authorized, besides large local issues, especially in New England, before its depreciation excited any very considerable alarm. It soon, however, became evident that the only way to stop the depreciation would be to stop the issues; and Congress made very persistent but ineffectual attempts to substitute for further issues a system of loans on paper bearing interest. At the same time they sought to sustain their failing credit by a resolution that their bills "ought to pass current in all payments, trade, and dealings, and be deemed equal in value to the same nominal sums in Spanish dollars"; and that all persons refusing to take them ought to be considered "enemies of the United States," upon whom it was recommended to the local authorities to inflict "forfeitures and other penalties." The States were also advised to make these bills a legal tender, to make provision for the redemption of the first six millions, to avoid the further emission of their own local bills, and to take measures to draw in those already out.[1] The loan system failing, Congress reluctantly had recourse to the press which printed the paper money, and the next ten millions increased the depreciation decidedly. The paper was still lawful tender in payment of debts; and notwithstanding the confusion of contracts, the universal high prices, the sufferings of the poor, and the gains of the artful and unscrupulous, Congress felt obliged to give currency to the most wretched sophistries, to refer the existing depreciation mainly to "want of confidence," and to laud the paper as the only kind of money "which cannot make to itself wings and fly away! It remains with us, it will not forsake us, it is always ready at hand for the purposes of commerce, and every industrious man can find it!" The rest of the story is soon told. Before the end of the year 1779, the remainder of the two hundred millions, which, in the vain hopes of stopping the depreciation, Congress had

[1] Hildreth's United States, chap. 35.

beforehand announced as the limit of the issues, was put out, and the press was allowed to rest. The value of the money was then about $38\frac{1}{2}$ for one. The States were now advised to repeal all laws making the bills a legal-tender, and the scheme of the "new tenor" was devised, by which the old bills were to be drawn in at the rate of forty for one, and funded in government bonds bearing interest. This was the finishing blow, and the paper soon dropped out of circulation altogether. Just before the Revolutionary army in camp at Newburgh had combined to refuse it, and its circulation was wholly stopped, it exchanged for cash at the rate of one thousand for one. One thousand for one is $99\frac{9}{10}$ per cent. below par, and the prices of commodities were as ridiculously high as the value of the paper was pitifully low. A man in New England or New York would pay five hundred dollars for his dinner, and never ask the landlord to reduce the bill. I heard the story in my childhood of a certain gentleman well known in those parts, who stuffed his sulky-box with continental bills and then sallied forth to purchase a cow!

At this juncture the rudiments of a better system appeared. For nearly a hundred years the Bank of England had been issuing paper payable on demand in gold and silver. Alexander Hamilton had been a close student of English history and of English finance, and he conceived that the same thing might be done with advantage in America. In 1780, when he was only twenty-three years old, he wrote a letter to Robert Morris, a wealthy and influential member of the Continental Congress, and afterwards the Continental financier, in which, after showing the causes of the depreciation of the currency, and the necessity of a foreign loan, he furnished a matured plan of a bank, by means of which the loan might be so applied as to reëstablish the public credit and become the basis of a redeemable currency. This was, as I believe, the first suggestion of a banking institution for America. Hamilton's idea was briefly this: Public credit there was none; an established government there was none; the Continental Congress was exercising the unlimited functions of a revolutionary government; under these circumstances the only way to create public credit was to unite with it the private interests of moneyed men. Establish then a bank which shall be the fiscal agent of the government; obtain, if possible, a foreign loan, and deposit it in cash in the bank; let half the stock of the bank be subscribed by wealthy men, who can reasonably look for a fair profit on their investment; let government hold the other half and have half the profits; then let the bank issue bills on its cash basis, consisting of the loan, the private subscriptions, and the product of the Continental taxes as they are gradually paid in. Thus the bank, and all subscribers to its stock, and all holders of its bills would be directly interested to uphold the government and its credit. Community would be equally benefited, since it would have a relatively sound paper for ordinary commercial purposes.

Mr. Morris found his duties as Continental financier sufficiently embarrassing; and in the fall of 1781 brought forward a scheme for a national bank, partially embodying on a small scale the ideas of Hamilton. Congress sanctioned the plan, and the

Bank of North America, the first bank in this country, was established in Philadelphia. Mr. Morris, in behalf of the general government, subscribed nearly two thirds of the capital stock of $400,000, and naturally took the entire control of the institution. The reason why individuals subscribed so little is to be found in the distrust with which paper money of all kinds had come to be regarded. Capitalists did not believe there would be any dividends, and the people were afraid the paper would depreciate in their hands. Under these unfavorable circumstances the bank went into operation in January, 1782. Every effort was made to produce a public sentiment favorable to the credit of the bank, and its bills were the first paper handled by Americans which was convertible into coin at the pleasure of the holders. Being made receivable at the Federal and State treasuries in payment of taxes and duties, and being cautiously issued at first, the bills soon came into such circulation that the bank was able to declare dividends on its stock from twelve to sixteen per cent. per annum. Who ever heard of capitalists who could resist sixteen per cent? The bank opened its books for new subscriptions, and the stock went up without difficulty from $400,000 to $2,000,000.

We must here dismiss the Bank of North America, the parent of all our institutions of the kind, with the remark that, although it was chartered by the old Congress as a national institution, such doubts were entertained of the competency of that body to incorporate an institution within a State, that a charter was soon after procured from the legislature of Pennsylvania; and also, that its connection with the Continental treasury ceased, on the retirement of Mr. Morris from the office of financier. It continued, however, as a State bank; and it flourishes still in a green old age among the banking concerns of the Quaker City.

Till Mr. Morris's Bank of North America commenced operations in January, 1782, all the paper that had been issued in the country, whether by the colonies as such or by the central authority represented at first by the revolutionary government and afterwards by the confederation, was irredeemable paper, and illustrated the universal financial law that such paper, unless issued under very favorable circumstances and strictly limited in quantity, will depreciate in spite of everything. The bills of the Bank of North America were convertible into gold and silver at the pleasure of the holders, and they mark, therefore, an epoch in the monetary history of the country. Some silver coins had been issued in Massachusetts as early as 1652, and continued to be struck at the colonial mint for about thirty years, but the pieces all bear the dates of 1652 or 1662; and these pieces, now known and prized as the "old pine-tree coinage," were the only public coins of any description minted in the country itself until after the close of the Revolutionary war. They were shillings, sixpences, threepences, and twopences. Both silver and copper coins were, however, minted in England for the use of the colonies; and in 1722 a patent was issued by George I. to one William Wood to make coins for colonial use out of pinchbeck, in pursuance of which he had the conscience to make thirteen bright shillings, or thereabouts, out of a pound of brass. It is refreshing to add that the colonists had the sense and spirit utterly to reject Wood's money. In 1786 actual coinage of copper coins took place under State authority, in Vermont, in Connecticut, and in New Jersey. The same year witnessed the adoption in the old Congress of Jefferson's plan for a decimal currency, and the establishment of a mint under national authority, and three hundred tons of Federal copper cents were contracted to be struck the following year.

When the government went into operation under the present constitution, in 1789, besides the Bank of North America, two others had been established, the Bank of New York in New York, and the Bank of Massachusetts in Boston. These three were all, and their circulation was mostly confined to the cities in which they were located. Except the copper cents just spoken of, there was no such thing as a national currency, and the new government had not sufficient credit to make it practicable to rely on the aid of private lenders. Hamilton was now Secretary of the Treasury. In pursuance of the duty of his office, he presented to Congress in December, 1790, his celebrated report, recommending the establishment of a Bank of the United States. In this report, which at once gave Hamilton a European reputation, two points were specially argued: first, that such an institution would afford through its bills great facilities to trade and to domestic exchanges; and, second, would furnish the new government a convenient paper medium for its monetary transactions, and be a resource for temporary loans The first point respected the people, the second the government.

There can be no doubt, I think, that in the circumstances of that time a national bank was expedient and beneficial. There was then no confidence, no credit, no currency, and no commercial relations established with foreign nations by which gold and silver could flow into the country. As an institution of loan, the bank gave credit to the extent of its means to all who had good security to offer. As an institution of circulation, it furnished a convenient, a convertible, and a national money. As a governmental fiscal agent, government could borrow of it on an emergency, and pay at its leisure from the proceeds of the imposts and taxes. The fullest acknowledgment, however, of the benefits of such an institution at that time does not at all commit one to the defence of any such institution now. Circumstances have utterly changed. No well-established national government can afford to add to its many and higher functions the delicate duty, so much more appropriate to private bankers, of loaning money to the people on interest according to its notion of their solvency; and, in a republic especially, where hostile parties alternately administer the government, loans would be sure to be made for partisan purposes, and corruption find the bank a ready tool.

The constitutionality of Hamilton's plan was stoutly denied in Congress. The first-rate abilities and growing reputation of that eminent statesman had already awakened jealousies both in Congress and in the cabinet. Nevertheless, a bill, in substantial accordance with the views of the Secretary passed both houses by large majorities. Washington, before signing it, required the written opinion of his cabinet on the question of constitutionality. Hamilton and Knox took the affirmative; Jefferson and Randolph the negative; the President, as often, sided with Hamilton, and signed the bill.

On New Year's day, 1853, I had the great personal pleasure of calling on the widow of Alexander Hamilton, who survived him just fifty years. Turning the conversation on her husband's connection with the government, the old lady remarked with enthusiasm,—" My husband gave you a bank. Jefferson thought we ought not to have any bank. and Washington rather thought so, too; but my husband said we must have a bank; and one day he said to me, 'My dear, you must sit up with me to-night, and write for me;' and I sat up all night, and I wrote it out with my own hand, and the next morning he carried it to Washington, and we had a bank!" This last was pronounced not without exultation. Fortunate old lady! The daughter of one of the purest and most magnanimous of the Revolutionary patriots, Gen. Philip Schuyler, and the wife of another, peerless among the statesmen of his time; who herself lived to see the complete success of the work to which her father and husband were among the chief contributors.

With a charter that was to run twenty years, with a capital stock of $10,000,000, $8,000,000 of which was subscribed by individuals, and $2,000,000 by the United States, and the whole of which was subscribed, with a surplus, within a few hours, the first

United States Bank went into operation at Philadelphia, in July, 1791. Notice this feature of the stock. Hamilton had just before persuaded Congress to assume the State debts incurred in the war of the Revolution, and to fund them, together with the certificates of the public debt, into one new and compact debt. Three fourths of the subscription of individuals to the bank stock must be in these new government stocks which bore six per cent. The demand for them, thus created, brought them instantly up to par; so that the bank was made a means, incidentally, of establishing the credit of the United States, — all its paper was now at par. This splendid success of Hamilton's financial schemes, together with the unexpected income from the new tariff, accounts in part for the immense popularity of the man; and justifies the strong expression of Daniel Webster, who said, on one occasion, that Alexander Hamilton raised the public credit of the United States from the dead.

During twenty years, the term of its charter, the operation of the first United States Bank appears to have been healthful and beneficent. It furnished a paper money secured by government stocks and by cash that was current at a uniform value all over the country; its loans, under the circumstances of the time, gave a sharp spur to industry and commerce; while its dividends to stockholders never fell below eight, and frequently rose to ten per cent. It is not to be wondered at, therefore, that as the time approached for the charter to expire, the stockholders were anxious for a renewal. They applied for such renewal, offering to pay the government a million and a quarter for the privilege of continuance. It was alleged against the bank, on the other hand, that the stock was now largely owned by foreigners, which was true; and that the directors had sometimes made, or withheld, loans, for party purposes, which was doubtful. The real cause of the opposition to the renewal of the charter was this: Instead of the three State banks in existence when the national institution was chartered, there were now (1811) eighty-eight State banks, in some of which the States as such held stock. These banks and their friends supposed that it would be for their interest that the national bank should go out of being; that, in that case, they should obtain the custody and management of the national funds, and furnish the country the currency, which the national institution had furnished. The charter was defeated, in the House by one vote, and in the Senate by the casting vote of the Vice-President, George Clinton. The bank was obliged to wind up its affairs. It did so speedily and honestly. This was in 1811.

Undoubtedly the paper of the first national bank was very fair money, and certainly superior to the bills of the new State banks, for the creation of which there was a sort of mania in the country so soon as it was ascertained that the national institution could not be rechartered. Many of these went into operation on the strength of little or no *bona fide* capital. They issued their notes freely, and the chasm caused by the withdrawal of the national circulation was soon filled up, and more too. As a necessary consequence, the whole circulating medium became depreciated, and the currency came into dreadful disorder throughout the country. In the fall of 1814, there was a general stoppage of all the banks in the United States, except those in New England. The notes of the New York city banks were ten per cent. below par; those of Philadelphia, eighteen; of Baltimore, twenty; of Pittsburg, twenty-five. All this illustrates the simple financial truth, that money is not a commodity of which an unlimited quantity can be absorbed by business, but is an instrument for a certain specific purpose,— namely, to facilitate the exchange of existing commodities and of services all ready to be exchanged, and only waiting for the presence of the medium to consummate the transfer; and whenever more than enough for this purpose is put out, whether it be specie or paper, a diminution in value of every part of it is inevitable; on the same principles precisely as, when the market is permanently overstocked with sewing-machines, there will be an inevitable decline in their value. Money is good for the purpose for which it was invented, and useless for any other.

In this state of things Mr. Dallas, then Secretary of the Treasury, recommended to Congress the establishment of a new United States Bank, modelled after the first, with a charter for twenty years, with a capital stock of $35,000,000, the bank to pay the government a bonus of a million and a half for the privilege of coming into being. It was thought that a strong central and national institution, on which the State banks, now increased in number to two hundred and forty-six, might lean for support, would enable them shortly to resume specie payments, and to go on thereafter on better principles. The bill organizing the bank was engineered through the House by John C. Calhoun. It went into operation in 1816, just after the close of the last war with England, when the reviving enterprise and enlarged business of peace seemed to open up before it a prosperous career.

The new bank was not, however, at first, fortunate in its management. It pushed its paper into circulation with reckless eagerness. In the course of one month it increased its discounts from three to twenty millions, and in nine months its discount line was thirty-three millions. The results were what might have been expected,—prices universally high, a spirit of speculation everywhere rife, and gold leaving the country by shiploads. The bank soon fell into difficulties, and public opinion turned more or less against it. Although under the abler and more careful management, first of Langdon Cheves, and then of Nicholas Biddle, the bank recovered its stability, it never enjoyed quite the same confidence and credit as the first bank.

This was not wholly its own fault; for in 1829, seven years before its charter was to expire, Andrew Jackson commenced his famous contest with the bank, which he kept up without intermission till the charter expired in 1836. Under this presidential and consequent congressional fire, the bank can hardly be said to have had a fair chance. Andrew Jackson had sworn its death by the 'tarnal—his usual oath—and Andrew Jackson was not a man to be thwarted. In his annual message in 1829, he gave the directors fair warning that there would be "constitutional difficulties" in the way of their securing any extension of their privileges, and in 1832 he vetoed the bill to recharter the bank. The next step was to remove from the custody and management of the bank the public moneys. Three years before the charter expired he requested Mr. McLane, the Secretary of the Treasury, to remove the national funds from the custody of the bank, and to place them in certain selected State banks. Mr. McLane declined to order the removal. Whereupon Mr. Duane of New York was appointed to the treasury. But Mr. Duane, no more than his predecessor, could see his way clear to remove the deposits. When made to understand that it was the determination of the President to have them removed at all hazards, he explicitly refused to lend himself for the purpose. The President removed Mr. Duane, and appointed Roger B. Taney, the late Chief Justice, as Secretary of the Treasury. He proved more flexible to the will of power, and immediately gave the required order. The consequences of this step in the circumstances were immense and mischievous. The discount line of the bank was at the moment over $60,000,000. The public deposits were $10,000,000. The sudden withdrawal of this sum affected credit and disarranged business to a remarkable degree, and caused intense excitement all over the Union.

The next movement in the "great experiment," as it was sarcastically called in the politics of the day, was the issue of the famous specie-circular, which directed the receivers of the public money to take nothing but gold and silver in payment of the public lands. Speculators and others had been making large purchases of western lands, expecting to pay in paper money. The specie-circular came upon them like a clap of thunder. Their consternation was vast, and the circular, coming as it did, shortly after the removal of the deposits, made confusion worse confounded.

General Jackson went out of office, and the second bank went out of being the same year; but the inaugurated movement was completed by Mr. Van Buren, who effected the complete divorce of the government from all banks and fiscal agents whatever, first, by directing the State banks which now had the keeping of the public moneys, to distribute them as surplus revenue among the States; and, by the sub-treasury scheme, in pursuance of which the United States received in payment of all dues, and paid out in all disbursements, gold and silver only. I believe in gold and silver money, or their equivalent in representative paper which can be instantly converted into them, and do not question the patriotic aims of the administrations concerned, but there was something headlong and violent in this transition from the traditional policy of the government to the new system.

From 1836 to 1862 there was no national money in the United States, except the coin; the paper currency was furnished by a number, increased at last to over fifteen hundred, of joint-stock banking companies, under the sole authority of the States. These, under various and often conflicting regulations, manufactured and issued money for the people. This money, as a whole, was never a safe, a uniform, an economical currency. It was subject to alternate contractions and expansions which spoiled it as a measure of value. It was never able to stand the shock of the commercial crises which it powerfully contributed to bring on. Money is an implement, and a costly implement, and the functions it has to perform cannot be performed by cheap, penny-wise, pound-foolish substitutes.

Two kinds of paper and two kinds of coin had preceded the issue of the bills of the first United States Bank. The first kind of paper were bills of credit issued first by the individual colonies, and then by the confederated continent, always inconvertible, and consequently always depreciating; the second kind of paper were the bills of the three State banks at Philadelphia, New York, and Boston, convertible, and so far forth excellent; but circulating mainly in their respective cities only. The first kind of coin were the pine-tree silver-pieces of Massachusetts, minted two hundred years ago, and the copper pieces struck under State authority about the time of the adoption of the constitution of the United States, simultaneously in Vermont, Connecticut, New Jersey, and Massachusetts; the other kind of coin being the copper cents nationalized by the old Congress, and which came into circulation while the convention was sitting which framed the constitution under which we live.

As soon as the new government had got fairly under way, the more pressing questions of the tariff, the national bank, the organization of the departments, being disposed of, the national mint was put into practical operation at Philadelphia. The laws relating to the mint were enacted during the session of 1792, and the first Federal coins of silver issued in 1794, of gold in 1795. It is to Jefferson that the country is indebted for the decimal scale of currency, so superior in convenience to all other monetary subdivisions. He had proposed a matured plan for the coinage, with the dollar for the unit, and the decimal subdivisions of dimes, cents, and mills, and the decimal multiple of the dollar, the eagle, while he was a member of the old Congress in 1785; and the Congress had adopted his plan the following year, and, as has been said, some copper cents were minted on the Federal standard; but nothing more was done till 1792, when the new Congress reaffirmed the resolutions of the old, readopted Jefferson's denominations, and put our existing mint into working order. There was a curious debate in Congress at the time as to the devices which the coins should bear. As the bill came from the Senate, where it originated, the gold and silver pieces were to have on one side the figure of the eagle, which the Continental Congress long before had adopted as the national emblem, and near this, the legend "United States of America." This was for the obverse of the coin, and so far nobody had any objection. For the reverse, the bill proposed that, in accordance with the usages of all nations from the time of the earliest known coinage, the impression or representation of the head of the President of the United States for the time being, together with his name, order of succession in the presidency, and the date of the coinage, should be stamped. This was strongly objected to in the House, as savoring of monarchy. The President's head on the coin was deemed by some a dangerous thing for the republic, and the proposal led to a sarcastic and even acrimonious debate, and was at length defeated in the House by a vote of twenty-six to twenty-two, in which the Senate was afterwards obliged to concur, and a proposition made by Key of Maryland was carried, to substitute a figure of Liberty instead of the obnoxious head of the President; but under precisely what sort of a figure to represent Liberty was then the difficulty, and at the next session Elias Boudinot of New Jersey, afterwards the director of the mint, endeavored to get substituted for the emblematic figure of Liberty the head of Columbus, but in vain; the Republican party was bound that the figure of Liberty and no other should go on the coins, and it went on, and we have here the history of that benignant looking lady, whose pretty face we used to see familiarly enough before the war, and whose acquaintance we hope to resume in the good time coming.

It may be asked how we came to have the dollar as the unit of our monetary system. The word dollar is derived from a German word which means valley, and was first applied to coins in consequence of this circumstance: in the mining region of Bohemia, at a place called Joachimsthal, (Joachim's valley,) silver-pieces of one ounce weight were coined and came into circulation about 1520 as Joachimsthaler, and then for shortness thaler; this became dalera in Spanish, and in English dollar. The thaler is still the German money of account, and the Spanish milled dollar became so famous in the world of commerce, and so familiar to our fathers in their dealings with the West Indies and the Spanish

American colonies, that our Congress adopted it as the best known and most convenient unit of money. The word dime is a corruption of the Latin *decem*, ten; cent a contraction of the Latin *centum*, hundred; and mill a contraction of the Latin *mille*, thousand; so that our denominations are philosophical as well as convenient, each one in order being and being designated a tenth part of the one above.

The mint of the United States is one of the most interesting institutions in the country. It was established at Philadelphia in 1792. While it was still doubtful where the ultimate seat of the national government would be placed, the citizens of that beautiful city were strongly in hopes of being able to persuade Congress permanently to abide in their town, in which the old continental body had first met, in which independence had been declared, and which, more than any other, was popularly regarded as the headquarters of the national Union. A notable instance of log-rolling legislation, the first in our history, transferred the capital of the country to the banks of the Potomac, but the good people of the Quaker City have nevertheless always retained the mint, as a memorial of their earlier position in the history of the government.

By the law establishing the mint, the chief officer was to be styled a director; and the ingenious David Rittenhouse, a self-taught mathematician, who had run several years before, by the help of instruments all of his own construction, the most difficult part of Mason and Dixon's line, was shortly after appointed to this post. The act stipulated that all bullion brought to the mint should be coined gratuitously, but when coin was delivered in exchange for bullion on the spot, one half of one per cent. was to be charged as seigniorage. The coins were to be the eagle, the half-eagle and the quarter-eagle in gold; the dollar, half-dollar, quarter-dollar, dime, and half-dime in silver; the cent and half-cent in copper. The weight of the eagle was to be 270 grains troy, alloyed according to the English standard, one part in twelve; and the dollar was to weigh 416 grains, alloyed one part in nine and nine-tenths. The sub-divisions of these coins, gold and silver, were to be in all respects proportional to their units. At that time, in France and in Europe generally, the current relative value of gold and silver was considered one to fifteen, and the act of Congress established that as the ratio of the value of the two metals to be maintained at the mint; but, from this clause of the law, there followed important consequences, which were not foreseen, since that was not, at least in America, the true ratio of their value at that time, and being a decided undervaluation of gold, the gold coinage did not come into any circulation. It was really worth by the ounce more than fifteen ounces of silver; but, as the mint only reckoned it equal to fifteen ounces of silver, it was more valuable out of the circulation than in it, and it was therefore always exported in preference to silver, in payment of foreign balances, especially after France and the rest of Europe had changed the relative legal value to one to fifteen and one half. After that, an ounce of gold, estimated in silver, was worth three and one third per cent. more abroad than at home, and, of course, under the circumstances, it would not circulate in the home currency. The cheaper money will push out of circulation the dearer the world over. From the organization of the mint till 1817, over five millions and a half dollars in gold-pieces were coined, and very little indeed of it came into permanent circulation, for the simple reason that it was really worth more than it was counted to be worth by the regulations of the currency. It would, therefore, pay to melt it up, because it was worth more as bullion than as coin.

This state of things continued, the silver circulating freely but the gold scarcely circulating at all, till the attention of Congress was called to the subject, and a law passed substantially rating gold in relation to silver at one to sixteen. The weight of the eagle was reduced to 258 grains from 270, and the alloy increased to one part in ten from one part in twelve. This increased at one jump the legal valuation of gold $6\frac{68}{100}$ per cent. as compared with silver, which remained as before. As the former ratio was a decided undervaluation of gold, so the law of 1834 as decidedly overvalued it; and the working of a beautiful natural law became immediately apparent, by which the current of the metals was reversed, silver now passing in preference to Europe to liquidate the balances of trade, and gold coming from Europe to the United States, where it was about three and one quarter per cent. dearer than in Europe, while silver was about three and one quarter per cent. dearer in Europe than in the United States. The metals go where they have the most consideration in exchange.

Dr. Robert M. Patterson, who was the director of the mint from 1835 to 1851, under whose direction the present admirably improved machinery of the mints was introduced, and who thereby developed their capacity from a coinage of $5,000,000 to $63,-000,000 per annum, drew up a new code of mint-laws, which was enacted by Congress in January, 1837, by which the previous complicated legislation was all superseded, and on which the mint has been substantially administered ever since. In the first place, the French standard of fineness of nine tenths for both gold and silver was adopted, that is to say, one part alloy in a whole of ten parts. Since its adoption by us from the French, this decimal standard of fineness has been adopted also by several other nations for their new coins, and thus some important steps have already been taken towards a most desirable end which is yet to be realized in the future, a universal currency for commerce. This change in the standard of fineness necessitated a change in the weight of the silver coins, if the established relation of one to sixteen was to be maintained. Accordingly the weight of the silver dollar was reduced from 416 grains to 412½, without changing its weight in fine silver. The weight of the dollar has remained at that figure ever since, but the smaller silver coins have been, as we shall see, still further reduced in weight, and the refusal of the dollar-piece to circulate has been another good illustration at our own very doors of the universal law that the cheaper money drives out the dearer.

At different times since 1837 new denominations of coins have been added to our national series; of gold, the double-eagle, the three-dollar, and the one-dollar piece; of silver, only the three-cent piece, which has never been popular, and will be superseded by the new three-cent copper piece. In 1853 very interesting alterations were made in the character of our silver coins; up to that date the laws made both the gold and silver money a legal tender to any amount; and it was consequently optional with the debtor to pay in the cheaper metal, which ever it might be; and as experience was proving that the relative value of the two was not constant but variable, and that the legally established ratio of one to sixteen was depleting the currency of silver, it was then determined to make gold alone the legal tender, except to the extent of $5; to cease coining silver for individuals, and only coin on government account such sums as seemed to be in demand for purposes of change; and to reduce the weight of the half-dollar and its subdivisions so that their nominal value should be considerably above their real value as compared with the silver dollar, and thus their exportation be prevented. Accordingly the weight of the half-dollar has been reduced from 206¼ grains to 192 grains, and of the smaller coins in proportion. A silver dollar has always weighed 371¼ grains fine, a dollar in parts now weighs $345\frac{6}{10}$ fine; and accordingly the dollar is worth $7\frac{42}{100}$ per cent. more than a nominal dollar's worth of the smaller pieces. The relative value of gold in silver is now 1 to 15.6; a gold dollar, therefore, weighing 23.22 grains pure, is worth $2\frac{43}{100}$ per cent. less than a silver one, and $4\frac{81}{100}$ per cent. more than a dollar in small silver. The result of these measures has been to establish gold as the real standard of the country, and to make silver entirely subsidiary to that. The copper coinage of the country consists now of four pieces; of which the one and two cent pieces are composed of 95 parts copper, 3 tin, and 2 zinc, and are respectively legal tender for debts not over four cents; while the three and five-cent pieces are composed of 75 parts copper and 25 parts nickel. 3 cent pieces are legal tender for 60, and 5 cent for 100 cents. The five-cent piece is minted after the French metric system, weighing precisely five *grammes*, and five of them laid along in order measuring exactly a *decimetre* in length. The minting of this piece is the first official recognition, embodied in act, on the part of the United States, of the excellence of the metric system.

It now remains to characterize, so far as it circulates money, the national bank system, and also the present condition of the entire currency.

When Secretary Chase assumed the Treasury Department in the spring of 1861, the state of the country, and, of consequence, the state of the finances, were appalling. Mr. Buchanan's administration had just been trying to borrow a few millions of dollars of the people, and had only succeeded in securing a very small sum, and that at the enormous rate of twelve per cent. interest. The clouds of war which had been gathering black and sullen all the winter, soon broke in wrathful peals over the head of the new administration. The country must be defended, as well as the ordinary expenses of the government met; an army must be raised, equipped, put into the field, and paid. We do not propose to follow the Secretary in his general financial embarrassments, expedients, and resources; but it is needful to our present purpose to say that, owing to the unexpected delays and disasters of the war, and to the consequent want of confidence in the public mind, he found it extremely difficult to borrow the sums necessary to be had in order to meet the expenditures of the government; and that in his first annual report to Congress, in December, 1861, he recommended, principally for the sake of facilitating the negotiation of loans, the organization of banking associations, whose circulation should consist only of notes, uniform in character, furnished by the government, and secured as to convertibility into coin by United States bonds deposited in the treasury. It is clear that if such associations should be formed, it would make a market for the national bonds to the extent in which they should invest their capital stock in them as security for their circulation. Above all things, at that time the United States wanted to borrow money. It must borrow or perish; and therefore a national banking system, based for security on the national debt, would open a market for some hundreds of millions of the evidences of that debt, and put a corresponding sum of immediately available funds into the hands of the government.

This proposal of the Secretary, involving, as it did, the winding up of the State banks as such, found at first but little favor in Congress or among the people. The banking interests of the eastern and middle States, particularly of the State of New York, from whose State bank system the idea was mainly and by acknowledgment borrowed, were especially hostile to the scheme. In his second annual report, in December, 1862, the Secretary iterated his recommendation, and enforced it at length by arguments drawn from the necessity of effecting immediately more extensive loans, from the character of the currency for soundness and uniformity thus furnished to the people, from the convenient agencies which such banks would furnish for the deposit of public moneys, and from the firm anchorage which such a system would give to the union of the States. These arguments, which found a response especially emphatic from the Western States, coupled with the assurance of the Secretary, that, if Congress should concur in his views, though conscious of the great difficulty which vast, sudden, and protracted expenditures imposed on him, he thought he should still be able to maintain the public credit and provide for the public wants, induced Congress to frame and pass "An act to provide a national currency secured by a pledge of United States stocks, and to provide for the circulation and redemption thereof." The act was approved by the President February 25, 1863.

Every bank organized under it invests its own capital stock in the bonds of the United States, bearing interest. These bonds are transferred to an officer of the treasury, called the comptroller, at Washington, who holds them as security for the redemption of the bills of such bank, but who pays the interest on them to the bank itself, so long as the bank redeems its bills promptly and violates no provisions of the organic banking law. Ninety per cent. of the amount of such bonds thus deposited with the comptroller, provided the bonds be estimated at par value and bear interest at a rate not less than five per cent., is then furnished by the treasurer to the bank in circulating notes, engraved and registered by the United States; unless the capital stock of the bank be more than $500,000 and less than $1,000,000, in which case only eighty per cent. of the capital is furnished in notes; and if the capital be between $1,000,000 and $3,000,000, only seventy-five per cent.; and over $3,000,000, sixty per cent. These notes thus received by the banks, they issue to the people in ordinary loans and payments, and they are required by the law to keep on hand at all times twenty-five per cent. of their aggregate average circulation and deposits in lawful money of the United States, with which to redeem their notes on presentation. Thus the convertibility of the notes is dependent first on the solvency of the association, and, if that fails to redeem them, they are speedily redeemable, after certain formalities are gone through with, at the treasury of the United States; and so many of the bonds belonging to such bank, deposited with the comptroller of the currency as security for the redemption of the notes, are then to be sold as shall reimburse the United States for such redemption; so that it is almost impossible under the law that the bill-holders of any national bank can ever suffer any loss. The United States holds the capital of the bank in its own hands, and is thus enabled to guarantee the convertibility of the bills. At the same time the system secures the manifold advantages of private capital, private enterprise, and personal sagacity and integrity, in the matter of loaning money, securing deposits, and general management of the banks.

The superiority in every respect of this scheme of banking to the fast and loose system which has prevailed in this country so long, is very apparent. In the first place, perfect publicity of the affairs of every bank is provided for in the organic law, and cannot be evaded. Every bank in the principal cities must publish a statement, under oath, at the beginning of every month, of its exact condition, and forward it to the comptroller; and the other banks must do the same every quarter, and the comptroller is to publish abstracts of these reports every quarter; so that everybody can know the state of each bank in particular, as well as the state of the whole circulation. In the second place, the whole amount of the circulation cannot be increased at the will of the banks or the will of the comptroller, or in any other way except by an act of Congress authorizing such increase; so that the system is not so liable to those sudden contractions and expansions which have been the bane of our paper money hitherto. In the third place, the government pledges itself to receive these bills for taxes, excises, and all other dues, except customs' duties; and makes them legal tender in all payments which itself has occasion to make, except the interest and principal of the public debt. If, to these provisions, there be added another, requiring all the banks to redeem their bills in New York, as well as at their own counters, the bills will be undoubtedly uniform in value all over the country, and debts can be paid by them through the post-office, or otherwise, without the mediation of any bank or the payment of exchanges. In the fourth place, it is to be noticed, that the United States absolutely guarantees the full payment of these notes, not simply as a trustee holding securities for the purpose, but as a principal pledging the public faith.[1] In the fifth place, besides the absolute security of ultimate redemption, the ratio of lawful money required to the aggregate circulation and deposits is much higher than has hitherto prevailed in practice throughout the country. The ratio required of all the banks in seventeen of the principal cities of the Union is twenty-five per cent., and of the banks elsewhere fifteen per cent. This fifth point is subject to a material deduction to be made shortly. Add to these reasons this other, that the homogeneousness of the money circulating among them, in connection with a common creditorship towards the United States Government, is an additional bond binding the States and the people together, and tending powerfully to neutralize the centrifugal forces which are always at work in large societies and governments.

But we shall get an idea too favorable to the new national banking system, unless we look also at its dangers. The money which these banks are to circulate is, after all, nothing but credit money, and will be liable in some degree to the disorders which are inseparable from every form of credit. Credit is not payment, but a promise to pay. The promise may be good, it may be sure to be fulfilled; but it is not, and never can be made, the same thing as fulfilment. These bills bear upon their face the acknowledgment that they are promises to pay, and not the pay itself; and men are so constituted, and society is so delicately organized, that times are liable to come when men shall have a general distrust of mere promises,

1 Walker's Science of Wealth. Page 233.

and shall desire to see them changed into fulfilment. If a panic should ever arise in regard to these notes, and a general desire be manifested on the part of the holders to convert them into cash, it is evident hat many of the banks would be obliged to suspend specie payments, since they are only required to hold twenty-five per cent. of their circulation and deposits in cash, and this ratio, as a general thing, is not likely to be exceeded. It is true that their notes cannot all come back at once for redemption, nor indeed any very considerable proportion of them, since, unlike the circulation of the State banks, they will pass freely beyond the boundaries of States and sections, and become necessarily very widely diffused; yet general confidence is a thing so sensitive, and credit money is in its nature such, that an absolute freedom from panics and from supensions cannot rationally be predicted. They are liable to come: it will be strange if they do not come.

In the second place, the legally required ratio of lawful money to liabilities is largely weakened, as the law now stands, by the provision that "bank balances and clearing-house certificates shall be deemed to be lawful money." As far as the immediate convertibility of the notes is concerned, it is evident that this clause neutralizes to a large extent the natural effect of the required ratio. Bank balances are not cash. If real, and not fictitiously created, they are a part of the assets of the bank, but their virtue is too remote, in most cases, to help any bank sustain a "run." What is wanted in order to convert notes and to allay a panic is not assets, however good they may be, but specie itself. While, therefore, this clause was a concession to the banking interests, it clearly jeopardizes those of the people. In fact, the framers of the law were so anxious to make it acceptable to the interests arrayed against it, that large dividends can be much more safely predicted from it for the banks than prosperity and security for the people. Thus far in their history the redemption of these notes has been a mere mockery. They have been redeemed, if any one has desired it, in United States legal-tender notes; that is to say, one credit has been redeemed by another credit no better than itself.

But the most imminent danger that threatens this system is the facility with which Congress may expand the circulation. This danger, always impending, has already struck once. By the law of July 8, 1870, the original limit of $300,000,000 of circulation is overpassed, and $54,000,000 additional authorized. When the war broke out, the paper money of the whole country, North and South, was only $202,000,000;[1] the maximum ever reached was only $214,000,000 in 1856, and at the same time a maximum of $138,000,000 in coin;[2] it would be difficult to give a solid reason why the country needs more money now than then; but this law of 1870 not only allows 18 per cent. addition to the national bank-bills, and authorizes the transference of $25,000,000 more from old banks to new,—an expansion while the process lasts,—but also authorizes a new kind of banks called *coin-banks*, not limiting their number or the capital to be invested in

1 Report of Secretary Chase.

2 *Hunt's Merchant's Magazine Year-Book*, 1870.

them, virtually pledging the government to redeem, if necessary, their notes in gold, and only requiring them to keep 25 per cent. "of their outstanding circulation in gold coin of the United States." This legislation in every part of it is unfortunate. It increases a bulk of currency already much too great; it puts in hazard the new banking system before it has fairly become settled; it puts off indefinitely the day of specie payments; and it adds an entirely new kind of money to kinds quite too numerous before. Probably no other nation ever had so many sorts of money at one time as are legal now in the United States. Let us see how many kinds of money we have.

1. *Coin money.* But even here there is great confusion, and dissimilarity in value. The silver dollar, although no longer the standard of account, is still coined at the mint, is still legal tender for debts to all amounts, and is worth much more than the gold dollar, and more still than a nominal dollar's worth of smaller silver; while the baser coinage is of two varieties, copper-nickel, and copper-tin-zinc, of differing intrinsic and legal tender value.

2. *Coin certificates.* Persons may deposit gold coin and bullion in sums not less than $20 with any treasurer of the United States, and receive therefor certificates, which are redeemable at sight and receivable for duties on imports. Government may also issue certificates in payment of interest on the public debt; but the amount issued to depositors and as interest must not be more than 20 per cent. of the gold then in the treasury.

3. *Bills of coin banks.* These are much like the

old State bank-bills, except that they have the indorsement of the United States. The Comptroller of the Currency may issue to any association making a deposit of bonds, as security, notes of different denominations not less than five dollars, to an extent not exceeding 80 per cent. of the par value of the bonds deposited. These notes rest back for redemption on one quarter of their own amount in coin. One dollar presented for payment in coin will practically withdraw four dollars from circulation, thus introducing an element of hazardous fluctuations.

4. *Legal tender notes.* These were issued in 1862 and 1863 to the amount of $450,000,000, of which $356,000,000 are still outstanding. They are the largest element in our present currency, they bear no interest, they are irredeemable, and have always been much depreciated as compared with coin.

5. *Fractional currency.* $50,000,000 in denominations less than a dollar are authorized by law, and about $40,000,000 are now in circulation. They are redeemable in legal tenders in sums not less than $3, and receivable in sums less than $5 for debts due the United States, except for duties on imports.

6. *National bank bills.* About $311,000,000 of these are now in the hands of the people. As they are redeemable in legal tenders, their value is equal to those and equally depreciated as compared with coin.

Thus the present currency of the country is made up of six different kinds of money, embraces three distinct dollars of differing value, each of which is legal tender for debts in all sums, and amounts in all to $900,000,000 more or less. It is too much in quantity, and most of it inferior in quality. The demand for more currency, which has not even yet spent its force in some parts of the country, is as senseless a demand as ever was raised. It proceeds from the old misapprehension of the nature of money. Money is only a tool, — a value tool, whose sole work is to help exchange other values, — and men confound the tool with the values, and think there is a lack of the former when what is really lacking is the latter. "The cry that currency is deficient is for me pure moonshine. I do not know when currency is ever deficient, except when people who have wages to pay on Saturday night are short of silver coin. I know of no other instance of deficient currency. What is the test of insufficiency? That a man who can pay for coin or a bank-note cannot get one; but when did such a thing happen? Not in panics even. There is always a plenty of currency in every panic; for in every panic those who require coin or notes, and can pay for them, can invariably procure them. No one, in any panic, ever is prevented from buying a railway ticket, because he cannot procure a sovereign, which he has means to pay for; no one, who needed gold for exportation, failed to get it, if not at the bank, still at the gold dealers, if he has the means of purchasing. A man may hold consols and be determined to sell them at any price rather than go without gold, but consols are never sold because gold is deficient, but because a debt must be paid, and it will not be paid in gold. An invasion of England would no doubt make gold scarce, because people would prefer gold to the notes of a bank, which the enemy might seize. But that event would fall within my formula. The use of gold would be actually increased by the invasion. But the use of gold is not increased by the lending and borrowing, the repaying or the settling up of the money market. Currency is not the tool of lending in the market. Theoretically every creditor might call on his banker to-morrow morning at ten o'clock to pay his debt in gold, — then of course gold would be insufficient for the work: but such an event is morally impossible. The rule is always the same. The quantity of tools needed depends on the work; and the grand fact to realize is, that borrowing, lending, investments, discounting of bills, and the like, are not worked by currency, and that currency has nothing to do with them, except to an extent utterly insignificant."[1]

But there are those, who, admitting that the present volume of currency is excessive, nevertheless think that business will soon grow up to it, that prospective transactions will healthfully absorb the whole of it, and that the simple force of national development, without contraction of its volume, will bring our depreciated currency to par with gold. This position mistakes the method in which business is practically done. Increase of business does not necessarily imply increase of currency at all. The business of the whole world is largely done, increasingly done, by the use of a commercial expedient called SET-OFF, by which one debt is made to pay another debt, and so the mass of debts liquidate themselves, and little currency is needed. It is the principle of the clearing-house. London has become the clearing-house

[1] Manuscript letter of Bonamy Price to General Garfield.

of the whole world, the place where international debts are exchanged against each other, and in the quarter ending March 31, 1870, £1,006,932,000 of checks and bills passed that clearing. British business has increased threefold at least in the last quarter of a century, but British currency has increased but little, even if it has increased at all. The bank-note circulation of the two islands is just about £40,000,000, and there is doubtless something more than that of coin in bank and private store. Money, though vastly important *as determining the denominations of value*, does after all but the *driblets* of business, the bulk of transactions being done by set-off. Even bank-notes, when truly convertible, have usually a short interval between issue and redemption. The average life of a Bank of England note is reckoned to be less than three days. Let us hear another word from Bonamy Price: "Goods are very little exchanged by currency, — I mean coin and notes. Setting off of debts against each other does the work. Just analyze an investment. Take this case. I make a profit of £1000 by selling iron to America. I wish to invest it. I am paid by a bill which implies that some Englishman is a debtor to some American. I send the bill to my banker. He gets it paid, — not in currency, but by a setting off of debts at the clearing house. I buy a railway share, or a lot of American cotton. I pay for it by a check on my banker, who now owes me £1000. He pays that check again, not in currency, but at the clearing house. The result is that I made £1000 by selling iron, and I have the proceeds in a railway share or cotton, and currency has not done one iota of the operation."

In opposition to the complexities, uncertainties, and endless losses of our present currency, my friend, Mr. Amasa Walker, advocates what he calls a *mercantile currency*, that is, a paper money issued by banks, and based dollar for dollar on specie actually in reserve. He would have but one kind of money, and that kind this. As he admits, such a money would be local and conventional, but it would also be as invariable in value as specie, and more convenient. But as this plan requires the minting and maintaining of as much or more specie than would be required if specie were the only money, as it would always be difficult to secure that all the banks should always have as much of coin in reserve as of paper circulating, and as the element of credit enters into the nature of such paper money, I cannot think his scheme is preferable to my own.

Considering the state of public opinion, and the usage of the more enlightened commercial nations, one should speak on this subject with caution, but for myself I do not believe that paper money, in any variety of it, ever made a nation, on the whole, richer or happier. Let the money of the nations be gold and silver coins; let these be minted on some universal scheme for commercial convenience; let nothing be used as a measure of values but the denominations of these coins; then, in connection with such money as a basis, money which will hold its units, whether pound, dollar, or franc, as invariable as such measures can be kept, let there come in the various expedients of paper credit, such as certificates of deposit, bills of exchange, checks, drafts, or what name soever they may bear, and most, if not all, the conveniences of paper money will be secured, and none of its fluctuations and disasters experienced. These forms of paper would not be money, although they might be made to perform much more than they do now one of the functions of money, that is to say, they would serve in large and distant transactions as a medium of exchange, but they never could disturb, as paper money usually does, the measure of value. Under this system banks would still be necessary for the purpose of loaning money, buying and selling credits, making collections, and so on, *but they would not manufacture and issue money.* Thus the two legitimate spheres of money and of credit will be kept entirely distinct.

CHAPTER XII.

ON CREDIT.

POLITICAL ECONOMY is the science of exchanges but there are certain exchanges which have this peculiarity, that the transaction is not then and there ultimately closed, but one (or both) of the persons exchanging relies on the good faith of somebody to fulfill in the future a promise expressly or impliedly made in the exchange. This peculiarity is very important to be considered, and gives rise to all those phenomena which pass under the general name of Credit. Debt and Credit are correlative terms. There is no debt without credit, and there is no credit without debt. The whole subject of credit is best unfolded by considering what is involved in the relation of debtor and creditor. This is wholly a personal relation; it always involves the element of future time, and is founded on the *belief* of one of the parties in a virtual promise made by the other. Hence the term credit from CREDO, *I believe*, and the corresponding term debt from DEBEO, *I owe*. Two other terms sometimes used in this connection are so ambiguous as to require explanation, namely, the terms *loan* and *borrow*.[1] If I loan a book to my friend, I expect him to return to me that particular

[1] For this point and some others in this chapter, not contained in my previous editions, I am indebted to Mr. Macleod's "Banking," *passim*.

book, and I do not alienate to him my ownership in it at all; but if I loan him ten dollars, I alienate to him completely my property in that money, and only expect him to return me an equivalent at some future time. In the last case there is credit and debt, but not in the former case. So of the word borrow. I may reclaim from a neighbor a borrowed tool, even without his permission; but I may not take back ten dollars he has borrowed from me, because I happen to find his purse. I have a claim on him for ten dollars, but he must pay me voluntarily, or be compelled by legal process. This illustrates what is said above, that the relation of debtor and creditor is a personal relation. It has nothing to do with any specific commodity. It is substantially a claim of one *person* on another *person*, and is based on good faith only.

This claim, however, of the creditor on the debtor is just as much property as anything else is property. The right to demand from the debtor at some future time an equivalent for what the creditor renders is the service which the creditor receives from the debtor at the time of the exchange. It is a clear case of value. Each renders to the other satisfactory equivalents. The right to demand a future equivalent is the present equivalent for the sake of which something else is rendered. All our definitions apply here perfectly. Considered as a mere case of value, the transaction is ended; but, considered as to the nature and basis of the exchange, the transaction is not yet closed. It follows, then, that *Credits or Debts are Rights not yet realized;* but which are, nevertheless, constantly bought and sold. What lies between creditors and debtors may be called indifferently debts or credits: it is of vital consequence to *persons*, whether they owe or are owed by others; but the *rights* alone become the subject of exchange, and the terms merely relative to persons become indifferent. The amount of transactions in credits is immense in every commercial country, and is becoming constantly greater. Not only are the exchanges very common in which the right to demand future payment is one of the services rendered, but the exclusive traffic in debts — exchanges of one form of debt for another — has already reached gigantic proportions in all parts of the world. In order that this form of exchanges may take place, it is of course needful that there should be a general confidence in the public mind; in other words, a general expectation that such debts will be promptly paid. As indicating a common honor and financial ability among business men, and as facilitating the production of services of all sorts, this state of general confidence is so desirable in the sphere of exchange, that great pains should be taken that nothing occur to destroy it. Credit-exchanges are naturally more sensitive than any other, since they walk by faith and not by sight. For reasons to be adduced shortly, they are more liable to be unduly multiplied than other exchanges are. The credit system is a great blessing to mankind, but, like all other great blessings, is very likely to be abused.

The right to demand a future payment of something from somebody is a species of incorporeal property well guarded by law; and, though itself intangible, is commonly, but not necessarily, re corded on paper. The paper is the evidence of the right, and not the right itself. These paper documents are termed Instruments of Credit, and are of two kinds: first, Promises to pay, and second, Orders to pay. We will first look at these principal forms of Credit, and then at its advantages and disadvantages.

(1.) Book Accounts. A charge in a trader's books is both a current and a legal evidence that the person charged has received a certain service, and has virtually promised to render the sum charged as a return service. This is the most common of the forms of credit; and if the person charged fails of his own accord to complete the exchange thus commenced, the law, in the absence of any proof to make the charge suspicious, collects it, if possible, and forcibly completes the exchange. The convenience of this form of credit is so great that it is not likely ever to be disused; and as between people who deal much with each other is very useful, inasmuch as their respective book accounts are set against each other in settlement, and only balances are required to be cancelled in money. It is for the benefit of both creditor and debtor, however, that such credits should be short in time, and such settlements frequent, since thus only does the creditor realize the gains of the exchange, and the debtor keep fair his mercantile name. If it be difficult or impossible to follow strictly the excellent financial maxim, "Pay as you go," the next best thing to that is, "Go and pay." The gains of an exchange are lessened, or its terms become more onerous, just in proportion as delay in its completion is experienced or expected. Book accounts are subject also to this disadvantage as compared with other forms of credit, that their number and amount as against any person are less likely to become publicly known, and therefore he is more likely to be trusted in this form by others beyond the point of his solvency and their safety.

(2.) Promissory notes. These are issued by individuals, corporations, and nations. They are usually on interest; and in this case, if the principal be considered secure, and the interest be promptly paid, the element of time is comparatively a matter of indifference, because the interest is compensation for delay, and is frequently the motive on the part of the holder of the note for rendering that service of which the note is evidence. When such promissory note, or other form of credit, is payable to bearer, it may run a devious round, may play a part in many a transaction; but it is in reality nothing but a general warrant entitling the holder, in view of some original service of the claim for the return of which he has become in some manner possessed, to take his satisfaction for that service whenever he will. It is like the land warrants, given by the United States, entitling the holder, in return for military service rendered, to locate his acres on any unoccupied national land within the national boundaries. As a warrant, its function ceases so soon as the acres have been chosen. Credit passes into payment. The private notes of individuals and corporations are payable in money, and if in credit-money, this itself ends in something that is not credit, and thus the circuit of exchange is completed.

When the United States borrows money, it gives

the lender a promissory note on interest at a certain rate, both principal and interest being payable at certain specified times. These notes are called indifferently bonds, stocks, or funds. The government issued in 1862–1865, both inclusive, about $2,500,000,000 worth of them, in return for money loaned to it by the people, and they bore interest at rates varying from 5 to $7\frac{3}{10}$ per cent., and were payable at periods varying from three to forty years. The bonds designated as "five-twenties," bear gold interest at six per cent., and the government reserves the right to pay the principal in five years, and pledges itself to pay it twenty years from date. So of the "ten-forties." The "seven-thirties" were so named, not from the time of payment, but from the rate of interest, which was $7\frac{30}{100}$ per cent., payable in legal tenders for three years, when the principal was payable in the same, or fundable in six per cent. gold-bearing bonds, at the option of the holders. So ready have the American people been to loan money to their government for the past few years, and take these bonds as security, that the treasury has experienced very little embarrassment from the want of money, although the expenditures have been at times over $3,000,000 a day. In the course of one week in the spring of 1865, ninety and odd millions of dollars were subscribed to a national loan. It is believed that the history of national borrowing presents no parallel with the late success of the United States in realizing money in the way of loans. The largest English loans ever made were made in 1812 and 1813, during the wars with Napoleon and the United States. In these two years the British exchequer borrowed $534,000,000, being an average of $22,250,000 a month, and pronounced that a wonderful financial achievement, as it was; but, from an aggregate of national wealth not larger than England's then was, though from a larger population, the United States realized in four years from loans three times as much at least in gold value, and at an average rate of interest but little higher than England then paid, which was five per cent. and a fraction.[1] The treasury notes commonly called greenbacks are promissory notes not on interest. They were made a legal tender for all debts public and private except duties on imports and interest on the public debt.

(3.) Bank-bills. Bank-bills are a form of promissory notes not on interest, and thus differ from the notes of ordinary corporations; but the bank offers, as a sort of compensation for the privilege of circulating notes not on interest, to convert them into coin on demand of any holder. It is this proffered convertibility into coin that enables the promissory notes of a bank to circulate as money, while the notes of other corporations and individuals equally solid and solvent do not circulate as money. It must be borne in mind, however, that the offer to convert them into cash does not essentially alter the nature of bank-notes; they are a form of credit; and although they are commonly issued against another form of credit, namely, against the interest-bearing notes of individuals who resort to the bank for discount, this only complicates the exchange without changing its nature. It is an instance of exchanging one form of credit for another which happens to have a greater

[1] Appleton's Annual Cyclopædia, 1863. Article "Finances."

currency or validity than the first, and for this superiority of the bank credit the individual credit pays an interest, in other words, is discounted; and such exchanges of one form of paper credit for another, with or without a premium, may go on indefinitely; as credit money, such paper may serve as a medium in many exchanges; but ultimately, and before the entire series of transactions is closed, such paper is to be exchanged for something that is not paper; it is redeemed in cash, or gives a claim to something no longer credit which is in reality the return service for the original service rendered.

(4.) Bank Deposits. Mr. Macleod gives the following definition of a banker: "*A banker is a trader who buys money, or money and debts, by creating other debts.*" A merchant is a dealer in commodities; a banker is a dealer in credits. The word *bank* meant originally a mass, an accumulation; as we still say, a *sand-bank*, and the *banks* of a river. When first applied to commercial transactions, as it was in Venice as early as 1171, it meant a common contribution of money then made by the citizens to the state; and also the *place* where commissioners paid the interest on this loan, and the shares in it were transferred. Both of these meanings inhere in the modern word bank. A bank is a place to which the money of other people is brought, as well as the banker's own; and hence we speak of banks of deposit: it is a place in which one form of credit is exchanged for another form; and hence we speak of banks of discount: it is frequently a place where promissory notes, designed to circulate as money, are issued; and hence we speak of banks of circulation

These three are the main functions of banks; and of these, the two former are, while the third is not, essential to banking. The central idea in banking is this: the banker receives his customers' money, and renders to them in return a credit, that is, a right to demand from him an equal sum at a future time. The evidence of this right is entered upon the banker's books, and thus becomes a DEPOSIT. The ownership of the money passes completely from the customer to the banker. The latter has the right to do just what he pleases with it; but he must be ready to respond to his customer's call, when the latter demands, not his own money, but so much of his banker's money. A deposit, therefore, is not the thing deposited, but a credit. The banker buys money with credit.

The motive that leads the customer to intrust his funds to the banker is the desire, not to have those specific funds kept safely, (for, the moment they have passed into the banker's hands, they are his absolutely,) but to have the right to call on the banker for such sums (not to exceed the deposit in the aggregate) and at such times as may suit his own convenience. He has such confidence in the integrity and solvency of the banker, and finds it so practically convenient to have dealings with him, that he prefers a credit on him for the amount to the possession of the money itself. The motive of the banker to receive his customers' funds on these terms is the fact that he can safely use a large portion of these funds in other operations in credit profitable to himself, and at the same time be sure of being able to meet his customers' calls for money He finds by experience that many of his customers wish always to have a balance in his hands; that while some of them are constantly drawing on him for cash, others of them are as constantly depositing with him in cash, and that consequently he can use with safety a part of the money he has purchased with his credit to purchase other credits with.

(5.) Discounted Notes. This brings us to the second essential function of banking, the discounting of paper. The banker uses his cash to buy credit, as well as his credit to buy cash. The credits that he buys are either notes of hand or bills of exchange, the former are promises to pay and the latter orders to pay. The form makes but little difference to the banker. His chief concern is with the genuineness and financial solidity of the names upon the paper to be discounted. Manufacturers and wholesale merchants usually sell goods *on time*, as it is called, say three months. A debt is thus created. The manufacturer or wholesaler is creditor and the jobber or retailer is debtor. But a debt is property; and the creditor in this case wishes to avail himself of his property at once for further production; so he either takes a note from his debtor, or draws a bill upon him, and this piece of property is ready for sale. The banker buys it, that is to say, the creditor passes over to him the right to demand payment of the debtor at the end of three months, and receives from the banker either money or so much of the banker's credit, that is, a deposit in the creditor's favor on the banker's books. For furnishing this creditor either with ready money or a more available credit in lieu of his mercantile paper, the banker charges a percentage. This is DISCOUNT. Discount is the difference between the face and the price of the paper. This is the chief source of profit in ordinary banking. When the paper matures, the banker realizes from the debtor its full face. The following is the form of a bankable note: —

> $1000. NORTH ADAMS, Mass., *Nov.* 10, 1871.
>
> Three months after date I promise to pay to the order of Joshua Swan, one thousand dollars, payable at the Adams National Bank, value received.
>
> Due Feb. 10/13. LEANDER ALLEN.

Joshua Swan's name on the back of this paper, and the requisite government stamp, make it, if the parties are "good," a legal and acceptable note for discount. Two names are usually, not always, requisite; but paper is discounted on the strength of all the names that are upon it.

It is thus in part through the purchase of discountable notes for money that banks derive their character as money-lenders. Also, such reserve sums as they do not wish to invest in negotiable paper, on account of the time involved before such paper matures, banks frequently loan on call to those who have salable collateral securities to pledge. So far forth they become direct money-lenders. The following is the form of such pledge: —

$5000. TROY, N. Y., *Nov.* 10, 1871.

On demand we promise to pay to the Bank of Troy, or order, five thousand dollars, for value received, with interest at the rate of six per cent. per annum, having deposited with said bank, as collateral security, with authority to sell the same, at the Brokers' Board, or at public or private sale, or otherwise at said bank's option, on the non-performance of this promise, and without notice, —

10 shares N. Y. Central,
55 do. Mich. Southern. JOHN SMITH & Co.

The buying of paper for money is mainly done in England by another class of dealers called bill-discounters, and is coming to be done somewhat in this country by retired merchants and others; though most of our banks continue to do it in connection with their function of issue. It is more in accordance with genuine *banking* to buy paper with credit, that is, by passing the price of the paper to the seller's credit in the form of a deposit. These deposits are promises to pay on demand. They are the customer's property, and the banker's promise.

We now come to two other forms of credit, which are virtually *orders* to pay.

(6.) Bills of exchange. A bill of exchange is a written instrument designed to secure the payment of a distant debt without the transmission of money, being in effect a setting off or exchange of one debt against another. Thus, suppose A in Boston owes B in New York $1000, and another party, C in New York, owes A in Boston a like sum; it is not necessary that A should send the money to B to cancel his debt, and C send the money to A for a like purpose; the two debts, by means of a bill of exchange, are set off against each other, and both transactions are closed without sending any money from one city to the other. A draws a bill upon C, directing him to pay B $1000, and sends this bill to B, who, if the bill be drawn on sight, presents it to C for payment; if on time, presents it to C for acceptance, who then pays it at maturity. An acceptance is written upon the face of a bill, as an endorsement is upon its back. A is called the drawer of the bill, C the drawee until he has accepted, and then the acceptor, and B is the payee. It is not often that the same person, as A, happens to owe another person in a distant place, as B, exactly the same sum as is owed him in that place by a third person as C; but by two bills of exchange, one drawn by each creditor on his own debtor, and then set off against the other, substantially the same advantage is reached as if it always happened so. Nearly all these bills come into banks in the way of ordinary business, either for discount or collection, and are adjusted through bank balances. The following is the form of an inland bill of exchange: —

$3000. PITTSFIELD, Mass., *Oct.* 1, 1871.

Four months after date pay to the order of John Kent three thousand dollars, value received, and charge the same to account of DAN STORRS & CO.

To ELI TRIPP, Boston, Mass.

Kent endorses, Tripp accepts, the stamp is affixed, and the bill is negotiable. Sometimes bills are drawn to the order of "ourselves," in which case the drawers also endorse. Not infrequently a bill passes through several hands, which may either be by successive endorsements, specifying to whom payment is to be made, or by what is called an endorsement in blank, by which is meant that the payee or subsequent holder, to whom the bill has been endorsed, merely writes his own name upon the bill, which is equivalent to making it payable to bearer. The remarkable convenience of bills of exchange in adjusting debts between distant places has already brought them into very general use wherever the necessary basis for them in commercial integrity is supposed to exist; and every year is witnessing an extension of their use in all commercial countries. Bills of exchange are either payable at sight, or after an interval fixed in the bill itself; and are either inland or foreign bills. Bills which have some time to run before maturity are frequently discounted by bankers or other money lenders, that is to say, the payee transfers the bill to them, receiving the amount, minus interest for the time it has still to run; and the bill thus serves the important function of enabling a debt due from one person to be made available for obtaining credit from another. It is a principal part of the business of banks to buy in this manner bills of exchange, either real bills, or accommodation bills, so called, which only differ from the others in that there is no real debt between the drawer and drawee, and collect them at maturity, thus securing bank interest on all money paid in purchasing such bills. The bills are discounted on the joint credit of the drawer and acceptor. It is evident that the use of bills of exchange, especially those which pass from hand to hand by endorsement, dispenses with the use and transmission of large amounts of money, and, as between distant places especially, is one of those economizing expedients of credit which are the birth of modern civilization and a sound mercantile honor.

Very similar are foreign bills of exchange in their functions and usefulness. Commercial relations between two countries, say for example, France and England, always give rise to a mutual indebtedness of their merchants, and if these debts were all to be paid by the actual sending of money to and from, there would have to be a constant and expensive outward and inward flow of the precious metals in respect to each country, which necessity is neatly obviated by the use of bills of exchange, and coin is only transmitted to settle the balances on whichever side there is an excess of debt. French dealers are always sending goods to England, and English dealers goods to France; and for what they send to England the French merchants draw bills on the parties to whom the goods are consigned, and the English merchants draw similar bills on their debtors in France; these bills are bought up by bankers or brokers in either country, and exposed again for sale to any parties who may have debts to pay in the other country. Thus bills on London, in other words, on English debtors, are always for sale in France; and bills on France, that is, on French debtors, are always for sale in London; the mutual debtors of the two countries, therefore, instead of sending coin to cancel their debts, buy and transmit these bills. As I wish to make the course and par of international exchange very plain to my readers, I will give a particular illustration. Suppose Pierre & Co., of Paris, send a cargo of wine to Barclay & Co., of London, worth £5000; the London firm thereby becomes indebted to the Paris firm to that amount, and Pierre & Co. draw a bill on Barclay & Co. for £5000; if they themselves have no debt to pay in London, they sell this bill to a Paris broker (if the exchange be then at par) for its face, minus interest for the time it has to run; and this broker is now ready to sell the bill again to anybody in Paris who has a debt to pay in London; and the person in London who receives it in liquidation of a French debt to him, presents it at maturity to Barclay & Co. for payment. A bill drawn in London for a cargo of hardware sent to Paris, is similarly negotiated with a London broker, and finds its way similarly to France, in payment of some English debt, and ends its career when it reaches the French firm on which it was originally drawn. We are now in position to understand clearly what is meant by the par of exchange. The merchants in Paris, who have debts due to them in London, draw bills of exchange for the amount of these debts, and, through the agency of middlemen or brokers, go into the market to sell these bills to other Paris merchants who have debts to pay in London. If the former set have a larger amount to sell than the latter have occasion to buy, in other words, if there be a larger amount of debts due from London to Paris, than from Paris to London, then the competition of the sellers of bills on London will lower their price somewhat in the market, in order, as usual, that the supply and demand may be equalized. In this case the par of exchange is disturbed, a bill on London for £100 may not sell for over £99, and the exchange is then said to be one per cent. against London, or, which is the same thing, one per cent. in favor of Paris. The par of exchange, therefore, between two countries, depends upon the substantial equality of their mutual debts; and if an exchange unfavorable to either continues long, and especially if the discount on its bills be sufficient to cover the charges of the transmission of specie, gold will begin to flow from the country against which the exchange has turned, and the equilibrium of payments, and hence the par of exchange will be restored. Also, the par tends to restore itself, without the sending of specie, in this way: if bills on London are at a discount in Paris, for the same reason that they are so will bills on Paris be at a premium in London, and therefore there will be a direct encouragement to the extent of the premium for exportations from England to France, because on every cargo sent bills can be drawn and sold in London for a premium; but the more bills on Paris thus offered, the more the premium disappears, and the par of exchange is restored so soon as the debts thus contracted by France are equal to the debts due her from England. At the same time, and so long as the discount on London bills continues, there is a discouragement to further exportations from France to England, because the bills drawn in virtue of such cargoes can only be sold below par. Here is another instance of a magnificently comprehensive law by which Nature vindicates her right to reign in the domain of exchange. It is through this law, stimulating exportations on the one side, and slackening them on the other, that most of the casual disturbances of the par of exchange are rectified; but if, notwithstanding this, the disturbance continues obstinate, it indicates one of two things as true of the country against which the exchange has turned: it has either made over-purchases of the other country beyond the power of its ordinary exports to cancel, or the money in which the bills drawn on it are liable to be paid is an inferior money. In the first case, the only proper remedy is an export of gold to pay off the old scores, and a more prudent method of purchasing in the future; in the second case, which is well exemplified in the instance of Amsterdam, cited in a preceding chapter, the remedy is to raise the currency to a good specie standard. When the rates of exchange were first established between England and the Colonies, the Mexican dollar of commerce was equal in value to 4*s.* 6*d.* English, £1 = 4.44 dollars, and the par of exchange was established at that rate. U. S. dollars have always been less valuable than that Mexican dollar, and while the old par has remained the standard, the real par has been changed by each change in our coins. Our present dollar contains 23.22 grains of pure gold; the English pound contains 113.001 grains, consequently the true par of exchange is $4.8665 to the £, and is expressed by 109½ instead of the old 100. The par of exchange between France and the United States is 5 francs

17 centimes for \$1; and between France and England, is 25 francs 20 centimes for £1.

(7.) Checks. Formerly, in England, and in other countries as well, every considerable dealer kept his strong box, and when he had occasion to make payments, told down the solid cash upon his own counter. Afterwards, the goldsmiths of London solicited the honor of keeping in their vaults the spare cash of the merchants, who in their payments among one another came to employ checks drawn on the goldsmiths, and at the shops of the latter the principal payments in coin were effected. The later introduction of banks brought along with it the custom, now continually widening in commercial countries among all classes of people, of keeping one's funds with a banker, and making payments by orders, or checks, upon him. When the person making the payment and the person receiving it keep their money with the same banker, there is no need of any money passing at all in the premises, the sum being merely transferred in the banker's books from the credit of the payer to that of the receiver. The banker is quite willing to do this business for nothing, and even to allow the depositors a low rate of interest on all balances remaining in his hands, in consideration of the privilege he enjoys of loaning such proportion of the sums as he deems safe to other parties at a higher rate of interest. In the large cities, by an arrangement called "the clearing-house," substantially the same benefits are secured as if all the people of the city kept their cash at the same bank; inasmuch as all the checks drawn on each of the different banks, and passing in the course of the business day into other banks, are assorted before evening at the clearing-house, and set off as far as possible against each other, leaving only balances to be adjusted in money. The London clearing-house was established in 1775; lately, the clearing-house itself, and the bankers and firms dealing with it, all have accounts at the Bank of England, and balances formerly settled by money are now settled by simple bank transfers. Checks may pass from hand to hand by endorsement; but in business towns it is more usual for each man to draw his own check to make payments, and pass in the checks he receives to his banker. Checks are bills of exchange with some differing legal incidents. So are drafts. A bill of exchange drawn by one banker on another has usually in this country been termed a draft. So far of the instruments of credit. Some of the advantages of credit have been already anticipated in the discussion of its principal forms; but we will now instance more specifically a few of these advantages.

1. There are some men, and particularly young men, who have integrity and industry and skill, but no capital; and when such men are enabled to borrow money to start themselves in business, or to enlarge a business already in successful operation, the general interests of production, as well as their personal interests, are subserved by such credit, because in all probability capital thus passes from hands which are less to hands which are more able to use it productively. Those who are best able to make capital tell are generally those who are most desirous to obtain it, and frequently those who can offer the best secu-

rity for its replacement. Nothing is to be said against, but everything in favor, of such a loaning of capital as shall bring it, under safe conditions, from the hands of the idle, the aged, those indisposed, or those incompetent to use it productively, into hands at once competent and honest. Such credit is a benefit, and only a benefit, to all the parties concerned, and to society at large. The operators retain something of profit after replacing the capital with interest; the lenders receive more than if their capital remained idle, or they employed it themselves; and society is benefited by a more complete development and rapid circulation of services. Despite all the instances of broken faith, it is still an honor to human nature that men do so gain by good character the confidence of their fellows that they are, and ought to be, trusted with capital on their simple word or note; and it is the glory of free political institutions, that under their influence, more than elsewhere, young men with no other dower than integrity and purpose do rise, by the help of so slight a stepping-stone as this, in crowds, to the high places of opulence. In the point of view, that thus all the available capital of the community is brought out into productive activity, too much can scarcely be said in favor of joint-stock companies, whose managers are known to be men of probity, which gather up the driblets of unoccupied capital here and there, and, combining them, enter upon paths of profitable production, which individual enterprise cannot tread. Too much cannot be said in favor of savings-banks, which take the surplus earnings of the poor, and not only keep them safely, but pay a fair interest on each deposit, and loan the aggregate at a higher rate on choice securities, thus stimulating frugality in a wide circle of depositors, and at the same time aiding production by opportune loans to the best class of borrowers. Here too come in life-insurance companies, which illustrate the advantages of credit in a most gratifying light, and whose action I hope to see extended to larger and larger classes of men, since it tends to transmute low and selfish cares into a noble care for those who are to come after, who might otherwise be left penniless dependants, and by elevating and enlarging the views of men, to make them better producers and better citizens. In this category of the advantages of credit come also the ordinary bank discounts, made for short periods only, holding the debtor to the strictest rules of payment, only professing and only enabled to help customers over the transient hard places in their business, and not to furnish the funds on which the business is mainly conducted. Sums drawn from the banks on credit should only form a part of the circulating capital of a business, and never be put into the form of fixed capital. The passing necessities of a business having an independent basis of its own can be safely and conveniently met by bank discounts. So far as the capital stock of a bank is made up of small subscriptions, it has the advantage just spoken of, of calling otherwise idle sums into activity; and so far as no undue privileges are accorded to it by law, there is no branch of industry more legitimate and beneficial than banking. It is no essential part of the functions of a bank, that it manufacture and issue money; the money it loans should be the national money; and if that, unfortunately, be credit money, the element of credit in the money should be sharply discriminated in the public mind from that element of credit by which the bank loans it to its customers. Bank credits are good, but that does not prove that credit money is good; and it was one ground of the viciousness of the late banking system of the United States, that the different kinds of credit involved in it were inextricably interwoven with each other in the common apprehensions, and when the money failed utterly, as it did repeatedly, to answer the purposes of money, people could not exactly tell whose fault it was.

2. There is another class of advantages in credit, which do not depend so much on the transfer of capital from less to more productive hands, as on the facilities which credit affords in economizing the general operations of exchange. Here the advantages are derived from the convenience of settling accounts arising out of exchanges, rather than from the character of the exchanges themselves. Look, for example, at bills of exchange. They serve to settle up the accounts arising from the commerce of two continents, with but little transmission of money from either, and with but little loss of time. Bills drawn in New York on London are usually payable at sixty days' sight; and the merchant dispatching a ship is able to realize at once the value of her cargo, minus interest for the time his bill has to run; he is indeed still liable in part to see that his bill is ultimately paid by his drawee; but the commercial integrity of the leading houses in all countries is with justice so firmly believed in and acted on, that on the

whole but little anxiety springs from this source. It is one of the noble things in international commerce that men trust each other across the oceans, and lay millions of value on the faith of a single firm. Inland bills of exchange equally facilitate settlements within the country itself; and checks contribute to the same end even more simply, passing readily in payments wherever the parties are known, and, though credit, doing the work of money more conveniently, and within certain limits as safely as money itself could do it. The face of a check drawn to the amount of his deposit in favor of another depositor is transferred in the banker's books from the credit of the drawer to that of the payee. The banker is released from one debt by creating another of equal amount. The drawer is released from a debt by causing another debt to be transferred to the payee. The payee is paid by the drawer by the receipt of another debt. Thus we see that a release from a debt is the same thing as a payment in money; and we saw in the paragraph on bills of exchange that the mutual release from debts is the same thing as a reciprocal payment of debts.

3. It is not strange that some thinkers and writers, seeing these unquestionable benefits of credit even within the peculiar sphere of money itself, have come, like Herbert Spencer and many others, to think and teach that credit might answer all the purposes of money. It is certain that it answers some of the purposes of money. Suppose A has bought of B $100 worth of goods, and B has bought of A $125 worth of another kind of goods. Three ways are open to close up these transactions. A may pay

B and B may pay A in money. This would take $225. A may pay B in money, and B may send it back with $25 more. This would take $125. Or A and B may mutually balance books, and B pay the difference in account. This would take $25. It is clear, that, as one or other of these methods prevails in practice, the quantity of money required to do the business of a country is very different. So in international trade. Foreign bills of exchange lessen enormously the quantity of money that would otherwise have to be transported. Credit *does* take the place of money in part. Can it take the place of money entirely? I think not.

We have defined credit as a right not yet realized. The denominations of money are certainly needful in order to *measure* this right; and I do not see how the denominations of money can be maintained at all separately from the use of money itself as a medium. Moreover, great as is the undoubted power of credit, it waits for something beyond itself; it waits for realization. I do not see how realization can come without the use of money, at least to settle balances. Further, there always have been hitherto in all commercial countries longer or shorter periods during which there was a general reluctance to accept the ordinary instruments of credit in exchange. Money, and much of it, was then found to be indispensable. The very advantages of credit itself, which have now been explained, are dependent on this, that there be underneath it, to support and limit it, a solid basis of value-money, in whose denominations value can be reckoned, in whose coins the balances of credit can be struck, and whose presence secured everywhere by natural laws alone can enable fulfillment to join hand in hand with promise If ever credit should usurp the whole domain of money, a tolerable standard of value would be no longer possible, credit itself would lose its foothold, and the vast balloon of promise, sailing for a while through the blue, the joy of projectors and the wonder of credulous spectators, would descend on a sudden collapsed and ruined to the earth.

This is the place to notice the much mooted question whether deposits are a part of the currency. It will have been observed that I have not used the word currency in these discussions in any technical sense. I do not accept the common distinction made between money and currency, namely, that the former is coin, and the latter the aggregate of the current forms of credit. Current usage of language in this country recognizes bank-notes as money equally with coins; and regards the possession of a *generalized* purchasing-power, by means of which something circulates among all classes of the people as a medium in their exchanges, as the sole characteristic of money. I think in this case language hits the mark. If so, deposits, though they may be currency if one cares for the word, are not *money.* A deposit is as much the banker's promise to pay as the bank-note is, but the two promises are quite diverse in their action. The note passes from hand to hand indefinitely in payments, legally liquidates debts at once, and is likely enough not to return to the banker for years. A check, on the other hand, drawn on a deposit, though it may pass by indorsement through a number of hands, yet in practice rarely makes but one payment, is legally discriminated from the bank-note, and comes back to the banker almost immediately. Checks are a useful form of credit, much less liable to abuse than bank-notes, but they lack that peculiar quality that constitutes anything to be money. Besides the two essential functions of banks, receiving deposits and discounting bills, they perform a variety of other legitimate operations in credit. They buy and sell debts of all sorts. They sell their own drafts on distant places. Our new national banks have done an immense business in the national bonds. They have been instrumental in diffusing these bonds among the people. They collect for their customers the coupons at maturity. They are the factors of the government in exchanging, for those who desire it, one species of bond for another. For the most part, all these dealings of bankers in debts, — and their aggregate amount is enormous, — must be enumerated among the advantages of credit.

There are some natural disadvantages in credit. The first is, that when it is much given by dealers to consumers, the reverse results take place from those already characterized, and capital passes out from the hands of productive operators and becomes temporarily unavailable as capital. When an industrious artisan or merchant has trusted out $1000 to dilatory customers for six months or a year, it is so much withdrawn for so long from his active capital, and to make up the consequent loss of profit there must be an addition to the prices of his wares, and besides some bad debts belong to such a system, and there must be an additional price to compensate this, and thus the customers who pay promptly bear a part of the proper burden of the delinquents, who at least do not wholly escape, inasmuch as they ultimately (if they pay at all) pay a price enhanced by their own delay. If the current profit of capital be ten per cent., and the merchant sells and gets returns five times a year, something less than two per cent. profit may be charged to each article, but if he only gets returns at the end of the year, ten per cent. must be put upon everything. Hence the excellent maxim, "Quick sales and small profits."

But the principal disadvantage of credit is seen in its action on prices through increased demand, and in its consequent tendency to produce commercial crises: and this chapter will be concluded by a presentation of this subject, together with a brief discussion of the proper method of dealing with the national debt of the United States.

The cause of commercial crises is, in general, an undue expansion of credit; or, to use an equivalent expression, a disproportion between the amount of debts and the available capital in the loan-market, or elsewhere, to meet those debts.

A man's whole purchasing-power is made up of three things: first, the property in his possession; secondly, the value that is owed to him; thirdly, his credit. He can buy value with these three things; and his power to buy is exactly measured by the sum of these three things. But while the first two are limited and ascertainable, the third, credit, is in a certain sense unlimited. Being based upon confidence, which is itself a variable quantity, a man's credit at one time may be vastly greater than at another, compared with his real property; and, if he have the reputation of doing a safe and regular business, and is favored by circumstances, he will find himself sometimes able to buy on credit to an extent out of all proper proportion to his capital. Instances are given of dealers, who, in times of speculation, have effected purchases to an extent seventy or even one hundred times greater than their capital. And on the other hand, in times of panic, men of known character and of financial solidity find it impossible to borrow a dollar.

Now money acts upon prices only by being offered in exchange for commodities; but we have seen that commodities may be purchased by credit as well as by money; when, therefore, credit is offered and received for commodities, it has the same influence upon prices, as when money is offered and received for them. The form which the credit assumes to effect the purchase is a matter of indifference, whether bank-notes, checks, bills of exchange, or book-credits, what acts upon prices is the credit, in whatever shape given, or whether it gives rise to transferable paper or not.

It follows from this, that whenever there is an extension of credit for the purpose of purchasing, there will be a corresponding rise of prices. He who employs both his cash and his credit in purchasing, creates a demand for the article to the full amount of his money and credit taken together, and raises the price proportionally to both.

There might be a simultaneous rise of price in several commodities, and a considerable spirit of speculation manifested in these, if there were no such thing as credit and all business were done by ready money; but there could not be a general rise of prices as to all commodities; for, while men spent more money on the few commodities, and they rose in price, they would have less money to spend on other commodities, and these would not rise, but rather fall. It is only when credit can be used freely, and increased purchases can go on in all departments at once, that there can be a rise of prices as to all commodities, and a universal spirit of speculation.

At such times, and while prices are still rising, men seem to be making great gains; those that sell while the fever is on do make great gains; and they not only use their credit freely, but they really have more credit to use, from the very fact they seem to be prosperous. Everybody wishes to extend his operations to the utmost limit, in order to realize the greatest possible gains. Everybody wishes to use not only all his money, but all his credit. Everybody desires accommodation, and accordingly everybody gives accommodation. All forms of indebtedness are greatly increased. Promissory-notes, bills of exchange, book-credits, are indefinitely multiplied in all directions.

It begins now to be perceived in certain quarters, that the thing has been overdone; speculative purchases cease; prices begin to fall; holders of commodities are anxious to sell; this very anxiety makes the price decline still further; holders rush into the market to avoid a still greater loss; and, as nobody wishes to buy when a market is falling, prices go down, down, down. Their inflated wealth collapses in the hands of the holders; a panic often sets in, more unreasonable, if possible, than the previous over-confidence. Men must realize something from their property; they sell it therefore, frequently, at almost any sacrifice; but the small amounts of money thus realized, and all the loans which can be extorted for unusual rate of interest, now when credit is almost destroyed, are totally inadequate to meet the immense mass of debts contracted when confidence was high. Property for which a man gave his note for $10,000 is now worth but $1000, but that fact does not annihilate his debt, or erase his name from the unlucky paper; he is still bound for the $10,000. And as the mass of paper, greatly augmented during the period of excitement, comes to maturity, how can it be met? It cannot be met. There is not disposable capital enough in the loan-market to meet it, even if it could be made available. But those who have capital hold on to it. They do not know whom to trust. Everybody seems to be losing, and many are failing all around them, and they will not loan. Those men therefore who have these debts to meet have no resource. They could borrow indefinitely a few months before, but now they cannot borrow a dollar. They besiege the banks with which they deal, sometimes piteously, and sometimes bitterly, for accommodation. But the banks cannot help them. These men must fail. There is no help for it. Thousands do fail in every revulsion. Distress, more or less extensive, is the invariable consequent of the series of events called a commercial crisis. That series is constituted somewhat in this manner: first, business a little brisk; second, confidence and credit enlarging; third, a spirit of speculation; fourth, a vast increase of all forms of debt; fifth, the revulsion, or what may be called the cascade of discredit; sixth, stagnation and distress.

A national debt is a mortgage upon the national property and income. It is sometimes considered as a blessing, but is more generally and truthfully regarded as a burden. It is not denied that incidental advantages may spring up in connection with it. The bonds, which are the evidences of the debt, open a convenient form of investment for presently inactive capital and for trust-funds of all kinds. There can be no doubt, I think, that certain classes of persons holding these national obligations are won to a stronger loyalty and become firmer friends to stability in government; but this consideration applies mainly to new governments, and to those temporarily endangered. Both England and the United States now make a portion of their public debt the basis of a national system of banking; but it is very questionable whether this can be mentioned among the incidental benefits of the debt. Again, "a moderate debt adds to the credit of a nation, and its ability to raise money in an emergency, for bankers and capitalists are more ready to take such securities as they are in the habit of dealing in."[1]

The burdens of a national debt are very apparent. During the fiscal year closing June 30, 1867, the United States paid out in interest $143,781,592; and between the 1st September, 1865, and the 1st November, 1867, it paid towards the principal of the debt $266,185,121. These vast sums came out

[1] Communication from Sidney Homer.

of the industry and income of individuals. They came through taxation of individual proprietors of value; and taxation to any such degree as this is a great disturbance to industry, and gives rise to an army of officials who consume a considerable percentage of all they collect. The collection of the internal revenue for the fiscal year 1867 cost $7,712,089. Moreover, the various expedients of taxation, which are always practically unequal in their operation, give rise to irritation and political agitation, and even sometimes to threats of repudiation, especially when the occasion has gone by under which the debt was contracted, and a generation is called upon to liquidate a debt which it had no agency in creating.

And here the vexed question arises, how far one generation has a right to throw upon succeeding ones the burdens of a national debt? I answer, that it has a very limited right indeed. The opposite doctrine tacitly implies that succeeding generations will have no occasion for extraordinary expenses of their own, and therefore may rightfully be made to contribute to the extraordinary expenses of this generation. But it is pure assumption to take for granted that the next generations will not have, of some kind or other, as much occasion for an extraordinary effort in the way of defence or of improvement as the present generation has had. It is an illusion to estimate what has now to be done as of much more importance than what will have to be done. Therefore to throw our burden forward on another generation that may have its own peculiar effort to make, just as great and just as imperatively called for, is an unwarrantable procedure. The view that has prevailed in practice, that a great war-debt for example, might be cast with facility upon posterity, has given rise to needless and expensive wars; and *they* have been called upon to pay who perceive the utter inutility of the expenditure. Thus bitterness has been added to burden. Besides, it will be found to have been commonly true, that each generation has been able of itself to meet the cost of whatever the providence of God has fairly called upon it to do. Sufficient unto the day is the evil thereof: conversely, the day thereof is sufficient for its own evil. The present generation of American citizens has been called on to do a great and necessary thing in suppressing a civil war, and in eradicating a social institution that was thoroughly bad. The expense of doing this has been enhanced by timid counsels in the field, by class-legislation in Congress, and by bad financiering in the Cabinet; but the debt, vast as it is, and unnecessarily incurred as a portion of it was, can all be paid off, must all be paid off, by the generation that incurred it.

How can this desirable result be best reached? First of all ought the United States legal-tender notes to be called in and cancelled. They are a portion of the unfunded debt, and no interest accrues upon them, but they have been mischievous and wasteful in their effects upon industry and business. Their introduction would not have been so harmful, if, contemporaneously with it, Congress had forbidden the further circulation of State bank bills. These latter were largely increased along with large issues of the national notes. The currency became thoroughly debauched. The measure of value became as variable as the drift of the winds. Prices became universally and abnormally high. Business became feverish, and speculation rife. When, after a long interval, the State bank bills were retired under a heavy tax, the national bank bills were ready to take their place, and these, together with the legal-tender notes and fractional money, now swell the volume of the currency to above seven hundred millions ($700,000,000) of paper money, every dollar of it practically irredeemable, and every dollar of it depreciated (September 30, 1871) thirteen per centum. The country is suffering in every one of its leading interests, domestic and foreign, from the influence of this inferior money. Trade is languishing; and the poor especially are experiencing the truth of the oft-quoted remark of Mr. Webster, that the most successful expedient ever devised to cheat the laboring classes of mankind is irredeemable paper money. Let, then, the national legal-tender notes be steadily withdrawn. They have cheated creditors, and relieved debtors of their just obligations. They have made it impossible for other forms of value-money to come into circulation. Their presence in the currency depreciates the value of the national bank bills, and puts off the day of specie payments. Let their career of mischief be concluded.

In respect to the funded debt, we are paying the interest promptly, and somewhat reducing the principal. Some of the six per cent. bonds have been refunded in five per cents, and thus the burden of interest has been lessened; but, after all, the vital question now is, not How shall we pay off or refund the bonds? but, How shall we pay off the greenbacks?

The bonds are not due yet for many years, but the legal tenders have already been due many years, and the government still dishonors its own promises to pay. Greenbacks are promises to pay gold dollars, and have no other possible meaning, and government is every day culpable while it does not take efficient measures to redeem these promises. Once in position to do this, the question late agitating the country about paying off a part of the bonds in greenbacks answers itself. How can a promise to pay be the same thing as the pay itself? And how can a nation pretend to fulfill one set of promises by compelling its holders to accept another set of promises? The only proper basis of a promise is the free trust of the receiver in the good faith of the promisor. To *compel* men to accept a *promise* is a monstrous incongruity. To make the greenbacks a legal tender was bad enough; to pay off the bonds with them would be enough worse. No! The greenbacks must first be paid in gold to every man who demands gold on them; this is absolutely necessary to national good faith; and then the bonds, if the principal be paid at all, which is not absolutely necessary to national good faith, since the terminable bonds may be changed into Consols with the consent of the holders, must be paid in gold to the last farthing.

The price of the bonds, since they bear gold interest, has always been higher than the price of the greenbacks, in gold. Still, the bonds have not been, till very recently, at par. The average cost in gold of all government purchases of six per cents between May, 1869, and March 15, 1871, was exactly $92.18 for each $100 bond.[1] All the different issues of six

[1] *Hunt's Merchant's Year-Book*, 1871.

per cents are now at or above par, and the ten-forty five per cents are worth about 97 cents on the dollar. The government itself realized from the original sale of most of these bonds much lower figures in gold value than even these. On the whole, the value of the evidences of the public debt is appreciating.

The debt itself is now about $2,300,000,000. The English debt is a trifle less than $4,000,000,000, much of it in the form of Consols, whose peculiarity is, that they never fall due, so as to be a claim for the principal against the government; but are, after a day fixed, always redeemable at the will of government at par. The ordinary price of Consols, which bear three per cent. interest, is about 94. The advantages, to a government, of a debt always redeemable, but never payable, are obvious at first sight. All our funded debt issued before 1865 is made payable on a day certain. The so-called Consols of 1865, 1867, and 1868, are payable not more than forty years from date; while the new bonds of 1870 are Consols proper, redeemable, the five per cents after ten, the four and a half per cents after fifteen, and the four per cents after thirty ye That they may be paid in gold will require an economical administration of government; an avoidance of intervention in the affairs of our neighbors, and of entangling alliances with foreigners; a free commercial system, under which duties shall be adjusted only for the most productive revenue; and a constant and onerous home taxation.

CHAPTER XIII.

ON FOREIGN TRADE.

The principles which determine the question of foreign trade have been already unfolded in these pages. It is only because their application to the wider field of international exchanges has been contested by some persons, while conceding their validity within the boundaries of the individual nations, that it is now needful to bestow upon the subject a separate treatment, to demonstrate that the laws of exchange are universal and not partial, and to attempt to answer with candor and thoroughness the objections that have been raised to the conclusions established by the almost unbroken unanimity of political economists who have written during the last hundred years. Here, as everywhere else within the science, the safe appeal lies to the common sense of men. A writer whose simple object is to reach the truth, and who has no interest, real or supposed, in defending or overthrowing a dogma, will not confuse the understanding of his readers, and his own, by leaping at once into the most complicated phenomena which the domain of exchange exposes to the observation of an intelligent science. He will take the simplest cases first, will display familiarly the principles applicable to them, and then with the clue well in hand, will pass on, and can be followed through the most intricate portions of the subject. It is not owing so much to any inherent difficulties of the subject-matter, that the question of foreign trade has been the vexed question of the late centuries, as it has been owing to a false method pursued in discussing it; a method which, however favorable to the apparent establishment of current maxims, and however approved by men of interested views, can never be made useful in the investigation of truth. It may be considered as a point already well settled by experience, that no man's sagacity is sufficient to guide himself or others to any sound conclusions on this field, who takes his stand at the outset amid the whirl of interlocking phenomena, and then endeavors to work himself out through the entangling meshes which surround him at every step. Happily, there is no need of any such procedure. Man is man, motive is motive, and exchange is exchange; and the apparent chaos of commerce can be resolved through these alone into harmony and order.

In our fourth chapter it was put, I believe, beyond the reach of controversy or cavil, that the only reason why men ever exchange services at all, is on the ground of a relative superiority at different points. This relative superiority at different points was shown to depend in individuals partly on natural gifts, partly on concentration of mind, or muscle, or both, on a single class of efforts, and partly on the use and familiarity in the use of the gratuitous helps of Nature aiding that class of efforts. The tailor makes the blacksmith's coat, and the blacksmith shoes the tailor's horse, for no other reason in the world, except that each has a relative advantage of the other in his own work, and therefore there is a mutual gain in their exchanging works. To pretend that there would be any exchange between them, in case the blacksmith could make coats as well as the tailor, and the tailor shoe horses as well as the blacksmith, would be to assert that man acts without a motive, and that exchanges take place without a gain. It was also shown in the same connection, that the greater the difference of relative advantage, the greater the gain of an exchange, because each purchases the service of the other at the rate of his own highest efficiency. To recur to the same example, while the efficiency of the tailor and the blacksmith each in his own trade remained at 6, the efficiency of each in the trade of the other being at 5, there was only a gain of 2 to be divided between them; but when by concentration and application the efficiency of each in his own trade rose to 15, his efficiency in the other remaining at 5, there was a gain of 20 to be divided between them. When the relative superiority of each over the other in his own trade was low, the gain, though sufficient to justify the exchange, was small; but when the difference of relative advantage increased, just in that ratio did the exchange become more profitable to both. The obvious inference from this, then drawn, and now repeated, is, that every person who exchanges with others is directly interested in the highest efficiency and success of their efforts as well as his own. The diversity of relative advantage at different points exhibited by different nations, and consequently the gains of international exchange, were expressly reserved at that point to a later stage of our inquiry That stage is now reached.

The various countries of the earth have received from the hands of God a diversity of original gifts, in climate, soil, natural productions, position, and opportunity. This diversity exists for a good design, and can never be substantially reduced by man, even if there were, as there is not, any good reason for desiring to reduce it. Besides original diversity in these respects, there has been developed in the history of the inhabitants of these countries, a diversity of tastes, aptitudes, habits, strength, intelligence, and skill to avail themselves of the forces of Nature around them. These differences are somewhat less inherent and more flexible than the others, but they exist, and always have existed, and in a greater or less degree always will exist; and it is on these diversities, original, traditional, and acquired, that international commerce depends; it never would have come into existence without them, and it would cease instantly and completely were they to fade out. Men do not engage in foreign trade for fun; they engage in it for the sake of the mutual gain derivable to both parties; they desist from it so soon as that mutual gain disappears; and there is no mutual gain in any series of exchanges, unless each party has a superior power in producing that which is rendered, compared with his power in producing that which is received. We will suppose a trade between England and France in cottons and silks, England sending cottons to France, and France sending silks in return. When and how long will this be a profitable trade? Then, when efforts bestowed in France upon silks will procure, through exchange with England, more of cottons than the same amount of efforts bestowed in France upon cottons will produce of cottons directly; and then, when efforts bestowed upon cottons in England will procure more of silks, through exchange with France, than the same amount of efforts bestowed in England upon silks will produce of silks directly. So long as there is a difference of relative efficiency in the production of the two commodities in the two countries, so long, setting cost of carriage aside, may there be a profitable exchange of the two. To make such an exchange profitable to both parties, it is not at all needful that the cottons exchanged for the silks shall have cost the English as many days' labor as the silks may have cost the French; or that the silks shall cost the French as much as the cottons cost the English; it is not a question of the absolute cost of either commodity to the parties producing it; but a question of the relative cost of that produced in either country compared with what would be the cost of the other commodity were it to be produced in that country. The question for the Frenchman is, Can I get more cottons by working on silks for a month, and then trading with England, than I can get by a month's work on cottons at home? And the question for the Englishman is, Can I get more silks by making cottons, and then trading with France, than I can get by trying to make silks at home? As this point is fundamental, and determines the whole matter of foreign trade, it shall be illustrated arithmetically. Suppose that cottons costing $100 in England exchange for silks costing $80 in France: is that a losing trade for England? Not necessarily. Is it a remunerative trade for

France? Not necessarily. It depends simply upon this: whether $100 expended in England in the manufacture of silks will produce as many and as good silks as can be obtained for $100 by exchange with France? If it will, depend on it, that $100 will never go to France to buy silks. If it will not, and silks are in demand in England, then, clearly, the trade is advantageous to the Englishman. If the cottons costing $100 in England, and obtained in exchange for silks which cost but $80 in France, can there and then be made for $75, France makes a losing trade (but only by supposition), though she gets what cost $100 for what cost but $80. My readers will perceive, that it is not the absolute cost of commodities to the countries producing them that determines their value in foreign trade, but that cost relatively to what would be the cost of the return commodities were they to be grown or manufactured there. A demand in each country for the product of the other is of course presupposed in the illustration.

If this general representation be just, and I think every thoughtful person will concede it, then it follows, that, setting aside a greater cost of carriage, foreign trade presents no elements peculiar to itself, but only the same elements which domestic trade presents; and consequently, that the same laws and limitations applicable to domestic exchanges are applicable also to foreign exchanges. As in every other exchange, so here, there are two efforts, represented in this case by the cost of the respective commodities, — the cottons $100, and the silks $80; there are two desires, — the desire of the Englishman for silks, and of the Frenchman for cottons; there are two estimations, — the estimation of the Frenchman of the effort in silks required to obtain the cottons by exchange compared with the effort required to obtain them directly, and the Englishman's estimation of his effort in cottons necessary to procure the silks in exchange, compared with what would be the effort needed to manufacture the silks in England; and, finally, as always, two satisfactions.

Now let us further suppose that while the cottons cost $100 in England, it would cost $120 to manufacture there as good silks as can be made in France for $80; and that while the silks cost but $80 in France, it would cost $96 to make cottons there as good as the English can make for $100. On this supposition, France can make both silks and cottons at a cheaper absolute cost than England can. But does that destroy the motive and the gain of an exchange between the countries in these two articles? Let us see. By exchange with England, France gets for $80 in silks, cottons which would otherwise cost her $96, — a handsome gain of 20 per cent.; England gets for cottons costing her $100 silks which would otherwise have cost her $120,— another handsome gain of 20 per cent. Though France can make each commodity for less absolute money than England can make either, there is a diversity of relative advantage, and therefore there might be in this case, as there is actually in many such cases, a profitable trade. The efficiency of France in making silks, relatively to that of England in making silks, is in the ratio of 80 to 120,— a difference of 50 per cent.; while the efficiency of France in making cottons, relatively to that of England in making the same, is only in the ratio of 96 to 100, — a difference of $4\frac{1}{6}$ per cent. In the majority of cases, doubtless, foreign trade takes place in articles, in the production of one of which each of the respective countries has an absolute advantage over the other, but an every way advantageous trade may be carried on in articles in the production of both of which one nation shall have an absolute superiority over the other, provided only that this superiority be relatively diverse in the two articles, as has just been shown. This is an effectual answer, as I take it, to the clamor of some, who object to importing articles which might be made at home for the same sum of money as foreigners expend in making them; admitted, that they might be so made; does it follow that the country importing them would get them as cheaply by making them itself? By no means does that follow. By the supposition, the importing country has an efficiency in making those articles equal to that of the foreign country; but it may also have a superiority absolute or relative over that country in the production of other articles which that country wants in exchange; if so, the exchange complained of may go on to the manifest profit of both parties. Our general supposition a little changed will put this case in its true light: France can make cottons for $100 which it costs England also $100 to make; shall she give up her trade with England in silks and cottons, because she can make cottons as cheap as England can? She had better not. Let the exchange go on; for $80 in silks she gets cottons which would otherwise cost her $100, — a gain of 25 per cent.; England gets silks for $100 which would otherwise cost her $120, — a gain of 20 per cent. as before. Let no nation be in haste then to drop a trade, because it thinks it can make the article received in exchange as cheaply as the other nation makes it, so long as it has an advantage over the other, absolute or relative, in making the article rendered in exchange; and when that advantage ceases, the trade will drop of itself.

What will be the extreme limits of the value of cottons and silks in a trade between England and France under the conditions supposed? And when will a third nation be able to undersell either in the ports of the other? The extreme value of French silks in English cottons, will be 80 and 96; they cannot fall below 80, because they cost the French that to produce them; they cannot rise above 96, because at that rate the French can make cottons, and there would be no gain in exchanging. Nations, no more than individuals, will get themselves served at a greater effort than that at which they can serve themselves. If a given effort does not realize more through exchange than it would directly, then the exchange ceases of necessity, as fire goes out for lack of fuel. The extreme limits of the value of English cottons in French silks, will be 100 and 120, for reasons precisely similar. Therefore the highest profits possible to both nations, under the conditions of the trade, are 20 per cent. each. France would be glad to take the cottons at a return of 80, at which rate her gain would be 20 per cent.; and she cannot under any circumstances offer quite 96, at which rate her gain would disappear No third nation, therefore, in a trade of silks for cottons, can expel the French from the English ports, until it is prepared to offer nearly 96, or more, in silks in return for English cottons; that is to say, until its efficiency in making silks relatively to that of England in making them, presents a greater difference than the difference of efficiency between France and England in making silks, that is, greater than fifty per cent. A greater difference of relative advantage, and nothing else, will enable a third nation to undersell France in such a trade. England would be glad to take the silks at a return of 100, at which rate her gain is 20 per cent.; and she cannot possibly offer quite 120, because at that rate her gain would wholly vanish. She could be undersold in the French ports, under similar conditions, and not otherwise, as the French in her own ports, as just now indicated. We have seen that the diversity of relative advantage in the production of the two articles in the two countries is in the ratio of 50 to $4\frac{1}{6}$; France has an absolute advantage in the production of both commodities; the trade proceeds simply on the basis of this relative diversity; and no nation can take away the silks of France from England, or the cottons of England from the French, either with other cottons and silks, or any other commodity, except on the basis of a diversity, absolute or relative, greater than this. Here is the whole doctrine of one nation's underselling another in the ports of a third. It can do so under conditions of greater relative efficiency, and not otherwise.

So far we have considered only their relative cost of production as determining the value of articles in foreign trade. But we know that the element of desires also helps to determine all value. We come now to illustrate what is sometimes and properly called "the Equation of International Demand."

If the demand for French silks in England just answers to the demand for English cottons in France, so that the silks offered by France just pay for the cottons offered by England, then, cost of carriage aside, the gains of the trade will be equally divided between the two nations, each will realize 20 per cent. profit, because neither will have any motive to lower the value of its commodity below its highest value; France, from its point of view, will offer 80 in silks and get 96 in cottons; England, from her point, will offer 100 in cottons and get 120 in silks. Demand and supply are equalized at a point of value most favorable to both parties, and really determined by the relative cost of production. This case of equalization, though possible, is likely rarely to occur in practice. On any terms of exchange first offered, there is likely to be a stronger demand in one country for the product of the other than in this country for the product of that. This will lead to a change of value, and a new division of profits. The product for which the demand is less will find its market sluggish, and in order to tempt further and brisker exchanges, will be compelled to offer more favorable conditions. He who enters a market in quest of what is more in demand with a service in return which is less in demand, will have to lower his terms, or not trade. The equalization of supply and demand will only be reached in this case, by quickening the demand for the commodity now less in demand, through an offer of better terms in trade.

Thus, if the demand for French silks in the English ports be slack, in comparison with the demand for English cottons in France, at the rate of exchange first established—80 for 96, the French merchant has no resource, if he wishes to continue the trade, but to offer more silks for the same amount of cottons, say, 85 for 96. If this reduction prove sufficient to cancel the account in cottons with the account in silks, then the trade will go on on this new basis for a while, the equalization of supply and demand has been reached through a new valuation of the commodities, and there is now a different division of the profits. France gains now only 13 per cent. by her trade with England, while England gains 27½ per cent. in her trade with France. Under these new terms of exchange, it is possible that silks may again become heavy in reference to cottons, and a new decline take place in their relative value. If the French are obliged to offer 90 for 96, in order to obtain the cottons they want, their profits will sink to 5⅔ per cent., while the English profits will rise to 35 per cent. If, in any contingency, the French were compelled to offer in the neighborhood of 96 in silks for 96 in cottons, the trade would cease of course, just as every other transaction ceases when the motive for it ceases. Of course, the cottons are just as likely to become dull in reference to silks, as the silks to cottons, and in this case England must lower her demands, and thus surrender a larger share of the profits to France. By the play of supply and demand, within the outermost limits drawn by the relative cost of production, is the value of articles determined in foreign trade; and no degree of complication in the variety of articles, or in circuitous exchanges, affects, for substance, these fundamental principles. For example, if, instead of one article, as cottons, England sends two articles, or ten, to France in payment for silks, she will send in preference that article in which her labor is relatively most efficient, so long as the French demand will receive it; then, when obliged to lower on that down to the point at which her next most available article stands, she will send that in quantities regulated by the demand for it; and so on to the end. No matter whether the articles be one or many; no matter whether the trade be a direct, or an indirect, trade; the profits in all cases will depend, first upon the ratio of the cost of what is rendered to what would otherwise be the cost of that received; and secondly, upon the relative intensity of the two demands. The greater the relative efficiency of any nation in producing an article of export, and the stronger the demand for that article in foreign ports, the more profitable does the trade become to that nation. The precious metals, whether produced at home, or obtained from other nations by another series of exchanges, stand here in the same relations as other commodities, and are frequently the most profitable articles that a nation can export. The terms of international exchanges, then, between any two nations, are so adjusted, as to equalize the demand for their respective products, and cancel the debts mutually incurred.

It follows from all this by a necessary inference, that what a nation purchases by its exports, it purchases by its most efficient labor, and consequently at the cheapest possible rate to itself. Only those things, for the procuring of which a nation possesses decided advantages relatively to other nations, and relatively to its own advantages in producing directly what is received in return, are ever exported; and hence, the return cargoes, no matter what they have cost their original producers, are purchased by this nation as cheaply as if they had been produced by its own most advantageous labor. This is a wholly impregnable position, and the advocates of restricting foreign trade are challenged to try their hand a little at its defences.

We see also, at this point, what to think of those people who deem it needful that each nation should be able to "compete" with other nations in everything. Why are not these people consistent enough to apply their favorite doctrine of "competing" to domestic exchanges also, and demand that the clergyman shall have facilities for "competing" with the lawyer, the tailor with the blacksmith, the farmer with the manufacturer, the publisher with the author? Will these people never learn that all exchanges, domestic as well as foreign, depend on relative superiority at different points, and that a nation which should try to make its success in production equal at all points, would be as foolish as an artisan trying to learn and practise all trades at once? Suppose the nation to succeed, what then? It would supply its wants at a certain average efficiency of effort; whereas, by a thorough development of all its own peculiar resources, it could command by exchange the products of the world at a cost not exceeding that of its own most productive and efficient exertion. In one word, whatever justifies individuals in selecting diverse paths of production according to their capacities and opportunity, the same justifies the nations in fully drawing out their own best capabilities under the conditions in which God has placed them, and then, exchanging what costs them little for what would otherwise cost them much, in enjoying all that the world offers at the least expenditure of irksome effort. Such action promotes the common good of all the nations, and makes the best of all accessible to all, and arms each with the power of all; while the opposite action, by lessening the diversities of relative advantage, so far forth incapacitates all for exchanges which are at once profitable and stimulating.

Closely connected with the one just cited, is another narrow and superficial notion, happily less prevalent now than formerly, namely, that new improvements in machinery, or other enhanced facilities of production, realized in any nation, are a disadvantage to other nations in their trade with that nation. Let us examine this point. Suppose France, by new methods of silk culture, to become able to make the silk which before cost $80 for $50, cottons in France, and silk and cottons in England, remaining in natural cost as before, does France alone gain the entire advantage of the increased cheapness of silk? We will see. The production of silk in France is greatly quickened by the cheaper methods, more is produced, more is carried to England to buy cottons with, but at the old rate of 80 for 96 the English will not take any more silks, and the French, who can now abundantly afford it, since their nominal 80 is really 50, will offer more silks for 96 in cottons, in order to tempt a brisker and broader sale. They offer, say, 96 in silks for 96 in cottons, and if that reduction of value of silks in cottons be enough for the equalization of the respective demands, the trade will go on on that basis, at least for a time; and as there is now a larger difference of relative advantage than before, there will be, as always in such cases, larger profits to be divided between the two parties. The 96 now offered in silks to the English is really only 60 in cost to the French, so that the French gain in the trade is largely increased; they now get for what costs them 60 what would otherwise cost them 96, a clear gain of 60 per cent. Before the new methods of silk culture were introduced they gained only 20 per cent. But the English have also gained largely by the ingenuity and diligence of their neighbors. Before, they gained only 20 per cent. in the trade at best; now they get for what costs them $100 that which otherwise would cost them $144, a clear gain of 44 per cent. Indeed, it might easily happen, through the changes in international demand, that even a larger share of the benefit of the French improvements should accrue to the English than to the French themselves; the share of the French all the while being large, and much larger, than if, greedily endeavoring to keep all the benefit, they refused to trade at all. Thus we reach again, from another outlook, a grand doctrine of exchange, that each party is benefited by the progress and prosperity of the other. The only way in which all nations can share in the benefits of the thrift and enterprise of each other, is through mutual international exchanges; and when each nation sees to it that it has a few commodities at least for which there is a strong demand among foreigners, and in the production of which themselves have a strong superiority, it may rest assured that it buys all it buys from abroad, gold included, at the cheapest rate to itself, and shares a part of the prosperity of every nation with which it trades.

It is now time to look at the cost of carriage, thus far allowed to sink out of sight for the sake of greater simplicity of view. This is an important element in international exchanges, and one which must not be neglected, although Mr. Carey unduly enlarges upon it with a view to prejudice a free exchange. Certainly, it costs something to carry any goods abroad, and to bring back a return, and we may be assured that if such return goods could be procured as cheaply without incurring such expense, the expense would never be incurred. The fact that all expenses connected with carriage are gladly borne by the merchants who carry on the trade, shows that the gains of the trade are so great as not only to pay freights and insurance, but also to leave a good margin for profits. Mr. Carey does not get around this stubborn fact. What use is it to pile up calculations to show that the expenses incurred in carriage, if applied to production at home, would secure as good goods and more of them? If they would, why do they not? Have not men common sense? Is not self interest a tolerably strong motive-power? Is it needful to invoke the mighty arm of law to compel men to act in accordance with their pecuniary interests? Mr.

Carey would restrict foreign trade, because it costs so much to carry it on. Is that wise, in case the gains after all largely overbalance the cost? If they did not overbalance it, would the trade go forward? If the cost be large, as it is, that is a good reason to desire its reduction, if possible; to labor for increased facilities of transportation, for cheaper freights, and better rates of insurance; but to argue for forcibly stopping a trade by legal enactment, because it costs those so much who freely undertake to carry it on, does not strike me, and, I believe, will not strike my readers, as a sound argument.

Which nation, a party in foreign trade, pays the costs of carriage? Or does each pay them in equal proportion? The aggregate cost of transportation to the foreign market is so much added to the cost of production, and is a deduction of so much from what would otherwise be the whole gain of the exchange; but it is not true that each party necessarily pays the whole of his own freights, and therefore, that the party carrying bulky articles is at a disadvantage compared with the other. He may or may not be at a disadvantage. That will depend on the effect of the new expense, however divided, on the demand in the respective countries. Suppose, that in the outset England pays the whole cost of carrying cottons to France, and France the whole cost of sending the silks to England; but as cottons are many times more bulky than silks proportionably to value, a larger bill of freights would fall to England; and cottons would therefore fall relatively to silks; but cottons and silks both have risen absolutely, that is, with reference to a given effort, or with reference to a money standard. Suppose that France, instead of 80 for 96, now has to give 82 for 96, and England, instead of 100 for 120 now has to give 105 for 120. The French gain in the trade is reduced by cost of carriage from 20 per cent. to nearly 18, and the English gain from 20 per cent. to nearly 14; but it is by no means certain that the trade would go on on these terms; the enhanced price of silks might well deaden the demand for them in England, more than the relatively less enhanced price of cottons in France would affect the demand for them. Silks have risen in England 5 per cent., but cottons have risen in France only 2½ per cent.; it is therefore every way likely that thereafter the demand for cottons will be stronger than the demand for silks, and if so, the French will have to offer better terms, or, what is the same thing, be obliged to pay a part of the English freights; so that there is nothing in the true state of the case to justify the conclusion jumped at by some people that they who carry heavy goods are at a disadvantage compared with those who carry light goods. That will depend on the equation of international demand. Nothing in the nature of things hinders, that each party shall in effect pay the freights of the other, or one even really pay the freights of both.

These, then, are the essential principles of foreign trade, brought out, it is hoped, as clearly and consecutively as the relative and complicated nature of the transactions will allow; and in the light of these principles it is very clear that foreign trade is just as legitimate as domestic trade; that it rests on the same ultimate principles in the constitution of man and in the providential arrangements of Nature; that the profit of it is mutual to both parties, or it would never come into being, or, coming into being, would cease of itself; that to prohibit it, or restrict it, otherwise than in the interest of morals, health, or revenue, must find a justification, if at all, outside the pale of Political Economy; that to say to any body of men who wish to render purely commercial services to foreigners, to receive back similar services in return, that such services shall neither be rendered nor received, is not only to destroy a certain gain, but also to interfere with a natural and inalienable right.

Unfortunately, the old mercantile system, which was so wise as to believe that gold and silver were the only objects of real value, taught also, in coincidence with its fundamental belief, that foreign trade ought to be so regulated and restricted as to bring in the largest possible quantity of the precious metals; that each nation ought to sell much and buy little in order to grow rich; that bounties ought to be given to exporters to encourage them to sell, and prohibitions laid upon importers to prevent their buying; and that the introduction, through exchange with foreigners, of articles which might be produced at home, should be by all means prevented by law, no matter what advantages for producing them foreigners might have, or what advantages the nation itself might have in producing that which the foreigners would be glad to take in exchange. The mercantile system as such, is long ago dead and buried, but it has left one of its progeny behind it, of no better birth than its parent, which has not yet found its predestined death and burial. This is the doctrine sometimes euphoniously and courteously denominated Protection to Native Industry, a designation however not in the least indicative of its real nature. This doctrine, now fairly expelled from England and Germany, still lingers feebly in some other parts of Europe, and, though steadily declining in the United States, is still strong enough here to control the present national legislation. It has been reinforced, of late years, by the very respectable authority of Mr. Carey, some of whose points will be considered in the sequel; and by one or two other persons whose opinions are entitled to a respectful consideration; and the prevalence of the doctrine in the popular mind, particularly in New England, is still such that I deem it useful to examine the topic at some length, preferring to do so in the way of replying to the main objections urged against the opposite doctrine of a free commerce, especially as Protection so called acts at present wholly on the defensive. Some of the objections are of a popular character, and I shall feel at liberty to subject them to a popular refutation; while such as profess to be scientific, will, it is hoped, be met by a scientific method at least equal to their own.

Let us see precisely what a tariff is. The origin of the word will throw light upon the thing. The southernmost point of the Peninsula of Spain, which juts down into the narrowest part of the Straits of Gibraltar, holds a town named Tarifa. Here, during the Moorish domination, a castle was built, and all vessels passing through the Straits were stopped and compelled to pay duties at fixed rates; whence the word *tariff* in English and other languages. It will be perceived at a glance that a tariff is only another name for a tax. It is the special form of tax which governmen s levy on goods brought in from other countries. It may be legitimately imposed for the sake of a revenue to support government; it may be a species of robbery, or black-mail, as in the historical instance just cited; or it may be levied for the sake of Protection, so called; but for whatever purpose imposed, it is always and simply *a tax on the exchange of goods.* How anybody can intelligently suppose that a system of *taxes* can be so cunningly adjusted as to become a positive productive agent, a spur to the progress of society, they must explain who suppose so. I myself once supposed so; but it was when I was in ignorance of the real nature and operation of such taxes. A careful study of the principles of this science, with a noting of the records of experience in this matter, has convinced me, as it has thousands of others, that Protective duties, so called, are nothing in the world but burdensome taxes laid upon industry; that they always have been, and always will be, deeply detrimental to the true interests of society. The word "Protective," as applied to a tariff, is full of deception. A tariff in its very nature is restrictive, obstructive, prohibitive.

The first main distinction to which I call attention, is that between a protective tariff and a revenue tariff. Upon this point a great confusion exists in the common mind. *A revenue tariff is a schedule of taxes levied on imported goods with an eye to equitable taxation only.* If such taxes are to be productive, they must not interfere essentially with the bringing in of the goods, that is to say, they must be levied at a low rate, so as not much to discourage importations, or encourage smuggling at all. Also, experience has shown that it is not needful, in order to derive a large revenue, to lay even low rates upon all goods imported, but only on certain classes of them, so as to burden at as few points as possible the ongoing of international exchanges. The prosperity induced by commercial freedom enables a country to import vast quantities of the articles subjected to the tax, so that large revenues come from low rates levied at few points. Also, these taxes ought to be laid on articles, if possible wholly, at any rate mainly, procured from abroad and which are not produced also at home; otherwise, the incidence of the tax on the portion imported will raise the price also of the portion produced at home, and the people will pay more in consequence of the tax, than the government gets in revenue. A proper revenue tariff, then, lays low duties on comparatively few articles, which are wholly or mainly procured from abroad. The most advanced nations of Europe now lay their tariff-taxes in accordance with these three principles.

But the purpose of a protective tariff is totally distinct from this. *A protective tariff is a schedule of taxes levied on imported goods with a design to raise the price of certain home commodities.* To reach this end, the duties are laid by preference on goods which are both imported and also produced at home, thus violating one of the fundamental principles of a revenue tariff. Also, to be protective, the duties must either be so high as to exclude the foreign goods altogether, and thus give the domestic manufacturer the complete monopoly of the home market, which is the perfection of Protection, or at least high enough to raise the price of the foreign goods to the point at which the home manufacturer is desirous of selling his own. These high duties, certainly for a time, discourage importations, and thus violate another of the fundamental principles of a revenue tariff. But the effect on revenue is not the worst effect. The main effect designed, and that actually follows, is to raise the price to all consumers, in order that a factitious advantage may accrue to certain home manufacturers. When most successful, the effect is to transfer money from the pockets of the many to the pockets of a few. I do not stop at this point to demonstrate the economical folly of this, my object being now to show the idea that always underlies protective duties. Also, since if one home producer receives an artificial advantage under the tariff, many others may lay an equal claim to it, tariff-taxes for Protection come to be levied upon a great many articles, thus violating the third fundamental principle of a revenue tariff, by interfering with exchanges at many points instead of a few.

Now, can these two systems of revenue and protection, which are so distinct and apparently incompatible, be combined together? Can there be a revenue tariff with incidental protection? One thing seems to be certain: Protection fully carried out would annihilate revenue, since the foreign goods would then be prohibited; and a system looking only to revenue, making the people pay only what government gets, would have no protection in it. If this be so, is there any reason to suppose that less degrees of protection would not be only less hostile to revenue? Is it not of necessity, looking at the *nature* of the two systems, that the point at which protection begins is also the point at which revenue begins to diminish? It is not denied that a tariff with protective features in it may be made to yield much revenue; but can it do this without making the people pay much more than the revenue? It is the interest of revenue that government shall get all that the people are made to pay in consequence of a tariff-tax. It is the interest of protection that the people shall pay much more in consequence of a tariff-tax than the government gets. Revenue is only received on the foreign goods that come in. Protection is only secured as the foreign goods are kept out; or are so raised in price as also to raise in price the corresponding domestic goods; which makes the people pay more, while the Treasury receives less. Therefore, the conclusion is unavoidable, that a revenue tariff with incidental protection is a solecism.

The fundamental reason why low duties on imports produce a larger aggregate revenue than high duties is found in the condition of society, which is like a pyramid standing on its broadest base, each of whose horizontal sections is more extended than the one above it. Those persons able to purchase an article at five dollars are more than twice as numerous as those able to purchase it at ten dollars; and those able to buy it at one dollar are probably ten times as many as those who would buy it at five dollars. An official list of taxable incomes in the Tenth District of Massachusetts lies before me, and selecting one town at random, I find one income over $40,000, three over $30,000, seven over $20,000, nine over $10,000, thirteen over $5,000, twenty-nine over 2,000, and seventy-eight over $1,000. A lower duty, therefore, on any article is likely to bring it within the reach of a wider circle of consumers; and for many to pay a low duty is better for the revenue than for a few to pay a high duty. Of course the exact limitations must be found out by experience. Alexander Hamilton long ago, in one of the papers of the Federalist, called attention to the fact that high duties will not make large revenues, any more than a large multiplier will make a large product. The multiplicand is an important factor in both cases. A subordinate reason why low duties are favorable to revenue is, that they destroy smuggling.

Free Trade is the opposite of Protection so called, and not of Customs duties properly levied for revenue. All taxes are paid out of the gains of exchanges; and there is no objection, on principle, to international exchanges paying their share of the taxes. Provided it be economical for the government to collect, and equitable for the people to pay, taxes in this form, it is just as legitimate to tax foreign as domestic exchanges. Some free-traders think it would be wise to abolish custom-houses altogether, and tax domestic exchanges only: the most, of whom I am one, see no objection in tariff-taxes levied at low rates on comparatively few articles of general consumption, which are wholly or mainly procured from abroad. This is the common and acknowledged meaning of the term Free Trade.

(1.) I shall now attempt to answer some objections. One of the most common of these has been, that Free Trade is a theory: "It is all very well in theory, but it will not work well in practice"; as if there can be a good theory that works ill in practice! A theory that does not work well in practice is a bad theory. The way to tell whether a theory is good or bad is to test it by practice. Everything that is done at all, unless by mere chance, is done on *some* theory; and it is certainly better that things should be done on a good theory than on a bad one. What makes a theory good? Simply because it corresponds with and explains the facts. Newton's theory of gravitation is a good theory on this ground, and no other. If a man objects to any theory, let him bring facts, principles, any truth whatever, to disprove it, and he shall be welcome; but do not let him delude himself and others by supposing that he can concede the theory to be good, and then safely denounce the practice. A theory is good because it is good in practice, and for no other reason.

There have been so many unfounded theories broached on all subjects, that the term has fallen into some reproach, and it is for this reason that the charge is brought against Free Trade, of being a theory: but there is nothing in the world more respectable than a good theory proved by solid arguments and verified by facts. I am prepared to show, however, that the charge of being a theory falls with far greater force against the doctrine of protection than against the doctrine of freedom. Free Trade can hardly be said to be a theory at all. It is the natural state of things. If you and I wish to exchange commodities for our mutual benefit, there is no theory or doctrine in the premises; we exchange, and that is the whole of it. If a Massachusetts fisherman wishes to exchange his dried cod with a West India sugar planter, and the trade is mutually beneficial, what theory is involved? They exchange, each is richer than before, and that is the whole of it.

If now some one steps in between you and me, or between the fisherman and the planter, and says, "You shall not trade!" he is bound to tell the reason why. The burden lies upon him. Let him bring forward his theory of restriction, and justify it. Let us hear the arguments and see the grounds that justify the prohibition of an advantageous trade! You see the burden of proof lies upon the advocates of restriction. It is the advocates of restriction that drag in a theory which interrupts the play of natural laws,—which says to men who wish to trade, "You shall not trade!" Commerce is no game of strife, of fraud, of overreaching. Its benefits are reciprocal and mutual; otherwise there would be no commerce. The freights of the navigating interest, and the gains of the merchants, are but a very small part of the benefits of commerce; the variety of commodities and of comforts which every commercial nation enjoys, by exchanging its own surplus products for the surplus products of its neighbors, is the substantial advantage of trade. When now this beneficial interchange is going forward, or, if the artificial barriers were thrown down, would be going forward, who is he that takes upon him to curtail and to prohibit it? Who is he that thinks himself competent to manipulate the unchanging laws of trade?

It is conceded by everybody that a free exchange of commodities within the same country is highly beneficial: what makes it suddenly cease to be beneficial as between foreign countries? Does the mutual benefit of an exchange depend upon the accident that the parties to it are citizens or subjects of the same government? The south end of Vermont trades freely and advantageously with its neighbors across the line in Massachusetts; is there any good reason why the north end of Vermont should not trade just as freely and advantageously with its neighbors across the line in Canada? These are questions which the theory of protection, in my opinion, cannot satisfactorily answer.

(2.) I pass to a second current objection, namely, that if we admit foreign goods freely, we thereby employ the labor of foreigners, and so far diminish the wages of our own laborers. Let us see if this is so. Foreign articles are certainly wrought by foreign labor; do we, then, by buying them employ foreign labor, to the prejudice of our own laborers? We are obliged to pay for everything we buy, — are we not? In what do we pay? Clearly, in the products of our own labor. We employ our own laborers to produce the articles which we exchange for foreign articles. We pay for our imports by our exports. Our exports are created by home labor, and the only possible way for us to obtain the results of foreign toil, is to offer in exchange the results of domestic toil. A commercial nation, therefore, not only does not, but it cannot employ foreign labor. The more it buys of foreigners, the more home labor it must employ to create the articles with which it pays for what it buys. We must remember that the exports, taking the years together, must and do balance the imports. Free Trade, therefore, can by no possibility discourage home labor, or diminish the wages of laborers; and, as a matter of fact, labor is best rewarded, other things being equal, in the freest commercial countries.

I deem it important thoroughly to demolish this objection, for it has been considered the stronghold of the advocates of Protection. I admit that a protective tariff may stimulate a certain branch of manufacture, may concentrate capital in it, may call laborers into it, and even for a time increase the wages of those laborers. But competition will very speedily reduce wages in that department to the average level in other departments, and unless it can be shown that restriction increases the general wages-fund of a country, — that fund that is designed for the payment of labor, — it is in vain to claim that it can increase the general wages of labor. Capital and laborers may indeed be withdrawn from one employment to another by artificial stimulus, but is there any general gain in that? While the one is stimulated, is not the other depressed? I have seen upon the ocean the wind blow up a wave, but I always noticed a depression behind it. The general level of the ocean is not raised, however high the waves rise.

Now how can the free interchange of commodities lessen the demand for labor or the rewards of labor? You are employing a hundred men. You wish to obtain a certain quantity of cutlery. Does it make any difference to you or to the wages of your men, whether you employ them directly in making the cutlery, or in making buttons with which you can purchase the cutlery from abroad? If, by employing them in making buttons you can purchase more and better cutlery, (and if you cannot, there is no temptation to an exchange,) is it not plain to reason that it is better for you, and that you can afford to pay them better wages, than if you employed their labor less effectively directly upon cutlery? This is but an instance, but it involves the principle. There is, there can be no discouragement to domestic labor in the freest international exchanges. Every foreign purchase necessitates the employment of domestic labor to create that with which the purchase is made, thereby enlarging the demand for laborers, and thus tending to increase their wages. The tendency of Free Trade is directly the reverse of that alleged in the objection; because the varied objects of use and elegance offered to our desires by international commerce, stimulate labor to create that with which to buy them.

We know now how to answer those who say, that if we should trade freely, with England, for example, we should bring down wages in this country to the English standard. This is too hollow a bugbear to frighten sensible people any longer. To say nothing of the principles just explained, and others equally conclusive, that combine to scout it, the facts in the case would seem to settle the whole question. We have traded with England for eighty years, largely, increasingly, and from 1846 to 1861, almost freely, and yet wages have not constantly declined in America, and never stood at a higher figure than when the Morrill Tariff was passed in 1861.

(3.) But if the doctrine of Protection be so false, and have no single solid argument in its support, why have so many nations acted on it, so many great men, among others, Daniel Webster, believed in it? This objection I am bound to notice, for it has had no small influence. To estimate its force rightly, two things must be remembered: first, that the doctrine of protection is an inheritance from the remote past, an outgrowth from a confessedly false dogma, which, being then universally received and acted on by the nations, has given this, one of its corollaries, whatever validity custom and prescription can give; and, secondly, that there has always been a rich and influential class of men in the commercial countries who have supposed that their interests were subserved by the practical application of the doctrine. In respect to Daniel Webster, the first great speeches which he made in Congress, speeches that foreshadowed his great fame, were delivered in 1814. These indicate, as any one may read in Benton's Debates, Vol. V., a strong hostility to commercial restrictions of all kinds. He opposed, and New England with him, the protective tariff of 1816. His speech of 1824, in opposition to the higher rates proposed in the tariff of that year, is in reality one of the best free-trade argu ments ever made. If he left, four years afterwards, this high ground of truth and principle, to occupy the lower ground of what he deemed expedient, it was owing to political stress of weather, to a change of policy on the part of Mr. Calhoun and other southern statesmen, to a supposed necessity of fostering manufactures on which New England under factitious inducements had embarked on a large scale. Mr. Webster never justified restriction as a principle; his commercial instincts were too strong for that; he always attempted to justify his course by peculiar and factitious circumstances; almost half of his congressional life had passed away, before he could be brought to vote for levying high duties; and although he afterwards brought forward, in defence of the position thus assumed, arguments which Political Economy pronounces unsound, and although there doubtless mingled in with his motives a desire to gratify powerful constituents and friends who were directly interested in high duties, there is abundant reason to believe that his defection from sound principles was never so radical as has been commonly supposed.

It is not difficult to see why there have always been so many advocates of the system of restriction. It is an old system. It is a system some of the arguments for which are superficially plausible. Above all, it is a system which many enterprising and prosperous men have considered as essential to their pecuniary interests; and when such men demand a champion, eloquence and arguments are never long wanting. As a matter of fact, the legislation of the world has been largely controlled by such men, and that too, not always in the interest of the masses. It is more than doubtful whether manufacturers as a whole class have ever been permanently benefited by protective duties, or rather, it is certain that they have not been; but they have supposed that they were, and some of them have been, prodigiously benefited; and they have acted, and are acting, on that supposition, and the power of such men over public opinion is very considerable. As a class, they are intelligent and rich, and can easily combine to influence opinion and legislation. But even if they were benefited, as a whole, by protective duties, what sort of justice is it to take money out of my pocket and put it into theirs? I object to that. My mickle, and your mickle, and our neighbor's mickle will make a very pretty muckle, — a small tax on all consumers of protected goods will reach a very handsome sum; but what valid claim can the manufacturers lay to it? They are a very deserving class, and consequently prosperous; but it may be respectfully submitted that they do not need unequal legislation in their behalf. They are not a needy generation, but are well to do. The list of incomes on which a United States tax is paid, late annually published throughout the country, puts this fact beyond the shadow of question. In most sections of New England, they are the only men of large incomes. Now, it is no objection to these excellent men that they are rich, and getting richer; they are rather deserving of all honor for their enterprise and vigor and success; but it is conclusive on this point, that they no longer need, even if they ever needed, any special protection from the government. Let them stand on the same level of advantage with other men, let them enjoy no unequal privileges, and everybody will rejoice in their prosperity. At present, they occupy a false position, fatal to their own genuine self-respect, and to the hearty congratulations of their fellow-citizens. By far the larger part of the industrial interests of the country have no special protection at the hands of government; and is it possible that these shrewd and able men who own and run mills and foundries, are willing to acknowledge that they alone of all the citizens are unable to render valuable and remunerative services to society without an artificial and governmental prop at their back?

(4.) This brings us to another objection, namely, that, were it not for protective duties, our manufactures would collapse, or as it is sometimes phrased, other nations would take all our manufacturing away from us. The first thing to be said about this is, that we do not manufacture for the sake of manufacturing, but for the sake of the product, — it is not the process that we care about, but the product; and even if it could be shown, as it cannot, that free trade would lessen the manufacturing, that would not be so deplorable, provided we obtained by it for the satisfaction of our wants as many or more manufactured products. Satisfactions, and not efforts, are ultimate in the field of exchange. In the second place, it is needful to look at the meaning of the word, manufactures. So far, I have used it in the loose popular way by which it has come to mean practically in this country the processes by which cotton, wool, and iron, are rendered available for various human uses. These more prominent interests are currently meant under the terms manufactures and manufacturers; but of course the terms properly include a wide range of efforts beyond these, indeed almost all forms of industry not agricultural, and not primarily mental. Now to say, in the broad sense, that protective duties are necessary in order that manufactures may succeed, is to make a statement which can be shown to be false. What is the magic of a protective duty? This, that it says to men who would otherwise come to our shores to trade, "You shall not bring those commodities you were about to bring, nor take away those commodities you were about to take in exchange." People commonly look only at the first part of what is said, and console themselves by thinking, if foreigners are not allowed to bring those goods, somebody will make them at home for us. But this is only half of it. Those branches of manufacture, or of agriculture, as the case may be, which were furnishing the goods wherewith to pay for those commodities about to be imported but now prohibited, lose their market. If we will not buy, of course we cannot sell. If we prohibit importations, we thereby necessarily prevent exportations; that is to say, we take away their market from those who manufacture or grow the goods which would be exported. We depress a profitable branch of manufacture by taking away its market, for the sake of introducing or fostering a branch which is by supposition and confession unprofitable.

The advocates of protection do not claim that branches of business which would otherwise be profitable and self-supporting should be protected, but only the weak and less profitable kinds; and so to bolster up these, protective duties virtually destroy other branches of industry, which only ask that their natural market shall be let alone, to maintain an independent and profitable existence. It is impossible to characterize in terms of respect so short-sighted and miserable a policy. How can a free commerce depress manufactures, when every nation must manufacture or grow a dollar's worth at home for every dollar's worth imported from abroad? How can high duties foster manufactures as a whole, when their very first effect is to cut off from their market all those manufactures which would otherwise have gone abroad with a profit, and their second effect merely to stimulate up to the general level of profit those which it is claimed will not otherwise yield a profit?

The French manufacturers in 1861 were afraid that if the barriers of restriction were thrown down, as proposed in Mr. Cobden's treaty, their business would suffer from English competition. The result has shown how futile were their fears. A large part of the manufactures of either country are admitted into the other with perfect freedom, and the duties on most of the rest very materially reduced; and the French manufacturers have found, as the American at no distant day will find, that there is nothing which stimulates manufactures so much as a broad market, — not merely a home-market, but a world-market. The French sent to England, in 1863, 1,076,-000,000 francs worth of goods and received back within a trifle as much in return, which was almost a quarter of what they sent and received to and from the rest of the world. It is as the friends and not the enemies of manufactures that we demand the abrogation of restrictive duties. Manufactures as a whole can never reach their point of just expansion, until this professedly discriminating, really repressing, and only at a few favorite points stimulating, system shall be abolished.

But it is said, that England can work up cottons, and Germany wools, and the North of Europe irons, cheaper than we can. Those who have followed me thus far through this chapter, now know that absolute cost of production has little to do directly in foreign trade. But if it be true that these commodities, or any others whatsoever, can really be obtained by us by a less expense of effort through exchange than directly, is there a decent reason why we should prefer to get them by the hardest when the easiest way is open? We may be assured that we shall not get them without being obliged to pay for them, and to pay for them will require a fair expenditure of effort and skill. If foreigners have the advantage over us in some things, we have the advantage over them in many things, and all exchange and the profits of it depend on relative superiority at different points.

(5.) I pass to an objection much urged by Mr. Carey, and others, namely, that the United States, without the aid of protective duties, will be confined to agricultural pursuits, and no diversity of employments, so essential to full social life, will come into play. But the truth is, diversity of employments is rooted in human nature, and in the circumstances amid which God has placed men, and so far is it from law being necessary to foster this diversity, that law is powerless to prevent it! While we were colonies of Great Britain, the laws were very strict against domestic manufacturing of almost all kinds, and yet long before the Revolution, the various branches of manufacture were introduced and prosecuted in spite of the laws: clothiers' mills went up along the mountain streams; wool and woollens were exported; in 1721 "New England had already six furnaces and nineteen forges. The product of iron was still more active in Pennsylvania, whence a supply was furnished to the other colonies."[1] The manufacture of steel was also attempted. Parliament felt itself called on to pass laws again and again prohibiting under severe penalties these incipient manufactures, sometimes making them liable to summary destruction as "nuisances." As soon as a branch of industry becomes profitable, and suitable to the conditions in which a community is placed, nothing but extreme vigilance can prevent its springing into being. Men naturally, spontaneously, under the pressure of necessity render to each other such services as are in demand, and as are possible to be rendered in the state in which they are placed. Foster manufactures artificially? They will come in naturally and inevitably just so fast and so far as they ought to come in. They are as natural to men as agriculture. They require capital indeed, and on a large scale, a large capital. So does agriculture. Capital is the growth of time and of frugality. No

[1] Hildreth's United States, vol. ii. p. 297.

new society can come at once into all the forms of industry which adorn an old established State; there must be a gradual growth of capital and of skill, and as these increase, one branch of industry after another comes in, and finds a stable foothold; and as capital further increases, and the rate per cent. of capital goes down, it becomes profitable to do many things which it would be sheer folly to do at an earlier period. When every dollar of the capital of a country can realize a clear gain of ten per cent., is there any sense or reason in withdrawing a part of it into occupations which can only yield six per cent.? "But we must have diversity," says Mr. Carey. Certainly, we want diversity, but only a natural diversity, in which each branch can stand on its own legs, and not find it necessary to tax all its neighbors in order that its own profits may equal the average of theirs. The theory of a protective tariff is this: that certain unprofitable branches of business shall be cared for by the State, that is to say, the citizens shall be taxed to bring up the profits of these to the general standard of profits. Is a diversity, thus secured, a profitable diversity? Would it not be better for all concerned not to enter at present upon forms of industry that by confession do not pay? "But," urges the advocate of protection, "if they do not now pay, they will pay by-and-by." How do you know that they will? The fact that they do not now pay, is not of itself good proof that they ever will; and at any rate, it strikes a good many people that it would be better to wait till that time comes, and to enter upon branches of industry just as fast as they become profitable, and no faster.

It seems strange to me, that Mr. Carey, whose general confidence in man and in nature is so justly strong, should find his confidence desert him just at this point; should show so much impatience with a natural progress of diversity and association; and should vehemently invoke the assistance of law to help on diversity within a sphere for whose general freedom he is a distinguished champion. He is less consistent than the famous charioteer, who, when his horses ran away down the hill, trusted in Providence until the breeching broke, and then gave all up for lost. Mr. Carey trusts in Providence, and does well; but all at once, when to other passengers as clear-sighted as himself there are no signs of anything giving way, he shrieks out that the breeching is breaking, Providence is inadequate, we must have recourse to Protection.

The idea that the United States, with a greater variety and abundance of natural resources than any other country on the globe; with an industrious, and enterprising, and skilful people; with mountain streams which leap to the wheels of industry with a song; with forests and coal-fields, and mines; with marts and markets, and navigable lakes and rivers; with a genius for traffic, and a keen eye to profit,— the idea that the United States is to be reduced to a mere farming country, unless government can be coaxed to tax foreigners and citizens in behalf of some branches of manufacture which are asserted to be otherwise unprofitable,—is too ridiculous for serious refutation. Why, no nation of the earth has such facilities for manufacturing: the raw materials are here; the food is here in abounding measure; the instruments are here in water, wood, and coal; cattle and horses and pastures are here; everything is here which a nation can ask for with which to produce either directly that which is wanted, or directly that with which to purchase at the cheapest rates what is wanted from abroad; and if God shall give us grace to mind our own business, to avoid entangling alliances and wars, to get and keep a sound money, and to rise above the silly jealousies which have hitherto restricted trade, we shall yet be the beehive of the nations, the chosen home of the industrial and civilizing arts.

(6.) But Mr. Carey endeavors to discover a distinction between commerce and trade. He says: "The words commerce and trade are commonly regarded as convertible terms, yet are the ideas they express so widely different, as to render it essential that their difference be clearly understood. All men are prompted to associate and combine with each other, — to exchange ideas and services with each other,—and thus to maintain commerce. Some men seek to perform exchanges for other men, and thus to maintain trade."[1] This attempted distinction plays a very important part in Mr. Carey's system; he is returning to it perpetually; and according to it, commerce increases as trade declines, the trader is a foe alike to commerce and society, and lives "by appropriation," and restrictions ought to be laid on trade in order "to establish perfect freedom of commerce throughout the world." He complains that hitherto "commerce has been sacrificed at the shrine of trade." Now, I have no hesitation in affirming that this for-

[1] Social Science, Vol. I. p. 210.

midable looking distinction is for the most part destitute of any basis of difference. Let us examine it. They who exchange services with each other, says the distinction, practise commerce, while they who perform exchanges for other men are mere traders. The distinction is made to turn on the ownership of the services exchanged: if the principals exchange for themselves, that is commerce; if they employ agents to do it for them, that is trade; if a merchant freights his own ship with his own goods and takes them to a foreign port, and takes care to exchange there with real owners only for what he wants in return, that is commerce; but if he employs a supercargo to manage his sales and returns, then it is trade. If a middle-man buys the cargo outright, and sells to another middle-man on the other side who is real owner of the return services, that is commerce under the definition; while in domestic exchanges all bargains mediated by employees is trade under the definition. This, to say the least of it, is putting a fine point on commercial transactions; and, so far as I can see, is totally irrelevant in a general doctrine of exchanges. Exchange is exchange, and the laws of exchange and the profits of exchange remain unaffected by any such distinction. *Qui facit per alium facit per se.* If I employ an agent to do any portion of my business for me, it is because I think it profitable to do so, and there is an exchange of services between him and me for that purpose, but the exchanges which he effects in my name as principal are in nature the same as if I effected them myself. If Mr. Carey wants to say that exchanges would be more profitable if there were no costs of carriage, no clerk hire, no intermediate services of any sort, there is nobody to dispute with him; but since exchanges cannot be carried on to any extent without these agencies, what is the use of quarrelling with Nature and Providence? The transporter is just as much of a producer as the grower or transformer,—he renders a valuable service, and must be paid for it of course. As soon as his services can be dispensed with, and no loss accrue, they will most assuredly be dispensed with; but to say that people shall not employ such an agent if they think their interests subserved by employing him, can hardly be reconciled with any adequate notions of freedom or of exchange. All sorts of services are in order in exchange. All sorts of talent are available. If a man has not capital to do business for himself, let him begin by doing business for others. If a man can furnish a ship, but cannot freight her, there is no serious objection to his furnishing a ship. Let the merchant freight her, and let them divide profits on the return. If a distinction between commerce and trade be allowed, for which I see no ground whatever, each, at any rate, is swallowed up in the higher unity of exchange, and becomes amenable to the principles already unfolded.

It is in this connection, that Mr. Carey exalts the policy of Colbert, the famous finance minister of Louis XIV., who certainly did much for the prosperity of France, and well deserves the fame which posterity is so ready to accord. But to refer the immense industrial impulse which France received at that time in any considerable degree to the restrictive duties laid by Colbert on foreign trade, is an instance, by no means single in Mr. Carey's books, of a fallacy called by the logicians *post hoc ergo propter hoc.* It is most unsatisfactory and illogical to be told that one thing came after another and therefore was caused by it. Colbert did many things much better worth the doing than to lay prohibitory duties. He swept away, so far as lay in his power, all the obstacles to the freest interchange of commodities within the realm of France. He abolished the interminable internal tolls and duties. He simplified and reduced the taxes. Says Henri Martin, — "We are struck with admiration to see Colbert begin by reducing an impost thirty-three per cent., on the increased product of which he founded in great part his hopes. Trampling on the routine of the exchequer, he had comprehended that consumption increases in equal or even greater proportion to the abasement of duties that weigh on consumable objects, and that the public treasury does not lose what the well-being of the people gains."[1] He abolished superfluous offices, and introduced economy, and, as far as possible, honesty into every department of the State. He emancipated the Communes from their old burdens, and forbade their incurring new debts. He renovated the whole industrial and financial system; and France began mightily to prosper. But he was also in part, unfortunately, a disciple of the mercantile system. He laid heavy duties on foreign goods, which of course provoked foreigners to lay similar duties on the products of French industry. Martin himself, with whom Colbert is a hero, acknowledges this consequence. It has never been proved, and never can be, that the high duties contributed to the then prosperity of the

[1] History of France.

French; the weight of bare authority is about evenly balanced on the question; but he who follows reason and science in the premises will not hesitate in his decision.

(7.) It has been often urged, that we must have a restrictive tariff because other nations have a lower rate of interest and profits, and more abundant capital than we have. It is fair to presume that they who say so know that foreign trade depends only very remotely on the absolute cost of the articles exchanged. If they do not know this, they are ignorant of the one fundamental proposition of commerce, and their reasonings as a matter of course cannot reach correct conclusions. If familiar with this proposition, they should see that any reference either to lower interest of money or to lower wages is, in this connection, entirely irrelevant. It is a matter of indifference to us what the goods we buy from abroad cost their producers, whether they paid high wages or low wages, high interest or low interest; we do not care about the absolute cost of production of anything we buy; the question of interest for us is how much of the home commodity must we give for it, and what does the home commodity cost us. The simple question that determines foreign trade is this,—would the commodity, if produced here, cost more than that commodity with which we buy it? If it would, then we profitably import it; and this, without any reference to its cost to the foreign producer. Whether he pays high wages or low wages, high interest or low interest, whether capital is abundant there or scarce, has little to do with this question of a profitable exchange of commodities, and justifies, in no conceivable manner, the restrictive system. California has much higher wages and a much higher interest than New England; does she need, therefore, to prohibit New-England ships from entering the Golden Gate? Is it for her interest to put restrictions on New-England goods? Does New England, because wages are lower here, get more than her share of advantage in the California trade? If not, no more would England or India in a trade with us. We trade with all the world: some parts have a higher rate of wages and interest than we; some parts have a lower rate; so far as that matter is concerned our trade may be equally advantageous with them all.

To this law of foreign trade there is, however, a single not unimportant exception. When two nations go into the market of the world with the same commodity, to buy gold and silver, then the absolute money-cost of that commodity is, as between the two, an important question. That one of the two nations whose wages are lower, and whose rate of interest is less, in the manufacture of the common commodity will, in a trade for gold, under-sell the other — that is, can afford to give more of its commodity for an ounce of gold, because its commodity has cost less in gold. This is clear, and it is the only case where foreign trade is determined by the absolute cost of production. But our objectors get no crumb of comfort here; for in the first place, the commerce of the world is not a commerce for gold and silver, but a commerce of commodities, in the exchange of which relative cost is the only principle. And in the second place, when two nations go intc the market of the world for gold, they rarely carry the same commodity, but carry, each its own peculiar commodities, in the production of which it has the greatest advantage. They have a strong motive to do this always, for that which they have the greatest advantage in producing will buy all other commodities, gold included, at the cheapest rate. Here too the relative cost decides. And in the third place, if two nations do carry the same commodity into the same market to buy the same gold, and the nation whose wages and profits are higher is thereby at a disadvantage in the trade, how is a restrictive tariff at home to help that matter? The true remedy is to cultivate our own peculiar advantages to the highest point, and carry those commodities abroad to buy our gold, and not endeavor to compete with our neighbor in the same commodity. High wages and high profits are a vast national advantage; restrictive systems tend certainly to reduce them; but shall we throw away a great advantage enjoyed by all laborers and all capital in all departments, in order to compete with less fortunate nations in a single trade with a single commodity? The folly of this is patent; especially as the United States is a gold-producing country, and not only supplies herself with gold, but half the world besides. The United States produced in the twenty years from 1848 to 1868, $1,255,000,000 of the precious metals.[1] Besides, is it not a little strange to hear the doctrine seriously propounded that we are put at a disadvantage in foreign trade, and that restrictions are made necessary, because on the whole we are making so much

[1] J. Ross Browne's Report, 1868.

money? If the current rate of interest and profits is so high with us, it shows that we are doing well on every hundred invested! One would suppose that capitalists might be content with such high profits! At any rate, one would think that the disadvantage in trade would rest with those who get the less returns on their investments, rather than with those who get the larger returns!

If there be a lack of capital, or a lack of skill in any country, what is the remedy? A protective tariff? If all the capital of the country is now taken up by branches of industry already existing, of what advantage is it to introduce a new branch which can only come into being at the expense of the old by withdrawing capital from the old? The capital is already taken up. Let it abide in its freely chosen channels. If the capital of the country is not all taken up, then certainly new branches of industry will come in, will come in of their own accord; you cannot keep them out. Every kind of business, which, under present circumstances, is profitable, will be carried on, and those that are not profitable we do not want.

If the restrictive system could increase the capital of a country, then it might with some show of reason be defended, but it would be a difficult task, I think, to show how the capital of a country can be increased by stopping a profitable commerce.

And just so of skill. If the new branch of manufacture for which skilled labor is wanted is carried on abroad, the laborers can be easily imported. An assurance of higher wages and constant employment has brought and will bring again skilled laborers from every country in Europe. Restriction cannot give us skill, since all experience has shown, and common sense testifies to the same point, that skill will be best developed under the freest competition — under circumstances where everything depends on relative skill, rather than where very little depends on it; where a high price, artificially created, is sure, whether skill be exercised or not. The sharp spur of emulation added to the keen impulse of interest, will most assuredly carry skill to its highest point. Nor is there any danger that our enterprise and skill will be overwhelmed by foreigners flooding our markets with cheap goods for the sake of strangling that branch of business on which our enterprise and skill are occupied. Commerce is an exchange of commodities for commodities for the mutual advantage of the parties. Exchange is always a reciprocal act; when a man sells he buys, and when he buys he sells. If a foreigner brings goods to our shores he always carries away in effect a corresponding value from our shores. The only motive he has to bring anything hither is that he may carry something hence. He sells to us, and in the very act buys from us; we buy from him, and in the very act sell to him. The commercial use of bills of exchange only disguises without altering this fact. Now to allege, as is often done, that foreigners will flood our markets at a loss to themselves, in order to discourage our manufacture of that article, is to ignore the motive from which commerce springs. Certainly they whose alleged profits are so much less than ours can ill afford such an operation as this; and until some well-authenticated case is given of foreigners willing to submit to a present loss in the hope of a future and problematical gain; until some well-authenticated case is given of a rising manufacture, adapted to our circumstances, and profitable in itself, being ruined in this way; until the case is given of magnanimous dealers sacrificing present gains for uncertain benefits to accrue in part to their fellow-dealers, freighting ships to America to bring nothing back; I shall beg leave to think that a thing so contrary to the interests of capital, to the laws of trade, and even to the principles of human nature, has not occurred in the past, and is not likely to in the future.

(8.) A further objection to free trade remains to be briefly considered. It is this, and it has been urged with some plausibility and much pertinacity, namely, that every nation ought to be independent of others in all the more essential articles of life; and therefore protective duties ought to be laid in order to compel the nations to make or grow all the articles of prime necessity for themselves. The objection divides itself into two parts, the postulate and the inference, and it shall be considered in that order and relation. First, every nation ought to be independent of others in respect to the supply of its more necessary wants, such as food, clothing, means of defence and offence, and so on. But what is it to be independent? I suppose it means, in this connection, to be sure of getting what is wanted under all contingencies. But is an individual man to be regarded as "dependent," and as likely to lose his bread, unless he devote himself to the growing of food directly? If he only has wherewithal to buy food, I take it that he is just as "independent," just as likely to get it, as if he produced it himself; and so a nation which has products to offer which are in demand in the world without, is very sure of getting whatever it wants, provided it is anywhere to be bought, and is, in my apprehension of it, in a very "independent" position. Protectionists have degraded language and degraded exchange by trying to make it appear that a man and a nation are reduced to conditions of dependence whenever they find it for their interest to buy; but the truth is that there is nothing dependent in buying and selling; the parties stand on a footing of perfect equality towards each other; each is at the same moment buyer and seller; one is as independent as the other, and nobody can be more so than either, except the savage and the hermit, who live in a state of isolation. Moreover, every nation does of course devote itself directly to the supply of its principal wants, and always continues to do so, unless it appears that it can supply those wants more cheaply through exchange. If it can supply them more cheaply through exchange, it becomes, in my judgment, more "independent" by doing so; more independent of irksome effort, and more sure of getting its wants supplied, since now it draws its supplies from a wider surface, from any point in the wide world where such supplies are to be had and where its own products are in demand. So far as food is concerned, this objection sounds but poorly in the mouths of protectionists, who are the men perpetually bemoaning the prospect that every nation, unless it follow their advice and lay protective duties, will be exclusively agricultural.

But the inference is even less defensible than the postulate. Let it be admitted, for argument's sake, that to buy is to be dependent, and that every nation loses a part of its independence by every act of foreign exchange by which it obtains its necessary supplies; does it follow that protective duties are the true remedy? No. Prohibition is the barrier to hold up before the waning independence of the nation. Why allow a thing to go forward under more onerous conditions, which under less onerous was proving fatal to independence? If for the citizens to import freely be so disadvantageous to their independence, how disastrous must it be to have the importations still go forward under a tax in addition, which the citizens must pay!

The late insurgent States of this country furnish a capital illustration of the fact that war and a stringent blockade cannot prevent exchanges from going forward, when there is wherewithal at home to pay for goods, and goods abroad which are wanted at home. The United States maintained a thousand vessels, more or less, along the coast of the insurgent region, to intercept all trade; but there was cotton within which the English wanted, and goods without which the insurgents wanted, and the exchanges went on, with great hazards and frequent losses indeed, but went on for four years, to an immense amount of transactions.

(9.) The last objection to a free commerce that will be noticed here is the one that has been so pertinaciously urged in the "New York Tribune," namely, that the higher paid labor of this country makes it impossible for us to trade freely with those nations in which a lower rate of wages prevails. This objection has more than once been impliedly answered in these pages; but it requires, and can be given, a specific refutation. There is a fallacy that pervades every article on the subject in the newspaper referred to that has fallen under my notice. It is one of the many fallacies that have their lurking-place around the word "*wages*." It is admitted that the rate of wages rules higher in this country than in European countries, and all good citizens, I believe, rejoice that the reward of laborers is high here, and desire it to become higher rather than lower in the time to come. But a high rate of wages does not necessarily import *a high cost of labor*. This was demonstrated at length in our chapter on Cost of Production. The cost of labor to the capitalist is made up of three elements: first, the nominal rate of wages; second, the efficiency of the labor; and third, the dearness of the commodity in which the laborer is paid. It would seem to be a patent fallacy to confound one component with a resultant of three components; and yet the writer in question invariably proceeds in his discussions as if a high rate of wages means a high cost of labor. He uses the former term as if it were synonymous with the latter. The arguments proceed, and the conclusions are reached, on the assumption that the cost of labor is higher in this country than in Europe, while all that is asserted in the premise, and all that is true, is, that the nominal rate of wages is higher. The logical force of the process and the security of the conclusion are destroyed the moment it is perceived that rate of wages and cost of labor are two very distinct things. It is fortunate for the United States that the two things are distinct; for while the rate of general wages is higher here than in Europe, the cost of general labor is lower here than in Europe. The unmixed evils of a debauched currency are perhaps disguising this truth at the present moment, but it is a truth nevertheless that cannot be questioned when the light of the following considerations is cast upon it. (1.) The cost of labor must be lower in this country than in Europe because the rate per cent. of capital is higher. Labor and capital alone conspire in production. *Profits are the leavings of the cost of labor.* If, therefore, on every hundred invested the rate of profit is higher, the conclusion is unavoidable that the cost of labor is lower. (2.) To account for this lower cost of labor, we have (*a*) The fact of the greater efficiency of labor. The greater the efficiency of labor, other elements as before, the less its cost to the employer. Labor is more efficient here, because the motives to labor are stronger and higher, because the general tone of things is more energetic, and because labor, all departments being considered, is more *generally* armed with labor-saving appliances. We have (*b*) The usually cheaper cost of that in which labor is paid. Abroad the laborer is paid in gold and silver. Here he is usually paid in a depreciated currency. Besides this, the price of general commodities even on a gold standard is usually higher here than abroad. Therefore the cost of even gold to pay his men is less to the employer here. We have (*c*) The fact that fewer persons are employed, in establishments that do equal work, here than there. There there are more supernumeraries, more persons more or less pensioned by the establishment, more gradations in authority, more wages of superintendence. Here, the fewest possible number of persons is employed, there is comparatively little superintendence, and each person is put upon his or her full power of work. These three considerations, (and others might be mentioned,) sufficiently account for the lower cost of labor here, since they more than overbalance the excess in the rate of wages paid; which excess, other things being equal, would enhance the cost of labor. The balance is decidedly on our side, as is shown by the current rates of profit and interest. Indeed, the excess in nominal wages paid is not so great as is commonly supposed, allowance being made for the different currencies. A skilled artisan in England earns eight shillings sterling per day, that is, two dollars in gold. Our own skilled artisans earn not much more. "The English agricultural laborer who earns fifty cents or two shillings sterling per day, earns say three pounds per month, and pays about this sum for the annual rent of his cottage. Now the laborer in this country seldom pays his annual rent by a month's wages." [1] Our Bureau of Statistics gives the wages of 14 classes of operatives in woollen mills in England, and the corresponding wages here reduced to gold. Our average is only 21.89 per cent. higher than theirs.

Edward Harris, a great woollen and cotton manufacturer of Rhode Island, says that only 20 per cent. of the cost of his fabrics is labor: 80 per cent. is materials and machinery. If so, England's advantage over us in woollen wages, *conceding to her la-*

[1] Sidney Homer.

borers equal efficiency, is only 21.89 per cent. of 20 per cent., or $4\frac{1}{3}$ per cent. in the whole cost. But pauper-labor is notoriously very poor labor to those who employ it. It is one of our grand advantages that our labor is *not* pauper-labor, but the opposite of it. Low-wages countries are always afraid of the competition of high-wages countries, and justly so. It is the competition of *England* that is most feared on the Continent of Europe, though English wages are the highest in Europe. With our still higher wages we have wrested many an industrial triumph from England herself; and if we had as good a money and as free a commerce as she has, our competition would be more feared by her than that of any other country.

I have now answered, with what success the reader must judge, every considerable argument that I am aware of as urged in this country against the policy of a free commerce. I have a few brief objections to add to the opposite doctrine of Protection.

(1.) It is no part of the proper province of government to undertake to redistribute the rewards of industry. Government has a right to take a part of the fruits of every man's industry for its own maintenance; but when it goes beyond this, and forcibly takes a portion of the fruits of one man's industry to reward another man's industry, it steps out of its true sphere. Every man has a right to all the rewards of his own industry, except as to that part which government takes in legitimate taxation. No government is wise enough, or ever will be, to say how much of the results of my labor I shall contribute to my neighbor to remunerate his labor

Congress has nothing to say about that. Congress is bound to give us both the benefit of equal laws, and then to leave us both to take care of ourselves. It is no part of the duty of Congress to see that any set of men whatever are making money. When, therefore, any branch of industry, in the exigencies of business, is depressed, for the leading men in it to go to Congress with their tale of woe, to induce that body to lay a tax for their relief on their neighbors, to empower them to pass round the hat in the community, like mendicants, and compel other men to drop their contributions into it, is as pitiful on the one side as it is extra-governmental on the other. The American people are patient, but they have borne with this sort of thing about as long as they will bear with it.

(2.) It is a second objection allied to the first, that the protective scheme is wholly a matter of finesse. If *all* interests were "protected" and "protected" alike, the issue of all the distributions and redistributions would be that all would stand relatively as before, but worse off by the losses of the process. Therefore it becomes a struggle of interests; and each interest, or combination of interests, endeavors both to get itself "protected" and that the rest shall not get "protected." The woollen men, for example, are anxious for high duties on foreign woollens, but are much less anxious for high duties on foreign wools. The wool-growers, however, do not see why they are not as much entitled to "protection," that is to say, to rob the public, as the woollen manufacturers. It would be difficult for anybody to see why they are not as much entitled to it. Which, then, shall get the better of the Committee of Ways and Means? That is the question. It is a question of lobbies, of influence, of indirect or direct bribery. So of other interests. The fact is, that the leading interests protected have been obliged to yield so much to the pressure of other interests with equal claims to protection, that, with a few exceptions, no classes would be benefited so much by the abolition of all protection as would they. They have purchased the right to pluck the community at one point by conceding to other parties the right to pluck them at a dozen different points. The woollen manufacturers, for example, have to pay a considerable duty on foreign wools, a high duty on foreign machinery, and an enormous tax for protection on every pound of iron they use. If now the principle of protection were abandoned, they would be relieved of all the contributions levied on them by others, and the public would be relieved of the contribution levied on it by them. It would be a relief all round. The interests of the manufacturers are coincident with the interests of the public. The product cheapened by the abolition of all these high duties, as well those which the manufacturers have *to pay* as those which specially protect *them*, would find a vastly extended market, not at home only, but also abroad; and such depressions in business as the woollen men are now suffering from would become rare indeed. Those branches of business, and they are numerous and important, which have never had a syllable of protection in the United States, have been the most prosperous and are now the strongest. They have to send no delegations to Washington. They expend the ingenuity and the money which protected interests spend in artifices, in the development of their business; and they have found, what the others at no distant day will find, that honest industry and skill are better in the long run than the highest strategy of the lobby.

(3.) Protection is a wasteful way to reach the end ostensibly proposed by it. It is claimed to be needful to encourage weak branches of business. Let us suppose for argument's sake, what would be folly to concede in reality, that it is desirable for the public to encourage a presently unprofitable business. How can it most cheaply and most certainly do this? Clearly enough, by offering a direct bounty on all that is actually produced. Let the public know what it gets for what it gives. Suppose the article wanted be hats. It is unprofitable at present to manufacture hats, but the public thinks it desirable to introduce the manufacture at the expense of the people. Very well. Let the government offer to pay outright from the public chest, say $2, for all hats of a certain quality made in the country. The bounty would be paid only so far as the manufacture was actually carried on. This stimulus would be explicit. All would be open and above-board. Everybody could see what was done, and what it was done for. This would be demonstrably the cheapest and most certain way to encourage hat-making. For suppose, on the other hand, the protective method be adopted, and a duty of $2 apiece be laid on foreign hats to encourage the home manufacture. Every consumer now pays an extra $2 for his hat, but there is no assurance that anybody will go into hat-making. Nobody is pledged to do it. It will depend upon the comparative prospect of making money in that, or other business, whether that business is continued and developed under the duty. Suppose, however, that the home market is one half supplied by the home production, and one half by the foreign article enhanced $2 in price by the duty. Suppose the market takes 2,000,000 hats. Then $4,000,000 are paid by consumers to encourage hat-making, when $2,000,000 in bounties would encourage it to the same extent. Unless the duty be so high as to keep out the foreign article altogether, there is a good deal of money paid by the people for hats that does not encourage hat-making. The system is wasteful. Why then is it preferred? It is preferred for the same reason that the fisherman prefers water a little muddy to fish in. The destined prey cannot see the operation of things so well! Protection is a cover under which the people are cheated. Is it strange, then, that the people grow indignant?

(4.) Protection makes a promise at the outset which it rarely fulfils. Special interests ask for protection to enable them to "start," holding out the promise that they will soon be able to walk off alone. Unluckily, the facts all show that that time, in their judgment, never comes. The interests which are the most highly protected in the United States at this moment, "started" in Massachusetts more than two centuries ago! The manufacture of linen, woollen, and cotton cloth was begun in Massachusetts in 1638, in Rowley, by some families from Yorkshire;

and became so remunerative in less than three years that several acts of the General Court designed to stimulate it were repealed.[1] The manufacture of woollens began in Massachusetts 232 years ago, and yet in the year of our Lord 1870, under an enormous protective duty, higher than was ever before levied in this country on that class of goods, we are told constantly that "*this immense industrial interest is in immediate danger of being destroyed by foreign importations!*" Do not these facts, and they might be multiplied indefinitely, throw a little discredit on the promises of protection? "We shall soon be able to go alone." Yes: *but when?* The duty on foreign iron is unprecedentedly high at this moment, and yet we read out of an unquestionable authority that, in 1676, "as good iron was made as any in Spain" in Massachusetts, and that there were "six forges for the making of iron in the colony."[2] The absurdity of this strong point of protection is apparent the moment its principle is attempted to be applied in domestic trade. If a new Boston dry goods' house should set up in Franklin Street alongside the old established houses there, and modestly charge its customers fifty per cent. additional on all goods, so as to enable it to "start" and to "compete" with its neighbors, it requires no prophet to predict that the "run" of its trade would be in the wrong direction. Young men, sometimes with little capital, are starting every year in all branches of business, by the side of old firms in settled business, and they succeed by dint of tact, skill, and industry. The

[1] Palfrey's History of New England, Vol. II. page 53.
[2] Palfrey, Vol. III. page 299.

United States will succeed by dint of the same and not otherwise. Let us hear no more, then, of this deceptive talk about "starting." *Credat Judæus Apella.*

(5.) Protection always gives birth to smuggling, and other frauds upon the revenue. Secretary McCulloch, in his Report for 1866, estimates these for that year at $92,000,000. The country will do well to ponder over this instructive official commentary on the principle of high duties. "Gentlemen," said Sir Robert Peel to the House of Commons in 1842, "what is the use of fixing our rates so high as to allow the smuggler to underbid us?" Smuggling has always accompanied high protective duties, and always will. Laws and vigilance have been unable to prevent it. Laws and vigilance are unable to prevent it now. To evade honest taxation is a high crime against society. To evade laws passed, not for revenue, but to foster class interests at the expense of the many, is a much less crime. It is a rude attempt to right a wrong. Government is the first and main offender. Let it yield to all men their just rights, including the right of free exchange subject only to fair taxation, and it will have no occasion to harry smugglers, and spend millions of the people's money in useless vigilance. To levy such high duties as either to prevent importations or to encourage the smuggler is a gross mistake. The country loses its revenue, the honest importer his business, the public morality becomes corrupted, and the manufacturer is not ultimately protected.

(6.) Protection defeats itself. Tariff-taxes, like other taxes, reappear in higher prices of commodities. If these taxes be high, and many, as they must under a system of protection, nothing can hinder high ranges of general prices. But such is a good market to sell in. As soon, therefore, as high tariff-taxes have had time to work out in high prices, foreigners can pay the high duties and still sell and undersell in such an artificial market. With this principle all facts agree. It accounts for the constant clamor for *more* protection. It accounts for this, that importations are never permanently stopped by high duties. Such duties make prices artificial, business precarious, losses inevitable, and "protection" self-destructive.

It is always pleasant to be able to confirm one's reasonings with facts, to clench the nail driven home by a logical process, with a blow or two from the hammer of actual experience. It is fortunately possible to do this in regard to free trade. The Greeks and Romans, though the latter at times stopped the exportation of specie, never dreamed of putting obstacles in the path of ordinary traffic. At Athens, all exports and imports were subject to a duty of *two per centum.* In the ports of her subject allies, Athens laid a duty of *five per centum,* in lieu of tribute. When, in a few exceptional cases, she laid *ten per centum,* it was denounced as downright extortion. The ports of Rome and Italy sometimes enjoyed a perfectly free trade; but generally, in them, and in the ports of the provinces, a revenue tax of *five per centum* was levied under the Republic, and *two and a half per centum* under the Empire.

England in the year 1842 abandoned for substance the doctrine of protection, and seven years later abolished a main feature of the system in the discrimination till then maintained in favor of her own ships over those of foreigners in her own ports. There is nothing now to hinder American ships from competing on equal terms with English vessels in the coastwise carrying-trade of England itself. The English tariffs are adjusted with a view to revenue merely; and in the late special commercial treaty with France, the duties were thrown off entirely from a portion of French manufactures, and materially reduced on most of the rest. England claims, through the mouth of her responsible ministers and statesmen, to set before the nations an honest example of free trade; and invites them, as I believe, in good faith, to follow her in the path which she has opened up for herself. The force of this example is frequently sought to be parried by alleging that England reached through protection a point of prosperity at which she was well able to dispense with protection. This is neither ingenuous nor true; since the men who have persuaded the English government to abandon the principle of protection, are the men who have demonstrated the economical folly of the principle under all circumstances; and have shown that England maintained the policy so long at a loss to herself as well as her neighbors. Other nations can say, if they please, "We will maintain protection as long as England did, and then follow her example in giving it up." But if they do this, they will do it at a loss, as England did, and too late bemoan their folly, as England does. Said Mr. Gladstone, Chancellor of the English Exchequer, in 1856, — "There is one domestic feature which I wish it were in our power effectually to exhibit to the governments and inhabitants of foreign countries. They know by statistics, which are open to the world, the immense extension which our commerce has attained under and by virtue of freedom of trade, and the great advancement that has happily been achieved in the condition of the people; but they do not know what it has cost us to achieve this beneficial, nay, blessed change; what time, what struggles, what interruptions to the general work of legislation; what animosities and divisions among the great classes which make up the nation; what shocks to our established mode of conducting the government of the country; what fears and risk, at some periods, of public convulsion. *These were the fine and penalty we paid for long adherence to folly.* We paid this fine and penalty upon returning to the path of wisdom, which too late we wished we had never left. It is not easy to calculate its amount, but if it could be exactly reckoned, and fully exposed to the eyes of other nations, our juniors in trade, it might supply them with a timely warning against imitating our former errors, and with the best encouragement to the adoption, before they become entangled in the creation of artificial interests, of our recent and better example."

But it is said, as if that were sufficient to condemn free trade, that England adopted it out of pure selfishness. Of course she did; and other nations will also adopt it from the same motive. No other motive is appropriate in the premises. The idea, disseminated by protectionists, that it requires a millenium for free trade to work in, is wholly fallacious; it requires an enlightened selfishness, and nothing more; and it is one of the grand wonders of Providence, that the elements of society are so wisely prearranged, that, within the sphere of exchange, the welfare of all is promoted through the enlightened selfishness of each. Trade is always selfish, just as much so under freedom as under protection; it is a sphere all whose operations are subject to the legitimate control of conscience, but it is not, and never was designed to be, a sphere of sympathy and benevolence: these have a sphere of their own, above and beyond the sphere of exchange. When a man gives, let him give, and enjoy the luxury of doing good; when a man buys and sells, let him honestly, but with an eye to self-interest only, buy and sell and get gain.

The number of tariff-taxes in England in 1842 was 1150; in 1870 it is only 33. The customs revenue has kept very steady under the successive remissions of these taxes, and is about the same now as then, namely, £22,500,000. Of these 33 articles taxed, 5 yield over 92 per cent. of the revenue, and 10 more most of the rest, showing that a large revenue may come from few articles of exclusively foreign production, as sugar, tea, coffee, tobacco, wines, fruits, and liquors. Under this remission of tariff-taxes and repeal of the navigation laws, the exports and imports of Great Britain, which in 1842 were but little in excess of their average of the previous forty years, have now increased threefold; British tonnage entered with cargo more than threefold; foreign tonnage, fourfold; shipbuilding, threefold; exports per capita between 1854 and 1868, from

£3 10*s.* 2*d.* to £6 0*s.* 9*d.*; imports per capita in same interval, from £5 10*s.* 2*d.* to £9 2*s.* 6*d.*; exports of cotton, nearly threefold; of linen, fourfold; of iron and steel, fivefold; of leather, sixfold; of haberdashery, nearly sevenfold; of woollen yarn, eightfold; of woollen manufactures, fourfold; of machinery, tenfold. Wages have increased at least 25 per cent. in all skilled employments, while hours of labor have been abridged and staple articles of food reduced in price. Paupers have decreased from 1 in 11 per capita to 1 in 20.[1]

The year 1860 is memorable in the history of England for the negotiation and ratification of the French Commercial Treaty, and also as the year in which the remaining duties, avowedly of a protective character, were repealed. The results to France of the relaxation of her own duties are only less brilliant than those to England, as she has less fully embraced the system of freedom. Comparing 1860 with 1868, the volume of French commerce increased from 562,825,000 francs to 1,435,000,000 francs; French exports to England from 331,775,000 to 847,200,000 francs; the export of butter to England from 2,500,000 to 52,000,000 francs; of eggs, from 7,000,000 to 38,000,000 francs; the whole export of wines from 800,000 to 4,000,000 gallons; the whole manufacture of silks, woollens, and cottons, from 92,800,000 to 265,139,000 francs. French manufacturers were afraid of the competition of England, which they professed to be unable to withstand. The result has shown, however, that, in the eight years, France has sent to England four francs in manufactures to one franc received from England in

[1] Librarian Board of Trade, Charles [illegible] England, et al.

manufactures. The explanation of this is partly due to the fact that the French have learned better than any other people the money value of elegance. They have learned that Beauty is a source of Wealth, and so they not only adorn their capital, and have made it by far the finest city in Europe, attractive as a resort to all the world, but also they contrive to make all their handiwork beautiful, and thus control in many things the markets, as they do also the fashions of the world.[1]

The Zoll-Verein, or Revenue-Union of the German States, presents a splendid example of the prosperity which follows in the train of free exchange. The rate of imposts on foreign goods is varied from time to time by the Zoll-Verein Congress, but ten per cent. is the maximum, and the interests of the revenue are consulted in adjusting the rates below that: since 1851 the raw materials coming from abroad are admitted free, or nearly so. The proceeds of these duties go into a common treasury, and are then distributed among the various members of the Union on the basis of their population. Every member without exception now receives a larger revenue than it did before it joined the Zoll-Verein. The city of Hamburg, a chief distributing point for the imports, is a sort of bonded warehouse under the system. The dutiable articles are arranged in thirty-seven classes; and the simplicity of the rates, the lowness of the rates, and the fewness of the articles charged with rates, stand in striking contrast to these points in the present tariff of the United

1 This thought was suggested to me by my late lamented friend, Sidney Homer, of Boston.

States. The revenue under the Zoll-Verein in 1868 was 27,347,156 thalers, which was 13 per cent. more than in 1867. Of this, 31.11 per cent. was from coffee, 11.66 per cent. from leaf tobacco, and 6.92 per cent. from salt. Thus 49.69 per cent. was from three articles: 9 other articles yielded 26.92 per cent.; and 25 articles yielded 91.24 per cent. of the whole. Iron, steel, and their manufactures, are admitted on easy terms, pig iron at 6 cents, and loop, rolled, and hammered iron, iron and steel wire, and cast steel, at 42 cents per cwt., but the home production of iron within the Zoll-Verein has increased steadily with the increase of the importation of foreign iron; so of other staples; an interesting proof that the relatively free introduction of foreign articles does not depress, but rather stimulate the production of similar articles at home, provided there be fair natural advantages.[1] Only 152 articles are taxed.

Our last example shall be Belgium. The perfect free trade which Belgium enjoyed in the sixteenth century gave an impetus to her industry and to her commerce which placed her at that period at the highest pitch of commercial prosperity. From 1792 to 1814, that country was controlled by the French, who applied to it the protective system with extreme rigidity. From 1814 to 1830, Belgium was united with Holland, and the two had in common a customs' tariff based on a *maximum* duty of 3 per cent. on raw materials, and 6 per cent. on manufactured goods. It was during this period that the modern manufactures of Belgium were brought into exist-

[1] Zolltarif des Deutschen Zoll-Vereins. I am indebted for a copy of this to the kindness of our minister at Berlin, Hon. George Bancroft.

ence, and made that astonishing progress which was demonstrated by an exhibition of national industry in 1830. A violent revolution, based on a difference in race, language, religion and traditions, then separated the Belgians from the Dutch, and the former reimposed upon themselves a protective system with such results in revenue and trade and industry, that M. Frère Orban, then and now Minister of Finance, came forward in 1851, and declared his intention gradually to remove from the tariff every duty that could be called "protective." With this view, a new tariff went into operation in 1855; and another, actually fulfilling that intention, in 1866; so that now, a tariff is maintained solely for revenue; and an almost universal public opinion finds fault with it, not that it is so free, but that it exists at all. The chambers of commerce in Belgium have *unanimously* passed resolutions advising the government to raise the revenue now raised by duties in some other way, and thus introduce a PERFECT FREE TRADE.[1]

I have dwelt the longer on this question of free trade, because it is a practical one now in this country, for whose right solution every citizen should be anxious. Some additional light will be thrown upon the subject in each of the three remaining chapters.

[1] Letter of M. Vander Maeren, of Brussels, April 10, 1868. M. Vander Maeren is a manufacturer, member of the government, and well known as a writer on economic subjects.

CHAPTER XIV.

ON THE MERCANTILE SYSTEM.

There have been three epochs in the progress of the science of Exchange. Each of these has been marked by a theory of its own, of which the two earlier were radically incorrect, yet prepared the way for the third and true system. We have already sufficiently considered the first of these theories, which assumed that gold and silver are the only wealth, and, consequently, that the only way for a nation to grow rich was to foster the importation and prohibit the exportation of the precious metals. The second commercial theory was more refined and complicated; we have already spoken of it as the Mercantile System, and partially explained its fundamental principle. The principle was to preserve the balance of trade, to make the exports greater than the imports, so that the balance should come back in gold and silver. The whole system is based on the absurd supposition that a merchant will carry abroad goods worth at home a certain sum, merely that he may bring back goods and money worth as much. Why, on that principle, should he carry forth goods at all?

The nature of trade, as mutually advantageous, was not understood. After every fair mercantile transaction, both parties are richer than before. The more genuine exchanges there are between two countries the better, because the motive for an exchange is always and everywhere the mutual interest of the parties. The benefit of the exchange is shared by both, otherwise there would be no exchange.

But the Mercantile System led each nation to suppose, that, by manœuvre and finesse, it could obtain more than its natural share of advantage. England, for example, in her trade with France, found that, by natural tendency, she bought as much of French wines and silks as she sold France of hardware and woollens. Instead of being satisfied with a legitimate and mutually advantageous trade, the English, under the promptings of the Mercantile System, say, "This will never do. This will never do. There is no balance in our favor. We must sell to France more than we buy of her, or else we get no balance of trade." Accordingly restrictions are laid on some French goods. Their introduction is either prohibited, or heavy duties are levied on them, in order to lessen the quantity imported. This is done in the hope of selling to the French as much as before, but of buying less, this is, less French goods; so that the difference must be paid in gold and silver.

All that was mighty well! But unfortunately the gold and silver, even if they should get it, was no whit better than the French goods, and would probably go right back to France in the purchase of such goods. And unfortunately also the French were adepts in the Mercantile System; they wanted a favorable balance too. They must sell more than they buy. Their exports must exceed their imports. Why not? And accordingly they prohibit some species of English goods, or burden them with a heavy duty; the English retaliate by new restrictions on the products of French industry, and are again in turn retaliated upon. Thus they go on tinkering and tormenting trade in the vain hope of some imaginary balance!

Because England and France are adjacent, and because their natural productions and acquired industry are so very diverse, they are naturally to an immense extent mutual buyers and sellers. France is gifted, perhaps as much as any country upon earth, in point of soil, climate, and natural productions. She produces with the greatest facility, and in the greatest abundance, wines and the cereal grains; and has unusual advantages also for the culture of the mulberry and the manufacture of silk.

England is not thus blessed by Nature; but she has freedom, and industry, and energy, and skill; these have made her for centuries the greatest manufacturing and commercial country in the world. She has always had those things to sell which France wanted to buy, and has always wanted to buy those things which France has had to sell. Exchanges between two such countries are natural and inevitable. If the governments undertake to forbid them, then the business will be done by smugglers, though with hazard and loss.

Now, the Mercantile System disturbed and well-nigh destroyed this natural and profitable trade. To be sure England could buy her wines of France much cheaper and of better quality than of Portugal; but then it was thought that the balance of trade with Portugal could be made more favorable than that with France; and accordingly, in 1703, the wines of Portugal were admitted upon the payment of a duty $33\frac{1}{3}$ per cent. less than the duty paid upon French wines; and the woollen cloths of England, which had been prohibited in Portugal for twenty years, were to be admitted upon terms of proportionate advantage. Up to that time the light claret of France had been the beverage of the wine-drinkers of England. Thereafter the more intoxicating port became what Daniel Defoe calls "our general draught." It was a point of patriotism for the Englishman to hold firm to his port.[1] An economic blunder was followed, as usual, by moral disadvantage. Five generations of English gentry — for the preferential duty was not abolished till 1831 — paid tribute in increased drunkenness to the balance of trade. The habit of taking strong stimulants was established; coarser tastes became the fashion; and even now sherry must be mixed with brandy to be acceptable to English palates. To drink worse wines at a higher price, to incur a habit which is a national disgrace, were not the only consequences; for the French, to retaliate and to restore the balance, prohibited English woollens. Thus the French lost the best market for their wines, and the English the best market for their woollen goods, which the French must now purchase elsewhere at an enhanced cost. It was a dead loss all round, — a gratuitous loss without any compensation whatever.

[1] Knight's *History of England*, v. 267.

Some very instructive laws — instructive in their folly — were passed in England to foster the woollen trade, with an eye to an ultimate balance. A law of 1666 required all *shrouds* to be made of wool.[1] Another law to the same effect but more stringent issued in 1677. This was amended three years later by an enactment, that all corpses, except those of persons dying of the plague, should be buried in shrouds made of *pure* wool, under a penalty of £5. This law was repealed in 1814.

To encourage wool involved discouragement to flax and cotton. A table-linen, called huckaback, began to be extensively made in England about 1700. It encountered great opposition. It was held, that Providence had appointed the woollen manufacture as the special employment of the island, and that the most acceptable sacrifice was that of the flock. Ireland might grow flax and make linen, as some compensation for the injustice that had been committed towards her in absolutely prohibiting the importation of her cattle. Cotton was also coming in. As early as 1719, printed calicoes of English production had become not only fashionable but common. Clamor alleged that the manufacture of light woollen stuffs would be ruined; and so an Act was passed in 1721, to preserve and encourage the woollen and silk manufactures, by prohibiting the use and wear of all printed, painted, stained, or dyed calicoes, in apparel, household stuff, or furniture. Of course such legislation was nugatory; but here is the evidence, among many other proofs, of the supreme ignorance and folly of law-makers, who,

[1] 18th Charles II. chap. 4.

from the earliest days of the loom and the plough in England, have struggled to regiment all industry — to encourage or to prohibit — to determine what wages laborers should be paid, and what should be the profit of capitalists — to crush rising industries by taxation — to compel the people to eat dear food for the supposed benefit of the landowner — and, finally, to find out that the nation was never so universally prosperous as when its industry was wholly left to the care of itself, under the guidance of God's natural laws.[1]

So far was this regulating mania carried at times that almost all legitimate commerce ceased between England and France. So reluctant was the one to buy of the other, so fully were the statesmen of each under the influence of the prejudice that the prosperity of their neighbors was incompatible with their own, that Parliament, in William and Mary's reign, decreed that the French trade was a nuisance; and Adam Smith tells us that, in his time, that is, less than a hundred years ago, smugglers were the principal importers of British goods into France and of French goods into Britain.

(1.) The laying extraordinary restraints on the importation of goods from those countries with which the balance was supposed to be unfavorable, was one device of the Mercantile System to increase the quantity of gold and silver in that country. It was unfortunately not the only nor the worst one.

(2.) An obvious second expedient was to prohibit altogether, or to burden with very high duties, the introduction of all such goods as could be produced at

[1] Knight's *England*, v. 26.

home. If we can produce the articles at home, then we shall not have to import them, and that will help the balance. Under the influence of this feeling, England, damp and cold, in the very teeth of Nature's protests, undertook to rival France in the culture of silk. Heavy restraints were laid on foreign silks, and the monopoly of supplying the home market was given to her own manufacturers. Certainly, silk can be made in England, of a somewhat inferior quality and at a somewhat greater cost than in sunnier climes. To overcome these disadvantages, what was needed was the healthy stimulus of competition. If things had been left to take their natural course, and foreign silks had been admitted freely, the home manufacturers would have been put upon their mettle to discover improved processes, to invent machinery, to make up the disadvantages of Nature by expedients of Art. The plant never becomes hardy and strong that does not root itself amid the breezes of heaven; so neither does a branch of business grow up into self-sustaining and vigorous life without the stimulating breezes of competition. Of this the case in hand affords an excellent illustration. For more than a century the silk manufacture of England, fenced round and protected, as it was called, by these restrictive and prohibitory duties, languished, pined, and at times almost expired; for the simple reason that the manufacturers, instead of relying upon their own invention, skill, and energy, looked to the government for support, and to an artificial monopoly; and it would have remained till this day inferior in design and in every other good quality, had not a great statesman,

Mr. Huskisson, who was denounced as "a hard-hearted political economist," made a partial beginning, in 1826, of that system of free trade which has raised this particular manufacture, as so many others, to an eminence which utterly disregards every danger of foreign competition. The duty on foreign thrown silk was then reduced from nearly fifteen to five shillings per pound; and on raw silk from nearly six shillings to three pence per pound. The consequence was that then first the English silk culture began to thrive; it has thriven from that day to this; the duties have been successively lowered, until, in 1860, the duties on foreign silks of every kind were abolished by Mr. Gladstone; and that England, which was to be ruined in 1826 by the importation of foreign silks, has been exporting for years silk of native manufacture to the extent of about $10,000,000 annually.[1]

As an illustration of the mischiefs which the Mercantile System everywhere introduced into the realm of industry, let us look at this instance a little more closely. During the continuance of the monopoly, the English consumers of silk were obliged to pay a very high price for an inferior article. To whose benefit did this high price accrue? It was designed to accrue to the benefit of the home manufacturer. The sole object in laying the prohibitory duties was to prevent importations, and to leave the home market entire to the home manufacturer. Precisely at this point we see how the whole doctrine of Protection grew out of the Mercantile System. The Mercantile System wished to repress importations for the sake of the balance of trade; but if needful

[1] McCulloch's Dictionary, ed. 1869; Knight, v. 21.

articles cannot be imported, they must be made or grown at home; and in order to be made or grown at home, the makers or growers must be encouraged. The monopoly of the home market was precisely this encouragement; and it is owing to this single circumstance that influential classes in every mercantile community have supposed themselves benefited by this monopoly, that the doctrine of Protection has lingered so long in the general mind. It is easy, however, to see that this benefit is in most cases wholly imaginary; and that the high prices paid by the consumers do not, on the whole, strengthen the manufacture, as has been supposed. If the government had gone further, and given those who had already commenced the culture of silk the monopoly against their own countrymen as well as against foreigners, so that nobody could engage in the manufacture except those already engaged in it, then, indeed, these would grow rich at the expense of their countrymen. Government would take money out of the pocket of every consumer of silk, and put it into their pocket, and the whole benefit of the high prices would accrue to the manufacturers alone. But governments have rarely gone so far as this. They have excluded foreign competition, but not prohibited home competition; and the result has been, that the high duties which excluded the foreign goods, and the consequent high prices of the domestic product, have drawn many men and much capital into that business, in the hope of an extraordinary profit. The business has been artificially stimulated, and capital has been thrust into it which would not have gone of its own accord. The thing has been overdone, and the feverish home competition, in its anxiety to reap monopoly prices, has brought down prices far below the paying figure. The business has collapsed from its very inflation; and thus alternate chills and fever have shaken the life out of it.

But the Mercantile System, and the restrictive policy that sprung from it, obtained universal currency. The statute-books of every nation in Europe are defaced by the absurdest laws and regulations respecting manufactures and commerce. Also, the artisans in the cities and towns were formed into guilds, that is, incorporated societies, and to each guild was given the monopoly of the market, in its branch of industry. No man could practise the art of a shoemaker in Antwerp or London without the consent of the guild of St. Crispin; and the guild itself determined the number of apprentices to each artisan, the years he should serve, the conditions under which he might become a master; in short, determined everything respecting the trade by constitution and bye-laws. The governments, justly regarding these artisans as the most industrious and deserving of their subjects, granted them many privileges, which, however, were no less contrary to sound principles than the rest of the system. That they might obtain cheap provisions, the export of corn was forbidden; and thus agriculture was prevented from selling its products in the best market, wherever that market might be found. That they might obtain the raw materials of their manufactures cheap, the export of these was strictly forbidden. The tanner and currier, for example, must sell his product to the "gentle Craft of Leather," and had no other market.

The general doctrine of fostering exportation was infringed on in these instances, because it was thought that there would be a greater ultimate export of manufactured products, if the raw materials of these were forbidden to be exported, and cheap provisions were secured to the artisans.

In order to encourage agriculture, most European countries, in accordance with the doctrines of the Mercantile System, passed corn-laws forbidding the importation of foreign grain, each nation wishing to raise its own subsistence from its own soil. The consequence of this was that the landholders secured the monopoly of supplying the home market with food; which of course greatly enhanced the price to all consumers, especially in times of scarcity. The increased price of bread, which rich and poor must pay alike, was but a part of the evil consequences. No nation is so sure of its subsistence, when it endeavors to raise the whole of that subsistence at home, as when it leaves the channels of importation open for foreign supplies. When the trade in corn is free, the dearth in one country is instantly supplied by the superabundance of another, and that by natural laws as beautiful and invariable in their operation as the laws that govern the heavenly bodies. Interference with natural law in no direction is so mischievous and culpable as in this. Is it not plain to common sense that that nation is most likely to obtain its food with regularity and in plenty which draws its supplies from the widest surface? Massachusetts, for example, does not begin to feed her own population; but does any one suppose her people are any more likely to starve on that account? She can buy food with the products of her industry. Her calicoes and cassimeres, her hardware and cutlery, her nick-nacks and notions, will buy wheat not only in the marts of the West, but in Poland and Russia as well. She is sure to be fed, because she has wherewithal to buy food; more sure to be fed than if she compelled the industry of her people to abandon the more profitable mill-stream and factory, shop, and foundry, to extort from these rocky hill-sides the reluctant grains.

England, too, in 1849, removed the last vestige of corn-laws from her statute-book, and now imports flour freely from the Black Sea and from the Baltic, from France and from the United States. Who supposes that, if England did not raise a kernel of wheat, she would not be as certain of her daily bread as the people of Poland or of Michigan? But one may say, in case of war, she had better raise her food at home. But it is absurd to suppose that any nation would be at war with all the world at once; and we may be assured that the portion not belligerent would be eager to furnish the supplies. And besides, plenty of wheat would enter England if the English only wanted it, though all the navies of the world should blockade the fast-anchored isle. Every creek and headland would be alive with the silent and secret but busy agents of a clandestine trade.

The simple consideration that condemns this second expedient of the Mercantile System, namely, the prohibiting the importation of such commodities as can be produced at home, and the Protective policy inseparably connected with it, is, that it involves a dead loss to the productive powers of the world. There is in the world a certain amount of capital and a certain amount of industry. These, if left to their own keen sense of interest, will make the aggregate amount of production in the world as great as that amount of capital and industry can make it. If, then, a free commerce distribute this aggregate production over the earth in accordance with the simple law of supply and demand, we shall have not only the greatest production, but the most perfect distribution.

But if now government steps in, and withdraws capital and industry from their freely chosen posts of activity, prohibits exchanges that would otherwise be made, and commands commodities to be manufactured or grown in localities where they would not naturally be manufactured or grown, then certainly the aggregate production of the world is lessened, and its distribution is less perfect.

(3.) The Mercantile System had two other expedients which were frequently employed to subserve the ends of its grand principle. For the sake of increasing the exports, and thus improving the balance of trade, bounties were given to encourage the export and sale of native fabrics in foreign markets. A bounty, we understand, is a sum of money paid outright by the government to the exporters of native fabrics, in order to enable them to sell their goods as cheap or cheaper than their rivals in the foreign market. England, for example, was so anxious to sell her goods to foreigners, that she regularly paid her merchants for selling the goods at a loss. "The price of these goods in that market," says the merchant, "will not reward my capital with the ordinary profit." "Never mind," says England, "sell away, and I will make up your loss by a bounty!" Was not that a rare and brilliant way of enriching the country? By natural laws, a branch of industry ceases as soon as it becomes unprofitable; but by the system of bounties a trade was perpetuated of which the expense was greater than the returns, of which every operation destroyed a portion of the capital employed in it. The loss was made up to the operators by government; in other words, the people were taxed to pay it.

(4.) The fourth and last expedient of the Mercantile System was to help the balance of trade by founding colonies, that the mother country might enjoy the monopoly of their trade, and force them to resort exclusively to her markets. All the English colonies on this continent were bound by the rigid fetters of this colonial system. Up to the date of American Independence, Virginia and Massachusetts must buy most they wished to buy in English markets, and carry most they had to sell to English ports. Spain and France extended the same colonial monopoly, with even more of inflexibility, over their American and West India settlements; and it was considerations growing out of this colonial policy which gave birth to the American Revolution; and that war was waged not more for the interests of humanity than for the freedom of trade.

CHAPTER XV.

ON AMERICAN TARIFFS.

So long as the United States were colonies of Great Britain, their commerce was bound in the rigid fetters of the Mercantile System. We have already seen in the last chapter that colonies were one of the devices of the Mercantile System to secure a favorable "balance of trade." If the maxim be to sell as much as possible and buy as little as possible, then colonies, which could be compelled to receive the goods of the mother country, must be commercially valuable. Accordingly, all the commercial countries of Europe, and particularly Spain and England, adopted a colonial policy that sprung directly from this fundamental maxim. They valued their colonies as affording broad markets for the sale of products, and also because they could monopolize the articles produced by the colonists themselves. In general, the colonists were compelled to sell all they had to sell to the mother country, and to buy all they had to buy of the mother country; even though the articles thus bought were not the produce of the mother country, but must first be imported there and then exported thence to the colonies. Until the Revolution, a Boston ship, for example, could not sail directly to China for teas, but the teas must first be brought to England in British ships, must pay a duty there, and then be reëxported to the colonies.

As early as 1650 this monopoly system was entered upon by the then republican Parliament of England. The colonies had already overcome the difficulties incident to their first settlement, had begun to increase rapidly in wealth, and their commerce had become so considerable as to afford a temptation to restrict its freedom and to endeavor to make it peculiarly advantageous to the mother country. In the year 1651, the Republican Parliament passed the famous Act of Navigation. It had a double object, — to promote the interests of English shipping, and to strike a decisive blow at the carrying trade of the Dutch. It prohibited all nations from importing into England in their bottoms any commodity that was not the growth and manufacture of their own country. In 1660, by a memorable statute, the ordinance was reënacted, with additional clauses, substantially excluding foreign ships from American harbors, and sacrificing to English monopoly the natural rights of the colonists.

This Navigation Act is of great interest to Americans, because the American Revolution grew directly out of it. Says Bancroft, "American Independence, like the great rivers of the country, had many sources; but the head spring which colored all the stream was the Navigation Act." It was enacted that certain enumerated articles, which included all the principal productions of the colonies, could not be exported directly to any foreign country, but must first be sent to Great Britain, and there unladen, before they could be forwarded to their final destination. It amounted to the same thing as prohibiting all exports except to the mother country. The chief products of their industry the colonists could not export to any place but Great Britain, not even to Ireland; neither sugar, nor tobacco, nor cotton, nor wool, nor indigo, nor ginger, nor dye-woods, nor molasses, nor rice, nor peltry, nor ore, nor pitch, nor tar, nor turpentine, nor masts, nor yards, nor bowsprits, nor coffee, nor cocoa-nuts, nor whale-fins, nor hides, nor ashes.

Nor was this all. England constituted herself not only the sole market for American products, but also the sole storehouse for American supplies. The colonies must not only sell exclusively in British markets, but they must also buy exclusively in British markets. It was enacted, that "no commodity of the growth, production, or manufacture of Europe, shall be imported into the British plantations, but such as are laden and put on board in England, Wales, or Berwick-upon-Tweed, and in English-built shipping, whereof the master and three fourths of the crew are English."

The preamble to this statute, which was supplemental to the Navigation Act, is curious, and assigns as the motive of the restriction, "the maintaining a greater correspondence and kindness between the subjects at home and those in the plantations; keeping the colonies in a firmer dependence on the mother country; making them yet more beneficial to it in the further employment and increase of English shipping and in the vent of English manufactures and commodities; rendering the navigation to them more safe and cheap; and making this kingdom a staple, not only of the commodities of the plantations, but also of the commodities of other countries and places for their supply; it being the usage of other nations to keep their plantation-trade exclusively to themselves."

In close connection with these commercial restrictions, it was a leading point in the colonial policy to discourage all attempts of the colonists to manufacture for themselves. "That the country which was the home of the beaver might not manufacture its own hats, no man in the colonies could be a hatter or a journeyman at that trade, unless he had served an apprenticeship of seven years. No hatter might employ more than two apprentices. No American hat might be sent from one plantation to another. America abounded in iron ores of the best quality, as well as in wood and coal; slitting-mills, steel-furnaces, and plating-forges, to work with a tilt-hammer, were prohibited in the colonies as nuisances." Similar restrictions existed in respect to wool and weaving; no wool, or any manufacture of it, could be carried across the line of one province to another; and a British sailor, wanting clothes in a colonial harbor, was forbidden to buy there more than forty shillings' worth. The liberty of free traffic between the northern and southern colonies was grudged to the colonists; and any of the enumerated articles exported from one colony to another, were subjected to a duty equivalent to the duty on the consumption of the commodities in England.

So fully were British statesmen trammelled by the ideas of this colonial system, that Lord Chatham himself, the best friend the colonies had in England, did not hesitate to say from his place in Parliament that in a certain probable contingency, he would prohibit the colonists from manufacturing even a hob-nail or a horseshoe. And Lord Sheffield, at a later period, said, "The only use of American colonies is the monopoly of their consumption, and the carriage of their produce."

From this degrading commercial vassalage the Revolution set us free. One will have observed that the economical consideration that condemns the colonial policy is, that it violates this sound commercial doctrine, namely, that men should buy in the cheapest market and sell in the dearest, wherever those markets are to be found. If the mother country finds it necessary to employ prohibitions to draw the colony-trade to herself, it proves that that trade, if left to itself, would have found other and more profitable channels. If Great Britain could have furnished us with all commodities as cheaply as we could procure them elsewhere, then there was no need of prohibitions and penalties — we should have gone to her of our own accord, as unerringly as the needle points to the pole. If she could not furnish us as cheaply as others, we were wronged—it was a tribute and a tax. She made us buy in a dearer market, when a cheaper one was open.

So, if she could pay as much for our commodities as we could get for them elsewhere, there was no need of compelling us to sell to her; we should, in that case, sell to her inevitably. If she would not give what we could get elsewhere, then we were wronged; she made us sell in a cheaper market, when a dearer one was open. Her prohibitions then were either needless, or they were pernicious.

But it may be said that our loss was her gain,

that what we paid extra as consumers, was to them extra profit as manufacturers and merchants. But where is the justice of taxing one set of subjects or citizens for the benefit of another set of subjects or citizens? And how is the wealth of the whole to be promoted by a transfer of gains from one part to another part?

A deeper consideration condemns the colonial policy. Every country has certain advantages, which, if properly improved, enable that country to defy the competition of the world in certain branches of industry. If England could not sell as cheaply as others in the colonial ports, then she was employing her capital and labor at home less profitably than she might have employed them; for if she had employed them upon those branches of production for which she had natural and acquired advantages, no nation could have undersold her; and therefore, if a forced market in the colonies encouraged her to continue branches of industry that would otherwise have been abandoned, it was a permanent loss to her own productive power.

I do not believe that colonial monopolies ever enriched a mother country, on the whole. So perfect and compensating are economic laws, that the losses of one country can never contribute to the permanent gains of another. The highest commercial prosperity of one country implies and demands a corresponding prosperity in other countries. Commerce is exchange. The richer your neighbors are in all products, the richer you will become by your dealings with them. England's hereditary jealousy of the prosperity of France has been as economically foolish as it has been bitter and persistent. It is true of the family of Commerce, as it is of the family of Christ, "If one member suffer, all the members suffer with it."

A good commercial system was not one of the immediate fruits of the American Revolution. The first government established in this country, the government of the Confederation, which lasted from 1781 to 1789, was not gifted by the people with the power "to regulate commerce." This was one of the reserved rights of the States, which immediately began to use it in accordance with their own views of their own interests. Each State laid its own tariff, and undertook to regulate its own trade. The results were most disastrous. Great Britain, seeing that, as a nation, we were helpless commercially, not only refused to negotiate a commercial treaty with us, but by an Order in Council, peremptorily excluded our ships from her West India possessions, between which and the United States there had grown up, partly through some relaxations in the Act of Navigation, and partly in violation of that Act, a large and most profitable trade. We were in no position to retaliate. As a nation, we had no power to exclude her ships, and thus force her to a position of reciprocity. The States passed various and conflicting laws. If Massachusetts, for example, laid a duty on certain goods, and Rhode Island did not, very little revenue would Massachusetts draw from that source; the goods were imported into Rhode Island, and then smuggled across the border. Thirteen independent States regulating the commerce of our seaboard, induced endless confusion, and there was no power to remedy it. Our commerce, such as it was, was ruined.

To consult upon a remedy for this state of things was the specific purpose of the meeting at Annapolis, in 1786. Alexander Hamilton was there as a delegate from New York. He persuaded the delegates to decline entering upon the subject of commerce, inasmuch as it was connected with other great defects of the Confederation, to which their powers did not reach; and drew up an Address to Congress to call another Convention, with ample powers to go over the whole ground, and to devise a system adequate to the exigences of the country.

Thus was summoned the Federal Convention of 1787, which framed the Constitution under which we live, and which gave to Congress, that is, the nation, the needful power "to regulate commerce."

The new House of Representatives, under the Constitution, commenced at once to discuss and frame a uniform national tariff. It passed in 1789; and, with some modifications and additions passed in subsequent years, constituted what I shall call, for convenience, the Hamilton tariff. I name it so, because Hamilton, as Secretary of the Treasury, made an elaborate Report to Congress on the subject, and the tariff, as finally adjusted, bore in almost every part the impress of his moulding hand. This tariff lasted for twenty-five years. It was very successful. It admitted the principle of protection, indeed, but mainly as subordinate to revenue, and rarely for its own sake, and the general rate of duties laid was very low. For instance, in the original bill as passed, cotton goods were charged 5 per cent., iron goods

7½ per cent., and woollens 5 per cent. These duties were afterwards somewhat, but not largely, increased.[1] Pig iron bore no duty at all.

Now under this low tariff the revenue steadily increased, year by year. There was almost no fluctuation, but a steady annual growth of income from 1790 to 1808, when the Embargo was laid, which, of course, interrupted everything. During these eighteen years, the revenue gradually rose from $4,000,000 in 1791 to over $16,000,000 in 1808; and, what is of greater consequence, the ratio of income to population is still more striking. The revenue began at the rate of about $1,000,000 to 1,000,000 of people, and steadily rose during the eighteen years to about $2,500,000 to 1,000,000 of people.

If now we compare these eighteen years of a low revenue tariff with any eighteen years in our after history when we have had an avowedly protective system, we shall see that in the point of steadiness, and especially in the point of a steady increase, those eighteen years cannot be matched. They cannot be matched even by a comparison with the years 1846–61, during which we had ostensibly revenue tariffs; because although these fifteen years present fewer fluctuations than any fifteen years after the first, they were undoubtedly less steady in increased revenue on account of a scale of duties too high to be most productive, and also on account of the increase of the free list in 1857. Still, a fair comparison of those eighteen years, and these fifteen years, with the years intervening, and with the years subsequent to 1861, will yield all that is claimed in respect

[1] Hildreth's United States.

to the superiority of low revenue over protective tariffs in point of a steady and increasing customs' income. Till 1808 duties averaged $11\frac{17}{68}$ per cent.

But while I praise the Hamilton tariff, in comparison with those that came after it, I do not forget its defects. It borrowed from the old Navigation Act of England, and made unwise discriminations between foreign bottoms and American ships. Duties were 10 per cent. higher on goods imported in foreign ships. Tonnage was 6 cents per ton on American ships; 30 cents per ton on ships American-built but owned by foreigners; and 50 cents per ton on all others. These discriminations were designed to encourage the building of American ships, and to keep the carrying trade both coastwise and oceanwise to American bottoms. But it cannot be wise to put obstacles in the way of foreigners coming to our ports to trade. Neither do sound principles approve even the moderate margin yielded in this tariff to protection. The duties indeed were low, — they were scarcely a burden upon industry, — but neither on the other hand did they aid it. All above the best revenue figure was needless. If, with the great advantage of being able to escape the costs of transportation, together with the abundance of raw material, and the endless resources of agriculture, any branch of industry could not live without artificial help, then the proof is complete that it ought not to have been entered upon, and could not have been prosecuted, except at a permanent loss.

Our second tariff, passed in 1816, I shall designate as the Calhoun tariff. Then first we entered upon the protective system as such; and it is a curious instance of how times change and men change with them, that Mr. Calhoun, who afterwards became the champion of Free Trade, strenuously advocated this tariff, while Mr. Webster as strenuously opposed it. Till then the tariff question formed no element in our politics; if I may say so, nobody knew that we had any tariff unless he chanced to read the statute-book; and it was an evil day for this country when a purely scientific question became mixed up in passions and politics, and adhesion, on one side or the other, to what not one voter in a thousand ever began to comprehend, was made a test of party. From that day to this, no tariff question has ever been decided on its merits. Interests, sections, passions, have influenced every bill; and it is a part of the punishment, I believe, for prosecuting an artificial and false system in any department, that it is hard work to get out of it. New England generally opposed the Calhoun tariff, and the principle of protection embodied in it; so did a majority of the Southern members; but South Carolina, seeing the growing value of cotton, and anxious for a home market for the raw material, united with Pennsylvania and the Middle States in securing the high duties, especially upon cottons and iron. The duties were increased, on an average, 42 per cent. above the old rates preceding the war. Imported articles were divided into three classes: 1st, Those of which a full domestic supply could be produced; 2d, Those of which only a partial domestic supply could be afforded; and 3d, Those produced at home very slightly, or not at all. On the first class, the duties were fixed substantially at 35 per cent. *ad valorem.* On the second class, including cottons and woollens, the duties were 25 per cent., to be reduced after three years to 20 per cent. On the third class the rates were mostly fixed with a view to revenue only. Pig iron was now taxed $9 per ton.

In connection with the tariff, we copied again, and more largely, from the English Navigation Act. Importations by foreign ships were limited to the produce of their respective countries; and the coasting-trade, hitherto open to foreign vessels, was now restricted to those American owned and built. In one word, we entered fairly and squarely upon the career of restriction. Average duties 1816–24, 24½ per cent.

Our third tariff, that of 1824, we may call, if we please, the Clay tariff. That gentleman, though Speaker of the House at the time, took an earnest part in the debates, and was regarded as the most prominent advocate of what then first began to be called the "American System," that is, the system of high protective duties. Mr. Webster still opposed this system, made an elaborate speech in reply to Mr. Clay, and voted against the bill.

The bill increased the duties on protected articles very considerably; and is an excellent proof that interests that are petted, and legislatively protected, do not long remain satisfied with what they receive, but are soon clamorous for more protection. The Calhoun tariff gave these interests large protection, eight years run on, and they call for more; they get it. Are they satisfied? Why should they be? Instead of being taught to rely upon themselves, they have been taught to lean upon the government. The average of duties 1824–28 was 32½ per cent.

Four years after the Clay tariff, that is in 1828, was passed the "Tariff of Abominations," so called, in the politics of the time. The manufacturers of course had asked for more protection; but the opposition to the system was now strong; it could not prevent the passage of the bill, but it loaded it down with all manner of objectionable features, to make it as distasteful as possible to its advocates. A political design to make the protective system unpopular appeared, and was indeed avowed; but the friends of protection, in view of the higher duties on many articles, came to the conclusion to support the bill notwithstanding its odious features. They swallowed the whole with the best grace they could. Daniel Webster, after strenuous but fruitless efforts to reduce its "abominations," for the first time in his life voted for a bill involving the principle of high protective duties. In 1828–32, duties averaged 36½ per cent., and on dutiable goods only, 43⅓ per cent.

Four years later Mr. Clay went into the Presidential canvass against General Jackson upon the avowed platform of protective duties. He was beaten. The country seemed to indicate its preference for another system; and accordingly in 1833 our fifth tariff, called the "Compromise tariff," became a law. It adopted a sliding scale in reference to all duties that were over 20 per cent., providing for their gradual reduction on each alternate year, till 1842, when and thereafter the uniform rate on all these goods should be 20 per cent. on the home valuation. Mr. Clay himself brought forward this bill as a "compromise;" and it was also approved by Mr. Calhoun. Average duties 1833–42, 16 per cent., on dutiable 32.

During the next nine years the attention of the country was occupied by the great questions of a National Bank and the currency. On these and other questions the administration of Van Buren became unpopular and broke down; and the Whig party, coming into power, passed what I shall call the "Whig tariff" of 1842. It was a high protective tariff. Extravagant expectations were entertained in regard to it in the high political excitements of the time. Under it, millions of capital were seduced into manufactures, particularly of iron; and when the high duties were abolished, as they were a few years later, hundreds and thousands of persons were pecuniarily ruined. It is impossible to speak in terms sufficiently deprecatory of an artificial system that inveigles capital and laborers into branches of industry in which they never would have embarked of their own accord. Our whole course of legislation on this subject cannot be properly characterized in terms of respect. Congress has alternately inflated, and then punctured, the bubble. The average annual duties between 1842 and 1846 on the aggregate of imports was 22¾ per cent., and the average on the dutiable goods alone, 32½ per cent. These averages are all carefully calculated from the official table presented in Mr. Commissioner Wells' Annual Report of 1869.

In 1846 was passed what we will call the "Walker tariff," from Robert J. Walker, then Secretary of the Treasury. It reduced the duties on imports down to about the standard of the "Compromise" of 1833. It discriminated however, as the Compromise did not, between goods that could be produced at home and those that could not. It approached, in short, more nearly than any other, in its principles and details, to the Hamilton tariff, although the general rate of duties was higher. From that time up to 1857, there was a regular and large increase in the amount of dutiable goods imported, bringing in a larger revenue to the government. The surplus in the treasury accumulated, and large sums were expended by the government in buying up its own bonds at a high premium, for the sake of emptying the treasury. Under these circumstances the "tariff of 1857" was passed, decidedly lowering the rates of duties, and largely increasing the free list. The financial crisis of that year diminished the imports, and the revenue fell off $22,000,000. Duties on the whole imports for the fifteen years 1846–61 averaged 17¾ per cent., and on those goods subjected to duty averaged 22¾ per cent.

It only remains to speak of the "Morrill tariff" of 1861. I include under that designation, as previously under the designation of the Hamilton tariff, the various supplements and modifications passed in accordance with the leading idea of the original act. So reckoned, the Morrill tariff is the ninth in order. The difficulties growing out of the war ostensibly united all parties in the view of obtaining, if possible, more revenue to the government; but there was no agreement as to the means by which more revenue could be obtained; and the protectionists in Congress seized the opportunity of the withdrawment of the Southern members for discriminating in favor of the articles in which they were interested even to the extent of diminishing the revenue by very high duties which lessened importations. They did this too without any general popular call for such a step. The people had deliberately and repeatedly indicated their preference for the system of low duties. The policy of the country was supposed to be settled in that direction. There was indeed a mildly drawn resolution in the political platform of the party that triumphed in 1860 in favor of what is called protection; but very little, or nothing, was said upon that subject in the canvass; the people pronounced in their verdict upon a totally different set of questions from those involved in a protective tariff. When, therefore, the congressional protectionists, availing themselves of the absorption of the popular mind in the war questions, availing themselves also of the indignation against England on account of the supposed haste with which she had recognized the insurgents as belligerents, sprung a highly restrictive tariff upon the country, they did it in obedience to no general call, and with little reference to the general welfare. In view of such a war as that then impending, the relevant questions were, How can we get the most revenue with the least interference with the industries of the people? and, How can we distribute the tariff-taxes so as to burden the whole people as equally as possible? If these questions alone had influenced the representatives of the people, the Morrill tariff would never have been heard of. The instincts of a people, on the breaking out of a great war, are always favorable to commercial freedom. On the 6th of April, 1776, the Continental Congress opened the ports of this country to all the world not subject to the king of Great Britain. They abolished by that act British custom houses, and established no others in their stead. "Absolute free trade took the place of hoary restrictions; the products of the world could be imported from any place in any friendly bottom, and the products of American industry in like manner exported, without a tax."[1] Many nations have acted similarly in similar circumstances; but no nation, to my knowledge, on the eve of a great war, ever did as the United States did 1861, make it of set purpose more difficult to obtain supplies from abroad, and more difficult to sell abroad the products of native industry. It was a clouded thought, hovering in many patriotic minds, that what they knew would be immediately and immensely beneficial to some of their constituents would not after all be very harmful to the country at large, that carried through the tariff of 1861. But it was harmful to the country at large in a high degree. Enlightened public opinion abroad turned more or less against the country in consequence; the people were obliged to pay nearly or quite double on some of the necessaries of life what the goods were worth in a free market; some of them lost also their best chance of selling a part of the products of their industry; unusual inequality of fortune soon appeared among the citizens; while the duties were put so high that nothing like the revenue was received from them that might have been received. With a much larger revenue in gold, a people obtaining their cloths and iron and similar goods at something near European or Canadian prices, and general industry going forward under its natural conditions, the credit of the government would not have sunk so low as unfortunately it did

[1] Bancroft, 8th vol., p. 323.

sink. The new tariff was not honestly adjusted for purposes of revenue, and while it seemed to concede something in its free list to the demand for free trade, the concession was largely delusive, since many of the articles thus admitted free of duty went into manufactures protected by higher duties than have ever before been levied in this country. To put articles on a free list is of itself no boon to free trade; it depends upon the purpose for which they are put there; whether to benefit the whole people or only a few persons at the expense of the whole people. In all our recent tariff-legislation there is many a snare for the unwary.

The average range of duties on the entire imports from 1862 to 1869, was 34½ per cent., more than three times as much as the average under the Hamilton tariff when we were a young nation; and the average on dutiable goods during the same interval was 41½ per cent., a higher average than the history of the country elsewhere presents, except for the brief period covered by the tariff of Abominations.

I find on an actual count of them in an official copy of the present tariff that the number of distinct articles subjected to duty is 2317. Taking, for example, the year 1868, the following articles actually paid the following rates of duty per centum of the value of the articles: — common window glass, 49; pig iron, 55; bar iron, 66¾; cast iron pipe and stoves, 109; wood screws, 66; carpenter squares, 82; sheet lead and pipe, 54; lead pencils, 59½; plain unbleached cottons, 58¼; spool cotton, 65½; cheap gunny cloth, 81¼; white marble, 57; veined marble, 78¾; salt in bags, 80¾; salt in bulk, 108¼; rice cleaned, 82¼; rice uncleaned, 165¼; scoured wool, 94; washed wool, 121; blankets, (average all kinds) 81¾; one kind of carpets, 80; another kind, 91; another kind, 156½; Paris white, 285; white chalk, 833¼.[1] The average duty on dutiable goods for 1868 was 47.86 per centum.

But it is said that our present tariff is productive. Of course, if the people trade at all, such a tariff will be productive; about one half of the value of the dutiable goods imported goes direct to government! To say that it is productive is only to say that it is hard work to destroy the commerce of a great people. The question is, would not a reasonable system be even more productive? At present, the government indeed gets much; but the people *pay* a great deal more; inasmuch as the ground-thought of the whole system is to raise the price of favored domestic products through the tariff-taxes on corresponding foreign products. Some of these taxes exclude the foreign product entirely: in this case, the people pay much, and government gets nothing. In other cases, the people are made to pay five, and even ten, times as much in consequence of a tariff-tax as the government receives from it. Can such a system properly be called productive? In round millions of dollars the tariff produced in 1863 and onwards to 1871, as follows:—49, 69, 102, 85, 179, 176, 164, 180, 194, 206; the average for the ten years is $140,000,000. This is *per capita*, calling the population 38,000,000, $3⅔. The exact annual average of British customs revenue for the first eight years of this period was

[1] Report U. S. Bureau of Statistics, No. 29.

$114,167,402. The figures for 1870 are not at this moment accessible to me, and the tariff-income for the year ending March 31, 1871, was only $107,840,-970, but if we may call the average for the ten years $114,000,000, and the population 30,000,000, this will be *per capita* $3¾, showing that a simple tariff on 33 articles or less is more productive per head of population than ours is. A single specimen of the inequalities of which our present tariff is full, may be given here by way of illustration. *Ex uno disce omnes.* A supplemental act that went into operation on the 10th of August, 1866, provides, for the sake of increasing the duties, that the costs of transportation, shipment, commission, brokerage, and all similar charges, be added to the invoice value of imports to make up the value on which the duties shall be levied. This applies to all dutiable imports, except *to long-combing or carpet wools costing twelve cents or less per pound.* Why are they excepted? Cannot the carpet manufacturers pay duties as well as other people? They have a very high protective duty on their own completed product. They compel, through Congress, everybody to pay this duty on foreign carpets, and carry up the price of their own in proportion; and yet this tariff exempts their raw material from an increase of duty applied to all other dutiable goods whatsoever! Ten days before this clause went into effect, the Hartford Carpet Company declared a *semi-annual* dividend of 20 per cent.; and its shares were announced as worth $275 each, with the dividend off.

A new tariff went into effect Jan. 1, 1871. It

is, however, in principle and in details, nothing more than a continuation of the Morrill tariff of 1861. It does indeed throw off some of the present tariff-taxes, but it throws them off mainly from the revenue parts, and not from the protective parts of the tariff. It releases taxes as compared with 1869 to the extent of $26,054,748;[1] but the people would have been relieved vastly more if this amount of taxation had been removed rather from articles protected than from articles now taxed simply for revenue. For example, 77 per cent. of all this reduction of tariff-taxes is from tea, coffee, cocoa, sugar, and molasses; articles, all the taxes on which go direct to government, and raise the price of nothing else. Precisely those articles, therefore, are the ones to bear a heavy tax. The average decrease on 40 articles in the new tariff is 40 per centum; and the average increase on 10 articles (all protected articles) is 47¼ per centum.

In reference to our present tariff, and all such tariffs, I wish, in conclusion, to make a few general observations.

1. Such duties as these, laid for protection, are *always* laid at the instance, and under the pressure, of the special interests protected. No legislator, on general principles, and without solicitation from individuals, ever framed, or would ever have thought of framing, such a tariff as ours. This is true even of the very moderate protection accorded in the Hamilton tariff. It is overwhelmingly true, and at every point, of the immoderate protection of the Morrill tariff. Distinguished members of the Committee of Ways and Means have related to me at

[1] Report Bureau of Statistics, No. 10, Series 1869–70.

length the methods pursued to gain the sanction of that committee, and thus the ear and the votes of Congress. Those methods are scandalous. If they were generally understood by the people, there would be a speedy end of all such legislation.

2. The condition of ship-building and ship-owning in this country is the best practical commentary on the influence of protection in general. The system is here reduced to its lowest terms. The perfection of protection is prohibition. Our navigation laws prohibit the buying of foreign ships for the sole purpose of encouraging the building of domestic ships. Notwithstanding their absolute monopoly of the market under this law, such are the duties levied for protection on the materials that go into ship-building, that our ship-builders cannot build ships at a profit. It is illegal to buy them, and it is next to impossible to build them; and consequently our foreign merchant marine has fallen off about one half since 1860; and of 133 steamers regularly plying between the ports of the United States and Europe *not one wears the American flag*.[1] In 1860, our own ships brought in nearly two thirds of our imports; in 1870, less than one third. One half of the commerce of the world is now done on British ships: only one fifth on American ships.[2]

3. It is foolishly claimed by some that protective duties always shortly lower the prices of protected articles. If they do, where does the *protection* come in? Or, what is the *motive* for levying such duties? Or, why has the Onondaga Salt Company been selling salt for years in Canada at forty per cent. less

[1] *Hunt's Year-Book* for 1870, page 127. [2] *Ibid.*

than in Syracuse itself? Why did the same company offer salt to the fishermen duty off, and only sell it to landsmen duty on? Is pig-iron, is marble, is rubber-webbing, is salt, are wood-screws, are carpenters' squares, are coarse blankets, cheaper than in 1860? In a natural course of things they would be cheaper: according to the price-lists they are dearer; and it is an unnatural and iniquitous force that makes them so.

4. The proper way to deal with protective duties is to abolish them instantaneously and simultaneously. The abolition of a tax on industry can do no harm to industry. If every tax of every name in all the earth could be abolished to-morrow, what harm would ensue? Taxes are indeed necessary for the support of government, but even when wisely laid for that end they are a necessary evil. They take just so much out of what would otherwise be the gains of exchanges. But protective taxes are the worst possible form of taxes, and the only thing to do with them is *to abolish them.* When protective duties become numerous, as with us, they become a universal burden; and there are only a few protected interests themselves which would not be instantly relieved by their universal abolition. To taper off in protection is much like a drunkard tapering off in his cups. It would indeed be unjust to abolish a part of these duties, and leave the rest in force—to strike out, for example, the duty on woollens and leave the duty on wools,—they should all go by the board together. Science and experience alike demonstrate that this is the best way to do it. Protection cannot complain of it, for when did itself ever

give previous notice to the people that its taxes were coming? Edward Harris paid $58,000 in gold duties on wool bought, paid for, and on its way to this country, when the wool tariff of 1867 came in. If, however, ignorance and prejudice hedge the way to this simultaneous abolition, let the worst duties go first: those on coal (we have more coal in this country than all the world besides), on pig-iron, on lumber, on salt, on wool, on *materials* generally.

5. The changing tone of New England on protection is very noticeable. Many of her prominent manufacturers are earnest for free trade, and very few of the rest have much zeal for the opposite. They have found out that they have to *pay* more protection than they *get*. Exclusive protection of one interest is a very different thing from general protection of many interests. New England, accordingly, is swinging back to her old position. Unjust discriminations in duties are helping this forward. The duty on coal is an abomination in New England; so is the duty of about 110 per cent. on fine wools, while carpet wools come in for about 15 per cent.; and so is the fact, that of the whole cost of producing a yard of the finer woollens 76 per cent. has been paid out in duties. The English manufacturer, for example, is wholly relieved of these duties, and his advantage of four per cent. in labor, if it exists, is a mere nothing in comparison with his advantage of 76 per cent. in cost of materials. No wonder our woollen manufacturers are going forward under discouragement. The tariff is their foe, and they are becoming a foe to it. The shoemakers — the largest single interest in the United

States next to the farmers — are indignant at the tariff taxes on their lastings, webbings, and other materials. Much of the present dissatisfaction of labor in New England is derivable from causes which have their seat in the tariff, and that will ultimately feel the force of their opposition. Moreover, Boston is anxious to regain its ocean traffic, and an obstacle to this is the tariff.

6. The progress that public opinion generally throughout the country is making in this matter of duties is very cheering. Light is breaking in. The people are understanding better than ever before the nature of these taxes that are laid, not to produce revenue, but to prevent it. They are even asking whether Congress has any constitutional right to lay taxes for any other purpose than to *get money* with which "to pay the debts, and provide for the common defence and general welfare of the United States." The issue of present discussions both on the constitutionality and the expediency of "protective" taxes, is sure to be favorable to commercial freedom. The present tariff rests on false principles throughout, and cannot, therefore, be permanent. To relax commercial systems, and not to restrict them, is alone in accordance with the spirit of this age.

CHAPTER XVI.

ON TAXATION.

If the general views maintained throughout this book are conceded to be correct, we shall now reach with very little difficulty the true principles of taxation. Value resides in services exchanged; and since government is an essential prerequisite to any general and satisfactory exchanges, since it contributes by direct effort to the security of person and property, it justly claims from every citizen in return a compensation for the service thus rendered to him. I do not mean to say that government exists solely for the protection of person and property, or that all the operations of government are to be brought down within the sphere of exchange; government exists as well for the improvement as for the protection of society, and many of its high functions are moral, to be performed under a lofty sense of responsibility to God and to future ages; but the matter of taxation, by which government is outwardly supported, and by which it takes to itself a part of the gains of every man's industry, seems to me to find a ready and solid justification in the common principles of exchange. A tax paid is a reward for a service rendered; and because the service may have respected another generation as well as the present, it is possibly proper that the tax also shall be passed over in part to another generation to pay. The services which government renders to production by its laws, courts, and officers, by the force which it is at all times ready to exert in behalf of any citizen or the whole society when threatened with evil, are rendered somewhat on the principle of division of labor, one set of agents devoting themselves to that work; and, notwithstanding some crying abuses of authority which no constitution or public virtue have yet been found adequate wholly to avert, are rendered on the whole economically and satisfactorily. Taxes, therefore, demanded of citizens by a lawful government which tolerably performs its functions, are legitimate and just on principles of exchange alone.

The questions now arise, in what proportions shall the citizens contribute to the fund necessary to be raised by taxation? And in what manner shall these contributions be paid?

The common notion has been that, since every man's person is supposed to be equally protected by the government, a uniform poll-tax assessed on all citizens alike is right, and that for the rest, a man should be taxed according to his property. But what is property? No word has received a greater variety of definitions, or is less settled in definite meaning in the minds of men. The lawyers make a distinction between real property and personal property; and the law at present, though a man have neither real estate nor movables, yet taxes him on his income, on the rewards of his daily industry, regarding that as a species of property. And this too is just; because, as I think, the ultimate idea of property is the power and right to render services in exchange. Robinson Crusoe, while solitary upon his island, did not and could not have property, in the true sense of that word. It is not the fact of appropriation that makes anything property; it is not the fact that a man has made it or transformed it, that makes anything property; it is not the fact that a man may rightfully give it away, that makes anything property; but it is the fact that a man has something, no matter what it is, for which something else may be obtained in exchange, that makes that something property, and gives government the right to tax it. In other words, property consists in values, in a purchasing-power, and not in possession, or in appropriation, or in the esteem in which a man holds anything he has as long as it is his own. The test of property is a sale; that which will bring something when exposed for exchange is property; that which will bring nothing, either never was, or has now ceased to be, distinctively property. This view may not seem to be as novel as it is, or it may be prejudiced by its very novelty, but at any rate it carries along with it that strongest of the criteria of truth, that it simplifies and illumines a confused section of the field of human thinking; and at the same time justifies a practice which governments have reached, as it were through instinct, but which is continually a subject of cavil and complaint, the practice, namely, of taxing men who have neither real estate nor chattels, on their incomes from industry. Within a month an intelligent man was heard to inveigh against the injustice of the law which taxes the industrious man who works and gains an income, but takes little or nothing from the man unable or too lazy to work. Nevertheless the law is right in its action, and my neighbor was wrong in his strictures.

To the general question, then, in what proportions shall the citizens contribute in taxes to the support of government, the general answer comes, that they ought to contribute in accordance with the value of the services which they either do or might render to their fellow-citizens. Under the expression "might render" is not included any personal services not actually rendered, but only those forms of material property which might be exchanged for other forms if the owner saw fit to exchange them, but which he prefers for the present to keep in his own possession. It would not be fair, for example, to tax a professional man on services which his neighbors, or any other authority, think he might render, were he less indolent or more capable; but it is fair to tax any man on those forms of material property in his possession with which he may at any time he chooses render services in exchange. The right to tax on the part of the government is connected with the right to exchange on the part of the citizens, grows out of this, and is limited by it. This consideration, though it may exclude the propriety of a poll-tax, is consistent with all other forms of taxation, and gives unity to them.

I do not think that the common sense of mankind falls in with the opinion ably advocated by Mr. Mill and others, that persons of a large property or of a large income should pay taxes higher than the due proportion of their properties or incomes to more moderate properties or incomes. The transaction between the government and a tax-payer is itself a kind of exchange, and if the ground of it be, as I think it is, that government facilitates by way of protection all his other exchanges, then ought he to pay taxes proportionably to the amount of his exchanges actual or possible; and a man should pay on an income of $10,000 ten times as much, and no more, as a man with an income of $1000. Mr. Mill regards equality of burden as the true general principle of taxation; and as a rich man can pay more than his proportional share with perhaps less sacrifice than the poor man, therefore he ought to pay more than his proportional share. This principle, formerly embodied in the United States income law, has now been discarded from it; and a uniform tax of 2½ per centum is laid on the excess of incomes over $2000. The present law seems fairer than the previous law in this respect. The prejudice, however, against the tax led Congress to reënact it for two years only. Certainly taxes ought to be laid on equal and equitable principles, but the difficulty of determining for different classes of citizens what would be an equality of burden is so insuperably great, that one hesitates before accepting it as the true principle of taxation. On the whole, I am clear that the best available guide in practical taxation are these simple principles, that property is essentially a power to render services, and that taxation should be as nearly as possible proportionate to the degree of this power.

If, then, taxes are to be laid on services, thus subtracting a portion from the gains which accompany them, the question now arises in what way are they to be laid? They are commonly divided into two classes, direct and indirect. A direct tax is levied on the very persons who are expected themselves to pay it; an indirect tax is demanded from one person in the expectation that he will pay it provisionally, but will indemnify himself in the higher price which he will receive from the ultimate consumer. Thus an income tax is direct, while duties laid on imported goods are indirect. There has been a great amount of discussion on the point whether direct or indirect taxation be the more eligible form; but the reader of penetration will perceive that there is not at bottom any very radical difference between them; each is alike a tax on actual or possible exchanges, with this main difference, that men pay indirect taxes as a part of the price of the goods they buy, without thinking perhaps that it is a tax they are paying, and consequently without any of the repugnance that is sometimes felt towards a tax-gatherer who comes with an unwelcome demand. Thus indirect taxes are conveniently and economically collected. Especially is this true of impost duties; since one set of custom-house officers collect easily and at once the government tax which is ultimately paid by consumers all over the country. The taxes, by stamps, on banks and bankers, on gas companies, and very many others levied by the present United States internal revenue law, are indirect taxes, whereby the government gets in a lump what is afterwards distributed over many subordinate exchanges. The countervailing disadvantage of indirect taxation, however, is, that the price of the commodity is usually enhanced to an extent much beyond the amount of the tax, partly because it is a cover under which dealers may put an unreasonable demand, and partly because the tax, having to be advanced over and over again by the intermediate dealers, profits rapidly accumulate as an element of the price.

Direct taxes are laid either on income or expenditure. An income tax, if the exact amount of income could in all cases be ascertained, would be a perfectly unexceptionable form of taxation. The only sources of income are three: wages, profits, rents. I do not think that gifts are legitimately taxable; they lie outside the field of exchange; they spring from sympathy, from benevolence, from duty; and while exchange must claim all that fairly belongs to it, it must be careful not to throw discouragements into the adjacent but distinct field of morals. Hence, it may well be questioned whether legacies, bequeathments, gifts to charitable and educational institutions, and gifts to individuals proceeding from friendship, gratitude, or other such impulse, are properly subject to taxation. The property is taxable in the hands of the donor, and may be in the hands of the recipient, but the passage from one to the other ought to be unobstructed by a tax. Gifts then excepted, and plunder, which is out of the question, the sources of income are few and simple, and there is no great difficulty in every man's ascertaining about what his annual income is. Fraudulent returns should be promptly punished by an additional assessment and collection. The income law at present in force in the United States has perhaps been subject to less complaint than the manufacturers' tax, and other forms of indirect taxation; and it might become more and more productive every year, as the forms were perfected, and as the memory and conscience of the payers were quickened by the action of a healthful public opinion brought to bear through the annual publication (now prohibited) of the list of their returns.

Other direct taxes are on expenditure of some special kinds, such as those on horses, carriages, watches, plate, and so on, kept for personal use. As the difficulty of a tax on a person's whole expenditure is much greater than one on his whole income, inasmuch as the items are more numerous and more diffused, it is only attempted to lay a few taxes on some peculiar items of expenditure, such as those above mentioned; but as these do not reach all persons with any degree of equality, they are so far forth objectionable. A house-tax, levied on the occupier, and not on the owner unless he be at the same time the occupier, would be a direct tax on expenditure every way unobjectionable.[1] Taking society at large, the house a man lives in and its furniture are probably the most accurate index attainable of the size of his general expenditures. They are open to observation and current remark; they are that on which persons rely more perhaps than on anything else external for their consideration and station in life; the tax could be assessed with very little trouble on the part of the assessor; and it is well worthy the attention of our national legislature, whether such a tax, if more taxes should be needed, would not be more equal and more easy of collection than any others now open; or whether it might not with advantage take the place of some of the com-

[1] Mill, Chap. III., Book 5.

plicated and objectionable taxes now laid. Direct taxes have this general advantage over indirect, that they bring the people into more immediate contact with the government that lays the taxes, and subject it to a quicker supervision and more effectual curb, whenever its expenditures grow larger than the people think it desirable to incur; they have this general disadvantage over indirect taxes, especially over imposts, that the number of officials required to assess and collect them is much larger, thus swallowing up a part of the proceeds of the taxes, with this liability also of bringing the people into an attitude of hostility to the government and to its contemplated expenditures. But whether the taxes be direct or indirect, or whatever be their form, except it be a poll-tax, which is questionable at best, they are laid upon exchanges, and are designed to withdraw for the use of the government a part of the gains of exchanges. From this point of view, which gives unity to the whole field of taxation, some practical hints may usefully conclude this discussion and this volume.

(1.) Under the principle, it is very clear that credits are a legitimate subject of taxation. Whatever is bought and sold is properly enough taxed, if the needs of the government require it, and if such taxation would be productive and not too unequal. As values always spring from the action of individuals, so the incidence of taxes is upon persons rather than upon things; and the question is what can a man sell, or what has he already sold, on the gains of which sale the government may lay some claim? If I have a mortgage on my neighbor's farm, I can sell it at any time to a third party; it pays me interest *ad interim*, and I can collect it at maturity. Government therefore properly taxes me for that credit in my possession. It is a part of my property. The holders of the government bonds occupy an economical position exactly similar. They have a lien on the national property and income. The credits they hold are vendible commodities. They are a paper bearing interest. They can be collected at maturity. They are indeed exempted by law from municipal and State taxation. That was a legitimate inducement held out to everybody alike to invest in the bonds. But there is no reason why the nation, having withdrawn them from town and State taxation, should not itself all the more subject them to their fair share of the national burdens. The income derived from them should be taxed as highly as any other income. It is no longer any ground of merit, even if it ever has been, for persons to buy the government debt. It is a mercantile transaction, and should be so considered in relation to taxes. So of other mercantile credits. They are taxable.

(2.) A man's annual income, exactly ascertained, exactly measures the aggregate of the gains of his exchanges for that year; and, therefore, under the principle, an income tax is the fairest of all forms of taxation, and may perhaps, in time, be made to supersede all others. An income tax is new in this country, and it has become strangely unpopular, and will be probably discontinued; but the English have found it for twenty-nine years to be the most uniform, unfailing, expansive, and responsive to control of all their fiscal expedients. The rate has varied from four to sixteen pence to the pound of income.

In 1857 it realized $80,255,000. In 1866, ours also realized $60,894,135.[1] The Germans, too, are now applying an income tax. The publicity resulting is no objection at all; inasmuch as every man has a *right* to know that his neighbors are contributing to support the government *pro rata* with himself. In bearing up the burden of government all citizens are copartners, and in this view each has a right to demand a look into the books of the others.

(3.) Taxes in general, in order to be most productive in the long run, as well as discourage as little as possible the exchanges which would otherwise go forward, ought to be low relatively to the amount of values exchangeable. A high tax not infrequently stops exchanges in the taxed articles altogether, and of course the tax then realizes nothing to the government. As the only motive to an exchange is the gain of it, the exchange ceases whenever the government cuts so deeply into the gain as to leave little margin to the exchangers. The greater the gain left to the parties, after the tax is abstracted, the more numerous will the exchanges become, and the greater the nnmber of times will the tax fall into the coffers of the government. In almost all articles, consumption increases from a lowered price in even a greater ratio than the diminution of the rate of tax; so that the interests of consumers and of the revenue are not antagonistic but harmonious. On articles of luxury and ostentation, and on those, such as liquors and tobaccos, whose moral effects are clearly questionable, very high taxes may properly enough be laid, because their incidence will hardly tend to di-

[1] Report Commissioner Internal Revenue, Dec. 1866.

minish consumption, and it would scarcely be to be regretted if it did; but with this exception, duties and taxes should be levied at a low rate per cent., as well for the interest of revenue as of consumers. It is to be added, however, that the taxes even on these articles may be too high to meet either a revenue or a moral purpose. The internal tax of two dollars a gallon upon distilled spirits was of this character. Experience has demonstrated that a less tax will produce more revenue, and the drinking of whiskey, bad as that is, is less culpable than the endless frauds on the government provoked by the high tax.

(4.) Duties and taxes should be simple, and their amount easily calculable by the payer beforehand. The complication of specific with *ad valorem* duties is a decided objection to the present tariff. The latter is a duty of so much per cent. on the invoiced or appraised value of the goods: the former is a duty of so many cents or dollars on the pound, yard, gallon, or other quantity. There are too many practical difficulties connected with either form of duty to make it proper to combine the two upon the same article. To combine them thus is one of the devices of protection. On the whole, specific duties are preferable to *ad valorem* because they give less chance to frauds, and because importers, and others, can make their calculations easier on the basis of them. To be sure, this involves that high-priced grades of an article pay no higher tax than low-priced grades of the same; but this consideration is largely overbalanced by those of convenience and productiveness. Teas are taxed in this way both in England and the United States, in the former 1*s.* 5*d.* per pound, and in the latter 15 cents per pound. By the U. S. tariff, late gone into operation, tea is reduced from 25 to 15 cents. It will be interesting to note the influence of this reduction on consumption, and consequently on revenue. A similar reduction was made at the same time on coffee, cocoa, sugar, and molasses; and will be watched also with interest. The tax on cigars at present in this country is a good instance in point of the superior efficacy of simple taxation. Under the sliding scale of 1864, the receipts were small and the frauds gigantic: under the uniform rate of ten dollars a thousand the receipts increased; and good results have followed later changes. So far as is possible, taxes should be levied upon commodities once for all, and then an end. The opposite principle of taxing commodities every time they change hands throws an indefinite burden on exchange, whose weight cannot well be calculated beforehand, either by the consumer or by the government, through uncertainty as to the number of transfers. Exchanges indeed are the only legitimate subject of taxation, but not every specific and subordinate exchange. An attempt to tax all sales whatever was followed in Spain, and will be followed everywhere, by a sluggish indisposition to trade at all. Let the amount of the tax be definite, and let everybody be sure that when it is once paid government will produce no further claim, and industry will go along under heavy taxes better than under those nominally lighter to which uncertainty as to time or amount attaches. All the more advanced governments have been simplifying of late years their systems of taxation, and collecting their revenue at fewer points, and under more tangible conditions, in order to interfere as little as possible with a free industry and free exchange. England, for instance, has given up a great variety of taxes, and now collects her revenue about as follows: — (customs for 1871, on eighteen articles, all others admitted free, yielded £21,568,194), —

Customs, 32 per cent.	Stamps, 12 per cent.
Excise, 30 per cent.	Post-office, 6 per cent.
Taxes, 16 per cent.	Miscellaneous, 4 per cent.

(5.) Our internal revenue system has been greatly simplified and improved by recent legislation. If the tariff could be readjusted *on the same principle*, little would be left to be desired in our tax-system. The principle is, relatively low taxes on comparatively few things. The principle is simple: the problem is difficult; but wonderfully less so, the moment all attempts are given up to foster any branch of industry whatever. Our legislators are not called upon to foster any industries. They cannot permanently do it, if they try; and they do immense harm, while they try. Their duties would be easier, and better performed, if they looked solely to the best methods of *raising money* in such a way as shall least interfere with what would otherwise be the ongoing of exchanges in all directions. Duties that prevent importations, and the consequent exportation of domestic products in return; and duties whose direct effect is to raise the price of other articles than those on which they are levied; are objectionable, and, for the most part, can be dispensed with. In case duties are laid on articles, as spirits, which are also produced at home, there should be an excise on the home product equivalent to the tariff-tax on the foreign, otherwise the people will pay more in consequence of the tax than government will get. This subsidiary principle is important. Our internal revenue for 1871 was above 144 millions of dollars, bearing a much lower ratio to customs' revenue than the two sustain to each other in Great Britain.

(6.) Taxes and duties should be collected by the government in as economical a manner as possible, that is to say, the money should be kept out of the pockets of the people as short a time as possible, disbursement following quick upon collection. It is poor policy to gather taxes at the beginning of the year which will not be disbursed till the end of the year. Let the people use their funds till they are wanted at the treasury; and if the taxes do not then come in as fast as wanted, it is better to issue what are called in England exchequer-bills, and in the United States certificates of indebtedness, to be redeemed at the end of the year from the proceeds of the taxes, than to let the people's money lie idle in the treasury.

(7.) If the necessities of the State require it, government has the right to demand from all persons who are capable of making exchanges, and who do make them, something in the form of taxes. But it is every way better, when possible, that people of very moderate means should be exempted altogether from direct taxes; and the payment of indirect taxes is a matter more in their own option, since they are at liberty to buy much or little of those commodities subjected to an indirect tax. In this country at present, incomes not exceeding $2000 are exempted by the law. If a house-tax should be levied, all houses below a certain grade of style and comfort should be exempted, and the tax pass up by easy gradations from those just taxed to the palatial residences of the rich. In the present age of the world, the well-to-do citizens of every country are able to bear without too great difficulty the burdens of the government, and nothing tests better the degree of civilization which a nation has reached than the care and solicitude it displays for the welfare of its poorer citizens.

(8.) Who pays the indirect tax? Can the producer throw it wholly upon the consumer? Can the banks, for example, throw their taxes wholly upon their customers? Producers and dealers and bankers and companies add the tax demanded from them, and sometimes more than the tax under color of it, to the price of their wares. But it is not true that they can always realize the whole of this enhanced price. Generally they can, sometimes they cannot. If the article be one of necessity, or a luxury that has become equivalent to a necessity, and there be no other source of supply than the taxed one, then, as a rule, the tax falls wholly on the consumer, and is a matter of indifference to the producer or dealer. But the usual effect of an enhanced price is to lessen demand, and if the article is dispensable, or its consumption can be lessened, or it can be obtained elsewhere, the market will be sluggish under the tax, and producers or dealers will be likely to tempt it by lowering prices, in other words, by sharing the tax with consumers, and paying that share out of profits. This is the principle. Producers and dealers would rather the tax were off. Consumers generally, but do not always, pay the whole of it.

(9.) I append a scheme of national taxation, embracing both internal and tariff taxes, prepared and published by Mr. Edward Atkinson of Boston. I approve of it strongly in its principle, and in its main details. Experience, after its enactment, would doubtless suggest improvements: I should be glad to see it, with minor exceptions, enacted.

REVENUE.

	Internal.	Customs.	Total.
From taxes upon spirits and wines, as collected in 1870	$54,286,371	$8,071,699	$62,358,070
" " " tobacco, cigars, and snuff, as collected in 1870	32,348,707	4,227,707	36,576,414
" " fermented liquors, as collected in 1870	6,910,757	347,687	7,258,444
" " " manufactures of silk, as collected in 1870		15,410,770	15,410,770
" " by stamps (other than those on beer and tobacco), as collected in 1870	15,071,783		15 071,783
" " upon banks and bankers, as collected in 1870	3,342,104		3,342,104
" " " national banks, as collected in 1871	6,003,584		6,003.584
" " " sugar and molasses, as collected in 1870 } Allowance made for reductions in the Act of 1870.		33,000,000	33,000,000
" " " tea, as collected in 1870 }		8,000,000	8,000,000
" " " coffee, as collected in 1870 }		8,000,000	8,000,000
" " " fruits, nuts, spices, laces, embroideries, fans, toys, kid gloves, and other articles of luxury, as collected in 1870		11,000,000	11,000,000
Miscellaneous receipts, as collected in 1870	4,731,650		4,731,650
From taxes upon gas, and other small receipts, as collected in 1870	3,000,000		3,000,000
" duties proposed to be collected upon textile fabrics, china and glass ware, as far as possible in the form of specific duties, but at rates averaging twenty per cent. *ad valorem;* say on common or coarse goods, ten per cent.; on medium goods, twenty per cent.; on fine and fancy cotton, woollen, worsted, and linen goods, cut-glass, and fancy china-ware, thirty to thirty-five per cent. The present rate of importation of the fabrics named being now at the rate of over $110,000,000 in value per annum, the proposed average rate of twenty per cent. would yield (tariff)		22,000,000	22,000,000
Total revenue	$125,694,956	$110,057,863	$235,752,819

www.ingramcontent.com/pod-product-compliance
Lightning Source LLC
LaVergne TN
LVHW021309110826
845150LV00003B/526